CW00870729

The Secret Police and the Religious Underground in Communist and Post-Communist Eastern Europe

This book addresses the complex intersection of secret police operations and the formation of the religious underground in communist-era Eastern Europe. It discusses how religious groups were perceived as dangerous to the totalitarian state whilst also being extremely vulnerable and yet at the same time very resourceful. It explores how this particular dynamic created the concept of the "religious underground" and produced an extremely rich secret police archival record. In a series of studies from across the region, the book explores the historical and legal context of secret police entanglement with religious groups, presents case studies on particular anti-religious operations and groups, offers methodological approaches to the secret police materials for the study of religions, and engages in contemporary ethical and political debates on the legacy and meaning of the archives in post-communism.

James A. Kapaló is a Senior Lecturer in the Study of Religions, University College Cork, Ireland.

Kinga Povedák is a Research Fellow on the MTA-SZTE 'Convivence' Religious Pluralism Research Group at the University of Szeged, Hungary.

Routledge Religion, Society and Government in Eastern Europe and the Former Soviet States

Series Editor

Lucian Leustean is Reader in Politics and International Relations at Aston University, Birmingham, United Kingdom.

This Series seeks to publish high quality monographs and edited volumes on religion, society and government in Eastern Europe and the former Soviet States by focusing primarily on three main themes: the history of churches and religions (including, but not exclusively, Christianity, Islam, Judaism and Buddhism) in relation to governing structures, social groupings and political power; the impact of intellectual ideas on religious structures and values; and the role of religions and faith-based communities in fostering national identities from the nineteenth century until today.

The Series aims to advance the latest research on these themes by exploring the multi-facets of religious mobilisation at local, national and supranational levels. It particularly welcomes studies which offer an interdisciplinary approach by drawing on the fields of history, politics, international relations, religious studies, theology, law, sociology and anthropology.

12 The Albanian Orthodox Church
A Political History, 1878–1945
Ardit Bido

13 Orthodox Christianity and the Politics of Transition
Ukraine, Serbia and Georgia
Tornike Metreveli

14 Religion and Politics in Contemporary Russia
Beyond the Binary of Power and Authority
Tobias Köllner

15 The Secret Police and the Religious Underground in Communist and Post-Communist Eastern Europe
James A. Kapaló and Kinga Povedák

The Secret Police and the Religious Underground in Communist and Post-Communist Eastern Europe

Edited by
James A. Kapaló and Kinga Povedák

Routledge
Taylor & Francis Group
LONDON AND NEW YORK

First published 2022
by Routledge
2 Park Square, Milton Park, Abingdon, Oxon OX14 4RN

and by Routledge
605 Third Avenue, New York, NY 10158

Routledge is an imprint of the Taylor & Francis Group, an informa business

British Library Cataloguing-in-Publication Data
A catalogue record for this book is available from the British Library

Library of Congress Cataloging-in-Publication Data
A catalog record has been requested for this book

ISBN: 978-0-367-27999-8 (hbk)
ISBN: 978-1-032-05588-6 (pbk)
ISBN: 978-0-429-33146-6 (ebk)

Typeset in Times New Roman
by Newgen Publishing UK

Contents

Figures

Contributors

Igor Caşu is Lecturer at the State University of Moldova, Chişinău. His recent publications include "Exporting Soviet Revolution: Tatarbunar Rebellion in Romanian Bessarabia (1924)," in *The International Journal of Intelligence, Security and Public Affairs*, vol. 22, no. 10 (Fall 2020), 224–43. He is currently working on a book on the post-war famine in Soviet Moldavia, 1946–47 in a comparative framework.

Iuliana Cindrea-Nagy is a PhD student on the Hidden Galleries ERC project. Her main research interests include the history of religious minorities in Romania, especially Old Calendarists, Tudorists and Neo-protestant communities.

Aleksandra Djurić Milovanović is an anthropologist working as Senior Associate Research Professor at the Institute for Balkan Studies of the Serbian Academy of Sciences and Arts in Belgrade. Her area of expertise includes the relationship between religion, migration, human rights and minority groups. She is the author of *Double Minorities in Serbia. Distinctive Aspects of the Religion and Ethnicity of Romanians in Vojvodina* (Institute for Balkan Studies SASA, 2015) and co-editor of Orthodox Christian Renewal Movements in Eastern Europe (Palgrave, 2017).

Ágnes Hesz is Assistant Professor at the Department of European Ethnology – Cultural Anthropology, University of Pécs, and worked as postdoctoral researcher on the Hidden Galleries ERC project in 2018. She is the author of *Élők, holtak és adósságok. A halottak szerepe egy erdélyi faluközösségben* [The Dead, the Living, and their Debts. The Role of the Dead in a Village Community] (Balassi, 2012).

James A. Kapaló is Senior Lecturer in the Study of Religions at University College Cork, Ireland and Principal Investigator of the Hidden Galleries project (ERC Project no. 677355). He is author of *Text, Context and Performance: Gagauz Folk Religion in Discourse and Practice* (Brill, 2011) and *Inochentism and Orthodox Christianity: Religious Dissent in the Russian and Romanian Borderlands* (Routledge, 2019).

Ondřej Matějka is Assistant Professor at the Institute of Area Studies at Charles University, Prague (Czech Republic). He teaches courses on contemporary European history and methodology of social sciences. He recently co-edited "Planning in Cold War Europe. Competition, Cooperation, Circulations" (De Gruyter, 2018).

Szilvia Köbel is a Senior Research Fellow at Historical Archives of the Hungarian State Security, Research Department, and Associate Professor at Faculty of Law of the Károli Gáspár University of the Reformed Church in Hungary. She is the author of *"Divide and Rule!". The One-Party State and the Churches* (Rejtjel Kiadó, 2005).

Maciej Krzywosz is Assistant Professor in the Institute of Sociology at University of Bialystok, Poland. He is the author of "Cuda w Polsce Ludowej. Studium przypadku prywatnego objawienia maryjnego w Zabłudowie" [Miracles in the Polish People's Republic. Case study of the Private Marian Apparition in Zabłudów] (IPN Białystok, 2016).

Dumitru Lisnic is a PhD researcher on the *Hidden Galleries* ERC project. He holds a PhD in Contemporary History from "Alexandru Ioan Cuza" University of Iași, Romania and is the author of *Elitele Moldovei Sovietice: Recrutare, rețele informale, identități sociale și etnice în Bălți, 1940–41, 1944–50* (Editura Arc, 2019).

Éva Petrás is a Senior Research Fellow at the Committee of National Remembrance (NEB), Budapest. Her publications include studies and monographs in church history of different denominations in the twentieth century and recently in the history of the Hungarian communist state security. She is the author of *Álarcok mögött – Nagy Töhötöm életei* [*Behind the masks – the lives of Töhötöm Nagy*] (ÁBTL – Kronosz, 2019).

Corneliu Pintilescu is Researcher at the George Barițiu History Institute (in Cluj-Napoca) of the Romanian Academy. He is the author of *Justiție militară și represiune politică în România comunistă (1948–1956). Studiu de caz: activitatea Tribunalului Militar Cluj* [Military courts and political repression in communist Romania (1948–1956). Cluj Military Court: A Case Study] (Cluj University Press, 2012) and "The Reverberations of the October 1917 Revolution and the State of Siege in Interwar Romania" in Gerhard Besier, Katarzyna Stoklosa (eds.), *1917 and the Consequences* (Routledge, 2020).

Kinga Povedák is a Research Fellow at MTA-SZTE (Hungarian Academy of Sciences – University of Szeged) "Convivence" Religious Pluralism Research Group. She was a postdoctoral researcher on *Hidden Galleries* ERC project from 2016–18. She is the author of the *Gitáros Apostolok – A keresztény könnyűzene vallástudományi elemzése* [Guitarist Apostles – The analysis of Christian popular music] (MTA-SZTE, 2019).

Rasa Pranskevičiūtė-Amoson is Associate Professor at Vilnius University, Institute of Asian and Transcultural Studies, Lithuania. Since 2018, she is the President of Lithuanian Society for the Study of Religions. She has published on the material collected during her fieldwork on (post-)Soviet religiosity, alternative religious movements and subcultures (Vissarionites and Anastasians, communities of Hare Krishna, Buddhists, Pagan Romuva etc.).

Anca Şincan is a Researcher at the "Gheorghe Şincai" Institute for Social Sciences and Humanities of the Romanian Academy in Târgu Mureş. She was a postdoctoral researcher on *Hidden Galleries* ERC project from 2017–19. Her research interests include the recent history of East Central Europe, memory and remembrance, church history, religion, and politics on which she has published articles and book chapters. She took part as an expert in the Presidential Commission for the Study of the Communist Dictatorship in Romania for the chapter *Church/religious denominations under communism*.

Tatiana Vagramenko was postdoctoral researcher at University College Cork, Ireland (2017–19) and a George F. Kennan Fellow at the Woodrow Wilson International Center for Scholars, Washington, DC (2019). She is co-editor of *Hidden Galleries: Material Religion in the Secret Police Archives* (Lit Verlag, 2020).

Cristian Maria Vasile is Senior Researcher at the "Nicolae Iorga" Institute of History (Romanian Academy; Bucharest). He works on the Research Program Romania and Europe in XXth Century. He is the author of *Viaţa intelectuală şi artistică în primul deceniu al regimului Ceauşescu, 1965–1974* [Intellectual and Artistic Life During the First Decade of the Ceausescu Regime, 1965–74] (Humanitas, 2014).

Acknowledgements

This volume represents one of the key outputs of the project *Creative Agency and Religious Minorities: "Hidden Galleries" in the Secret Police Archives in Central and Eastern Europe* funded by the European Research Council (project no. 677355). We would like to thank Cseh Gergő Bendegúz, Director of the Historical Archives of the Hungarian State Security (Állambiztonsági Szolgálatok Történeti Levéltára–ÁBTL) for hosting the first project workshop in September 2017 where a number of the papers included in this volume were first presented. We also owe a debt of gratitude to the past and present Directors, Dragoş Petrescu and Constantin Buchet, and Head of Research, Silviu Moldovan, National Council for the Study of the Securitate Archives (Consiliul Naţional pentru Studierea Arhivelor Securităţii–CNSAS) for their support during the lifetime of this project.

Siobhán O'Brien, our Research Support Officer, deserves a special mention for her indispensable contribution to so many aspects of this project throughout its four years. Finally, we would also like to thank the following individuals for their support, advice and inspiration during the course of the project: Lavinia Stan, Cristina Văţulescu, Muriel Blaive and Sabrina Ramet.

Introduction

Reframing the religious underground

James A. Kapaló and Kinga Povedák

As one of the primary instruments of political control and social change both in the Soviet Union and in the satellite states in Eastern Europe, the secret police played a pivotal role in most, if not all, anti-religious operations launched during the communist period. They did so with specially trained, dedicated units established to counter the activities of enemies labelled as "clerical reactionary forces," "spies" or "saboteurs" and to prevent the pernicious influence on socialist society of superstition, religious charlatanry and economic exploitation; all of which were associated with the activities of the so-called religious underground. Following the establishment of Soviet power, and in close collaboration with the relevant government ministries, commissions and agencies, the secret police were charged with maintaining the social order, which entailed identifying, surveilling and infiltrating religious communities in order to undermine, eliminate or control them from within. As Soviet influence and domination extended into Central and Eastern Europe following the Second World War, anti-religious and anti-sect policies were adopted and enacted – in some cases wholesale, in others only piecemeal – by the new subject regimes and their own recently formed secret police forces.

In the context of the Cold War, the fate of religious leaders, Church institutions and ordinary believers became a cause célèbre of the West, where society was mobilized in the name of the defence of religion against atheism and an image was projected of defiant priests and pastors engaged in a serious game of cat and mouse with the secret police. This image of a religious underground, which was based on the testimonies and reports of religious dissidents and émigrés, was promoted by Radio Free Europe and Radio Liberty that claimed to be able to report on the realities behind the Iron Curtain but were themselves of course heavily biased by Western perceptions of what life must have been like there (Kasprzak 2004). Between the official Soviet narrative of the "victorious war against superstition" and the corresponding "religious narrative of martyrdom" (Kelly 2012, 305) which was disseminated in the West, there was a much more complex lived reality in which violent persecution and repression at the hands of the secret police formed only a part. Accommodation, compromise and collaboration were also central to this relationship. The religious communities that came to be referred to as the religious underground, however, were not devoid of agency; they were able to deploy creative means not only of avoiding arrest, foiling agents and uncover informers, but also to establish resilient, viable and meaningful lifeworlds beyond the strictures and confines of officially prescribed lives in the factory or on the collective farm.

Following the fall of the communist regimes in the region, scholars have gained a considerable, if also extremely problematic, new resource for the study of religions. In many states, the communist secret police left behind a vast archival collection that meticulously catalogued the complexity of their information gathering and repressive operations from brutal mass deportations, undercover operations and interrogations, to the subtle manipulations and creative fabrications of secret agents. The archives of the secret police have been at the heart of an urgent re-examination of the legacy of communism aimed at "clarifying the past, uncovering the truth, and furthering the search for justice" (Apor et al. 2017, 1). The truth and justice projects pursued through the archives have proven highly contentious, exacerbating the particular ethical and epistemological challenges that confront scholars of religions working with secret police materials. This volume engages the incontestable abundance and incontrovertible complexity of secret police archival documents with the aim of fostering new methodological approaches and comparative research on the complex intersection of religion and state security in the communist and post-communist context. The authors included in this volume recognize, however, that the secret police archives, especially when approached as standalone sources, have their limits. Several authors in this volume are at the forefront of endeavours to engage the archives in dialogue with other sources and their contributions draw on the archives of religious communities, contemporary testimonies and oral historical interviews. In addition to contributing to our understanding of the history of Church-state relations, of communist-era state security, and indeed of religion under communism in general, this volume also aims to inform our understanding of the role of memory politics in post-communist societies, questions of democratic rights and freedoms of minority groups, the roots and legacy of activism and dissent in the region and the very question of the value and status of truth and trust in contemporary society.

Comparative endeavours in relation to the varied experiences of communism in Eastern and Central Europe are relatively rare, and especially with regards to religion under communism (one notable exception is Ramet 1998), as most scholarship has, as Blaive (2018, 1) points out, tended to emphasize national exceptionalism over "a systematic approach to understanding communism as an international social phenomenon."

The diversity of the religious field in Central and Eastern Europe, with its mix of Catholic and Orthodox majority states, significant Protestant communities and its bewildering array of religious minorities and ethno-religious groups, has also mitigated against taking a regional approach in favour of pursuing research projects based on confessional particularity. Whilst regional studies of Orthodoxy, Protestant Churches or the Catholic Church under communism have explored the particular circumstances of their encounter with hostile communist regimes (see, for example, Kosicki 2016; Leuştean 2009; Michel 1991; Ramet ed. 1988, 1990, 1992), this volume, rather than drawing a distinction along confessional lines, approaches the diversity of religious activity targeted by the state through the lens of the "religious underground," a label that was used both by the communist secret police and by those resisting them. This term, which has both a literal and a metaphorical meaning, came to refer to all unregistered or legally proscribed religious communities that were the target of the secret police from the earliest days following the Bolshevik Revolution until well into the 1980s. We have drawn together studies from both the Soviet Union (Ukraine, Moldova and Lithuania) and a number of satellite communist countries (Hungary, Romania, Czechoslovakia, and Poland) as well as Yugoslavia in order to highlight the commonalities and divergent practices through time of the secret police in their anti-religious operations and to explore the various ways in which religious communities responded to them. The studies collected here deal mainly with Christian Churches and communities in the European territories of the Soviet Union and Eastern Europe (with the notable exception of Chapter 8 by Pranskevičiūtė-Amoson who explores the secret police campaign against Krishna Consciousness (ISKCON) in Lithuania).

Religious discrimination, ranging from the bureaucratic to the violent and genocidal, has been an integral part of human history up to the present day, even in democratic societies and the targeting of religious communities by state security agencies in the twentieth century was by no means limited to the communist world. Looking beyond Eastern Europe there are many obvious opportunities for comparative analysis and reflection. In the US, the FBI has in the course of the twentieth century targeted numerous religious groups employing many of the techniques we associate with communist dictatorships including mass surveillance and agent infiltration operations, propaganda campaigns based on fabricated evidence, and the widespread interpretation of religious beliefs as political dissent, criminal behaviour and, most recently, terrorism (Johnson and Weitzman 2017, 2). The processes by which, under the guidance and name of J. Edgar Hoover, internal enemies were produced by casting suspicion on progressive, pacifist and left-leaning religious groups resulted in the FBI policing "the borders between true and false religion" (Johnson and Weitzman 2017, 3) using means similar to those deployed by the KGB, which had been tasked with maintaining another religious boundary, this time between scientific atheism and the backward superstition and reactionary clericalism of religious people and institutions. In fact, the context of the Cold War, which in the West was frequently characterized as a crusade to defend religion, offers an important lens through which to view the securitization of religion in diverse times and settings.

The introduction to this volume was written in the spring of 2020 in the midst of the Covid-19 pandemic whilst many in the world were in so-called "lock-down." The quarantine under which large portions of the population of Europe and the wider world found ourselves included the introduction of new policing measures, surveillance by drones, road checks, monitoring of all public spaces and gatherings as well as the closure of most businesses. Places of worship were ordered to shut in a move that in post-communist Eastern Europe carried echoes from former times of the forced closure of churches during the communist era. Reports of neighbours spying on and informing on each other became widespread, as was the case also with police inspections of houses and gardens, and even the contents of the grocery shopping of those suspected of contravening the new regulations. The state and the media mobilized public support to prevent public health measures from being sabotaged by the dangerous actions of irresponsible citizens. In short, we witnessed how the role of the police could swiftly change in times of crisis and how the discursive strategies of the state could alter our perceptions of our everyday activities, of our friends, neighbours and colleagues. What a few short weeks earlier would have appeared implausible or ridiculous became a concrete and for some a painful lived reality. The opportunities for societal self-reflection at this juncture are enormous; How and why are we motivated to comply or resist when our freedoms are constrained? How resilient are we when confronted with restrictions that change fundamentally the pattern of our days and the rhythm of our lives? How do we respond to unpalatable "facts" and what motivates us to seek alternative truths to comfort ourselves or to shape our resistance?

Religious resistance and the formation of the underground

The term "religious underground" was deployed by the Soviet state as early as the 1920s to refer to religious communities that were denied registration or were legally prohibited. Its meaning, however, expanded to signify the many religious practices that were extralegal, that were discouraged by the state or that simply slipped from view. First Lenin, then later both Stalin and Khrushchev recognized that hasty anti-religious policies, if conducted without preparatory ideological groundwork, could easily lead to a strengthening of religious feeling and an increase in the number of unregistered groups (Fletcher 1970, 364; see also Lisnic, Chapter 1, this volume). Commenting on this dynamic in 1970, Fletcher (1970, 365) observed that "So long as believers are permitted legal outlets for their religious desires, their activities can be observed and, to some extent, supervised" but if these options are eradicated the challenge of day-to-day control "must be overcome by the most laborious process of investigation and liquidation." Fletcher, in his slightly simplistic characterization of this process, nevertheless makes a salient point, as worshipping legally and openly became impossible, or the compromises involved became intolerable to believers, the catacomb churches and clandestine forms of religious practice, from catechism classes to secret baptisms, and from apocalyptic chain-letters to secret pilgrimages, multiplied and became increasingly more creative. Therefore, in addition to the powerful religious institutions and figureheads that the regime had initially targeted and desired to topple, a whole raft of new innovative manifestations of religion became the target of the secret police and state propaganda. The religious underground, as Vagramenko elucidates (Chapter 2, this volume) "was the kind of discourse the Soviet secret police harboured and caused to function as true" through both the generation of knowledge and the direct exercise of repressive actions.

By placing the notion of the religious underground at the centre of focus of this volume, we aim to bring more sharply into focus the dialogical process that gave birth to a range of grassroots activities, local practices and lived religious lifeworlds that were both the target and the product of diverse repressive operations. As Glennys Young has highlighted in relation to the study of religion and politics in the Soviet Union, which we contend holds true for the other communist societies of Central and Eastern Europe, religion has been treated as "an object of Soviet political mobilization" (1997, 3) with little attention accorded to the ways in which religious agency shaped society, culture and politics. The varied and sometimes rich observations and representations of everyday religious life to be found in the archival documents of the secret police, which are central to the studies in the present volume, grant us the opportunity, notwithstanding their inherent problems, to explore questions that have heretofore been somewhat neglected.

Although we associate the religious underground with communist repression, it is important to note that covert religious communities predated both the Bolshevik Revolution in Russia and the communist takeover in Central and Eastern Europe. For centuries Orthodox dissenters in Tsarist Russia had been establishing secret networks and communities in isolated locations in order to avoid the attention of the authorities whilst in many states in the interwar and wartime periods, the policies pursued by nationalist and right-wing regimes aimed at homogenizing nation-states around the respective majority ethnic and religious identity produced their own local clandestine forms of religion. In this context, mainstream and majority religions often played a role in the repression of smaller and newer religious communities. In the 1930s and 40s, not only in the Soviet Union, but also across the region, arrest, detention in labour camps and deportation had become widespread means of dealing with banned religious groups and problematic leaders. By the time of the communist takeover in Romania for example, Old Calendarists, Inochentists, Jehovah's Witnesses, Adventists, and Baptists (see Cindrea-Nagy, Chapter 16, this volume) had developed tried and tested methods of avoiding detection, hiding their leaders or concealing their meetings in order to preserve their traditions (see also Kapaló 2019, 107–77). Likewise, in Hungary, Jehovah's Witnesses, Nazarenes and Seventh day Adventists had suffered similar repression (see Petrás, Chapter 5, this volume) and developed their own clandestine practices. Religious difference and innovation in this period, perhaps like at no other time since the Thirty Years War, had become associated with enmity towards the state.

Communist repression of religion was of course different in one key respect, namely the committed goal to eradicate totally religious faith and practice from society. Nevertheless, policies and strategies towards religion adapted over time, often for pragmatic reasons (Young 1997, 2). During the early years of Soviet power, policies towards religion were directed mainly at separating Church and state. The Separation Decree of 1918 seemed to level the religious field by granting equal legal recognition for citizens to profess any faith or none (Wanner 2007, 36) and this was followed by moves to reduce the economic power of the Orthodox Church and its control over education. Following the Thirteenth Party Congress in 1924, however, anti-religious policy changed in favour of propaganda as the main tool including public debates, exhibitions, lectures and publications (Wanner 2007, 39), although this went hand in hand with "rough methods" including physical attacks on Church property, clergy and laity (Young 1997, 3). Newspapers and journals such as *Bezbozhnik* (Godless) and *Antireligioznik* (Antireligious), dedicated to the publication of anti-religious and anti-sect propaganda were published and supported by the League of Militant Atheists, recruited to campaign and mobilize the people against religious institutions. The anti-religious campaigns of the 1920s, which were intended to liberate people from the grip of irrational belief and superstition were, however, a relative failure, especially in the countryside (Wynot 2004, 97–9).

Metropolitan Sergei's Declaration of Loyalty signed in 1927 marked a watershed in relations between the Soviet state and the Russian Orthodox believers. From this point forward, diverse groups that refused to accept the compromise or who were denied official recognition coalesced into a diffuse religious underground under the umbrella name of the True Orthodox Church (see Vagramenko, Chapter 2, this volume). 1929 saw the passage of new wide-ranging laws to regulate religion, including the Law on Religious Associations, which became "the principal normative source of Soviet restriction on churches" (Boiter 1987, 109). Amendments to the Constitution, effectively confiscated all Church property and turned it over to local authorities as well as criminalizing unregistered religious communities and public evangelism and prohibiting all forms of religious education and severely restricted publishing activities (Wanner 2007 48–9). These changes heralded in a much harsher period of "threefold secularization" designed to eliminate the role of religion in social, moral and political life that consisted of dismantling the Orthodox Church and its authority, removing religion from the public sphere and the propagation of an alternative Marxist materialist ideology to replace religious beliefs (Wanner 2007, 52). In addition to the use of propaganda and direct punitive action against individuals, including deportations and executions, the state also began to close and destroy places of worship. Starting with the Russian Orthodox Church but soon extending to other denominations and religions, thousands of churches and monasteries were closed and their buildings and land appropriated by the state. Monasteries were considered especially dangerous as places offering shelter to the "enemies of the people" (see Vasile, Chapter 13, this volume). By 1929, all monastic institutions in Russia had been closed producing the widespread phenomenon of vagrant ex-monastics who formed their own hidden communities and networks in both rural and urban settings (Wynot 2004).

Besides the direct mass repression of the Orthodox Church, the major upheavals of collectivization and grain requisitioning in the countryside contributed to an upswing in popular religious agency and apocalyptic expectation amongst the peasantry at large (see Viola 1990; Smith 2006) that bolstered membership of a whole range of emergent clandestine forms of religious community and practice. As Vagramenko explores (Chapter 2, this volume), the secret police referred to these prophetically and eschatologically inspired movements under diverse names including "Red Dragonists" or "the ecclesiastic-monarchist underground" amongst others.

The religious underground also expanded to include another important category of believers, the so-called sectarians. Despite the preferential treatment that many sectarian groups received in the first few years following the Bolshevik takeover when efforts were made to mobilize them in the class struggle (see Lisnic, Chapter 1, this volume), by 1923 the Communist Party of Ukraine had noticed that controlling sectarians was significantly more difficult than controlling the centralized and hierarchical Orthodox Church (Wanner 2007, 39; see Pintilescu, Chapter 4 and Petrás, Chapter 5, this volume). From the mid-1920s, groups such as the Seventh Day Adventists, Baptists, Evangelicals, Pentecostals, Nazarenes and Jehovah's Witnesses were also denied official recognition. These unregistered religious groups were, by their nature, difficult to keep track of and control (Baran 2014, 46); many of them had never been officially recognized or registered in the first place and hence there were no public records pertaining to them. Certain sectarian groups were considered especially dangerous because of their international connections and pacifist teachings, a stance that resulted in the Jehovah's Witnesses, especially, being the target of some of the most severe of repressive operations aimed at any group (see Caşu, Chapter 6, and Petrás, Chapter 5, this volume).

With the advent of the Second World War, however, Stalin was forced to reconsider his attitude towards the Russian Orthodox Church as he needed to strengthen "emotional loyalty to the state" amongst the populace (Dragadze 1993, 153). The new attitude culminated in the famous meeting between Stalin and the Bishops of the Orthodox Church that took place on September 4, 1943, at which an understanding was reached that normalized Church-state relations and allowed the Church to conduct normal activities. In Russia, at least for a time, Orthodox worshippers could once again attend church, perform services at home and take part in religious processions. Islam, which had similarly been suppressed before the Nazi invasion of the Soviet Union out of fear of pan-Islamic resistance, was also officially tolerated. By contrast, the so-called sectarians fared very badly in the immediate post-war period (Chumachenko 2002, 190).

All the states that fell under Soviet hegemony after World War II adopted this Stalinist model of Church-state relations where separation, in effect, came to mean total control, subordination and surveillance (see Petrás, Chapter 5, and Köbel, Chapter 3, this volume). In the 1940s and 50s, in the newly acquired or reoccupied lands of the Western Soviet Union and in the new satellite states, widespread closures of monastic institutions and nationalization of their property and land took place. The dissolution of monasteries gave birth to the widespread phenomenon in these countries too of forms of secret monasticism and the establishment of home-based communities of ex-monks and nuns witnessed earlier in Soviet lands (see Bögre and Szabó 2010; Hesz, Chapter 10, this volume; Kapaló, Chapter 12, this volume). In Moldova, the closure of all but one monastery in the republic in the period from 1958 to 1965 had the unforeseen consequence of breathing new life into already existing underground religious dissent movements. The mass arrest of Greek Catholic clergy in 1944–45 and the forced unification of the Church in Soviet Ukraine with the Russian Orthodox Church in 1946 was followed a few years later in 1948 in Romania and in 1950 in Czechoslovakia with the closure of their Greek Catholic diocese, in effect producing some of the largest catacomb churches and communities in the region.

Under these conditions, in order to secure the basic right to operate, Churches across the region were forced to make certain compromises with the state along the lines of Metropolitan Sergii's Declaration of Loyalty. Legal acknowledgement was granted in exchange for loyalty but as Köbel notes these "were technically contracts but served as political accords. Complete loyalty and political support were demanded from the religious leadership in exchange for their legality" (Chapter 3, this volume). The freedom to operate was severely curtailed and in relation to these concessions, as Köbel notes (Chapter 3, this volume), "every Church had an opposing, nonconformist layer." The nonconformists could be found in a wide variety of forms. In the Soviet Union, the attack on the Orthodox Church produced numerous and widespread "reactive movements" such as those described by Vagramenko (Chapter 2, this volume), whilst in communist satellite states there were, for example, problematic and outspoken critics amongst the clergy in the Protestant Church in the Czech Republic (Matějka, Chapter 9, this volume) and "clerical nonconformists" in the Catholic Church in Hungary who refused to obey their bishops (Köbel, Chapter 3, this volume). In Romania, such nonconformist factions and tendencies were labelled "anarchist groups" by the state (see Pintulescu, Chapter 4, this volume). In some cases, dissent within officially recognized Churches led to actual splits with nonconformists forming their own underground organizations as happened with the Seventh Day Adventist Church in both the Soviet Union and Hungary (Köbel, Chapter 3, this volume) and the Pentecostals in Hungary (Povedák, Chapter 11, this volume).

Therefore, besides the formation of genuine catacomb groups, many of those who opted to remain within the officially recognized structures of legally operating Churches continued to conduct activities that were no longer permitted according to new secular laws. Many forms of pastoral activity such as youth and community work, catechism classes, as well as the distribution of spiritual literature aimed at transmitting Christian values were now forbidden (Fejérdy et al. 2018, 446) forcing leaders, teachers and youth workers into clandestine forms of practice and secret methods of communication (see Hesz, Chapter 10, this volume). We should add to this summary of groups that comprised the religious underground, the small number of alternative, non-Christian movements that were active during the final decades of communism, amongst which were Tibetan Buddhist groups, various Pagan movements and Krishna Consciousness (ISKCON), all of which were closely connected to an existing broader "unofficial cultural field" that was receptive to alternative religiosities and spiritualities (see Pranskevičiūtė-Amoson, Chapter 8, this volume).

The Soviet satellite states also later mirrored the policies and actions of the Soviet Union with regard to the so-called sects of protestant origin. In the Hungarian context, as Köbel notes from an Office of Church Affairs report, they were considered "more dangerous than the historical Churches, because they don't have a definitive dogma but instead talk about whatever they want to" (Chapter 3, this volume) whereas in Poland as they were associated with the German minority, they were dispossessed and marginalized as "anti-Polish" elements (Flemming 2009, 118–19). Despite the appearance of a more lenient approach to religious minority groups, even after its break with the rest of the communist bloc in 1948, Yugoslavia also viewed sectarian groups such as the Nazarenes and the Seventh Day Adventists as "anti-communist and disloyal." They were seen as potential supporters of foreign intervention due to their international networks in the West and as a danger to the state due to their pacifism, which directly challenged a central doctrine of Yugoslav communism which considered all citizens as defenders of the state (Djurić Milovanović, Chapter 14, this volume).

A further distinct aspect of the religious life of the underground took shape amongst believers who found themselves in the labour camps, prisons and penal settlements. Periods of time in detention, which could last years or even decades, gave birth to creative expressions of spirituality which as Petrás (Chapter 5, this volume) illustrates with regards to Jehovah's Witnesses in Hungary resulted in a devotional life "enriched and deepened by the persecution." Time spent in labour camps and in exile also presented the possibility for witnessing and proselytizing amongst fellow prisoners and other exile communities, thus facilitating the spread of religious communities to far-flung places. The religious underground, therefore, was characterized by an extremely diverse set of actors, communities and practices, the lived experience of which was shaped by state security operations, surveillance and imprisonment. In the broadest sense, therefore, authors in this volume use the term religious underground to refer to religious communities, agencies and activities that evolved in large part to avoid detection and control.

The idea that underground religious activities, diverse as they were, constituted genuine resistance to communism has been questioned by some as an "idea made up by the regime" (Fejérdy et al. 2018, 445). Indeed, as Vagramenko argues (Chapter 2, this volume), the secret police, through their practices of documentation, intended to produce an image of clandestine religious practice as politically dangerous in order to justify the actions taken against them. Moreover, communist authorities tended to view any attempt to continue to transmit religious faith and belief as a political act of opposition (see Pintilescu, Chapter 4, this volume) despite the fact that Christians themselves may not always have understood their actions in such terms. According to this view, Christians who struggled to preserve their way of life and faith were not necessarily resisting communism but were rather engaged in the positive act of "building Christianity" despite the risks involved (see Fejérdy et al. 2018, 445). This perspective which emphasizes the significance of faith as opposed to dissent in discourses of religious agency during the communist era can be contrasted, as Wynot highlights, with another tendency amongst historians of the Soviet Union to "underestimate the depth of religious feeling amongst the laity" (Wynot 2004, x) rejecting the idea that peasant defiance of anti-religious campaigns constituted genuine resistance instead relegating it to a vague "desire to defend what was simply familiar and enjoyable" (Husband cited in Wynot 2004, x).

As chapters in this volume demonstrate, the responses of diverse religious groups to repression and control were as radically different as the groups themselves. From the outpourings of popular Marian devotion amongst Catholics in Poland, discussed by Krzywosz in Chapter 7, and the use of blessed food as a spiritual weapon against the regime, outlined by Kapaló in Chapter 12, to clandestine meetings in forests, meadows and baptisms on a public beach, described by Petrás in Chapter 5, religious agency and creativity took many forms, some spontaneous, others intricately planned and executed. As Pranskevičiūtė (Chapter 8, this volume) argues, in the context of aggressive anti-religious operations, the activity of groups such as Lithuanian Hare Krishnas, despite the fact that it did not "emerge as an open opposition to communist ideology" nevertheless constituted a form of resistance against the Soviet regime. As she points out, "almost every initiative of the believers eventuated in interference by the Soviet apparatus" (Pranskevičiūtė and Juras 2014, 4 cited in Pranskevičiūtė, Chapter 8, this volume). We should consider, therefore, these diverse responses as forms of resistance in so much as the concrete actions taken undermined or disrupted the state's ability to pursue its social, cultural, and economic policies; the motivation for these actions may have been other-worldly but the results were intended also to shape this world. Whether viewed as a positive act of building faith, Christian or otherwise, the realization of a socio-cultural alternative way of living or simply as a defence of tradition, the phenomenon of clandestine forms of religion reflected both conscious and unconscious forms of defiance, resilience and creative agency in differing measures. In this sense, we argue that religious resistance as witnessed in the underground activities of these groups should not be reduced to a mere construct of the regime nor to a simple unintended consequence but rather should be seen as a reflection of the complexity of life under communism (see Blaive 2019, 7) and of the worldview and agency of believers (see Baran 2014, 49), as well as an important object of research for scholars of religion.

Particular representations of the religious underground featured in the discourse of both sides during the Cold War; these representations were produced and projected by the secret police, as described above, whilst also being promoted and popularized by Western media and Christian dissidents. Through the titles of memoirs such as that of Romanian pastor Richard Wurmbrand's *In God's Underground* and of organizations such as *Underground Evangelism*,[1] whose mission territory was described as the "unregistered underground Church," the image of heroic priests and pastors defying the communist authorities, dodging the secret police, maintaining their faith in prison despite mistreatment and torture was powerfully propagated by Radio Free Europe and Radio Liberty. The religious underground, therefore, represents a co-construction that – it can be argued – served an important function for both sides. This discursive construct, however, also points to a complex, multidimensional, material and tangible "reality" that has become more visible in its diversity since the opening of the archives of the secret police. By approaching the problem of religious repression through the frame of the religious underground, rather than seeking to establish a stable concept or fixed category, we hope to encourage an interrogation of the boundaries between the regimes of truth operative during the Cold War and the lived realities of religious communities. In doing so, we highlight the "the borderline between collaboration and resistance, constructive criticism and subversion, culture and politics" (see Blaive 2019, 7) and encourage reflection on the moral dilemmas, pragmatic choices, emotional impulses and faithful actions of religious individuals and groups. There is enormous potential for further research on the alternative cultures, material and economic life, ritual practices, leadership and social organization in the underground as studies in this volume hopefully demonstrate.

The secret police

We have used the expression "secret police" in the title of this volume as a catch-all term. The nomenclature of the Soviet political police, and later that of the satellite states, presents a bewildering set of inaccessible names and acronyms. As Cristina Vățulescu (2010, 3) has noted, these included organ, agency, authority, service, section, commission, and administration. These are all terms that shrouded rather than revealed the nature of the activities the secret police carried out, which were, in fact, ones we much more readily associate with policing such as "surveillance, investigation, arrest and detention" (Vățulescu 2010, 3). In the Hungarian case, although numerous changes of name did not indicate a change in the methods of the secret police, nor indeed a change in their personnel; more often than not behind them lay a conscious political decision which might impact the future operations, power, and status of the secret police (Müller 2012, 9–10). Following Vățulescu's lead, we have selected the term secret police as the most appropriate because of the role that the "idea" of secrecy played in their activities and operations. The secret police were never truly "secret" of course as everyone knew of their existence; they presented what Vățulescu has called a "visible spectacle of secrecy" or a "histrionic secrecy" (2010, 3). Anthropologist Katherine Verdery has also challenged the stereotype or assumption of the secret police's invisibility; she characterizes it as a managed performance of secrecy rather than truly secret or invisible work. Officers could be seen, they were "the guys hanging out in places where potential 'dissidents' might congregate" (Verdery 2018, 284), they dressed a certain way and had the same haircuts. The very visibility of agents, who in some cases were surprisingly obvious and unorthodox in their approach (see, for example, Krzywosz, Chapter 7, this volume) was designed to have a prophylactic effect, acting as a deterrent and constant reminder of the watchfulness of the state.

In both the early Soviet and satellite contexts, the secret police were the key weapon in the pursuit of revolutionary social change with newly established secret police forces in Eastern Europe, modelled on and under the close supervision of Soviet advisers. Indeed, control of the secret police by local communist parties, with Soviet help, was the critical means by which they could eventually take control of government and the state. The degree to which these new security organs exercised freedom of action was determined, in part, by how secure and trustworthy Moscow perceived the communist leadership to be in each country (Verdery 2014, 8). Across the occupied states, the secret police were directly subordinated to the communist party rather than the government, with Soviet advisors and agents determining the structure, ideology and practical operational aims and methods of the newly established forces. In the German Democratic Republic (GDR), as in the Soviet Union, the Ministry of State Security and its secret police considered themselves "the sword and shield of the party," not defenders of the people or even of the state (Heidemeyer 2015, 10).

The brutal methods of the secret police were first employed in the interest of establishing the new ruling order and then in maintaining it. In the satellite countries, once the communist regimes had dealt with the immediate threat from the enemies of the past, including "fascist elements" and political figures from the previous regimes, they turned their attention to dealing with the future enemies of the new "democratic order." A statement in 1947 by a captain of the recently renamed and unified Hungarian secret police, the Államvédelmi Osztály (ÁVO), captures the significance of this change, "the difference lies in the shift in our priorities from the past to the future, that in the first place we no longer have to track down the past political enemies, regardless of the seriousness of their crimes, but the prevention of the realisation of the aims of those attempting to destroy the democratic state order" (cited in Müller 2012, 23–4).

Amongst the categories of new social enemies to be targeted by the secret police were the so-called clerical reactionary forces as the manifesto of the Hungarian Workers' Party (MDP) openly declared that "clerical reaction is political reaction painted in the colour of religion, and thus the fight against it is political in nature" (Köbel, Chapter 3, this volume). Religion was regarded by the communists as a façade or mask behind which political enemies were cloaked. From the late 1940s on, secret police agencies began to establish units dedicated to pursuing, surveilling and countering the activities of the clergy and Churches categorized as reactionary forces. In Soviet Moldavia, as Caşu describes (Chapter 6, this volume), in March 1946, when the MGB of the Moldavian Soviet Socialist Republic (MSSR) was created, as in other Soviet Republics, the special department dealing with religion was named department "O" and was responsible for operations against the clergy of legally registered religious denominations as well as anti-Soviet elements amongst adherents of sects, Jewish spiritual leaders and Zionists. In Hungary, following the creation of the Államvédelmi Osztály (ÁVO) in 1946, the 3rd Sub-department was dedicated to the surveillance of the Churches with its tasks described as "the gathering of information related to Churches, dissemination of information and prevention of the spying operations of Churches" (Müller 2012, 29). Such sub-departments at the central level, as was the case in Romania, were often mirrored at the regional level (Pintulescu 2018, 131).

Depending on the context, the relative danger projected onto various religious groups differed but communities that refused to participate in social and political life, that rejected civic duties such as the military draft, or whose members refused to compromise in terms of their proselytizing activities were considered high priority enemies. In rural contexts, the religious enemy was often assimilated with the principal class enemies in the countryside, the wealthy peasants or kulaks, who were targeted for opposing the collectivization of agriculture or for resisting grain requisitioning. In Hungary, especially following the Hungarian Revolution in 1956 (Kiss et al. 2012, 38), and in Czechoslovakia (see Matějka, Chapter 9, this volume), the danger of so-called "clerical reaction," was first and foremost associated with the Catholic Church. Nevertheless, the category could be and was expanded to include also other Churches. The Protestant Church in Czechoslovakia, considered loyal by the regime until the late 1950s (see Matějka, Chapter 9, this volume), was later targeted as a reactionary force in society, as were the so-called dangerous sects across the region (see Petrás, Chapter 5, this volume). Indeed, terms such as "Clerical reaction" were extremely elastic and could be applied to any religious group depending on ideological or political need at any given time (see Kiss 2012, 38).

Once the communist regimes had established their hegemonic positions, the role and operational priorities of the secret police shifted away from revolutionary change to the maintenance of the new status quo. One aspect of this was policing the new legal basis of Church-state relations. Based on principles adopted in the Soviet Union, policy towards religion was designed to appear to separate religious institutions from the state but in effect also aimed to control them from within. This "hostile separation" model, gave legal guarantees of freedom of conscience and equal treatment for all recognized religious institutions whilst placing them under the supervision of state offices or councils of religious affairs. In tandem with these other government bodies, the secret police were tasked with achieving total control in the religious sphere (see Köbel, Chapter 3, this volume; Şincan, Chapter 15, this volume, and Djurić Milovanović, Chapter 14, this volume).

The system introduced in the Soviet Union, and later in the communist satellite states, carried echoes of the strategies employed earlier in the Russian and Habsburg Empires (see Werth 2014). In Tsarist Russia, co-opting the Orthodox clergy to police itself, as well as wider society, was later employed rather effectively in some communist states. In Romania, Orthodox churchmen continued to police religious practice in line with the state's expectations, much as they had done in pre-communist times (see Vasile, Chapter 13, this volume). In order to secure near total reach in terms of information gathering and influencing the religious portions of the population, the regime recruited agents from amongst the clergy and leadership (as illustrated in Chapters by Krzywosz, Vasile, Cindrea-Nagy and Caşu in this volume); this practice was widespread, with collaborative priests' loyalty to the regime rewarded in various ways including lucrative leadership positions, career opportunities for family members, and places in university for their children.

The avowed desire to eliminate religion from society was balanced by a pragmatic realization that in certain contexts religious actors and institutions that had the potential to be suitably disciplined or had proven sufficiently tractable could be useful instruments in the pursuit of the regime's longer-term strategic goals, particularly in the post-war arena of Cold War global politics. The Romanian Orthodox Church, as Vasile explains (Chapter 13, this volume), benefited from the state's suppression of the Greek Catholic Church in 1948, whereby more than one million believers were coerced into changing their denominational allegiance. This move "amounted to a successful but paradoxical proselytism carried out by a self-avowed atheistic regime" (Vasile Chapter 13, this volume) to the benefit of the majority Orthodox Church, which the state considered easier to bend to its will. Some majority or mainstream Churches in the region enjoyed unrivalled access to the higher echelons of the party, whilst dissenters were increasingly marginalized and repressed. Indeed, repression by the state might result of from simultaneous charges of anti-communist activity and alleged heretical practices (see Vasile, Chapter 13, this volume). This model of Church-state relations adopted across the region, as Köbel (Chapter 3, this volume) describes in the

Hungarian context, facilitated a "flexible praxis" allowing the secret police to operate against individuals or groups at any given time based on low-level orders and instructions, or "backstage legislation," rather than on the basis of comprehensive laws that theoretically would protect freedom of conscience and religious practice.

In the post-Stalinist era, the secret police transformed from a violent repressive force into a highly effective "preventive institution" (Verdery 2018, 285) based on fear and intimidation rather than the overt terror of the past. But as Blaive (2019, 2) has explained, fear was not only an instrument of "political submission" utilized by the regime, but also a dimension of the relationship between those in power and the population, since the authorities "feared their people too" and had to take account of the changing external context. Pressure generated by the activities of dissidents and international appeals by members of the religious underground to international bodies contributed significantly to the pressure that the communist leadership experienced to relax its anti-religious operations and grant new freedoms.

As a result, as Köbel (Chapter 3, this volume) demonstrates, the legal status of Churches and religious communities could and did change over time. This often came about due to "changed external political conditions," which in Hungary coincided with Hungarian membership in the United Nations, the signing of the International Covenant on Civil and Political Rights in 1975, and, in the final years of communism, the state's desire to curry economic or political favour with the West and other important international trading partners. On the whole, policies towards religious groups from the late 1950s onwards balanced a range of factors, ensuring that the outward appearance of religious freedom was maintained whilst multiple forms of pressure were applied on institutions, clergy and believers.

Secret police operations

As the chapters in this volume demonstrate, the numerous shifts in state policy towards religious institutions and communities resulted in extremely diverse secret police operations. Whilst it would be impossible to capture the full scope of secret police operations employed against the religious underground, the chapters in this volume illustrate a range of operational methods and goals from their inception in the early Soviet context in 1920s Ukraine (Lisnic, Chapter 1), to the Stalinist-era mass repression from the 1930s to the early 1950s (Vagramenko and Caşu, Chapters 2 and 6 respectively) through the anti-religious campaigns of the Khrushchev-era (see Kapaló, Chapter 12 and Krzywosz, Chapter 7) right up to the closing decades of communism in 1970s Hungary (Povedák, Chapter 11, this volume) and 1980s Soviet Lithuania under the renewed anti-religious policies of Yuri Andropov, a former Chairman of the KGB (Pranskevičiūtė-Amonson, Chapter 8). The objectives of these diverse operations also varied tremendously, from the elimination of so-called enemies of the people and the "destruction of the prestige" of religious leaders to the suppression of local religious enthusiasm and the infiltration and manipulation of international networks and Churches. Although many studies exist on the organization, recruitment, operational methods and changing role of the secret police in various national contexts, the specific means by which these were applied or mobilized against the religious underground has remained understudied, particularly in a comparative frame.

As a number of the chapters in this volume demonstrate, the secret police's operational role combined the generation of information and the production of knowledge about the enemy with the implementation of policies designed to undermine, eliminate, or control their targets. These two distinct dimensions of their work were present from the very beginning of the institution. As Lisnic outlines (Chapter 1, this volume), in the early 1920s before the Cheka, the first Soviet secret police force, had built the capacity to generate information at the local level, the authorities relied on subordinate networks of County Departments of Secret Informers for their intelligence. As the secret police evolved, the information gathering and operational roles of the secret police were mutually dependent, "gathering information was shaped from the very beginning in order to produce evidence to legitimate future repressive measures" (Pintilescu, Chapter 4, this volume). This involved the ascription of political or antisocial, and therefore criminal, meaning to religious practices and beliefs through a "rhetoric of unmasking" (Vățulescu 2010, 24) that applied to all classes of social enemy, not just religious ones. Stalinism, as Vățulescu describes it, propagated a way of looking, a "watchfulness," or an "omnipresent call for vigilance" (Křišťál 1985, 108 cited in Matějka, Chapter 9, this volume), that required a peeling back of "the surface of reality in expectation of the worst" (Vățulescu 2020). The secret police were the main instrument through which this compulsion to unmask hidden hostile elements in society was achieved.

Until the late 1920s, significant differences existed between how enemies were perceived and constructed depending from where they were being viewed. In the first few years after the Bolshevik takeover, as Lisnic demonstrates (Chapter 1, this volume), conceptions of precisely which religious groups constituted the enemy could differ significantly between the political centre and the various layers of the bureaucracy, with officials associating "the idea of enmity with a set of obstacles which hindered the implementation of the policies they were in charge of." These agencies, Lisnic concludes, saw the "formation of different images of the same religious group at different levels of administration" (Lisnic, Chapter 1, this volume). This situation changed, however, as War Communism gave way to the period of the New Economic Policy in 1921.

By the 1930s, the means of construction of knowledge about religious communities had become much more sophisticated and centralized. Taking as her case study the model criminal files that were compiled on the True Orthodox Church, Vagramenko (Chapter 2, this volume), demonstrates how internal top-secret publications produced by the GPU, the State Political

Directorate as the Soviet secret police were known at the time, were compiled and disseminated. The construction of the ecclesiastic-monarchist underground in these model cases, which succeeded in unmasking simple peasants as "agitators" or "spies" in a highly organized underground network implicated in the machinations of "foreign intelligence agencies," illustrates the process by which "an alternative reality" could be created "where people and social relations got new roles and meanings" (Vagramenko citing Melley 2000, 42). Diverse pieces of information, both visual and textual, were systematically "dislodged from their initial context, *estranged,* and then re-assembled in a new way" in order to produce criminal evidence.

As the secret police vision and production of serviceable knowledge about religious leaders and groups became more sophisticated, study manuals and operational guides were produced that outlined Marxist historical critiques of religion and Church history based on the regime's idea of scientific atheism. These manuals supplied officers with the conceptual tools and vocabulary to enable them to "rewrite" religious meaning, actions and lives in their reports. These resources, which generally represent a synthesis of empirical experience gained in real operations with heavy doses of ideologically inspired fantasy, often bore inflated titles such as the manual authored by two Romanian secret police officers in 1983 entitled

> Aspects of the hostile activity conducted by autochthonous elements incited by emissaries of reactionary religious centres and organisations abroad. Measures taken by organs of the state security for the prevention and counteracting of enemy actions conducted under the cover of religion.[2]

In 1960s Poland, as Krzywosz notes (Chapter 7, this volume), the continued prevalence of miracles and apparitions, which were said to be caused by reactionary elements amongst the Catholic clergy, were deemed dangerous enough to warrant the production of a special manual dedicated to combating these forms of political insurrection allegedly disguised as popular devotion.

Such manuals supplied officers with political interpretations of religious history, terminology and expressions. In the example offered by Petrás (Chapter 5, this volume), terms that appeared in Jehovah's Witness literature such as the "realm of the Satan" and "This world is condemned and its days are counted!" were given political meaning. Such translations, however, in overwriting their original eschatological meaning, had the potential to mislead Hungarian secret police agents and so, despite the production of expert specialist materials, a lack of genuine theological and practical knowledge of religious practices sometimes directly hindered secret police operations. This was the case when Hungarian secret police officers failed to recognize the significance and incriminatory nature of a confiscated photograph of Jehovah's Witness believers seemingly enjoying a bathing holiday at Lake Balaton, which was, in fact, a photograph taken on the occasion of an illegal mass baptism (Petrás, Chapter 5, this volume).

Mistaken interpretations and false constructions composed and disseminated by acting secret police officers shaped the education of future officers. The highly flawed interpretation and characterization by the Czechoslovak StB (*Státní bezpečnost*) of the so-called New Orientation within the Czech Protestant Church described by Matějka (Chapter 9, this volume), which constructed a group of progressive left-leaning pastors and believers as "a second power centre" was "so persuasive that it became a pedagogical resource for students of the StB faculty of the Police University" and was reproduced in a number of master theses at the Police University. The manuals and theses composed about clerical reactionary forces, as Matějka points out in relation to the Czechoslovak case, may also have served as powerful tools of "self-legitimization" offering a platform on which to provide "arguments explaining the ongoing importance of the StB" and to justify "its relevance and raison-d'être in the context of *perestroika* and *glasnost*."

The specialist secret police publications discussed in this volume document the powerful imperative for all underground religious groups to conform to the image of an enemy constructed by the state, whether this reflected reality or not. By the 1930s, as Vagramenko illustrates (Chapter 2), the Soviet secret police characterized the religious underground as highly organized, politically motivated, and internationally connected and the secret police went to great lengths to visualize and materialize the invisible networks that constituted the underground according to their understanding and ideological need. In relation to some groups, such as the Jehovah's Witnesses (see Baran 2014, 49), the Soviet authorities were dealing with genuine underground networks as complex and organized as the state's projections but secret police understanding of other groups such as the extremely diverse groups of Orthodox dissenters (discussed by Vagramenko, Lisnic, and Kapaló in this volume), bore little relationship to reality, indeed secret police documents demonstrate how the regime got "caught up in its own internal falsifications" (Șincan this volume citing Kotkin, 2002: 36). This was the case with regard to the operation described by Matějka (Chapter 9, this volume) in which the Czechoslovak StB looked so feverishly for "a unified hostile headquarters" and firmly believed in the existence of "a second power centre" inside the Czech Protestant Church that their actions paradoxically contributed to its very formation. As Matějka concludes, the StB constructed the enemy so effectively that it "succeeded (at least partly) in creating it."

The repertoire of discursive strategies available to the secret police in unmasking religion was diverse but nonetheless highly formulaic. Anti-religious rhetoric across all of the communist states was based on the Soviet model with propaganda and operational campaigns following the shifts in policy in Moscow quite closely. One of the most significant means of producing or amplifying political guilt during the Cold War, was to accuse religious actors of being in league with the external enemies of the communist world, particularly with imperialist Western powers. Jehovah's Witnesses in Romania were charged with being members of a "conspiratorial group intent on subverting the regime, that was controlled directly from the United States, the centre of the capitalist world" (Pintulescu, Chapter 4, this volume), while in Yugoslavia, Nazarenes and Adventists were accused of enemy activity including "propaganda and espionage for foreign agents" (Djurić Milovanović, Chapter 14, this volume). As late as the 1980s, during a period of renewed concern over ideological decay within the Soviet Union, one leader of the Krishna Consciousness movement could be declared an agent of the CIA "specializing in ideological diversions, including subversive activities of imperialism against the socialist system" that were designed to "destroy the country from the inside" (Pranskevičiūtė-Amonson, Chapter 8, this volume).

The Catholic Church was also regarded as one of the main external enemies of communist governments. This was based on a number of factors including the highly centralized character of the Catholic Church led from the Vatican, over which communist regimes had little control, the ideological influence the Church wielded globally, but not least the Church's economic and social power in some satellite countries such as Poland or Hungary. As Árpád von Klimó relates with regard to Hungary, before the establishment of the communist system, the Catholic Church was the country's largest landowner, overseeing thousands of schools and controlling dozens of publishing houses and newspapers. It also enjoyed the support of lay organizations and associations counting hundreds of thousands of members (Klimó 2016, 51–2).

Central to the construction of knowledge and of political guilt of religious actors, as both Pintilescu and Vagramenko point out in their studies (see Chapters 4 and 2 respectively), was the wider network or set of social relations. People could be understood and incriminated "sometimes by simply invoking their membership in a 'counter-revolutionary organisation'" simplifying legal or bureaucratic procedures because, "instead of compiling individual criminal investigation files, they compiled group files" (Pintilescu, Chapter 4, this volume). The production of knowledge, therefore, in regard to the unmasking of the hostile activities of the clerical reaction, served a number of functions and produced a range of responses and significantly it could serve as a means to justify the perception that the work of the secret police continued to be necessary, thus shoring up its preeminent position as the defender of the people.

Religions and members of religious communities were targeted as part of a much wider process of identifying anti-Soviet or counter-revolutionary social elements, a process that reached extraordinary proportions in the mass repressions of the late 1930s to the early 1950s. In this period, entire social categories or portions of the population became targets of the NKVD, including former kulaks, "national elements" or untrustworthy ethnic groups, and petty criminals, with the aim being the total "excision from the body politic" of these population cohorts (Hagenloh 2009, 8). This approach, as Hagenloh concludes, eroded the distinction between civil and political crime and between civil and political policing (Hagenloh 2009, 10). Religious groups could, therefore, be routinely classified both as a political enemy and as a social, moral and even medical threat to society.

As Lisnic demonstrates in his case study of ethnic-Moldovan Inochentists in 1920s western Ukraine (Chapter 1, this volume), a "socially dangerous element" might combine suspect class identity with political, geographical, ethnic, and behavioural layers of guilt. Recidivism, or vagrancy, was one such suspect behaviour that was associated primarily with criminal activities (see Hegenloh 2009, 81–3) but formed also part of the construction of an image of certain religious groups as dangerous, such as wandering ex-monastics and preachers of various sects. In the case of Inochentism, the mobility of elements in the underground led to accusations of kidnapping and the sexual exploitation of young girls who had "disappeared" into the sectarian underground (see also Kapaló 2019, 229–37). Indeed, the invisible or secretive nature of the religious underground, which was in most cases, but not all, a consequence of the repressive policies of the state, enabled the shocking accusations based on secret police case files that appeared in anti-religious propaganda to appear plausible to the public, including accusations of child murder amongst Jehovah's Witnesses (see Baran 2014, 73). The charge of so-called "anti-human" and "anti-social" behaviour, and especially the risk this posed to young people (see Djurić Milovanović, Chapter 14, this volume), remained a central element of secret police discourse on the dangers of the religious underground. Even in the final years of the Soviet Union, KGB reports and the propaganda press represented members of the Krishna Consciousness movement as "antisocial people who used various drugs, organized orgies, and so on" (Pranskevičiūtė-Amoson, Chapter 8, this volume). As the chapters in this volume demonstrate, a religious identity as defined and constructed by the secret police had the potential, at various times and in different contexts, to weave together layers of political, class, ethnic, geographic, medical, and social behavioural guilt in the construction of a total enemy.

Knowing and representing the enemy was a necessary and integral part of direct repressive operations, which took various forms and could combine a range of measures or methods. Mass arrest and deportation to Siberia and other remote and inhospitable regions of the Soviet Union for resettlement and forced labour was one of the earliest instruments of mass terror employed by the Soviet state and is associated primarily with the Stalinist-era. This approach was applied widely to other cohorts of the population such as kulaks and suspect ethnic groups but religious communities also were sometimes the explicit target of such mass operations. An early example of the deportation of a religious community is discussed by Lisnic (Chapter 1, this volume) who demonstrates that the operation against Inochentists from Odessa Oblast in 1923 required the kind of top-down centralized planning that could be achieved only once communications had improved between various layers of the administration and the Joint State Political Directorate, or OGPU, as the Soviet secret police were called during 1922–34.

From 1929, the same year that the Law on Religious Associations was introduced heralding the mass, systematic closure of Orthodox Churches and religious institutions, OGPU was entrusted with running the entire Soviet penal system, the so-called Gulag, or Main Camp Administration (*Glavnoe upravlenie lagerei*), making such mass operations easier to co-ordinate. At the height of the Gulag system, Orthodox clergy, monks and nuns, members of the sects and underground religious communities were subject to extra-judicial arrest, sentencing and deportation usually involving a simple decision by *troikas*, headed by the local NKVD chief (by this point the NKVD had taken on the role of the secret police). In 1944, around 1,000 members of the underground True Orthodox Church were exiled in a single operation (Baran 2014, 59) but the largest mass deportation of a religious group, and also the final one before Stalin's death, targeted Jehovah's Witnesses. Labelled "Operation North" and planned and executed by the MGB (Ministry of State Security) officers on April 1, 1951, this operation deported more than 16,000 Witnesses to Siberia and Central Asia from Western territories of the Soviet Union including the Moldavian SSR (today's Moldova), Northern Bukovina in Western Ukraine and the Baltic Republics. Operation North coincided with operations against Jehovah's Witnesses across the communist satellite states that took various forms, including house raids and show trials (see Petrás, Chapter 5, this volume). Decisions by *troikas* or, as in the case of Operation North, by the Special Board (*Osoboe Soveshchanie*) of the MGB were, as Cașu points out (Chapter 6, this volume), extrajudicial and therefore technically illegal according to Soviet legislation and exemplify the flexible praxis employed by the communist state.

Stalinist-era repression of socially harmful elements also entailed the mass surveillance of targeted suspect populations. From the 1930s, following the OGPU's takeover of civil as well as political policing, surveillance, agent infiltration, and the registration of the population and its movements, became part of a top-down plan for a preventive system of population control. Although early attempts at covert operations and undercover surveillance had limited success in some areas (Hegenloh 2009, 13), the recruiting and implanting of undercover agents for surveillance and information gathering became an important element in secret police operational work targeted at religious communities. This policy resulted in a majority of leaders of Protestant groups in the Soviet Union engaging in some form of collaboration with the KGB (Vagramenko 2021, in production).

Immediately after the communist victory in Yugoslavia in 1945, secret police operations against religious sects with international ties combined surveillance work, or counter-intelligence, with covert infiltration and intelligence work. As Djurić Milovanović recounts (Chapter 14, this volume),

> During counterintelligence work, the agent had to be familiar with the teachings of the particular "sect," have detailed information on their organisational structures and methods of religious propaganda, follow

> closely the work and networks of the religious leaders and control religious activities and rituals that preached activities against the government.

In the course of their intelligence work, the agent had to "influence the sect's leadership towards working for the benefit of the country and being a model organisation." In Operation North, the Soviet MGB engaged in extensive agent infiltration (Chapter 6, this volume) and at the height of Hungarian operations against the Catholic Church following the Hungarian Revolution in 1956, 197 Catholic priests had been recruited as undercover agents (Kiss et al. 2012, 35) who succeeded in infiltrating "themselves into every organizational and functional aspect of the Church" (see also Köbel, Chapter 3, this volume).

The embedding of agents, as Caşu's case study (Chapter 6, this volume) illustrates, served a number of purposes. In the case of JWs in Soviet Moldavia, they could be used to determine whether targeted communities were aware of their impending fate. The use of several agents in a single group could also guarantee the accuracy of information gathered as well as assure the reliability of individual agents and informers. In the case of Operation North, infiltration of the community was part of a strategy designed both to facilitate the smooth realization of the deportation and to shape the behaviour of the community going forward. As Caşu suggests, the ultimate goal of the infiltration of the community, and the intentional omission of some JWs from the deportation, "was not to destroy the whole organization but to bring it under the control of the state security organs" and ultimately create the possibility to infiltrate JWs' international networks, thus extending the reach of the secret police beyond Soviet borders (Chapter 6, this volume). This case demonstrates that a combination of approaches by the secret police could be aimed at achieving more complex outcomes, in which control was deemed more useful than outright elimination.

Reliance on large numbers of informers, some highly trained and dedicated, others informal, irregular and unreliable, was characteristic of the post-Stalinist era. In Romania, for example, the number of informers rose from 73,000 in 1968 to 144,289 in 1989 (Stan 2013, 62). The operation against the Inochentist-Stilist community described by Kapaló (Chapter 13, this volume) demonstrates the contribution that might come from significant numbers of religious insider-informers that had intimate knowledge of the community and understood very well the beliefs that lay behind their practices. As the secret police operation against the pilgrimage to the Marian apparition site at Zabłudów in Poland in 1965 (Krzywosz, Chapter 7, this volume) shows, informers comprised a vital component of a complex operation that lasted over a period of two years. This multifaceted approach was applied in a remote rural context and, in contrast to the operation launched against Jehovah's Witnesses in Moldavia, was reactive rather than proactive. By the end of the operation the secret police, in collaboration with the Provincial People's Militia, included the surveillance of pilgrims arriving at the site of the Marian apparition, warning talks (so-called *profilaktika*), surveillance and intimidation of the visionary and her family, a propaganda press campaign, roadblocks to quarantine the local area, mass perlustration of correspondence, special radio links to headquarters, and direct violent intervention by the Citizen's Militia against those who gathered at the site. Local public sanitation authorities were also mobilized by the secret police in order to emphasize the personal health risk to pilgrims who were drinking the local spring water. The operation described by Krzywosz represents a total mobilization of every possible human and technological resource at the disposal of the secret police to put a stop to a spontaneous manifestation of religious devotion.

The success of the operation, as Krzywosz demonstrates, hinged on the ability of the secret police to recruit a wide range of informers from every segment of the local population, from amongst the pilgrims, from the local town, from amongst the priesthood and even from within the religious visionary's immediate family, thus ensuring that "the secret police had a full picture of married life, family and social relations of the Jakubowski family at their disposal." The ability of the secret police to "colonise" all significant relationships (see Verdery 2018, 183) and to intimidate and use to their advantage local relations, rumours and rivalries relied on the invisible work of the secret informers. In contrast, the secret police agents in this case were known and visible to the residents of Zabłudów. They were conducting, as mentioned earlier, a performative operation that was designed to be both threatening and preventative (see Vaţulescu 2010, 3).

The potential and methods used for recruiting informers differed, depending on the nature of the targeted Church or community. In Romania, as explained by Cindrea-Nagy (Chapter 16, this volume), the techniques used to recruit Orthodox clergy, who were offered protection or privileges against the threat of severe consequences if they refused to collaborate, differed from those employed when seeking to access the so-called neo-Protestant Churches, such as Adventists or Pentecostals, which could be infiltrated more readily by planting informers posing as new converts. In all cases, however, compromising information, especially relating to moral and sexual conduct was commonly used to blackmail and intimidate potential recruits (see Şincan, Chapter 15, this volume). Informers were often used to sow doubt and division within communities, especially amongst followers of the smaller Churches or sects (see Cindrea-Nagy, Chapter 16, this volume), as was the plan of the State Office in Hungary described by Petrás (Chapter 5, this volume) which intended "to split the loyal and reactionary segments within the sect" with the aim of offering legal recognition to the loyal wing of the Jehovah's Witnesses and make them join the Council of Free Churches. The secret police, however, were not always successful in recruiting informers as Matějka (Chapter 9, this volume) outlines in relation to the Czechoslovak secret police attempts to infiltrate the Czech Protestant Church. As this case demonstrates, attempts could backfire as they did when a group of Czech pastors publicly recounted their experience of being blackmailed to inform on colleagues. As a result, this operation failed and had the opposite effect instead encouraging "a new sense of loyalty and cohesiveness among Protestant opponents of the regime."

In terms of the chronology of anti-religious campaigns in the Soviet Union, the final phase came during General Secretary Yuri Andropov's term as General Secretary. As Pranskevičiūtė-Amonson (Chapter 8, this volume) explains, a range of operational means were employed including undercover agents and informers tasked with uncovering and disrupting lines of communication amongst ISKCON members within the Soviet Union, the application of "administrative legal and preventive warning measures," or so-called *profilaktika*, as well as house raids and arrests. Warning conversations or interviews were a common method deployed in Soviet Lithuania (see Harrison 2010), which as Pranskevičiūtė-Amonson recounts involved both intimidations, such as threats to expel them from an institute or other workplace, and incentives. As a result of the operations, "almost all original devotees had to quit educational institutions, and some of them lost their jobs" whilst others were imprisoned or committed to psychiatric hospitals where they were forcibly treated with psychotropic drugs.

In contrast to the picture created by the high profile cases discussed thus far, it is important to note that a large proportion of evidence from secret police archival sources, as Hesz (Chapter 10, this volume) illustrates, show us that a great deal of officers' time and attention was dedicated to documenting and prosecuting far less dramatic cases. Rather than uncovering complex organizations with ties to international centres, low-level economic activity by clergy or the recording of simple religious rituals such as marriages or baptisms that in most states, at most times, was frowned upon but not illegal, was the day-to-day work of many officers engaged with the clerical reaction. Secret police operations, which were oftentimes violent, callous and brutal, like the operations that targeted other segments of the population, were intended not simply to dominate but also to shape the population (see Hegenloh 2009, 11). Critical to our understanding of the aims and implications of these extreme attempts at social engineering are the archival records compiled by the secret police themselves.

Secret police archives and the politics of the religious field in post-communism

At the height of the demonstrations that swept East Germany in the autumn of 1989, attention was already turning to the secret police and their archives. Erich Mielke, the Head of the Stasi, began ordering the destruction of state security files beginning with evidence of illegal phone tapping and postal interceptions as well as the lists of names of unofficial informers and collaborators (Engelmann 2015, 176). In Hungary, in the months following the change of political system in October 1989, film footage emerged of the surreptitious destruction of secret police files precipitating the so-called Dunagate scandal (Uitz 2008, 58), whilst, in Romania, in the chaos of the days that followed the revolution in December of that year, there were several reports from various corners of the country of secret police documents being systematically destroyed or stolen (Stan 2005). Mielke soon followed up his initial order with instructions to destroy a much wider range of Stasi files including the shredding of sensitive Church Department documents (Engelmann 2015, 176). Protesters responded by storming the Stasi Headquarters to prevent their destruction.

In the years and decades that have followed, the fate of, access to, uses and methods of interpretation of secret police files have been at the heart of a range of historical questions, political debates, and public controversies. The opening of secret police archives constituted one of the most important aspects in the broad movement for transitional justice and remains the most contentious element in a "symbolic battle for the possession of the past" in post-communist Eastern Europe (Horváth 2008, 247). All the studies in this volume draw directly on secret police archives or engage with the critical questions that they provoke for researchers of the past and for religious actors in the present. As several chapters in this volume demonstrate, Churches, religious leaders and believers have become embroiled in the numerous controversies that surround the secret police archives in post-communist societies.

Access to communist-era secret police files coincided with the transformational influence of the "archival turn" in the humanities and social sciences. The archive, under the influence of Michel Foucault and Jacques Derrida, has come to be viewed as a critical mechanism of societal control exercised through the production and legitimation of historical memory. Viewed through these optics, aspects of human cultures are transformed, alienated, hidden and subverted through the mechanisms of the archive which in the process empowers some whilst divesting others of vital political, cultural and spiritual capital. In the context of post-communist Eastern Europe, historical memory, justice and truth-seeking have become shackled to the fate of and uses of the secret police archives. The peculiar and paradoxical hold that the archives have results from an "enduring belief in the authority of their holdings" (Vățulescu 2010, 13) in post-communism which comes despite the recognition that the materials they contain are the product of the ideological and social engineering projects of regimes whose methods were often illegal and immoral. Similar to the colonial archive, the communist-era archive, as Luehrmann alerts us, "never intended to be neutral or objective but to participate in transforming the reality it described" (2015, 32 cited in Vagramenko, Chapter 2, this volume).

Despite the vastness and incontestable richness of the secret police archives, access to previously classified archives does not necessarily bring with it deeper understanding or conceptual advances (Kotkin 2002). In Kotkin's words, these emerge rather from our relationship to the archives and the "worldviews and agendas" we bring to them. In this sense, the architecture and ideological furniture of the institutions set up to govern the archives in post-communism, as well as the ongoing societal perception and uses of the archives that these institutions have wittingly or unwittingly facilitated, shape how historians, anthropologists and sociologists conceive them and work with and through them. Studies of religion during communism and post-communism, whether historical, ethnological, anthropological, or sociological in nature, have only recently begun to reflect on the complex relationship between the archive, the subjectivity of the scholar, the politics of memory, and the contemporary struggle for political (and religious) capital in the post-communist world.

The uses of and levels of access to secret police archival documents differ vastly from one national context to another. The process began in the early 1990s in Czechoslovakia and Germany with the introduction of so-called "lustration" measures designed to vet those seeking political office or key administrative jobs through an examination of their past using the archives. Later, a number of post-communist states passed legislation on access to secret files and opened specialist secret police archival institutions, as in Lithuania (see Pranskevičiūtė-Amoson, Chapter 8, this volume) or institutes of memory, as in the case of Poland, that are dedicated to uncovering the legacy and activities of the secret police in the search for an "authentic" version of the past. Some countries in the region, such as Romania and Hungary, have well-established public institutions with almost two decades of experience of managing access to their holdings both by those who were targeted by the state and by researchers. Others, such as Ukraine and Albania, have only recently embarked on this process passing "de-communisation" laws, which have granted researchers access for the first time to secret police files. In Serbia on the other hand, as Djurić Milovanović recounts (see Chapter 14, this volume), despite a request from the European Parliament for the Republic of Serbia to fully open its secret police archives as part of the EU accession process, a lack of political will and the failure to pass the necessary legislation means that access is extremely limited.

The various institutions that have been established as custodians of secret police archives have taken on a range of distinct roles. Although the mandates differ from country to country, alongside the preservation and safeguarding of documents, they include the pursuit of processes of lustration or vetting for public office, the investigation and exposure of communist crimes including the exposure of former agents and informers, managing access of targeted individuals to their personal files as well as facilitating and developing research and education. The remit of these institutions, therefore, is oriented towards the future as well as towards the past (see Verdery 2014) as they form a central platform of projects designed to overcome the legacy of repressive regimes and to work towards justice and reconciliation in society. Significantly, as Vasile (Chapter 13, this volume) notes with regards to the Romanian case, such institutions were designed and intended to break the monopoly held by ruling elites "on the potentially toxic information found within political police archives" and to prevent, or at least reduce, the potential for blackmail and manipulation. Facilitating and producing research whilst also engaging in public education were also seen as important means of conveying "the moral complexities" of the holdings of the secret police archives which would in turn help "counter attempts at slander and vicious labeling of those who had, in fact, been victims of the Securitate" (Vasile, Chapter 13, this volume).

The implications of access, or indeed the lack of access, to secret police materials for Churches and religious communities have in some cases been profound. As Vasile (Chapter 13, this volume) and Cindrea-Nagy (Chapter 16, this volume) highlight in the case of Romania, responses to the challenges posed by the archives have varied greatly, often determined by the relative access of Church leaders to the corridors of power in post-communist politics and their ability to influence and shape public perceptions. Members of some smaller Churches in Romania, once the opportunity arose, sought actively to uncover the uncomfortable past relationship to the secret police and the communist regime in what Cindrea-Nagy (Chapter 16, this volume) describes as an act of "purification" or of "healing the sins of the past." This process offered the opportunity for former collaborators to seek redemption through confession of their sins – an opportunity that some but not all took up. This was made possible due to the approach unique to Eastern Europe of granting access to ordinary citizens, effectively democratizing truth-seeking (Stan 2013, 60) and allowing individuals and communities to determine for themselves how secret police reports were used and interpreted.

By contrast, the hierarchies of the Orthodox and Roman Catholic Churches in Romania, have pursued a very different policy of attempting to prevent evidence of collaboration or collusion in communist crimes from coming to light by using their political leverage to hinder the work of archival institutions and researchers (Vasile, Chapter 13, this volume). At the same time, the Roman Catholic, Greek Catholic, and especially the Orthodox Church hierarchies in Romania have engaged in the promotion of martyrs of the communist repression, mainly victims of the regime who suffered and died in prison (Cindrea-Nagy, Chapter 16, this volume), creating a "sacred narrative" of suffering in order to dominate public discussion and deflect attention away from revelations about Church leaders who had been secret police agents or informers.

In the case of the Czech Protestant Church, access to secret police archival documents has been equally divisive. As Matějka outlines (Chapter 9, this volume), a 2004 publication of StB documents that was distributed to every parish in the Church with the aim of helping Czech Protestants "come to terms with their past" became the cause of division within the Church over competing understandings of the "epic struggle with the StB" that older generations like to portray in contrast to the much more complex picture of cooperation and accommodation with the communist authorities that researchers have uncovered. As Matějka concludes, the interpretation offered by a group of secret police officers of the "trajectory of Czech Protestants between 1948 and 1989 has not stopped producing painful conflicts inside the Church milieu to this very day" resulting in a generational fault line between older members of the community who accept at face value the StB narrative and younger colleagues who have "tried to offer more differentiated interpretations of Czech Protestant history during the communist dictatorship based on critical work and utilising a vast array of sources (without exclusive preference for StB files)."

The activities outlined above carried out by or through the institutions in charge of secret police documents, rely on a "presumed credibility," on the part of researchers as well as the public at large, and of the archival documents compiled by the secret police (Pehe 2019, 208), which, as Apor et al. (2017, 4) point out, was reinforced by these institutions' claims "about their capacity to reveal the truth about the past based on their custody of huge amounts of material." The peculiar and paradoxical power of secret police archival documents, which continue to be viewed as sites of authenticity and credibility due in part to their once hidden and secret nature, makes them the quintessential means for legitimizing historical narratives and making claims about justice (see Apor et al. 2017, 4; Blaive 2019; Pehe 2019, 207) as well as making them extraordinarily powerful instruments of political control (see Vasile, Chapter 13, this volume). As the chapters in this volume by Vasile (Chapter 13), Cindrea-Nagy (Chapter 16), and Matějka (Chapter 9) demonstrate, the policies and agendas of the institutions that manage secret police archives have profoundly influenced how religious communities themselves have engaged with and conceive their past.

The dynamic that has emerged in the religious field in Romania, the Czech Republic, and elsewhere, as mentioned above, is the result of the broader phenomenon in post-communist societies that is linked to the de-communisation process as a whole, which has promoted secret police files as the vehicle through which to apportion blame to perpetrators and establish the innocence of victims. This highly polarized process, as Apor et al. (2017) argue, has produced a simplistic understanding of the moral complexity of the relationship between the secret police and those labelled as collaborators, and the ethical dilemmas faced by ordinary citizens who were threatened, blackmailed, or otherwise coerced into collaboration. Whether through attempts to prevent, delay, or restrict access to secret police archival documents or by embracing them as a potential source of closure and redemption, Churches, other religious communities, and individual believers have been forced to position themselves in relation to the archives. The various strategies pursued by religious actors have resulted, in some cases, in further internal strife whilst in others they have initiated a healing process. The absence of a clear "definition and epistemology of what constitutes both a victim and a perpetrator" has, as Blaive shows (2019, 3), perpetuated a culture of systemic blame of everything associated with the communist past and has obstructed more nuanced analysis of the moral complexities of individual cases.

Studying religions through the secret police archives

The peculiar significance and power of the secret police archives is in some senses amplified in the case of the documents relating to religious groups, which means that studying religions through them presents a number of distinct challenges as well as opportunities. Generally speaking, state and other archives, through their practices, establish their own authority by archiving that which is deemed worthy of preserving with the aim of determining how future generations should understand their past. Secret police archives, on the other hand, have systematically preserved a record of those whom the communist regimes judged as "unworthy," categorizing and producing knowledge about them to suit their ideological purposes. Due to the nature of the way the state, through its model of hostile separation, sought to expel religion from public life whilst also controlling (and defining) religious institutions from within, secret police documents disproportionately preserve records of the uncomfortable margins of mainstream religions, religious dissenters, troublesome rebels, and the religious competitors of the more compliant religious hierarchies, that also judged them as "unworthy." Groups that most official state archives systematically excluded and which the state most wanted to marginalize through its "knowledge" production and propaganda campaigns have been systematically and labouriously documented by the secret police.

The mass of documentation that exists is generally considered by historians to be more useful for understanding how the secret police "perceived individuals and groups and how the institution worked than for what historians usually consider to be their main task: reconstructing events" (Pintilescu 2018, 148). As Lisnic (Chapter 1), Vagramenko (Chapter 2), Matějka (Chapter 9), and others in this volume demonstrate, coming to grips with the discursive practices of the secret police is critical for understanding how enemies were perceived by the state and how the knowledge that was produced helped define operations and actions against these groups, thus shaping the daily activities of the secret police (see Pintilescu 2018, 126–7). The different categories of documentation produced by the bureaucratic processes of the secret police, however, offer opportunities for scholars of religions, and for members of surviving or descendent communities, to approach other questions that are specific to religious life.

In the absence of ethnographic data from the period, Hesz (Chapter 10, this volume) and Kapaló (Chapter 12, this volume) argue that secret police informer files have a particular value for research on everyday aspects of lived and material religion during communism. Despite the multiple voices, of the informer, the officer, the target, and the compiler, being layered together in reports, hints and fleeting glimpses of revealing everyday encounters and exchanges nevertheless offer insights into aspects of religious life as lived in the period. Examples cited by Hesz demonstrate how, despite inconsistent and contradictory information being very common, the vividness of some reports helps us grasp the agency of individuals and groups in their strategies of avoiding attention from the authorities or organizing their ritual life under the pressure of surveillance. In many cases, informers were themselves religious specialists who offered detailed and vivid accounts of religious ritual and belief in order to protect their targets whilst quietly fulfilling their duty to report. As Hesz outlines, approaching religion as a lived phenomenon and employing a vernacular religious lens to these bureaucratic documents, offer insights into how individuals navigated the strictures of the regime in the expression of their faith.

The vividness of informers' reports is sometimes matched by the visual materials that can be found in secret police files. As the chapters by Povedák (Chapter 11), Vagramenko (Chapter 2), and Krzywosz (Chapter 7) in this volume illustrate, in their attempts to incriminate and eliminate certain religious groups, the secret police preserved or created valuable visual and material traces of otherwise invisible clandestine communities. Inserted into the kilometres of shelves stacked with case files, the archives contain a hidden repository of confiscated religious materials such as leaflets, brochures, hymn sheets, diaries and community photographs – the ephemera of religious life. These sit alongside photographic images, graphs, maps and tables created by the secret police in the course of their investigations (see Kapaló and Vagramenko 2020). Oftentimes, groups such as the Nazarenes, discussed by Djurić Milovanović (Chapter 14) or the Inochentists discussed by Kapaló (Chapter 12), that due to their marginalized status, underground existence, or ambivalence towards the act of historical documentation, preserved few records themselves, can be found represented in great detail in the secret police files. Secret police archives, therefore, represent an important resource for understanding both how the totalitarian state constructed religious "others" in order to incriminate and control them and how certain religious communities chose to represent themselves in times of extreme repression.

As the studies by Vagramenko (Chapter 2), Povedák (Chapter 11), and Krzywosz (Chapter 7) show, as well as gathering confiscated materials, the secret police employed various photographic and graphic techniques as part of their construction of knowledge about and incrimination of religious groups. Vagramenko (Chapter 2) illustrates in her study of Soviet model criminal files, how specific visual forms of documentation and representation helped establish truths about the religious underground. Photography, in particular, played an important role in reinforcing the textual message of the file. Crime-scene photographs, discussed by Povedák (Chapter 11, this volume), were produced according to highly formulaic specifications that were often intended to capture the illegal economic activities of targeted groups (see also Kapaló 2019; Kapaló and Vagramenko 2020). The corpus of images in the archives, however, also includes a significant number of confiscated photographs that offer the researcher unique access to the self-representational practices of groups during communism. As with all other materials found in the archives, the photos we find there present both interpretational and ethical challenges. Employing the method of photo-elicitation, Povedák (Chapter 11, this volume) explores the advantages and pitfalls of working with descendent communities to redefine and recontextualize the photographic holdings of the archives.

Drawing on informer reports from an operation targeting Inochentist-Stilists in Romania in which the foodways of the community featured heavily, Kapaló (Chapter 12) explores the methodological potential of approaching the archives from a material religion perspective. Kapaló argues that certain secret police sources, especially those generated by insiders who acted as participants in the social and ritual life of communities, offer us an access point to the performative, material and somatic aspects of religious life. In response to the overwhelming tendency amongst scholars of communism to approach secret police materials from a solely discursive or constructionist approach, Kapaló suggests that when viewed through a material lens and situated within the broader religious context and lifeworld, the texts and images in the archives can reveal important, heretofore overlooked aspects of the transmission of religion in the underground.

Questions of morality, and especially sexuality, are also ubiquitous in secret police documents on religious life, as Şincan (Chapter 15, this volume) demonstrates in relation to Romania. Despite the communist regime's importation of a code of moral conduct from the Soviet Union, the moral standards that secret police officers used in policing religious groups betrayed a "hybridization" that drew on religious aspects and terms. The secret police, as Şincan's case studies demonstrate, were able to use information relating to an individual's moral conduct, whether genuine or fabricated, as a means of control with the Securitate officer acting "as moral censor and judge." The privacy of individuals targeted by the state was of course not respected by the secret police but today, for the researcher of religion under communism, the protection of the privacy of victims, especially with regard to issues of health and sexuality, is enshrined in law and shapes the practices of archival institutions. As Şincan's study demonstrates, this situation presents the researcher with a dilemma, as something that was so central to the way the secret police operated against religious actors, namely the use of coercion and blackmail based on questions of morality and sexuality, is extremely difficult legally and ethically to discuss in academic publications. In the post-communist context, the "breaking of the secrecy" that surrounded the archives (Stan 2013, 75), whilst serving to guarantee the break with the past and reassure citizens that surveillance had stopped, also granted the contemporary reader of a secret police file a "power over the individual" (Şincan, Chapter 15, this volume) that in its ability to shame, blackmail, and destroy reputations was cruelly similar to the power exercised by secret police officers. Those of us who study religions that were under the prying gaze of the secret police are increasingly called to reflect on our positionality. Thus, Şincan asks, "as the current readers of these files, are we imposing similar personal definitions of good and bad, moral and immoral onto behaviours and narratives in the archival documents?"

The archives of the secret police, despite their enormous significance for researchers and religious communities alike, have their limits. The problematic epistemological and ethical nature of secret police archival documents (and in some cases the lack of access to them), encourages or demands the use of alternative sources. Several of the chapters in this volume engage the archival data in dialogue with the archives of religious communities (see Pranskevičiūtė-Amoson, Chapter 8; Petrás, Chapter 5; Matějka, Chapter 9) and oral historical research (see Petrás, Chapter 5; Pranskevičiūtė-Amoson, Chapter 8; Matějka, Chapter 9 and Povedák, Chapter 11, this volume). The lack of access to secret police materials, as Djurić Milovanović (this volume, Chapter 14) outlines in her research on religious minorities in communist Yugoslavia, means that historians of religions have to glean as much information from the Ministry of Internal Affairs, the Ministry of Religious Affairs, the Ministry of Justice, and other public administration archives and triangulate this with ethnographic research with individuals and communities. Djurić Milovanović shows that such research "reveals not only the richness of preserved memory but also their personal archival material ..." including documents related to imprisonment or verdicts from the military courts, photographs, letters and books. In her case study of the KGB operation against ISKCON in Lithuania (Chapter 8), Pranskevičiūtė-Amoson also identifies the inherent problems associated with KGB documents which render them insufficient as sources when seeking to understand complex sociocultural processes such as the success of ISKCON in Soviet Lithuania. As Pranskevičiūtė-Amoson asserts, only through the utilization of interviews with individuals who were members of ISKCON and were targeted by the secret police can we gain insights into the real motivations of members of the movement and the actual activities of the KGB, which are often masked in the official reports and accounts.

Conclusion

In this introductory chapter, we have only been able to address some of the important historical points, theoretical questions and methodological insights that appear in the chapters of this volume. The challenges of working with the multidimensional and politically charged secret police archives, as this volume seeks to illustrate, are both epistemological and deeply ethical in character. Interpreting files, reports and images that are antagonistic towards their subject, couched in ideological language, formulaic, and misinformed or intentionally misleading, incomplete (or selectively withheld) has become the business not only of trained historians and lawyers, but also of journalists, politicians, and the general public who have pursued vigilante actions (Stan 2011) in the search for justice, truth or redemption. As such, overreliance on secret police materials can, and has, produced extremely distorted views of the past that have in turn shaped historical memory, political discourse and conceptions of justice and truth in post-communist society. The religious underground, which constituted the object of secret police operations being both produced and defined by them, however, was no mere mirage, metaphor or discourse but a lived experience bound by a material existence, social bonds and individual agency. It is the aim of this volume to encourage further scholarly reflection on the complex intersection of the secret police, and their archives, and the meaning and lived reality of the religious underground.

Acknowledgement

The research for this chapter was funded by the European Research Council (ERC) under the European Union's Horizon 2020 research and innovation programme No. 677355.

Notes

1 Founded in 1960, Underground Evangelism began by smuggling bibles into the Soviet Union and Eastern Europe. The organization still operates today under the name Mission Without Borders www.mwbi.org/about-us.

2 Aurel Zapodean and Nicolae Bordeianu (1983), *Aspecte din activitatea ostilă desfăşurată de elemente autohtone incitate de emisari ai unor centri şi organizaţii religioase reacţionare din străinătate. Măsuri întreprinse de organele de securitate pentru prevenirea şi contracararea acştiunilor duşmănoase desfăşurată sub acoperirea religiei* (ACNSAS D008712 vol. 1, 12).

Archival sources

Consiliul Naţional pentru Studierea Arhivelor Securităţii [National Council for the Study of the Securitate Archives] (ACNSAS), D008712, vol. 1.

References

Apor, Péter, Horváth, Sándor and Mark, James. 2017. "Introduction: Collaboration, Cooperation and Political Participation in Communist Regimes." In: *Secret Agents and the Memory of Everyday Collaboration in Communist Eastern Europe*, edited by Péter Apor, Sándor Horváth and James Mark, 1–17. London and New York: Anthem Press.

Baran, Emily. 2014. *Dissent on the Margins: How Soviet Jehovah's Witnesses Defied Communism and Lived to Preach About It*. Oxford and New York: Oxford University Press.

Blaive, Muriel. 2019. "Introduction." In: *Perceptions of Society in Communist Europe: Regime Archives and Popular Opinion,* edited by Muriel Blaive, 1–12. London, New York: Oxford Bloomsbury Academic.

Bögre, Zsuzsanna and Szabó, Csaba. 2010. *Broken Lives – Lifestories of Nuns During Communism* [*Törésvonalak – Apácasorsok a kommunizmusban*]. Budapest: Metem–Historia Ecclesiastica Hungarica Alapítvány–Szent István Társulat.

Boiter, Albert. 1987. "Law and Religion in the Soviet Union." The American Journal of Comparative Law 35 (1): 97–126.

Chumachenko, Tatiana A. 2002. *Church and State in Soviet Russia*. Armonk, New York, London: M. E. Sharpe.

Dragadze, Tamara. 1993. The Domestication of Religion under Soviet Communism. In *Socialism: Ideals, Ideologies, and Local Practice*, edited by Chris M. Hann, 148–9. London & New York: Routledge.

Engelmann, Roger. 2015. "Safeguarding the Stasi Files and Making Them Publically Accessible." In: *State Security: A Reader on the GDR Secret Police*, edited by Daniela Mükel, 113–19. Berlin, Federal Commissioner for the Records of the State Security Service of the Former German Democratic Republic (BSTU).

Fejérdy, András et al. 2018. "Religious Resistance: Forms, Sources and Collections." In: *The Handbook of Courage: Cultural Opposition and its Heritage In Eastern Europe*, edited by Balázs Apor, Péter Apor and Sándor Horváth, 445–71. Budapest: Institute of History, Research Centre for the Humanities, Hungarian Academy of Sciences.

Flemming, Michael. 2009. *Communism, Nationalism and Ethnicity in Poland, 1944–1950*. London: Routledge.

Fletcher, William C. 1970. "Underground Orthodoxy: A Problem of Political Control." *Canadian Slavonic Papers / Revue Canadienne des Slavistes*. 12 (4): 363–94.

Hagenloh, Paul. 2009. *Stalin's Police: Public Order and Mass Repression in the USSR, 1926–1941*. Baltimore: John Hopkins University Press.

Harrison, Mark. 2010. "You Have Been Warned: The KGB and Profilaktika in Lithuania in the 1970s." *Political Economy Research in Soviet Archives (PERSA) Working Paper* No. 62. https://warwick.ac.uk/fac/soc/economics/staff/mharrison/archive/persa/062.pdf

Heidemeyer, Helge. 2015. "The Ministry of State Security and its Relationship to the SED." In: *State Security: A Reader on the GDR Secret Police*, edited by Daniela Münkel, 10–19. Berlin, Federal Commissioner for the Records of the State Security Service of the Former German Democratic Republic (BSTU).

Horváth, Zsolt K. 2008. "The Redistribution of the Memory of Socialism: Identity Formations of the "Survivors" in Hungary after 1989." In: *Past for the Eyes: East European Representations of Communism in Cinema and Museums after* 1989, edited by Oksana Sarkisova and Péter Apor, 247–73. Budapest and New York: CEU Press.

Johnson, Sylvester A. and Weitzman, Steven (eds.). 2017. *The FBI and Religion: Faith and National Security Before and After 9/11*. Oakland, California: California University Press.

Kapaló, James. 2019. *Inochentism and Orthodox Christianity: Religious Dissent in the Russian and Romanian Borderlands*. Abingdon and New York: Routledge.

Kapaló, James, and Vagramenko, Tatiana (eds.). 2020. *Hidden Galleries: Material Religion in the Secret Police Archives in Central and Eastern Europe*. Berlin: Lit Verlag.

Kasprzak, Michal. 2004. Radio Free Europe and the Catholic Church in Poland During the 1950s and 1960s. *Canadian Slavonic Papers / Revue Canadienne des Slavistes.* 46 (3): 315–41.

Kelly, Caitriona. 2012. "Competing Orthodoxies: Identity and Religious Belief in Soviet and post-Soviet Russia." In *Soviet and Post-Soviet Identities*, edited by Mark Bassin and Caitriona Kelly, 229–320. Cambridge: Cambridge University Press.

Kiss, Réka, Soós, Viktor Attila and Tabajdi, Csaba. 2012. *How to Repress the Churches? A Textbook for Officers* [*Hogyan üldözzünk egyházakat? Állambiztonsági tankönyv tartótiszteknek*]. Budapest: L'Harmattan.

Klimó, Árpád von. 2016. "Vatican II and Hungary." In: *Vatican II Behind the Iron Curtain*, edited by Piotr Kosicki, 50–75. Washington D.C.: Catholic University of America Press.

Kosicki, Piotr H. (ed.). 2016. *Vatican II Behind the Iron Curtain.* Washington D.C.: Catholic University of America Press.

Kotkin, Stephen. 2002. "The State – Is It US? Memoirs, Archives, and Kremlinologists." *The Russian Review*. 61 (1): 35–51.

Křišťál, Miroslav. 1985. The Contribution of the StB towards the Limitation of Enemy Activities Inside the Evangelical Church of Czech Brethern and Their Abuse by Political and Church Opposition in Czechoslovakia and by Foreign Opponents ["Podíl orgánů StB na zamezování nepřátelské činnosti v Českobratrské církvi evangelické a na jejím zneužívání politickou i církevní opozicí v ČSSR, jakož i zahraničním protivníkem"]. Master Thesis, Vysoká škola SNB, Fakulta StB, Praha.

Leuştean, Lucian. 2009. *Eastern Christianity and the Cold War, 1945–1991*. Abingdon and New York: Routledge.

Melley, Timothy. 2000. *Empire of Conspiracy: The Culture of Paranoia in Postwar America*. Cornell University Press.

Michel, Patrick. 1991. *Politics and Religion in Eastern Europe: Catholicism in Hungary, Poland and Czechoslovakia*. Cambridge: Polity Press.

Müller, Rolf. 2012. *The Political Police in the Rákosi-era* [*Politikai Rendőrség a Rákosi-korszakban*]. Budapest: Jaffa Kiadó.

Pehe, Veronika. 2019. "Autheniticating the Past: Archives, Secret Police and Heroism in Contemporary Czech Representations of Socialism." In: *Perceptions of Society in Communist Europe: Regime Archives and Popular Opinion,* edited by Muriel Blaive, 207–22. London, New York: Oxford Bloomsbury Academic.

Pintilsecu, Corneliu. 2018. "The Production of the Securitate's 'Truth'." In: *Aus den Giftschränken des Kommunismus: Methodische Fragen zum Umgang mit Überwachungsakten in Yentralü und Südosteuropa*, edited by Florian Kührer-Weileach and Michaela Novotnick, 125–48. Regensburg: Verlag Friedrich Pustet.

Pranskevičiūtė, Rasa and Juras, Tadas. 2014. "Acting in the Underground: Life as a Hare Krishna Devotee in the Soviet Republic of Lithuania." *Religion and Society in Central and Eastern Europe*, 7 (1): 3–22.

Ramet, Sabrina P. (ed.). 1988. *Eastern Christianity and Politics in the Twentieth Century (Christianity Under Stress, 1)*. Durham, North Carolina: Duke University Press.

Ramet, Sabrina P. (ed.). 1990. *Catholicism and Politics in Communist Societies (Christianity under stress, 2)*. Durham, North Carolina: Duke University Press.

Ramet, Sabrina P. (ed.). 1992. *Protestantism and Politics in Eastern Europe and Russia: The Communist and Post-communist Eras (Christianity Under Stress, 3)*. Durham, North Carolina: Duke University Press.

Ramet, Sabrina P. 1998. *Nihil Obstat: Religion, Politics and Social Change in East-Central Europe and Russia?* North Carolina: Duke University Press.

Smith, Steve. 2006. "Heavenly Letters and Tales of the Forest: 'Superstition' against Bolshevism." *Forum for Anthropology and Culture* 2: 316–39.

Stan, Lavinia. 2005. "Inside the Securitate Archives." *Woodrow Wilson Centre for International Scholars, Cold War International History Project*. Accessed on 19 March 2020 www.wilsoncenter.org/article/inside-the-securitate-archives.

Stan, Lavinia. 2011. "Vigilante Justice in Post-Communist Europe." *Communist and Post-Communist Studies* 44: 319–27.

Stan, Lavinia. 2013. *Transitional Justice in Post-Communist Romania: The Politics of Memory*. New York: Cambridge University Press.

Uitz, Renáta. 2008. "Communist Secret Services on the Screen." In: *Past for the Eyes: East European Representations of Communism in Cinema and Museums after 1989*, edited by Oksana Sarkisova and Péter Apor, 57–79. Budapest and New York: CEU Press.

Wanner, Catherine. 2007. *Communities of the Converted: Ukrainians and Global Evangelism*. Ithaca, NY: Cornell University Press.

Werth, Paul W. 2014. *The Tsar's Foreign Faiths: Toleration and the Fate of Religious Freedom in Imperial Russia*. Oxford: Oxford University Press.

Wynot, Jennifer Jean. 2004. *Keeping the Faith: Russian Orthodox Monasticism in the Soviet Union, 1917–1939*. College Station, Texas: Texas A & M University Press.

Vagramenko, Tatiana. 2021. KGB "Evangelism": Agents and Jehovah's Witnesses in Soviet Ukraine. *Kritika*.

Vățulescu, Cristina. 2010. *Police Aesthetics: Literature, Film and the Secret Police in Soviet Times*. Stanford California: Stanford University Press.

Vățulescu, Cristina. 2020. "The Mug Shot and the CloseUp: Visual Identification in Secret Police Film and Photography", *Association for Slavic, East European and Eurasian Studies*, Virtual Conference/Webinar series "Political Police and the Soviet System", April 17, 2020.

Verdery, Katherine. 2014. *Secrets and Truths: Ethnography in the Archive of Romania's Secret Police*. Budapest and New York: CEU Press.

Verdery, Katherine. 2018. *My Life as A Spy: Investigations in a Secret Police File*. Durham and London: Duke University Press.

Viola, Lynne. 1990. The Peasant Nightmare: Visions of Apocalypse in the Soviet Countryside. *Journal of Modern History* 62 (4): 747–70.

Young, Glennys. 1997. *Power and the Sacred in Revolutionary Russia: Religios Activists in the Village*. University Park, Pennsylvania: Pennsylvania University Press.

Part I

Constructing the enemy

Historical and legal contexts

1 Shifting images of a harmful sect

Operations against Inochentism in Soviet Ukraine, 1920–23

Dumitru Lisnic

This chapter concerns anti-sectarian policies designed by local Soviet authorities in the early 1920s. The case that I analyze in the following pages exemplifies how a set of local events, perceptions and relations could produce an image of an allegedly harmful sect. This image went on to form the centre of propaganda narratives and repressive policies against this religious group throughout the Soviet period right down to the end of the regime. The case examined here shows how a set of contrasting archival images of a religious group were constructed at different hierarchical levels of the Soviet administration. This study aims to contribute to the already existing scholarship on early Soviet engagement with religion, which although impressively detailed with regard to the formation and evolution of the policing system and repressive mechanisms, does not explore the role of functionaries and police officials at the micro-level in shaping the regime's perception and understanding of specific cohorts of population targeted by repressive policies. My study is centred on the case of Inochentism, a religious movement that emerged amongst Romanian-speaking peasants at the beginning of the twentieth century in the northern part of today's Odessa Oblast of Ukraine. I identified a series of documents which shed light on the first encounters of the Soviet regime with this minority religion and contribute to our understanding of how at the local level the Inochentists came to be regarded as a hindrance to the Bolshevik project. In this study, I use the term "local" to refer to all levels of administration hierarchically lower than governorate/region centres, namely the village, *volost*, district, county and *okrug*.[1]

Inochentism is a religious movement that emerged from within Orthodox Christianity in the territories of the Russian Empire that had a Moldovan population. Numerous ethnic Romanian[2] peasants from the territories of today's Republic of Moldova and from Odessa oblast in Ukraine, beginning in 1909, began to follow the teachings of the charismatic monk Inochentie of Balta, from whom the movement took its name. Thousands of pilgrims gathered at the monastery of Balta, located in the northern part of today's Odessa oblast, where father Inochentie Levizor preached a message of repentance, extreme fasting and celibacy in preparation for the impending End of Days. He also performed mass confession and exorcisms (on early Inochentist practice see Kapaló 2019, 74–106). In 1912, the Russian authorities exiled Inochentie, giving rise to an intensification of apocalyptic expectation and narratives amongst his followers, which resulted in many of them selling their properties, adopting celibacy and moving to Lipeţcoe (Ukrainian *Lipetske*) near Balta, where they built an underground monastery and established an utopian communal society called "Gradina Raiului," the Garden of Paradise, often abbreviated in contemporary sources to "Rai." Inochentie was freed by the amnesty that followed the February Revolution of 1917 but died shortly after his liberation in December 1917 (see Kapaló 2019, 47–9).

The events described in this chapter unfolded in one of the Western peripheries of former Russian Empire, which was conquered by the Reds at the end of the Russian Civil War. The counties of Ananiev and Balta, located in the northern part of Odessa Governorate, were controlled by Denikin's forces until the first weeks of 1920, when the Red Army occupied these overwhelmingly rural territories. After the county of Ananiev was dissolved in 1921, Ananiev city and the surrounding villages were included in Balta county. A specific feature of the area where the city of Ananiev is located was that in the early 1920s the majority of its rural population was Moldovan (DAOO, fond. P-12068-1-171, 140).[3] According to archival documents, Moldovan peasants were considered more religious and less literate than their Ukrainian and Russian neighbours (AOSPRM, fond. 49-1-205, 21). The traditions, institutions and the way of life, or "the social space" (Viola 1996, 38) of Moldovan rural communities had been less impacted than other communities by the processes of modernization that penetrated the countryside during the first decades of the twentieth century. As a consequence, they were less involved in the new forms of economic production and in local political life. For example, according to a report from 1924, there were more Ukrainians than Moldovans among the *kolkhozniki* of the collective farms located in Moldovan villages from MASSR[4] (AOSPRM fond. 49-1-235, 6). In 1925, only 6.5% of the communists in MASSR were Moldovans (AOSPRM fond. 49-1-84, 59). Significantly, Rai, the Inochentist spiritual centre, was located on the territory of Ananiev county. In 1921, after an anti-Inochentist operation in September 1920, which resulted in the flight of a part of the Inochentists from Rai, the population of the Inochentist settlement was approximately 800 persons (ASBUOO 27146, 237). The followers of Inochentie of Balta also lived in other villages and they had a significant influence among the local peasantry. Additionally, numerous Inochentist communities existed in other counties from the south-western part of Soviet Ukraine and in Bessarabia, which was part of Romania at that time.

Anti-religious policy and Soviet countryside in the early 1920s

One of the most ambitious projects of the Bolshevik party was to transform Russia into an atheist country and to root out religion from its society. The law of January 21, 1918 on the separation of church and state had a special significance in this regard. Citizens were granted freedom of conscience and the right to not follow any religion, and any kind of discrimination based on confessional affiliation or atheism was outlawed. Churches and religious organizations were no longer to have the status of legal persons nor the right to property and as a consequence the buildings and religious items of all confessions in Russia were declared public property and they could only be used for religious purposes with the permission of authorities (Pospielovsky 1987, 133–4). In this first period of church-state relations between 1917 and 1920, the Soviet state attempted to seize the Russian Orthodox Church's proprieties and to destroy its institutional structures. Other religious groups were targeted only as part of a general policy of terror but the Orthodox Church, its clergy and churchgoing, in general, were under permanent coordinated pressure that aimed at eliminating its influence altogether (Walters 1993, 5–7).

During this period the Bolsheviks' policies of War Communism, which attempted to restructure Russian society and its economy through such measures as the ban on private trade and the nationalization of economic assets, caused extreme damage to the economy. The peasantry hoarded their agricultural products in response to low prices offered by the state and to the devaluation of the currency. In May 1918 the Bolsheviks began the forced requisitioning conducted by armed civilians and Red Army soldiers, who entered villages and deprived farmers of all their produce. In response, the countryside resisted in different ways including open rebellion (Pipes 1996, 195; 200; 205–6).

The violent policies of the Bolsheviks were not only driven by the shortages, but also by their ideology according to which the food crisis was caused by the resistance of socially hostile kulaks, imagined as the most reactionary part of the peasantry who exploited the poor farmers. In the post-revolutionary years, the food crisis in the Bolshevik-held territories worsened as a consequence of a number of additional factors among which was the ongoing civil war which ended in 1921. The main food-producing areas, such as Ukraine, Caucasus, Siberia and Volga, were under the control of White forces, leaving Bolshevik-held central regions of European Russia without needed supplies. After the winter of 1919–20, when the Red Army captured from the Whites large areas including important agricultural bases, the pressure on the peasantry did not decrease. Nevertheless, numerous peasant rebellions and the Kronstadt uprising forced the Bolsheviks to abandon the policy of War Communism and to implement the New Economic Policy (NEP) beginning from 1921 (Mawdsley 1987, 71–2; 242–3). The Tenth Party Congress in March 1921 decided to replace the forced seizure of agricultural produce with a limited marked exchange in order to mitigate the tensions in the regime's relations with the peasantry. Although this new policy aimed at stabilizing the situation in the country, harsh repressive operations were conducted by the Cheka (political police)[5] 18 months after the abovementioned party congress. In 1921, with the Politburo's approval the Cheka conducted numerous repressive operations against striking workers and political opponents. Up until mid-1922, peasants that resisted were subjected to the most brutal measures including punitive executions of members of rebels' families and hostage taking as well as tens of thousands of arrests and executions (Hagenloh 2009, 30–3).

In terms of anti-religious policy, the years of NEP can be considered as the second period of church-state relations (Walters 1993, 7–13), which is characterized by a partial decrease in state violence. A circular of the Central Committee from February 1922 and the Party Congress from April 1923 stressed the need to conduct strong anti-religious propaganda avoiding aggressive methods that would provoke the strengthening of religious feelings (Peris 1998, 32). Nevertheless, in 1921–22, the Orthodox Church faced aggressive assaults from the Bolshevik regime, which attempted to use the context of the famine in its anti-religious project. Although the Orthodox Church was involved in collecting relief and donated its own resources to support the peasants affected by the famine, Soviet authorities launched a campaign of seizing church valuables to help the starving. Numerous priests and believers resisted the seizure of sacramental items and were arrested or executed (Peris 1998, 26–7).

In contrast to the experience of the Orthodox Church, Vladimir Bonch-Bruevich, an influential Bolshevik leader, obtained the opportunity to prove his argument that so-called sectarians were a religious expression of social and political protest (Coleman 2005, 158). One of the first privileges granted by the Bolshevik state to sectarians was the decree in 1919 that freed the former religious dissenters of the obligation to serve in the army. On November 5, 1921, the People's Commissariat of Agriculture[6] made an appeal to sectarians and Old Believers from Russia and abroad, to settle on the lands confiscated by the Bolsheviks in 1917–21 and to create agricultural communes. According to the text of the appeal, the sectarians had a communist way of life long before the Revolution of 1917 and they had been persecuted by the tsarist authorities (Etkind 2013, 604–6). Through the granting of privileges to sectarian agricultural communes, and through successful work, they hoped to convince the peasantry that work in collectives was the best means of agricultural production. In April 1925, approximately 100 Evangelical Christian Communist communities and 20 Baptist ones were in existence. In these communities, the members worked the common land with common tools, and in some cases even lived in the same buildings and kept all their money in a common budget (Coleman 2005, 174–5). By the end of the 1920s, the party had rejected the idea that communism had any connections with sectarian beliefs. As a result, during the collectivization of agriculture, the campaign for the creation of kolkhozes was applied to sectarian agricultural communes in the same way as other peasant settlements (Etkind 2013, 626).

Local institutions of power in the early 1920s

The Reds took Ananiev under their control at the beginning of 1920. An essential part of the consolidation of Bolshevik control at a local level was the formation of a set of incipient institutions in order to prepare the ground and to administer the newly occupied territories under the extreme circumstances of ongoing military confrontations. The common way of establishing Soviet control in a territory after its occupation by the Red Army was to form a revolutionary committee (*revkom*). These committees had extraordinary powers and imposed martial law in the occupied territorial units. Among their duties was to unify and direct available revolutionary forces and to govern the territory, to initiate the formation of a local party committee, and to eliminate hostile elements (Easter 2000, 32). In the case of Ananiev county, the party committee was created on February 12, 1920, and it appointed a party member to the revolutionary committees of each *volost* and to the *revkom* of the county (DAOO fond. P-12233-1-2, 1–3).

After this initial stage in the organizational process at the local level, a large degree of decision-making power was concentrated in the committee of the party organization of the administrative units with its meetings attended by the heads of the most influential institutions and organizations, many of whom were part of its membership. The primary party organizations were the smallest party units which were attached to villages, institutions or collective farms, and which played multiple roles in the countryside. Their members were usually the heads of the village soviets, of the collective farms, and of other institutions and organizations. At the same time, they observed the mood of the villagers, the activity of the bureaucrats of non-worker social origins, and were empowered to arrest the regime's enemies. In numerous penal cases against religious minorities from the countryside, local communists were both informers and witnesses for the secret police. As A. Berelowitch and V. Danilov mention, institutional reports of village soviets and *volost* executive committees to higher authorities were the main source of information for the Soviet secret police regarding the state of affairs in the countryside because the secret police had not yet developed an efficient network of informers in rural areas in 1920–30s (2000, 10).

Other important local institutions were the executive committees[7] that took on the duties of local government, although their activity was under the tight control of the party. The majority of the specialists who in the early 1920s worked in the state bureaucracy were of "hostile social origins" or even fought against the Reds during the Civil War. Nevertheless, the Bolsheviks could not govern the country without the expertise of these bureaucrats who were placed under the permanent supervision of party members appointed to key positions in the administration (Heinzen 1997, 87).

The All-Russian Extraordinary Committee, or the Cheka, was established on December 7, 1917, based on the decision of the Soviet Government, headed by Lenin. The main task of this agency was to struggle against counterrevolutionary activity and acts of sabotage and to take punitive measures, including extrajudicial execution, against those who engaged in such actions. (Jakovlev 2003, 14–15). One of the objectives of the Secret Department of the Cheka, established on February 24, 1919, was to struggle against the "hostile activity of churchman and sectarians" (Jakovlev 2003, 17). On June 11, 1918, the

Conference of All-Russian Extraordinary Committee decided to expand its presence at the local level by establishing Cheka departments in each oblast, governorate and county (Kokurin 1997; 9). The earliest available documentary evidence I have identified mentions the existence of a Cheka department in Ananiev county from September 15, 1920 (DAOO, fond. P-12233-1-4, 13). Before the creation of secret police departments at the level of counties, the repressive policies of the regime were applied by the County Departments of Secret Informers.[8] On April 3, 1920, the Headquarters of the Red Army units that operated in the region together with the Odessa department of the Cheka ordered the formation of the County Departments of Secret Informers in the governorate. They were subordinated to the Odessa Cheka and to the local *revkomy*. They were to establish a network of informers in each village, collect data regarding criminality in the county and about the mood of the population, prevent peasant rebellions and struggle against any armed bands of insurgents. These departments were obliged to inform the Cheka about the situation in the county, and they had military detachments under their command. The only difference between the prerogatives of the local Cheka agencies and of these departments was that unlike the former, the County Secret Informer Departments could not sentence arrested citizens (DAOO, fond. R-2106-4-1, 1–4).

On February 23, 1922, the Politburo decided to abolish the Cheka and to replace it with the GPU, or the State Political Directorate, which had a similar structure and prerogatives (Jakovlev 2003; 24–5). This change was advocated by some Bolshevik leaders who wanted to limit the powers of the Soviet civil and political police. Unlike the Cheka, the GPU was subordinated to the NKVD[9] which had formally been accountable to the government, and the extrajudicial prerogatives of civil and political police were abolished. Nevertheless, political police was technically subordinated to the Politburo and Felix Dzerzhinsky, the chief and the founder of the Cheka, continued to head the NKVD. The legal framework imposed on the activity of police in 1922, however, was frequently ignored by officers. Although the police had its extrajudicial powers partially restored, it did not continue to enjoy the same freedom to conduct its struggle against real or perceived enemies as during the Civil War (Hagenloh 2009, 32–3; 35; 40).

In the realm of state repression, an important role was also played by civil police. After the Bolsheviks seized power, the decentralized and self-governed police forces were moved under the authority of the NKVD, created on November 10, 1917. In the context of the ongoing civil war, in March 1919, Felix Dzerzhinsky was appointed as head of NKVD, and the activity of the civil police (*Militsiia*) was subordinated to the Cheka (Hagenloh 2009, 25–6). In the NEP era, the civil and political police were separated in a few stages. In 1923, Dzerzhinsky was replaced by Beloborodov as the head of NKVD, and in March 1924 the OGPU was created as a separate political police structure with its Special Board authorized to conduct administrative sentences. In the following years the two police forces competed over the control of different domains of policing and over the exclusive right to conduct extrajudicial repression. Both *Militsia* and OGPU faced a shortage of staff and funding, and their presence outside of cities was scarce (Hagenloh 2009, 34–40; 42). The presence of militia forces in the northern part of Odessa province, as elsewhere, was also thin and varied from one territorial unit to another. For example, in Tiraspol county in 1921 there was a total number of 387 pedestrian militiamen and 23 mounted (TsDAVOV, fond. 5-1-618, 18.) which is not many for a territorial unit of its size.

The institutions introduced above constituted the main state and party organizations that operated at the local level. As we shall see, on the territory of the Ananiev county they played a major role in both shaping the regime's perception of Inochentism and in designing a set of local repressive policies against this religious group. The prejudices and perceptions produced by the various local authorities of Ananiev shaped the regime's understanding of Inochentism right up until the collapse of the USSR.

Insurgency and counterinsurgency in Ananiev county and the "problem of Rai"

The first repressive operation against the Inochentists conducted by the authorities of Ananiev county is a good example of how in the context of civil war and peasant rebellions, local functionaries constructed the image of an enemy, projecting onto the Inochentist community their fears and misunderstanding of the religious practices of this minority group. The monastery of Rai was besieged and liquidated by party workers and Cheka troops in September 1920. A number of accounts of this operation survived including a few archival documents and a number of propaganda articles.

As with the rest of Ukraine, Ananiev county was part of the battleground of the Russian Civil War. The county and the city of Ananiev were re-conquered by the Red Army from the Whites in the first weeks of 1920 after the Reds retreated from the area in 1919 (DAOO fond. P-12233-1-2, 1). Military confrontations, however, continued in the county of Ananiev after its occupation by the Red Army. The highest point of the anti-Bolshevik military resistance in the region following the defeat of the Whites came in April 1920. The forces of Zabolotnyi, a military commander of the Ukrainian Republic who operated in the area, took under their control the Bîrzula-Jerebkovo railway and occupied Ananiev. According to Bolshevik party reports, many villages from the vicinity of Ananiev formed armed detachments and sent them to support Zabolotnyi's forces. By the end of April, Zabolotnyi had been defeated (DAOO, fond P-3-1-13, 6) but he and his detachments continued to wage an insurgent war moving from one village to another and attacking the Soviet forces and officials.

In the northern territories of Odessa governorate, numerous insurgent groups continued their fight for the rights of the peasantry or for Ukrainian national cause against the Bolsheviks. According to numerous reports, anti-Bolshevik detachments were spread throughout the countryside where they enjoyed the support of the peasantry and they waged a partisan war against the regime. These detachments were very active, numerous and well-armed. For example, in March 1921 alone the insurgents conducted 52 raids in Balta county. As a consequence, the Soviet authorities lost 40 men, 20 horses and a significant quantity of grain (DAOO, fond. P-1-1-37, 3–5). Additionally, in the early 1920s in many villages, peasants rose up against the Soviet authorities. The best hiding place in the region for the rebels were the forests. Around Balta, Sovransk and Kruty, where there were large areas with forest cover, the insurgency was stronger than in other parts of the northern territory of Odessa governorate. According to party reports, the roots of the insurgency were in the peasantry's discontent with the grain requisition campaigns and with the abuses committed by Soviet officials (DAOO, fond. P-1-1-37, 3–7; 10–11).

Possibly because the authorities were so busy dealing with armed resistance in the countryside, party reports from 1920–21 contain less data on religious affairs than the documents from the following years. Nevertheless, from the first days after the re-occupation of Ananiev by the Reds, Soviet officials were very attentive to Rai. Numerous reports from the 1920s issued in Ananiev, Balta and Odessa, mention the existence of Inochentist communities such as this report by a party worker who visited a number of villages from the vicinity of Ananiev during the first months of 1920.

> By coincidence I was near the "Monastery Rai," which is located near Gandrabura. It was a holiday and approximately 2000 peasants gathered there. After the service, the priest made a speech saying "you are not humans but pigs and you do not need an authority. Now the country is ruled by pigs. We need a tsar." In the caves, *petliurovtsy* [fighters for the Ukrainian Republic] and weapons are possibly hidden. The caves shelter saints, and everywhere there is lying and thieves.
>
> (DAOO, fond. P-12233-1-22, 11)

Besides the reported sedition, the attention of the party worker was attracted to the underground monastic complex. The network of underground spaces built by Inochentists appeared to be a perfect hiding place that was beyond the control of the authorities. The perception that the Inochentist underground was a hideout for anti-Soviet elements took an official form in September 1920 when the party bureau of Ananiev county decided to take measures against Rai monastery and liquidated it because "... in 'Raiskij Sad' [...] counter-revolutionaries are hiding, [and] there is anti-Soviet preaching ..." (DAOO, fond. P-12233-1-4, 12; 18).

Eliminating any possibility of hiding was one of the main aims of the measures taken by the authorities in their struggle against the insurgency. For example, in order to make the forests from the region less suitable for sheltering anti-Bolshevik insurgents, by 1923 the authorities had replaced the forest guards with Red Army veterans (DAOO, fond. P-12068-1-18, 1). The colonization of strategic and border areas with veterans was a measure used by the regime to create social support in territories where it was most needed (Viola 2014, 56). For the local Soviet authorities in Ananiev, the elimination of the underground network of tunnels that were controlled by a monarchist sect (ASBUOO 27146, 12) was to prove of equal importance to the appointment of veterans to guard the forests.

The Inochentist underground was still a source of concern for local authorities in 1921, one year after the initial liquidation of the monastery. One of the most frequent questions asked by the secret police officers during the interrogation of the Inochentists arrested in 1921 was if they have a secret entrance to underground except the known ones that had been sealed by the authorities one year earlier (ASBUOO 27146, 62–224). The monastery of Rai and its preachers were the focus of the Soviet authorities, however, not only because of their underground monastery and anti-Soviet preaching. On September 6, 1920, a decision of the county party committee explains the need to take measures against the monks of Rai:

> About "Raiskij Sad," the Inochentist monastery where [unintelligible word] counterrevolutionaries are hiding, anti-Soviet preaching takes place, where because of [unintelligible word] against the kulaks, the wealthy elements of the countryside transport grain, clothing, money and valuables during the night.
>
> Resolution: It is necessary for Special Troika[10] to pay attention, especially to village Tocilovo, through which the kulaks of the surrounding villages like Lipetskoe, Baital, Gandrabura, Perelioty, transport their property during the night.
>
> (DAOO fond. P-12233-1-4, 12)

The text of this decision reveals that the economic activity of the Inochentist monastery whose active members were travelling through villages, preaching and collecting donations, was interpreted by local authorities in a manner that linked the Inochentist problem to the official narrative about the struggle against the kulaks. The Soviet regime imagined the kulaks as an "avaricious, bloated, and bestial" enemy from the countryside and it kulakized all peasants who opposed its policies (Viola 1996, 16) especially the requisition of grains, which was one of the main tasks of the local authorities. The gathering of economically significant donations by the network of Inochentist preachers gave rise to suspicions that the Inochentists constituted an organized kulak conspiracy and that the community held large quantities of agricultural produce and valuables in the underground monastery. Significantly therefore, in the early 1920s, in the period in which the central Soviet authorities were promoting a set of policies favourable to religious sectarians who they were encouraged to establish agricultural communes on the land provided to them by the state (Coleman 2005, 174–5), the Inochentist commune, on the other hand, was nevertheless perceived and labelled in the local context as an enemy.

One of the earliest propaganda accounts of the closing of the Inochentist monastery that I have identified is an article published in 1927 in the newspaper of the Central Committee of Party Organisation of MASSR, *Plugarul Roş* (The Red Ploughman). The article describes the liquidation of Rai in the following terms:

> [...] immediately after the counterrevolution was identified in Rai, and after the "holy fathers" began their fight against the Soviet authorities, Cheka undertook appropriate measures to drive them away, and indeed it forced them to leave. [...] The liquidation of Rai did not take place without casualties, without bloodshed. The first victim was the head of the Revolutionary Committee from Nanile [Moldovan name of Ananiev], comrade Anosov. Anosov was killed by Ionko, the brother of the most beloved women (nun) of Inochentie [...] who was the commander of the Bîrzu Railway Station [...] He took a group of Red Army soldiers and attacked Anosov [and his troops that besieged the monastery].
>
> (Lesi Gomin 1927, part 2–3)

According to the article in *Plugarul Roş*, during the liquidation of Rai two separate Soviet military detachments clashed with each other. We can make sense of this based on two contextual factors. Firstly, there were ongoing clashes locally between the authorities and bands of insurgents and secondly, a breakdown of communication between the detachments sent by Bîrzula railway administration and by the county administration might easily have happened as a consequence of the poor state of communication infrastructure.

An important figure in the propaganda history of the closure of Rai is Anosov, the secretary of Ananiev Party Committee. His death during the violent closing of Rai is confirmed by the fact that according to archival documents on the location of Rai monastery an orphanage was established which was named after the dead secretary Anosov (DAOO, fond. R-2106-1-151, 5).

In a recent unpublished interview with the son of one of the Inochentists who took part in the events, the details of whose account correspond in numerous ways with the archival data, Anosov died as a consequence of an accident.

> In 1920, Anosov came from Ananiev with his troops, surrounded the [Rai] Garden and opened fire on people. The people got scared and hid in the caves. Approximately 200 people entered the caves. [...] I do not know who informed the authorities in Kotovsk [the new name of Bîrzula/Bârzu] that a group of bandits killed people in the Garden [of Rai]. From Kotovsk, Alexandru was sent with his troops. He came to the hill and

> opened fire. Anosov got scared and started to run toward the forest and he was killed …
>
> (Interview by J. Kapaló with Damian Pavlovich Obrejenko 2014)

This oral history states that the Inochentists were not involved in the killing of Anosov. According to the interview, Anosov and other Soviet officials died as a result of an accidental exchange of fire between two separate armed groups of Bolsheviks and soldiers.

The political police criminal case file created during the repressive operation against the Inochentists in 1921 confirms some of the events described in the article from *Plugarul Roş* and in oral history. A document mentions that Aleksandr Ionko was a former tsarist officer who served as the vice commandant in Bârzula and who was arrested in 1920 but succeeded in escaping from the Cheka (ASBUOO 27146, 287). According to the documents from the same file, during the operation from September 1920, the authorities of Bârzula were misinformed by the Inochentists that the monastery had been attacked by a group of bandits who opened fire on civilians (ASBUOO 27146, 104). Accordingly, any statement that Aleksandr Ionko had connections with the Inochentists can be dismissed. In order to diminish the responsibility of local authorities for the incident which resulted in Anosov's death, propaganda accused the Inochentists of involvement in the killing of the secretary of Ananiev Party Committee.

A few weeks after the closure of "Rai," the Party Bureau of Ananiev county discussed some possible abuses committed by Podzakhodnikov, the military commander of the Cheka unit that had assaulted the underground monastery after Anosov's unsuccessful attempt to close the monastery. On October 15, 1920, at the session of the party bureau the events were described in the following terms:

> Comrade Podzahodnikov reports: The long attempts to convince them [the Inochentists] to leave the underground were unsuccessful. A secret water pipe was discovered and destroyed. This spread panic among the monks who proposed to leave the cave during the night time after the soldiers would withdraw. It was proposed that they should to do so within two days, otherwise harsher repressive measures would be taken. When leaving Rai, I ordered that weapons should be used in case of any excesses. […] During the night they undertook an attack on comrade Bondarshiuk, who threw the bomb.
>
> [Later,] comrade Podzahodnikov mentions the inefficiency of the commission and expresses his belief that harsher measures should be taken against workers [of Rai] who do not want to work. Regarding the permanent drunkenness of Bondarshiuk, Podzahotnikov mentions that the work in Cheka is very hard, and he himself uses to drink quite often and he allows his subordinates to do the same.
>
> (DAOO fond. P-12233-1-4, 18)

In this report, Podzakhodnikov, who was the superior of Bondarshiuk, defended his subordinate, who committed a number of abuses. Nevertheless, in its resolution, the Party Bureau of Ananiev county disapproved the permanent drunkenness of Bondarshuk and ordered the launch of an investigation regarding his conduct during the liquidation of Rai:

> Resolution: The causes of the closure of Rai should be made public. It is unacceptable that a party member is a drunkard. An investigation regarding the conduct of comrade Bondarshiuk should be made, and in case he is found guilty, he should be expelled from the party. Remove comrade Bondarshiuk from Rai. […] Make an official request to Odessa Governorate Party Committee to replace comrade Podzahodnikov because of his overwork
>
> (DAOO fond. P-12233-1-4, 18)

The decision of the bureau to launch an investigation and to fire Podzahodnikov reveals that his explanations did not correspond with reality or were perceived as doubtful. With regard to the population of the county, the bureau decided to start explaining the causes of the closure of the monastery to local citizens before the investigations into Bondarshiuk's conduct were complete. The repressive operation of 1920 appears to fit very well the context of War Communism. The so-called liquidation of Rai was characterized by chaotic, indiscriminate violence, by confusion and accidents which resulted in casualties amongst both civilians and officials.

The representation of the underground Inochentist monastery as a hideout for anti-Bolshevik fighters, which was never substantiated, became a central myth of propaganda narratives about this religious community. It was produced under the extreme circumstances of Civil War and peasant resistance to the Bolshevik regime with the local authorities projecting onto the Inochentists a set of fears related to their concerns for the regime's survival in the region. These associations produced a distorted image of Inochentists and triggered the repressive operation of 1920 in precisely the period in which numerous other sectarian communities enjoyed privileged treatment by the Soviet regime.

The contradictory policies of provincial and local authorities: the repressive operation from 1921

A second major anti-Inochentist operation was conducted in October 1921 when approximately 55 leading Inochentists from Rai were arrested and imprisoned, exiled or condemned to death (ASBUOO 27146, 4). The first operation against Rai had been conducted in mid-September 1920, approximately eight months after the occupation of Ananiev county by the Red Army and under the conditions of an ongoing struggle with peasant insurgency. In these extreme circumstances, the local authorities had more freedom to apply their own initiative than normal and indeed were even expected to do so. In this way, we can explain the local character of the first repressive policies against the Inochentists. Following this, as I will demonstrate below, during the next anti-Inochentist operation starting from the autumn of 1921, the initiatives of local authorities continued to play an unexpectedly important role. Under the extreme circumstances of anti-Bolshevik insurgency, permanent shortages and poor infrastructure, in both 1920 and 1921, local authorities were able to obtain a change in the decisions made by the provincial centre and succeeded in influencing, to a large degree, perceptions at the provincial level. Likewise, as the case of the operation from 1921 reveals, party members from rural areas collaborated closely with the police and in the case of the Inochentists produced an understanding of this religious group on which secret police officers would base their investigations.

The start of the secret police investigation was triggered by two main factors. The first one was an undated request by the commander of the border Cheka to the Balta county department of secret police to examine the situation in Rai because a number of Inochentists had been arrested transgressing the border with Romania (ASBUOO 27146, 279). The second, and main cause of arrests, was a series of requests and complains written by local functionaries. The discontent of the local authorities was caused by the return of leading Inochentists who had left the monastery of Rai in September 1920. In order to limit their influence on the rest of the population of Rai, the authorities established a state farm and Inochentists leaders were denied the possibility of becoming members (ASBUOO 27146, 11). The Inochentist leadership, in response, wrote a petition directly to the Odessa Governorate Department of Lands[11] in which they requested permission to create instead an Inochentist agricultural commune (ASBUOO 27146, 258–60; 305) of the type that other sectarian groups were being encouraged to form elsewhere (Coleman 2005, 174–5). The Inochentists obtained the approval of the provincial centre and at the general meeting of the inhabitants of Rai, the Inochentists elected the administrative bodies of the newly established collective farm with no communists among its membership (ASBUOO 27146, 29).

Following this, the head of the already functioning state farm, the communist Dicul, then went to Balta and informed the authorities about the difficulties faced by the administration of the state farm in Rai (ASBUOO 27146, 29). As a result, the county Cheka department made a request to Odessa to cancel the authorization to establish the Inochentist agricultural commune in Rai (ASBUOO 27146, 258). As a consequence of the request by the Cheka, the newly established Inochentist collective farm was liquidated and the leadership was arrested.

The main accusation against those arrested was inspired by Dicul's report about incidents that occurred at Rai according to which two distinct groups of Inochentists existed. The first one was described as the so-called Zinovievists, or the followers of Zinovie Gâştemulte, who were poor peasants believing that they could redeem their souls through work. Zinovie had the status of a prophet amongst this group. Zinovie's good relations with the administration of the local state farm are revealed by the fact that he was in charge of organizing, deploying and supervising the workers of the state farm. Nevertheless, as a religious leader Zinovie had only around 50 followers and the absolute majority of the inhabitants of Rai did not consider him a prophet. The second group, according to Dicul, comprised the Inochentists who were kulaks and the leaders of the liquidated monastery, who believed that they should not work but pray and opposed the state farm (ASBUOO 27146, 11; 93; 179). On Dicul's suggestion, therefore, it seems that the police officers invented a category of hostile inhabitants of Rai, who were labelled as kulaks and named "Inochentists." During the police interrogation of arrested believers, one of the main questions asked was to declare belonging to one of the abovementioned groups (ASBUOO, 27146, 109). This question reveals that the police officers and Dicul were aware of the various beliefs and practices of Inochentist community and how this manifested as resistance and attempted to impose on them a certain form of religious identity. Additionally, Dicul exploited the religious capital of Zinovie Gâştemulte in order to mobilize and control a part of the population of Rai. Dicul's account of the categories of inhabitants of Rai provided the secret police with a set of tools that allowed them to re-impose his authority on the collective farm. At the same time, Dicul's categorization was part of a codified request to not exile the entire population of Rai but just to reinforce order because the Inochentist settlement was important for the local economy.

The cancelation of the permission to create the Inochentist collective farm reveals a few very important features of centre-periphery relations in state and party apparatuses from Odessa governorate in 1921. Firstly, local authorities were capable of advocating for changes to decisions made in Odessa. Secondly, the leaders from Odessa did not yet have a good knowledge of the situation at the local level and of the events that had occurred in the northern part of the governorate since the occupation of this territory by the Red Army. The insufficient coordination of actions between local and provincial administrations was another problem. In certain matters, the provincial centre relied on the knowledge and on the experience of local functionaries, which enhanced the capacity of local authorities to influence the perceptions and decisions of the provincial centre. The difficulties faced by local and provincial authorities in establishing their control in the northern part of the governorate after its occupation, the ongoing activity of anti-Bolshevik insurgency and shortages of resources and poor infrastructure are all part of the explanation of these phenomena of centre-periphery relations.

From a local problem to a cross-border threat: a view on Rai from Odessa

In the previous sections, I have shown that in 1920 and in 1921 the initiatives and the perceptions of county authorities played a central role in the repressive operations launched against the Inochentists. The operations to deport the Inochentists (including the so-called Zinovievists) in 1923, was monitored by the authorities of Balta *okrug*[12] and by Odessa provincial centre. The deportation of the Inochentists in 1923 was part of a wider effort of provincial authorities to consolidate the state border and to cleanse the border area of dangerous elements. The argument of this section is that the analysis of the history and of the nature of Inochentism by *okrug* and provincial authorities from the perspective of a new set of policies and objectives and with more resources at their disposal added new elements to the image of this religious minority.

The OGPU, which succeeded the Cheka in 1922 as the Soviet secret police force, launched an operation against the Inochentists in 1923 that was a more top-down initiative than the earlier ones. It was constituted by a set of complex actions to identify and register Inochentist preachers and to then arrest and deport them (ASBUOO 5247). By 1923, the authorities perceived the Inochentists as a threat because of the cross-border character of this religious community. The majority of its members were, as already stated above, ethnic Romanians, a significant part of whom were Bessarabians who frequently transgressed the state border in order to maintain ties between their home communities and Rai. From the perspective of the regime, this created favourable conditions for the infiltration of foreign spies into the Soviet Union (ASBUOO 5247, 15; 22). Additionally, according to the ideas of "social danger" with which the police operated, the Inochentists posed a threat to the stability of the regime. As Paul Hagenloh observes, although in theory Soviet criminology associated the idea of social danger with class origin, in the early post-revolutionary years in its operations in urban areas the police linked this notion to recidivism and the lack of a defined place of residence (2009, 27–8). Although Inochentists were a rural religious community, they lived in a border territory, which like Soviet cities, was regarded by the regime as an area that needed to be cleared of dangerous elements. Therefore, because the police had conducted repressive operations against this religious minority in 1920 and in 1921 that had not resulted in the elimination of the movement, and because many of its members had a semi-itinerant way of life, the Inochentists closely fitted the category of socially dangerous.

The Provincial Party Committee from Odessa ordered the beginning of a new anti-Inochentist operation in the summer of 1923 (DAOO, fond. P-3-1-584, 8–9) and it sent reports about the activity of religious minorities to Kharkov, which was the capital of Soviet Ukraine at the time. According to the reports, Inochentism and other sects were spreading steadily because of the weakening of the Orthodox Church (DAOO, fond. P-3-1-584, 13). Surprisingly, the influence of the Inochentist leaders was also reported to be increasing because of the repressive operations from 1920–21, which had forced a part of them to leave Rai. As a party report from April 1923 mentions, in 1921 numerous Inochentist monasteries were established in the villages of Balta county by the believers who had left Rai. Another report shows that in the entire northern part of Odessa governorate Inochentist preachers-travellers had a significant influence on local peasants (ASBUOO 5247, 10; 13). The authorities decided to exile all Inochentists from the governorate and on July 10, 1923, the Executive Committee of Balta *Okrug* ordered the preparations for the anti-Inochentist operation to begin. The heads of the executive committees of the districts were in charge of registering the Inochentists from their districts (ASBUOO 5247, 22–3).

The anti-Inochentist operations started in the summer of 1923 (DAOO, fond. P-3-1-584, 8–9; 22), several months before the session of the Antireligious Commission of the CC of CP(b)[13] from November 26 in Moscow that ordered Ukraine's authorities to launch a campaign against miracles and to identify through police operations the cross-border ties between the organizers of the miracles and foreign anti-Soviet organizations (Stenograph №40 of the session of Antireligious Commission from November 26, 1923). Nevertheless, the accusations against the Inochentists of transgressing the state borders and the perception of the Party Committee of Balta okrug that Rai was at the centre of the phenomenon of the renewal of Orthodox icons[14] in Balta okrug (ASBUOO 5247, 163) fitted the patterns of the operation ordered by the Antireligious Commission in Moscow on November 26, 1923. Possibly, the deportations of Inochentists was one of the cases which prompted the decision of Antireligious Commission to take measures against the miracles in Ukraine. The anti-Inochentist operations from 1923 continued long after November 26 and probably some of its latter stages were adapted to the decisions of the abovementioned session of Antireligious Commission.

As already mentioned, the operation from 1923 was part of a number of measures aimed at securing the state border. These efforts were going on at the same time as a set of policies directed at the consolidation of the control by central authorities of the peripheries. For example, in 1923 with the authorization of the Central Committee of the Communist Party of Soviet Ukraine, the Balta Party Organisation was purged. According to the report, because of the proximity of the state border numerous unreliable elements had succeeded in entering the party (DAOO fond. P-3-1-584, 15). The purging of the elites and the cadre shuffling consolidated the control by the provincial centre of Balta. Among other policies that were aimed at the centralization of power was the administrative reform applied in Odessa governorate in 1923 (DAOO fond. P-12068, Inventory no. 1). As Gerald Easter mentions, regionalization, or the replacement of the old tsarist system of territorial division (governorate, county, *volost*) by geographically larger units (*oblast*, *okrug* and *raion*/district) was a strategy employed by Moscow to limit the influence of local cliques of functionaries and to impose over them the authority of elite factions that could control the distribution of resources at local level (2000, 76–9). This general consolidation of the control of the provincial centre over the local level explains the much greater knowledge of the "Inochentist problem" and of the general situation in the territory in 1923 than in 1920–21.

As a consequence of the increasing involvement of the authorities in Odessa in anti-Inochentist campaigns the representation of Inochentism in archival documents became more complex. In 1920, the monastery of Rai was imagined as a place of kulak conspiracy and as a shelter for monarchists and for counterrevolutionary bandits. In 1921, as mentioned above, a part of the Inochentists were declared kulaks and arrested as part of a police operation at county level. In 1923, when the investigations were conducted by the Department of Border GPU of Balta *okrug*, and based on the orders and instructions of the provincial authorities, the allegations formulated by police officers reflect their preoccupation with broader problems relating to security and stability of the Soviet regime and the border. If in 1920, the local authorities perceived the Inochentist underground as a hideout of the fighters for Ukrainian Republic (DAOO fond. P- 12233-1-22, 11), who were very active around Balta and Ananiev, then some of the police reports from 1923 reveal the concern instead with Romanian ethnic origin of Inochentists and the proximity of the state frontier with Romania, which was being frequently transgressed (ASBUOO 5247, 15; 22). At each level of administration, the officials associated the idea of enmity with a set of obstacles which hindered policies they were in charge of implementing. The result of these associations was the formation of different images of the same religious group at different levels of administration.

In 1923, the Border Department of GPU had access to more sources of documentary information in its investigations than the county department of the political police in 1920–21. Being interested in the cross-border nature of the movement, the Border Department of GPU could use sources from Romania in order to analyze the nature of the Inochentist movement. For example, an article from the Romanian newspaper *Glasul*, published on June 14, 1923, which refers to an underground church built by Inochentists in the village of Piatra, Orhei county, in Bessarabia, was quoted by the officers in their reports. According to the article, after the Romanian Gendarmerie conducted a series of arrests and searches of members of the Piatra community, they identified a group of 13–14 years old children suffering of sexually transmitted diseases (ASBUOO 5247, 121). Soviet authorities took very seriously the accusations printed in the Romanian newspapers and in 1923 they ordered a medical check-up of arrested Inochentists. The medics concluded that none of 67 Inochentists they checked had sexually transmitted diseases (ASBUOO 5247, 349). Articles such as the one in *Glasul* about the Inochentist community from Piatra containing accusations of murder, abuse and rape of teenage women were published in numerous Romanian newspapers from 1923 onwards. Contemporary *Siguranța* (the Romanian state security service) reports, however, dismissed these accusations in the media (see Kapaló 2019, 156–9). The Soviet political police, nevertheless, subsumed these narratives into their reports (ASBUOO, 5247, 122) and portrayed the Inochentist underground as a place where numerous crimes were perpetrated.

David Shearer suggests that in the 1930s the category of "socially dangerous element" began to have a broader understanding than in the 1920s (2009, 57–8) with cohorts of the population associated with it being regarded not only as a source of ideological contamination, but also as the cause of the spread of diseases (Shearer 2009, 60). Although the accusations from 1923 against the Inochentists are not the result of an already existing association of socially dangerous elements and epidemics, the case of the Inochentists nevertheless reveals the existence in the 1920s of a tendency by the regime to regard marginal and semi-itinerant populations as potential bearers of infection.

In the case of all three operations discussed above, from 1920, 1921 and 1923, the functionaries who produced the allegations against the Inochentists projected onto them their own preoccupations regarding possible challenges to their authority and stability of the regime, and their concerns about eventual obstacles to state policies that they were in charge of. Because of the differences between the attributions of the functionaries from Odessa and those of the local bureaucrats in Ananiev and Balta, the accusations from 1923 are different from those from 1920–21. Nevertheless, the secret police investigation file from 1923 subsumed an important part of the accusations formulated by the county authorities during the earlier operations from 1920 and 1921.

Conclusions

Local Soviet authorities and their superiors imagined the regime's enemies differently. Soviet functionaries constructed the enemy through the lens of the policies they implemented and from the perspective of the difficulties they were dealing with in their administrative processes. At the local and central levels, authorities dealt with different sets of problems and obstacles, and as a result they associated the idea of enmity with a different set of features. These variations can be observed more easily in the first years after the revolution because of the poor communication infrastructure between county administrations and provincial centres. Additionally, at the provincial level Soviet officials were concerned with broader problems of security and stability of the regime, and they had at their disposal more sources of information, which made their understanding of real or imagined enemies different from the accounts produced by local authorities.

In the case of Inochentists, the local authorities from Ananiev county produced an understanding of this religious group that remained at the centre of anti-Inochentist repressive policies and propaganda campaigns until the collapse of the communist regime. The earliest archival accounts of the Inochentists, which present them as a hindrance to the Bolshevik project and as a counterrevolutionary group allied with anti-Bolshevik forces of Petliura, were the product of the preventive policies of counterinsurgency conducted by the authorities of Ananiev in 1920. Likewise, the production of the negative propaganda image of Inochentists as a group of armed counterrevolutionaries was a strategy of local authorities to gloss over a number of incidents they were responsible for and which resulted in the death of a number of local officials and Red Army soldiers.

Acknowledgement

The research for this chapter was funded by the European Research Council (ERC) under the European Union's Horizon 2020 research and innovation programme No. 677355.

Notes

1 *Volost* was an administrative unit subordinated to a county, which existed in Imperial Russia and in early post-revolutionary years. The district (in Russian *район*) is an administrative unit geographically larger than the volost which it replaced after the Soviet administrative reform. *Okrug* was a territorial unit geographically larger than a district and a county but smaller than oblast or governorate. The old administrative unit of county was replaced by the *okrug*.
2 The majority of the ethnically Romanian population from the territory of present-day Republic of Moldova, from eastern parts of Romania, and from Ukraine, refer to themselves by the ethnonym Moldovans or Moldavians (in Romanian: *Moldovean or Moldovan*). A significant part of Moldovans from the territory of present-day Ukraine (Moldovans living around Ananiev and Balta included) do not consider themselves belonging to the Romanian ethno-linguistic group.
3 The majority of the population of the district of Ananiev, created in 1923, was Moldovan.
4 Moldovan Autonomous Soviet Republic was established in October 1924 as part of Soviet Ukraine, and it included parts of the territory of Ananiev and Balta counties, and a series of other territories.
5 The All-Russian Extraordinary Committee abbreviated as VChK, and commonly referred as Cheka, was the name of the Soviet secret police, which was created in 1917. The Soviet secret police was later known under a succession of different names, including OGPU, NKVD, MGB, and KGB.
6 Narodnyj Komissariat Zemledelija RSFSR.
7 Upravkomy.
8 Uezdnye Sekretno-Agenturnye Otdelenija.
9 People's Commissariat of Internal Affairs.
10 During the mass repressive campaigns "Troika" was the name of the extrajudicial boards which had the right to mete out sentences based on simplified procedures.
11 Gubzemotdel.
12 Balta Okrug included the northern part of today's Odessa Oblast and approximately two-thirds of the territory of the Republic of Moldova from the left bank of Dniester (commonly referred to as Transnistria). Balta *okrug* was created in 1923 (DAOO Fond P-12068, Inventory no. 1).
13 The Antireligious Commission of the Central Committee of CP(b) was created in 1922, and it formulated the antireligious policy in USSR.
14 The renewing (obnovlenie) of Orthodox Icons was a widely-spread phenomenon in Soviet countryside during periods of crisis. The Eastern Orthodox peasants perceived the renewing of icons, or when in a miraculous way the icons became new and clean, as an intervention of the divine power in their lives (Viola 1996, 53).

Archival sources

Arkhiv Upravlinnia Sluzhby Bezpeky Ukraïny v Odes'kii Oblasti [Archive of the SBU Office in Odessa Oblast] (ASBUOO), file no. 27146; 5247.

Tsentral'nyi Derzhavnyi Arkhiv Vyshchykh Orhaniv Vlady ta Upravlinnia Ukraïny [Central State Archives of the Supreme Authorities and Governments of Ukraine] (TsDAVOV), fond. 5, Inventory 1, file no. 618.

Arhiva Organizațiilor Social-Politice a Republicii Moldova [Archive of Social-Political Organizations of the Republic of Moldova] (AOSPRM), fond. 49, inventory 1, files no. 84; 208; 205; 209; 235; 821; 1815.

Derzhavnyi Arkhiv Odes'koï Oblasti [State Archive of Odessa Oblast] (DAOO), Fond P-1, inventory 1, file no. 37; fond P-3, inventory 1, file no. 584; fond. P-12068, inventory 1, files no. 16; 18; 114; 171; fond P-12233, inventory 1, files no. 2; 4; 22; fond. R-2106, inventory 1, files no. 1; 151.

Interviews

Interview, Damian Pavlovich Obrejenko, 2014. Interviewed by James A. Kapaló.

References

Berelowitch, Alexis, & Viktor Danilov. 2000. *Soviet Countryside through the Eyes of VChK-OGPU- NKVD. 1918–1939. Documents and Materials in 4 Volumes* [*Sovetskaja Derevnja Glazami VChK-OGPU- NKVD. 1918–1939. Dokumenty i materialy v 4 tomah*]. Institut rossijskoj istorii RAN, Dom nauk o cheloveke (Francija), Central'nyj arhiv FSB RF, Institut istorii novejshego vremeni (Francija), Moskva: ROSSPEN.

Coleman, Heather J. 2005. *Russian Baptists and Spiritual Revolution, 1905–1929.* Bloomington: Indiana University Press.

Easter, Gerald M. 2000. *Reconstructing the State: Personal Networks and Elite Identity in Soviet Russia.* Cambridge: Cambridge University Press.

Etkind, Alexandr. 2013. *Khlysts: Sects, Literature and Revolution* [*Hlyst: Sekty, literatura i revoljucija*]. Moskva: Novoe literaturnoe obozrenie.

Gomin, Lesi. 1927. "On the Journey to 'Paradise'" ["Cu călătoria la 'Rai'"]. *Plugarul Roșu*, 37–40 (4 parts).

Hagenloh, Paul, 2009. *Stalin's Police. Public Order and Mass Repression in the USSR, 1926–1941.* Washington D.C.: Woodrow Wilson Centre Press,

Heinzen, James W. 1997. "'Alien' Personnel in the Soviet State: The People's Commissariat of Agriculture under Proletarian Dictatorship, 1918–1929." *Slavic Review* 56: 73–100.

Jakovlev, Aleksandr. N. et al. 2003. Lubjanka: the VChK-OGPU-NKVD-NKGB-MGB-MVD-KGB agencies. 1917–1991 [*Lubjanka: organy VChK-OGPU-NKVD-NKGB-MGB-MVD-KGB. 1917–1991. Spravochnik*]. Moskva: MFD.

Kapaló, James. 2019. *Inochentism and Orthodox Christianity: Religious Dissent in the Russian and Romanian Borderlands.* London: Routledge.

Kokurin, Aleksandr. I. & Petrov, Nikita. V. 1997. Lubjanka: the VChK-OGPU-NKVD-NKGB-MGB-MVD-KGB agencies. 1917–1991. A handbook [*Lubjanka: organy*

VChK-OGPU-NKVD-NKGB-MGB-MVD-KGB. 1917–1991. Spravochnik], Scientific Editor R.G. Pihoja. Moskva: MFD.

Mawdsley, Even. 1987. *The Russian Civil War*. Boston: Allen & Unwin.

Peris, Daniel. 1998. *Storming the Heavens: The Soviet League of the Militant Godless*. Ithaka and London: Cornell University Press.

Pipes, Richard. 1996. *A Concise History of the Russian Revolution*. New York: Vintage Books.

Pospielovsky, Dimitry V. 1987. *A History of Marxist-Leninist Atheism and Soviet Antireligious Policies. Volume 1, A History of Soviet Atheism in Theory and Practice, and the Believer*. London and New York: Palgrave Macmillan.

Shearer, David R. 2009. *Policing Stalin's Socialism: Repression and Social Order in the Soviet Union, 1924–1953*. New Haven and London: Yale University Press.

"Stenograph №40 of the session of Antireligious Commission from 26 November 1923/ Protokol №40 zasedanija Antireligioznoj komissii ot 26 nojabrja 1923 g". In: M. I. Odincov, Zh. V. Artamonova, N. M. Volhonskaja, A. S. Kochetova, A. V. Lukashin, E. L. Subbota, *Konfessional'naja politika sovetskogo gosudarstva. 1917–1991 gg.: Dokumenty i materialy v 6 t. T. 1 v 4 kn. 1917–1924 gg. Kn. 1. Central'nye rukovodjashhie organy RKP(b): ideologija veroispovednoj politiki i praktika antireligioznoj propagandy,* Moskva: Politicheskaja jenciklopedija, 2017, 504–5.

Viola, Lynne 1996. *Peasant Rebels under Stalin: Collectivization and the Culture of Peasant Resistance*. New York: Oxford University Press.

Viola, Lynne. 2014. "Collectivization in the Soviet Union: Specificities and Modalities." In: *The Collectivization of Agriculture in Communist Eastern Europe: Comparison and Entanglements*, edited by Constantin Iordachi and Arnd Bauerkämper. Budapest: CEU Press.

Walters, Philip. 1993. "A Survey of Soviet Religious Policy." In: *Religious Policy in the Soviet Union*, edited by Sabrina Petra Ramet. New York: Cambridge University Press.

2 Visualizing invisible dissent

Red Dragonists, conspiracy and the Soviet secret police

Tatiana Vagramenko

> "And another sign appeared in heaven: behold, a great, fiery Red Dragon having seven heads and ten horns, and seven diadems on his heads."
>
> (*Revelation 12:3*)

> "Instruct the Ukrainian KGB to quickly prepare the arrest of L. or to compromise him, otherwise he will bring Armageddon to us"
>
> (*A marginal note on a KGB secret document*)

Introduction: materiality of common sense[1]

Rumours about the arrival of the Antichrist were increasingly spreading – the Red Dragon had come.

The turbulent turn of the twentieth century in Russia, the revolution of 1917 with the following Soviet repression of the Orthodox clergy and mass closure of churches and monasteries triggered the growth of popular Orthodox-based movements with apocalyptic and chiliastic visions. The images of Apocalypse had become a persistent popular cultural form particularly among Russian and Ukrainian peasants. Popular prophets and *yurodivye* yelled on the streets that the communists were putting the stamp of Antichrist on foreheads of those entering kolkhozes or participating in elections or the census; that men in kolkhozes would have common wives, and everybody would be sleeping under a common blanket; that children would be taken away from their parents; that aged people would be recycled for soap production; and human hair, instead of wool, would be exchanged for American tractors. People made coffins and performed funeral services on living persons (Demianov 1977, 25; HDASBU, fond. 16-1-206, 16–17; 16-1-45, 73–4; 16-1-206, 184–5). They were ready to meet the Apocalypse and these prophetical images of the world's end guided their perceptions of the swirling events of their day.

The Soviet secret police called them Red Dragonists – *krasnodrakonovtsy*, the church oftentimes branded them sectarians. Starting from the late 1920s and throughout the 1930s, the Soviet government undertook a series of "liquidation campaigns" against these popular religious movements, as part of their struggle with mass peasant rebellion. Multiple secret police operations were carried out against what would be called by then "the ecclesiastic-monarchist underground." Eventually, a powerful image of the enemy was constructed: "the base of the counter-revolution in the village turned out to be the coalition of the kulaks and churchmen" (HDASBU, fond. 13-1-383, 5–6). Thousands of ordinary believers (mainly peasantry) were repressed as members of the "insurgent counter-revolutionary ecclesiastic-monarchist Red Dragon-type (*krasnodrakonovskogo tipa*) organization." Popular eschatology was reclassified as political subversion; street prophesies of the Red Dragon were "converted" into the Red Dragon-type organization.

The image of the religious underground as an organized, networked, and politically subversive organizational structure (often associated with foreign intelligence agencies) became common-sense knowledge, proliferated by Soviet anti-religious propaganda, romanticized by émigré religious publicists, and often reappeared uncritically in later works. Exploring the truth or fiction of these constructions it is not my primary aim here but rather in this article, I look at the process of the shaping of common sense, trying to grasp the *materiality* of the emergence of the religious underground. I focus on the material background of these constructions, namely specific practices and documents that ensured the standardization of the image of the centralized religious underground organization, and I trace tangible forms – specific textual and visual tools – by which this common-sense knowledge was shaped.

With this in mind, I address documents created and archived by the Soviet secret police – the main producer of knowledge and social categories in the Soviet Union. I attempt here to undertake an archaeology of knowledge produced by the secret police on the pages of top-secret reports, penal case files, letter-coded files of secret investigation, and what I have called "model criminal files" related to the so-called ecclesiastic-monarchist underground. The analysis of epistemic practices is undertaken through the interpretation of the narrative and visual techniques deployed by the secret police in their documentation.

The chapter focuses particularly on one specific genre of documentation from the secret police archives, recently declassified in Ukraine. *Model criminal files* – published as brochures or circulated as typewriter copies – were internal top-secret publications of the GPU. They compile material from secret police operations, penal cases and closing indictments against members of the ecclesiastic-monarchist underground. Apart from that, they contain unique visual material, such as religious network schemes and photo-collages, produced by the secret police as aesthetic forms to visualize their constructions of the religious underground. Both textual and visual material are examined below as epistemic means in the creation of common-sense knowledge on the religious underground. By word and by image, they visualized or materialized some intangible forms of popular religiosity, turning the apocalyptic visions of the Red Dragon into political crime.

Using the theoretical perspective developed by Ann Laura Stoler (2009) and Katherine Verdery (2014), I read these documents as a site of knowledge production and "a repository of and generator of social relationships" (Verdery 2014, 5). In this framework, archive is understood as "a force field that animates political energies and expertise, that pulls on some 'social facts' and converts them into qualified knowledge" (Stoler 2009, 22). This approach to the archive as knowledge practice goes beyond the question of truth value through the interpretation of alternative "regimes of truth" that archival documents produced and operated. Likewise, to continue with this Foucauldian approach, the concept of the religious underground, which I scrutinize below, was the type of discourse the Soviet secret police harboured and caused to function as true. The truth is not outside power, Foucault argues, but is linked to the system of power, and "induces the regular effects of power" (Foucault 1977, 13). The regime of truth, produced by the Soviet secret police and carefully registered on the pages of their top-secret files, longed for an exclusive position of the absolute truth that induced a totalizing effect of power. In this way, the documents created an (alternative) reality of their own – they had, what Miriam Dobson and Benjamin Ziemann argue after Roland Barthes, "reality effects" (Dobson and Ziemann, 2009, 11). Sonja Luehrmann adds to this that Soviet-era archival documentation "never intended to be neutral or objective but to participate in transforming the reality it described" (2015, 32). The "reality effect" of secret police documents was to shape people's understanding of the world – the world, where clandestine practice of religious beliefs was considered to be politically dangerous. This, in turn, triggered the development of specific methods of control and domination, and forms of political action that determined popular religious life in the Soviet Union till the very end of its existence.

The claims for truth revelation become the main discursive framework of both Soviet secret police documentation and official anti-religious propaganda. This "terrible revelation" of hidden power relations, of an enemy disguised under the mask of a religious believer, of a terrorist organization hidden behind a rural religious community has a strong resemblance to conspiracy theories proliferating nowadays in many parts of the worlds. They are different, however, in the way they were produced and implemented. Both the popular eschatology of the Red Dragon and the Soviet representations of the Red Dragonist underground are treated below as two conspiracy theories – a popular conspiracy and a state-sponsored conspiracy. The clash of the two conspiracies exposed different interpretations of power and truth and their "reality effects."

Grassroots holiness: the arrival of the Red Dragon

The Russian Orthodox Church became the main target of Bolshevik politics soon after the revolution of 1917. The Church, as the instrument of the exploiting class, had to be removed from the political arena. What the

Soviet government perhaps did not anticipate was the scale of grass-roots religious turmoil and the extent of alternative forms of religiosity that would be triggered by the repressive political actions against the Orthodox Church establishment. These reactive movements required different political strategies.

In the 1930s, the majority of churches in the Soviet Union were closed and monasteries disbanded.[2] Thousands of disenfranchized priests with their families, and displaced monks and nuns were left homeless, banned from living in particular cities or were subject to immediate resettlement from areas of collectivization.[3] A significant part of population – along with many dispossessed kulaks – at once became uprooted and mobile. They wandered from village to village, begging or doing some casual day labour, clandestinely performing rituals and preaching about the arrival of the Apocalyptic Red Dragon and the Antichrist. The so-called "vagrant clergymen" brought to life numerous popular prophets and saints, *yurodivye* (holly fools), *klikushi* (shriekers), *starets* (elders), *prozorlivye* (forseers), and *bogoroditsy* (mothers-of-God) (HDASBU, fond. 16-1-206, 184). The phenomenon of popular prophetism proliferated, developing new forms, like *boliaschie* (holy ills), or *spiashchie* (holy dormants) (HDASBU, fond. 9-1-89, 101–3). They revivified mystical and eschatological beliefs, and fostered a charismatic environment particularly among the rural population (Demianov 1977; Viola 1990; Kizenko 2000; Coleman 2005, 151; Beglov 2008; Zimina 2010).

The Soviet authorities reported about the "epidemics of religious miracles" and "mass mystic psychosis" (Yashchenko 2008, 26; Babenko 2013; Tepliakov 2010). Religious miracles like the renewal of icons, of churches, and cupolas, popular prophecies, miraculous healing and the appearances of saints, icons, crosses and holy wells (with growing pilgrimage to places of miracles) became a mass phenomenon (Viola 1990, 756–8). "There was not a single village where a miracle hadn't happened," communicated the Ukrainian GPU in 1923; and the following year 586 cases of religious miracles were reported in Ukraine alone (Babenko 2013, 337–8). Visions of the Antichrist, stories of the punishment of godless communists, rumours about the appearance of members of the Tsar's family alive, the circulation of heavenly letters and magical letters of happiness, the proliferation of ecstatic and charismatic experiences during clandestine overnight praying – all these were reminiscent of a crisis cult.

Popular religious dissent movements were mostly spreading in the central Russian and Ukrainian countryside (on alternative urban popular religious revival of that time see Steinberg 1994). The followers of these movements were largely peasants, illiterate or with only a basic education, with a remarkable proportion of youth (particularly later, during the 1940s–50s), many active women in leading roles, and sometimes, in the absence of priests, with a practicing female priesthood (Pospielovsky 1995, 320; Kizenko 2000, 201). They did not form a theologically or organizationally unified phenomenon or a social movement in the proper sense of the term. It was rather constituted of dispersed communities and individual wandering booksellers, prophets and prophetess, priests and monastics united by a common apocalyptic vision of the world. On the pages of secret police files, they had multiple names: Ioannites, Fedorovists, Samosviatsy, Buevists, Stefanovists, Podgornovists, Suzdaltsy, Mikhailovists, Ignatievists, Inochentists, Enokhovits, Massalovists, Iliodorovists … or simply Red Dragonists. In the Central Black Earth region of Russia alone there were some 30 different group names that were defined as sects (Demianov 1977, 5). Attempts to describe and to classify the multiplicity of groups or to find their origins often lead to confusions. Some groups could have multiple names (e.g. Fedorovists were known, at the same time, as Red Dragonists, Massalovists, Samaritans, Samosviaty and Letuny); others joined the Old believers who had a long tradition of underground life (Demianov 1977, 5). Soviet secret police files offer clear evidence of these confusions. One religious group from Ukraine was repressed as Inochentists, but they had hardly heard about Inochentie Levizor, the founder of Inochentism (ASBUVO, 27921-fp). The writings of father John of the Kronstadt confiscated from believers was a reason to repress them as Ioannites, for the Soviet authorities equated Ioannites with father John's followers, in general (Kizenko 2000, 273–5).

They had different names and survival strategies: some cut off links with both "the world" and official church structures and built their churches and monasteries underground or in backwoods; others struggled for official registration and state recognition of their churches. What they perhaps all shared is the vision of the Red Dragon (red communists) and Soviet power as a sign of the coming Apocalypse.

Popular eschatology as conspiracy theory

The "anti-Soviet eschatologism" (A. B. Zhuravskii, cited by Beglov 2008, 86) remained a vibrant religious and cultural practice of what is often termed the religious underground decades. Many years later, in the 1950s, a KGB officer recollects his memory of two arrested women, True Orthodox believers. Dressed in a military uniform with a famous blue KGB service cap, he entered their prison cell. As they saw him, the women started crossing themselves and moaning: "Begone, begone, power of Antichrist! Keep away! Keep away! … Keep away Antichrists, you will burn in a fiery furnace!" (Sannikov 2002, 56).

Ordinary believers were reading the Biblical prophecy and the many apocryphal apocalypses that were available in popular chapbooks and manuscript notebooks in light of current events (Kapaló 2011, 127–37). They tried to understand and to interpret the hidden meanings of the dramatic rupture, linking the violent and devastating events of the First World War, of the series of revolutions, of the ensuing civil war of 1917–22, and of the Stalinist terror with an apocalyptic future.

This eschatological prophetic culture proliferated not only amongst Orthodox-based religious communities, but was also a characteristic of Russian and Ukrainian evangelical Christianity of that time. Ukrainian Pentecostalism, for example, developed a particular prophetic culture with a pronounced eschatological background. For many years, wandering Pentecostal prophets were a big concern of the Soviet secret police. By the 1950s, the Soviet authorities in Ukraine reported the surveillance of over 200 prophets and prophetess who were spreading apocalyptic views in Ukrainian Pentecostal communities (HDASBU, fond. 3-1-331, 191–228).

To use Mark Fenster and Lee Quinby, popular eschatology of post-Revolutionary Russia was both an all-encompassing narrative framework and a network of non-discursive practices that explained the past, the present, and the future for the masses (Quinby 1994, xv; Fenster 2008, 198). As Fenster argues, popular eschatology connects with and overlaps with conspiracy theory: "Although overtly spiritual, popular eschatology is implicitly political in its strong linking of a coming millennium to conservative political dogma" (2008, 15). Popular eschatology views historical and current events in terms of vast conspiracies led by knowing and unwitting agents of Satan (2008, 228). This form of popular apocalyptic vision, therefore, activated both religious and political agency. Being cut off from major church networks, with the priesthood and religious leaders repressed, ordinary believers attempted to make sense of a seemingly incomprehensible world. They developed both interpretive practices and survival strategies, while re-building their religious communities, distorted by waves of repression.

Waiting for the coming end, people dug out underground churches, built subterranean monasteries, constructed chapels in cellars of their houses, in barns and bunkers, and continued to practice their religion in private homes or in remote places and forests. In fact, the 1920s to the early 1930s (the years of the beginning of collectivization and mass repression, when the Red Dragonist movement flourished) was a period of popular religious animation. Church life blossomed. Few churches remained open, but they were full. Various sisterhoods, brotherhoods, and church councils mushroomed. They ran charity campaigns to help imprisoned clergymen, organized concerts of religious music, held theological lectures, meetings and overnight prayers (Lopushanskaia 1971, 69; Pospielovsky 1995, 164–6). Monastic life also experienced a revival in the novel form of secret monasticism (Wynot 2004, 131).

Shared eschatological feelings activated narrative agency, offering believers an active role in "the practice of historicizing" (Fenster 2008, 230–1) – they mobilized believers' creative agency to rethink and to reconstruct both ongoing events and the imagined future within the eschatological narrative. A Pentecostal prophecy manuscript, confiscated by the Ukrainian secret police in 1953, is a vivid example of this historicizing agency. The 15-page text, handwritten by a wandering Ukrainian Pentecostal prophetess, recycles Biblical images of Ashur and develops eschatology as a *narrative of tacit resistance* to the Stalinist terror:

> And liberty [*volia*] and freedom will follow soon; the days of freedom are approaching. For Ashur will be overthrown. And people will be called. I will call up people from many countries, and they will arrive and will

> [condemn] Ashur. The end has come, they call Ashur to death, for Ashur will be shot dead. Oh, oh, oh the storm will arrive for there will come the great bloodshed ...
>
> (HDASBU, fond. 6-60259-fp)[4]

Texts such as these were part of a political and spiritual struggle to represent and understand the world's order as the relationship between Bible-based prophecy and current events. In this way, they were dangerous indeed for emerging Soviet power. In the unfolding of its campaigns of repression against the popular and underground religious movements, the Soviet government did not merely *see* the political nature in popular religiosity, their reply to this popular eschatology was the creation of a giant conspiracy theory called *the ecclesiastic-monarchist underground*. The story began with the True Orthodox Church.

Red Dragon-type organization: the True Orthodox Church

Starting from the late 1920s, the eye of the Soviet state moved to grassroots religiosity. The Stalinist secret police launched a series of "liquidation campaigns" against popular religious movements that were scattered from Western Siberia up to the Northern Caucuses and Ukraine. The secret police often called underground home groups – "wild parishes" (*dikie prikhody*) or "hut groups" (*khatnicheskie gruppy*, from Ukrainian *khata*, peasant hut), as they were hidden, uncontrollable and in many ways spontaneous. They were as difficult to control as they were difficult to define.

Popular religious movements were even more difficult to deal with as they were comprised mainly of the peasantry. The exploited, and therefore presumably revolutionary, class, as it turned out, resisted socialist construction, such as dekulakization, collectivization, or industrialization. The peasantry had also smuggled their faith into the socialist reality.

> The village is infected with religious superstitions ... The church had solid ritual and domestic roots in the village ... Of course, within such a context, we could not, administratively and operationally, liquidate the church, that consisted of many millions of peasants,

says a 1930 top-secret circular letter (HDASBU, fond. 13-1-383, 2). But how then to categorize, within the class-based communist ideology, this spontaneous, multi-faced and persistent popular religiosity? How to resist or control these apparently chaotic movements of peasant believers (illiterate, impoverished, and historically the most exploited strata of society) that rejected the construction of socialist society and preached the arrival of the Red Dragon?

In order to channel the apparent religious turmoil into some communist-based ideological structures, the Soviet state applied its common technique of the re-invention (and revelation) of a hidden enemy, in this case hidden behind the mask of a religious peasant (Fitzpatrick 2005). The powerful image of the religious underground as a centralized and networked political organization soon began to form on the pages of secret police documentation and then in anti-religious propaganda. Thus, during the Soviet period, many of the underground religious communities would be united under the name of, and persecuted as, the True Orthodox Church that became one of the persistent images of the enemy. This was an umbrella term, widely used after the split within the Russian Orthodox Church (ROC). The term referred to the then-underground communities who did not accept the infamous Declaration of Loyalty to Soviet power signed by the ROC Metropolitan Sergii in 1927 and consequently broke up with the official church. Many of the popular religious movements, who became part of the True Orthodox Church, however, emerged well before the Revolution, hence, they were not formed as the direct consequence of the split. Moreover, as Pospielovsky argues, even among the communities called the True Orthodox or the Catacomb Church, not all of them rejected Sergii's Declaration and some remained loyal to the Moscow Patriarchate. Many chose (or were forced into) an illegal underground position simply because it was impossible to comply with newly created registration procedures and requirements for religious communities and groups (Pospielovsky 1995, 174–5). As the Church was splitting into multiple conflicting groups, ordinary believers often did not know who to follow. In the context of the mass closure of churches and oftentimes the absence of official clergymen, they had no other choice but to take care of their religious needs on their own, creatively adapting religious practices to changing circumstances.

A very different image of the True Orthodox Church, however, as a networked religious organization with a centralized leadership was cultivated by the Soviet secret police and by its off-spring – anti-religious propagandists. Few historians have questioned this construction but some acknowledged that the movement was heterogeneous. In 1973, the main Soviet "sectologist," Alexandr Klibanov, wrote that the history and the origins of True Orthodox communities, their composition and ideology still remained a blank page (cit. in Demianov 1977, 5–6). Lev Mitrokhin, studying True Orthodox communities in the Central Black Earth region argued that the local tradition cannot be generalized as a common phenomenon for the whole of Russia (cit. in Demianov 1977, 6). Soviet historian, Aleksandr Demianov, a former True Orthodox believer himself, conducted long-term ethnographic work among True Orthodox communities in the 1970s. Demianov's main argument was that True Orthodox communities, including the Ioannites he studied, lacked any centralization and even communication between themselves. They were constituted of scattered groups of believers, often unrelated to each other, with their own doctrines, ritual practices and different stances towards the Moscow Patriarchy and the official Church (Demianov 1977). Perhaps the most explicit in this view was Pavel Protsenko, a Soviet dissident and a publicist who collected oral history materials on underground Orthodox communities in the Soviet period. He argues (referring also to Solzhenitsyn's personal observations) that the True Orthodox Church as a centralized all-Union organization simply did not exist but was a myth most likely created by *Chekists* on the pages of criminal files (Protsenko 1998). Post-Soviet Church historians Dmitry Pospielovsky (1995, 324–5) and Alexei Beglov (2008, 40) also question the integrity of the True Orthodox movement. They also argue that Soviet policies expanded the scale of the religious underground by implementing state control over religion and by reducing the limits of legal religiosity.

Soviet policies not only triggered the development of popular religious movements, they also created a powerful image of the religious underground as a centralized and networked political organization. It was a sort of conspiracy theory that "organized" dispersed believers into a clandestine political network and that "converted" prophets, monastics or priests into agents and spies. Constructions like *the ecclesiastic-monarchist underground*, counter-revolutionary religious organizations, Red Dragon-type organizations, and even the catacomb True Orthodox Church were the product of the imaginative practices of the state. How these images were constructed and how they affected clandestine religious life and believers' survival strategies is a point of scrutiny below.

Crafting religious dissent: agitators, spies and couriers

> Soon these [anti-Soviet] elements became united into a set of groupings, at first separate and uncoordinated, but the longer it went on, the faster and the more intense they developed … [T]he anti-Soviet activities were increasing within these church groups, united later into the all-Union counter-revolutionary organization the "True Orthodox Church".
>
> (HDASBU, fond. 13-1-387, 3)

This was a typical narrative frame for the many trials against believers in the 1920s–30s, including the most resonant series of trials in 1928–31 against members of the True Orthodox Church – "the insurgent organization of clergymen." Among the 3,000 arrested, there were 600 priests; a few distinguished church intellectuals, including A. Losev and M. Novosyolov; and 12 bishops (Joseph (Petrovykh), Dimitry (Liubimov), Sergii (Druzhinin), Alexii (Bui) etc.) (Kosik 2009, 77–8). The rest were ordinary clergy, monastics and peasants from northern and central Russia, the Volga region, the Caucuses, and Ukraine.

The *snowball principle* allowed the authorities to construct a network of an all-Russia underground organization. Onto the core trial of a dozen church leaders and professors in Moscow and Leningrad, the secret police began to "attach" more arrests, revealing or constructing sets of social relationships between believers and communities. From the centre (Moscow and Leningrad), the snowball repression expanded to other places all over Russia, further to rural regions, particularly to those affected by peasant riots and mass resistance to collectivization.

To limit resistance, the state funnelled spontaneous popular movements and vernacular religious practices into known types (Verdery 2018, 292). Peasant communities, who resisted giving up their land and faith, and who were enthralled in apocalyptic feelings, eventually received proper social categorization within the all-Union network. An illiterate peasant believer turned into an "agitator" or a "spy" of the highly skilful underground organization, and sometimes represented as linked to foreign intelligence agencies. A wandering monk/nun or a popular prophet/prophetess was classified as a "courier" or "emissary," who disguised him/herself under peasant rags and bast-shoes or as dogsbodies (*chernorabochii*) (HDASBU, fond. 16-1-206, 95–6; 13-1-387, 29–30). Vagabond clergymen now became "travelling propagandists" (*raz"ezdnye propagandisty*) or "travelling agents" (*raz"ezdnaya agentura*), with their secret task to carry on propaganda against kolkhozes and Soviet power (HDASBU, fond. 13-1-387, 41).

A secret police file describes one of the dissenting religious groups: "The organization was built as an armed band; it had their own secret agents, couriers, observation posts, safe houses, clandestine rendezvous points (*iavochnye punkty*). They introduced passwords, codes and secret permits"; the whole group "had a character of a thoroughly conspiratorial underground organization, [and] had illegal monasteries with underground paths ..." (HDASBU, fond. 13-1-383, 4). This is an eloquent example of what Vățulescu calls *police estrangement* – a narrative technique that forcefully defamiliarizes popular religious practices and beliefs, presenting them from unusual angles and removing them from conventional context (Vățulescu 2010). Likewise, a self-denouncement – a centrepiece of Stalinist files – is composed following the principle of *self-estrangement,* controlled and forced confession that fully adopts the narrative strategies of the secret police (Vățulescu 2010, 167–86). A "forced autobiography" of Stefan Podgornyi, a monk and a *starets*, or elder, one of the most charismatic religious figures of that time, is among thousands of others in Stalinists trials that reveal, what Vățulescu argues after Bakhtin, a double-voiced discourse and "the role of the other in formulating discourse" (Vățulescu 2010, 43–4, 170). In one of his interrogations, Stefan told: "*Podgornovshchina* [Podgornyi movement], which I lead, gradually, with time, turned from a church organization into a political anti-Soviet organization ... The [political] education of ordinary members ... was clandestine, under the disguise of religiosity" (HDASBU, fond. 13-1-387, 56). From this *estranged* angle, peasant believers, who venerated *starets* Stefan as a prophet became members of a subversive clandestine political organization, and Stefan himself – a counter-revolutionary.

This was not a mere fabrication of facts about religious life, or "a jumbled mix of fantastic stories" (Vățulescu 2010, 44), it was the creation of an alternative reality, where people and social relations got new roles and meanings.

And what mattered here was the secrecy, the mask – *clandestine* social roles and relations. "People are no longer what they used to be," says Melley (2000, 42) and "are not who they seem," says Verdery (2014, xiv). This fundamental assumption of the hidden enemy disguised under the mask of a religious believer unfolded into a full conspiracy theory that the Soviet state produced, embedded and at the same time acted against. State-sanctioned conspiracy was the way of crafting religious dissent – it aimed to reveal hidden connections and relations between people and social actions. It was an effective political device to unite "the people" by labelling political enemies and expressing hostility towards the imagined "other" (Shinar 2018, 649; Fenster 2008, 11; Melley 2000, 8); it was "the most potent technology of exclusion" (Verdery 2014, 136). As such, it functioned as an effective instrument to implement a new social order.

Secret police model criminal files

But how were these conspiracy constructions actually assembled? What was their material background? What practices or documents ensured the standardization of the image of the centralized religious underground organization? Scrupulous work was hidden behind these constructions and Soviet secret police files, that have recently become more accessible thanks to the opening of Soviet-era archives in Ukraine, provide us with insightful materials that capture moments of Soviet conspiracy-making in motion. Countless secret police instructions, internal workshops, orders and reports produced the knowledge on religious dissent and ensured the standardization of this knowledge across the country.

Below I focus on the materiality of conspiracy constructions through an exploration of model criminal files, a specific genre of Soviet secret police documentation recently declassified and made available in the Ukrainian archives. These files offer a perfect angle to look at the combination of the verbal and the visual techniques and aesthetic representations of the religious underground network as developed by the secret police. Following Foucault, I engage in an archaeology of knowledge of *the ecclesiastic-monarchist underground organization*, tracing the production of knowledge as a unique combination (or in Deleuze's terms, a "practical assemblage") of visible and articulable, of discursive practices, of statements and non-discursive practices of visibilities (Deleuze 1992, 51).

In 1930, the Soviet secret police (called by that time the OGPU) in Belgorod, circulated a top-secret document. It was not a usual circular letter, a report or a directive, but a printed brochure – a model collective penal case. It contained reprinted parts of a closing indictment against the "insurgent, counter-revolutionary, monarchist, red-dragon type organization of Samosviatsy and Ioannites." Eleven volumes of the group penal case (kept today in the Central FSB archive in Moscow) were turned into a 94-page model case brochure. One of the copies of the brochure was sent to the OGPU office in Kiev, where,

80 years later, I was able read it (HDASBU, fond. 13-1-388). This document was not unique. During the 1930s, a number of similar model collective cases were published or circulated as typewritten copies between OGPU offices as top-secret documents. Some copies were also sent to local Party Committees. This type of secret police document was more than just a report or a demonstration of the OGPU's power and effectiveness to the Party and state authorities (as argues Babenko 2012). When I asked an archivist why a criminal file was published as a brochure, she answered: "But how else could our ordinary officers know anything about these sects? They had to work with them and these documents were supposed to facilitate their work."

This type of document was a sort of manual for the OGPU's struggle against various groups, collectively referred to as the all-Union counter-revolutionary ecclesiastic-monarchist organization. It was a particular "archival form" (Stoler 2009, 20) that transmitted a constellation of categories and techniques and trained secret police officers in the regions to produce homogenized and standardized knowledge through repeated formulae and frames. It contained everything a local secret police officer needed to know: articles of accusation; narrative style and a set of narrative formulas; forms of interrogation questions and "correct" responses; the historical outline and the social structure of the movement as perceived by the secret police, and evidence of its insurgent, counter-revolutionary activities. It introduced both social categories and the political practices that these categories marked. Using wooden language and ritualistic formulae, the file set up necessary categorizations such as anti-Soviet activity, conspirativity, counter-revolutionary unrest, an enemy disguised under the mask of religiosity, class struggle, liquidation campaign and denunciation of the enemy (Verdery 2014, 55). It also provided a repertoire of roles – "a cliché from an infamous stock of characters" (Vǎţulescu 2010, 38; Verdery 2014, 56) – couriers, emissaries, spies, counter-revolutionaries, terrorists, vagabond agitators and propagandists. A secret police officer read this all, underlined some points with red or blue, made marginal notes, and later recycled this in his own work.

The epistemic force of the document was in being a stencil to apply in similar cases. It was a tool to ensure the integrity of the knowledge, hence, the homogeneous and standardized repressive actions against such diverse groups of believers. The knowledge eventually transcended the walls of the secret police office. Regional Party committees also got copies of model criminal files like this one, which later were recycled in the Department of Agitation and Propaganda – the main producer of anti-religious propaganda materials. Hence, on the pages of anti-religious periodicals, like "*Bezbozhnik*," "*Voiovnychyi ateist*" or later in propaganda films, one would encounter literally the same formulae and narrative and visual techniques, even some confiscated religious material, recycled from their cooperation with the secret police.[5]

In this way, the model criminal file itself was a social agent, to follow Verdery (2014, 60). The file did not refer to a reality or existent social relations, but it produced the reality of the networking religious underground and envisioned nodes of social relations, creating enemies, terrorists, spies, conspirators, and insurgents out of ordinary believers.

Secret police bricolage

In addition to and alongside the narrative representations of the conspiratorial organization, the files also aestheticized them visually with some artfully created materials. The brochure opens up with a photo-collage of people on trial. The easiest way to visualize hidden religious dissent as a conspiratorial organization is to group them altogether in one picture. Figure 2.1 shows the photo-collage from a model criminal file on the Ioannites and Samosviatsy. The trial was against a hundred believers, mostly priests, monastics and some peasants identified as kulaks. They were accused as members of the "insurgent, counter-revolutionary, monarchist, red-dragon-type organization ... united to overthrow Soviet power and to restore the monarchy." (HDASBU, fond. 13-1-388, 1). The closing indictment says, they disseminated leaflets with the writings of father John of Kronstadt, spread the preaching about Red Dragons and the coming End of the World. By this, the file argues, they prepared the peasantry for mass protests against collectivization and other Soviet reforms.

The file groups believers into 11 "cells" and groups, each headed by a wandering monk or a nun, a prophet or a prophetess, a holy fool (*yurodivyi*) or a holy ill person (*boliashchii*). The photo-collage does not picture all the arrestees but visualizes the main idea – the network of former monks and nuns (most of those pictured were monastics) clandestinely united around a leader (a prophet or a holy ill person). Photographs of larger size pictured the supposed leaders of the cells. They are in centre place in the photo-collage. And their central position is emphasized by the fact that the secret police have not used arrest mugshots for these important figures, unlike for all other photographs. Leaders are dressed in their monastic and clerical clothing. In her photograph, Ekaterina Titova (central column, second top), who was a nun and a prophetess leading one of the underground monasteries, is dressed in her full monastic clothing. Andrei – a *boliashchii*, or holy ill person and local charismatic leader, a centre of gravity for believers in Belgorod – is pictured half-reclining, surrounded by flowers. The largest photographs located at the top belonged to a hieromonk, Feognost Pilipenko. His central position in the photo-collage was determined by his special role in the secret police construction. He was accused as a clandestine courier, who linked local sets in Belgorod and connected them with the central clandestine organization in Kiev.

The visual cues provided by the secret police invite us to read the photo-collages in this way. However, if we learn more about the case, we find out that neither Ekaterina Titova nor Andrei *Boliashchii*, nor Feognost Pilipenko was actually arrested, at least as part of this trial. Therefore, the secret police

Figure 2.1 Photo-collage from a model criminal file on the Ioannites and Samosviatsy (HDASBU, fond. 13-1-388, 1). ©State Archive Branch of the Security Services of Ukraine.

simply did not have their arrest mugshots. In creating the file and the photo-collage, the secret police used the materials at hand – in this case, some confiscated photographs along with arrest mugshots. Levi-Strauss' concept of *bricolage* seems to perfectly describe the secret police technique of producing knowledge. Using whatever is at hand, re-deploying different things in new combinations, subjecting them to its own logic, the secret police produced a new totalizing narrative. Confiscated photographs of some religious activists as left-overs of an extraneous cultural tradition and visual materials (arrest mugshots) produced by the secret police itself come together in this heterogenous repertoire used to create new meanings out of incriminating evidence. It does not matter whether Feognost Pilipenko was actually a leader of any popular religious movement or whether the nun Ekaterina headed an underground monastery. What matters here is that their large-size photographs can be re-utilized in the production of knowledge on the religious underground network and hence, in the revelation of the conspiratorial political network.

Likewise, the bricolage technique in Figure 2.2 utilized various confiscated photographs and grouped them around the image of bishop Avgustin (Beliaev) (HDASBU, fond. 13-1-391, 6a). A teacher, a manufacturer's daughter, an engineer, two priests (*pop*), a monarchist, a merchant's daughter and son, a former civil servant, a former merchant and an officer – all these discrete pieces from different cultures and social classes, divorced from their original contexts, have been meticulously collaged together. A drawing of a flag with a "God save the Tsar" slogan adds integrity to the image of a secret network produced out of miscellaneous fragments.

Religious network schemes

The religious network scheme was another visual technique to envision centralized religious organizations through complex sets of social links. Schemes from model criminal files were accurately made and printed using an advanced photo-printing technology. The images show the network of an insurgent religious and political organization from bottom to top. At the very bottom are "local (rural) cells" (*sel'skie iacheiki*) – basic religious groups located in farms, villages and settlements. A dot (triangle, circle, or rectangle) shows the number of arrested in a repressed cell. A shadowed sign signifies a "not liquidated" group still under surveillance.

A network scheme from the Samara OGPU (Figure 2.3) is perhaps the most elaborate one (though unfortunately it has survived only in a poor quality copy) (HDASBU, fond. 13-1-386, 1). It pictures a network of the counter-revolutionary organization in the Middle Volga region and its complex links of relations between cells and centres. Miniature images of churches indicate "basic cells" (*nizovye iacheiki*) centred around some churches that remained open. Basic cells are grouped and linked to form regional sets of cells. Circles twice crossed refer to local leaders – a kulak, a priest (pop), a monk, a bishop, or simply indicate surnames with no details. Regional sets of cells are linked

Figure 2.2 Photo-collage of confiscated photographs grouped around the image of bishop Avgustin (Beliaev) (HDASBU, fond. 13-1-391, 6a). ©State Archive Branch of the Security Services of Ukraine.

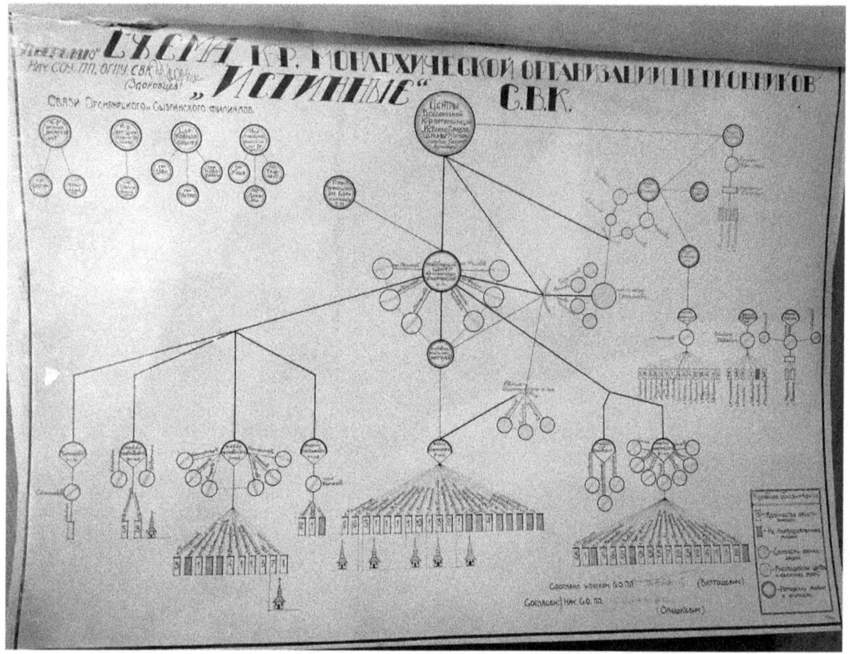

Figure 2.3 Network scheme of the True Orthodox Church from the Samara OGPU (HDASBU, fond. 13-1-386, 1). ©State Archive Branch of the Security Services of Ukraine.

to a senior centre of the "counter-revolutionary organization" in Kashirin region. This link is not direct, but is established through groups of couriers (*sviaznoi*), schematically pictured as shadowed circles. Through a similar group of couriers, the regional centre is connected eventually to the top – two all-union centres of the counter-revolutionary organization the "True Orthodox Church" – the political centre in Moscow and the administration centre in Leningrad.

An all-encompassing image of the religious network is finally deployed in Figure 2.4 (HDASBU, fond. 13-1-387, 49). The scheme is signed by Evgenii Tuchkov, the head of the so-called "Church department" of the OGPU and one of the leaders of the 1920s–30s anti-religious campaigns who headed secret police operations against the ROC and the ecclesiastical underground. The scheme "reveals" hidden connections of branches and cells in the entire country (Central, Caucasian, Black sea, Central Black Earth, Volga regions, Ukraine etc.). Shadowed circles refer to those cells and branches that had supposedly developed significant insurgent activities. The scheme gives two types of social connection: a direct link between the cells (full lines) and an indirect link (*kosvennaia sviaz'*, dotted lines). It is unclear what an indirect

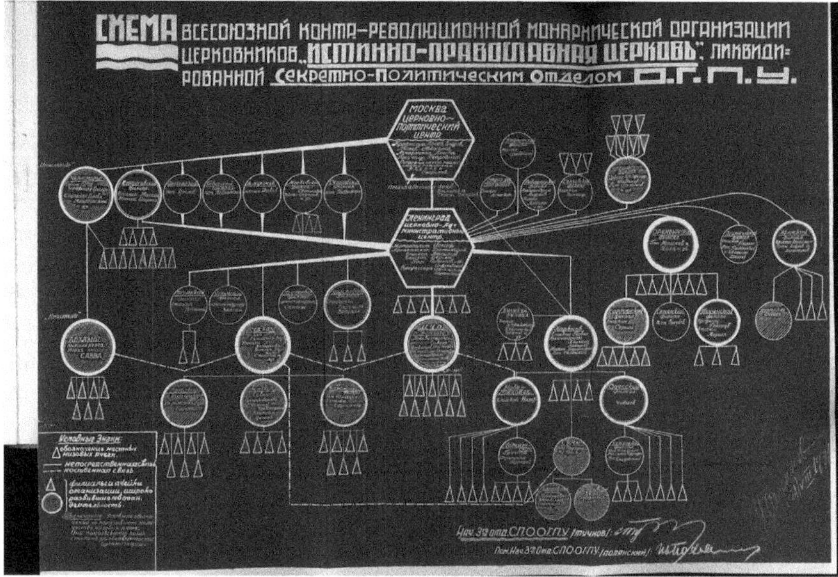

Figure 2.4 Network scheme of the True Orthodox Church signed by Evgenii Tuchkov, the head of the "Church department" of the OGPU (HDASBU, fond. 13-1-387, 49). ©State Archive Branch of the Security Services of Ukraine.

link means here (some kind of double-imaginative relation), but it allows for every group, branch and cell in the entire Soviet Union to be interconnected and at the same time subordinates them altogether to regional and superior centres. Two hexagons – two all-union centres in Moscow and Leningrad – crown the scheme. Thus, an ideal image of the insurgent, espionage, terrorist, counter-revolutionary, conspiracy organization was fully accomplished. It is pictured as a network, which is built not as a web but as a vertical hierarchical scheme where all links and dots come up to a centre. It is grounded on the assumption that a person is not an individual but a network node.

These schemes visually demonstrate Verdery's point when she claims that it is "not individuals but social connections that are the basic unit of [socialist] society" (2018, 244). When personhood is understood as the sum of relationships, as "composites of all the social relations running through them," then to know the network means to reveal the truth (Verdery 2014, 187). It was social networks but not individuals that the Soviet secret police operated with as basic categories. As Florin Poenaru points out, "In the Soviet system, the individual is never guilty as such, as an isolated human being, but always [as] part of a 'guilty' wider set of social relations" (cit. by Verdery 2014, 189–90). Comparing the Romanian Securitate's envisioning of networks with standard analysis of networks, Verdery observes that the latter "connects sets of dots (people) that pre-exist the line drawn between them," whereas the Securitate's networks did not link preceding dots: "they *created* the dots and connected them through lines whose vector was not the target's life but the Securitate's intentions" (Verdery 2014, 201–2, emphasis original).

To summarize, religious network schemes and photo-collages are visual representations of the socialist theory of personhood and network. They were "ideal constructions" within a broader narrative of the Stalinist conspiracy theory. The construction was totalizing as it both produced the knowledge of a giant conspiracy network and at the same time, deployed political actions to disintegrate the envisioned social relations, to cut off the links within the network. As the subsequent history of the Soviet secret police shows, the aim was not to fully destroy the network, but to place it under control, to re-forge social links within the network in a way that it would be the secret police and the communist party that would crown every pyramid of social networks, in Verdery's words (2014, 204), to become the ultimate network node.

Conclusion: clash of conspiracies

Eschatological beliefs proliferated in the Russian and Ukrainian countryside before and after the revolution of 1917 and particularly during 1920–30s anti-religious campaigns, when the majority of Orthodox churches and monasteries were closed, their property confiscated, clergy and monastics repressed or disenfranchized. Popular religious movements prophesied about the arrival of the Red Dragons, the communists, who would bring the End of the World. Envisioning apocalyptic images, people dug out underground churches and monasteries, told eschatological stories transmitted orally or circulated in handwritten notebooks, made folk icons, and wandered from village to village preaching about the Apocalypse. They were not unified into organizational structures, nor had they a common theology or religious practices. Some believed in John the Kronstadt as a prophet and a Christ saviour, others sought to restore broken links with the Moscow Patriarchy. Some adopted millenarian theology and ecstatic practices, or built an underground "New Jerusalem," others – joined Old Believer communities. They were scattered around the country, avoided elections, *kolkhozes* and other Soviet reforms, while reading historical and current events in terms of apocalyptic conspiracy.

The giant conspiracy theory of the ecclesiastic-monarchist underground network was a reply of the Soviet state to these popular religious movements. This was conceived as the means to control the spontaneous religiosity of peasant masses. The state conspiracy theory envisioned religious dissent as a hidden political power, as an organized, complex, and politically dangerous underground organization. The popular eschatology of the Red Dragon was eventually reclassified as a "red-dragon type counter-revolutionary ecclesiastic monarchist underground organization." The image was powerful as it had the effect of common sense and triggered a set of political actions that determined the religious lives of ordinary believers in the Soviet Union.

In this article, I have focused on the social categories the Soviet secret police produced and operated with while dealing with popular religiosity. I have undertaken an archelogy of the concept, "ecclesiastic monarchist underground organization" in order to look closely at how this concept was constructed and envisioned, and what kind of narrative and visual techniques were developed in order to ensure the integrity of the concept and its reality effect. Specific genres of Soviet secret police documentation – top-secret model criminal files and printed official reports on the so-called ecclesiastic-monarchist underground – provide insights into the layered process of knowledge production and social imaginaries of the state. Equating knowledge and power, secret police discursive practices can be seen as a site of the forging of power relations.

Using certain narrative forms, styles and visual techniques, the secret police drew an image of a dangerous network of enemies, producing a sort of common-sense knowledge out of this image. Model criminal files on the ecclesiastic-monarchist underground from the late 1920s–1930s can be read as manuals on the production of this kind of "common sense." Published as top-secret instructions for regional secret police officers, they provided epistemic tools to create the alternative reality of religious life in the Soviet Union. Both the verbal and visual materials were generic plots or building blocks in the construction of the knowledge on the religious underground network. Citations of witnesses and arrestees, religious network schemes, confiscated photographs, and arrest mugshots were dislodged from their initial context, *estranged,* and then re-assembled in a new way, finally moving into the field of criminal evidence. This is how the conversion of popular religiosity into political subversion was accomplished.

Notes

1 This research was supported by Irish Research Council, Government of Ireland, project "Religious Minorities in Ukraine from the Soviet Underground to the Euromaidan: Pathways to Religious Freedom and Pluralism in Enlarging Europe" (GOIPD/2017/764).

2 By the end of the 1930s, approximately 28% of churches remained opened in the entire Soviet Union (with only 9% of churches opened in Ukraine) out of some 50,000 churches that existed before the Revolution (Pospielovsky 1995, 168). In 1937–1939, there were over 9,500 underground illegal parishes (Beglov 2008, 68).

3 The new category *lishentsy* (disenfranchised persons) introduced by the Constitution 1918, included, among others, the clergy and monastics. They were deprived in their civil rights (to vote and be elected, to higher education, to live in certain cities, to occupy governmental position, etc.), as well social subsidies like housing or retirement. Priests paid 75% taxes from their "unearned" income (Pospielovsky 1995, 159).

4 See Vagramenko, Tatiana. "Confiscated manuscript of Pentecostal prophecy from Ukraine," *Hidden Galleries Digital Archive*, http://hiddengalleries.eu/digitalarchive/s/en/item/12.

5 Cristina Vățulescu (2010) gives an insightful analysis of the cooperation of the Soviet secret police and film production. For an example of such symbiosis of the secret police and anti-religious propaganda films in Ukraine see Vagramenko, Tatiana. "Secret police photographs of Ioannite community in Ukraine", *Hidden Galleries Digital Archive,* http://hiddengalleries.eu/digitalarchive/s/en/item/161.

Archival sources

Haluzevyi Derzhavnyi Arkhiv Sluzhby Bezpeky Ukrainy [State Archive Branch of the Security Services of Ukraine in Kyiv] (HDASBU), fond 3; fond 6; fond 13; fond 16.

Arkhiv Upravlinnia Sluzhby Bezpeky Ukraïny v Vinnyts'kii Oblasti [Archive of the SBU Office in Vinnyts'ka Oblast] (ASBUVO), spr. 27921-fp.

References

Babenko, Liudmila. 2012. "Special Operations of the Soviet Security Organs on the Liquidation of the Ecclesiastic-Religious Underground in the 1930 – Beginning 1950s" [Spetsoperatsii radians'kykh orhaniv derzhpezpeky po likvidatsii tserkovno-relihiinoho pidpillia u 1930 – na pochatku 1950-kh rokiv]. *Aktual'ni problemy vitchiznianoi ta vsesvitnioi istorii. Zbirnyk naukovykh prats' Rivnens'koho derzhavnoho humanitarnoho universytetu*, 23: 85–97.

Babenko, Liudmila. 2013. "The Cooperation of the Party-Soviet Organs of the State Security Services in the Struggle Against 'Religious Miracles' (1920–1940)" ["Vzaemodiia partiino-radians'kykh orhaniv derzhbezpeky v borot'bi z "relihiinymy chudesamy" (1920–1940)"]. *Z arkhiviv VUChK-GPU-NKVD-KGB*, 40–41 (1–2): 327–50.

Beglov, Aleksei. 2008. *In Search of "Ideal Church Catacombs". Church Underground in the USSR* [*V poiskakh "bezgreshnykh katakomb". Tserkovnoe podpol'e v SSSR*]. Moscow: "Arefa".

Coleman, Heather J. 2005. *Russian Baptists and Spiritual Revolution, 1905–1929*. Bloomington: Indiana University Press.

Deleuze, Gilles. 1992. *Foucault*. Translated and edited by Seán Hand. Minneapolis: University of Minnesota Press.

Demianov, Aleksandr I. 1977. *True Orthodox Christianity. The Critique of Ideology and Activity* [*Istinno-pravoslavnoe khristianstvo. Kritika ideologii i deiatel'nosti.*] Voronezh: Izdatel'stvo Voronezhskogo universiteta.

Dobson, Miriam and Benjamin Ziemann. 2009. "Introduction". In: *Reading Primary Sources: The Interpretation of Texts from 19th and 20th Century History*, edited by M. Dobson and B. Ziemann, 1–18. New York: Routledge.

Fenster, Mark. 2008. *Conspiracy Theories: Secrecy and Power in American Culture*. Minneapolis: University of Minnesota Press.

Fitzpatrick, Sheila. 2005. *Tear Off the Masks! Identity and Imposture and Twentieth-century Russia*. Princeton: Princeton University Press.

Foucault, Michel. 1977. "The Political Function of the Intellectual" (translated by Colin Gordon). *Radical Philosophy*, 17: 12–14.

Kapaló, James Alexander. 2011. *Text, Context, and Performance: Gagauz Folk Religion in Discourse and Practice*. Leiden: Brill.

Kizenko, Nadieszda. 2000. *A Prodigal Saint: Father John of Kronstadt and the Russian People*. University Park: Penn State University Press.

Kosik, Olga V. 2009. "The Collection "The Case of Metropolitan Sergius" and the Participation in it of the Martyr Mikhail (Novoselov)" ["Sbornik "Delo mitropolita Sergiia" i uchastiie v nem muchenika Mikhaila (Novosiolova)"]. *Vestnik PSTGU. II: Istoriia. Istoriia Russkoi Pravoslavnoi Tserkvi* 31 (2): 77–95.

Lopushanskaia, Elena L. 1971. *Bishops Confessors [Episkopy ispovedniki]*. San Francisco.

Luehrmann, Sonja. 2015. *Religion in Secular Archives: Soviet Atheism and Historical Knowledge*. Oxford: Oxford University Press.

Melley, Timothy. 2000. *Empire of Conspiracy: The Culture of Paranoia in Postwar America*. Ithaca, New York: Cornell University Press.

Pospielovsky, Dimitry V. 1995. *The Russian Orthodox Church in the 20th Century* [*Russkaia pravoslavnaia tserkov' v XX veke*]. Moscow: Respublika.

Protsenko, Pavel. 1998. The Myth of the True Church. [Mif ob istinnoi tzerkvi]. *Vestnik Russkogo khristianskogo dvizheniia*, 179 (5–6): 137–50.

Quinby, Lee. 1994. *Anti-Apocalypse: Exercises in Genealogical Criticism*. Minneapolis: University of Minnesota Press.

Sannikov, Georgii Z. 2002. *The Big Hunt: The Crush of the Armed Underground in Western Ukraine* [*Bol'shaia okhota: Razgrom vooruzhennogo podpoliia v Zapadnoi Ukraine*]. Moscow: Olma-Press.

Shinar, Chaim. 2018. Conspiracy Narratives in Russian Politics: From Stalin to Putin. *European Review* 26 (4): 648–60.

Steinberg, Mark D. 1994. Workers on the Cross: Religious Imagination in the Writings of Russian Workers, 1910–1924. *The Russian Review* 53 (2): 213–39.

Stoler, Ann Laura. 2009. *Along the Archival Grain: Epistemic Anxieties and Colonial Common Sense*. Princeton and Oxford: Princeton University Press.

Tepliakov 2010. "The Ioannites of Western Siberia in VChk-OGPU-NKVD Documents (1920–1940s)" ["Ioanity Zapadnoi Sibiri v dokumentakh VChk-OGPU-NKVD (1920–1940 gody)]". *Vestnik Tverskogo gosudarstvennogo universiteta. Seriia: Istoriia* 30 (4): 128–36.

Vǎţulescu, Cristina. 2010. *Police Aesthetics: Literature, Film, and the Secret Police in Soviet Times*. Stanford: Stanford University Press.

Verdery, Katherine. 2014. *Secrets and Truths: Ethnography in the Archive of Romania's Secret Police*. Budapest: Central European University Press.

Verdery, Katherine. 2018. *My Life as a Spy: Investigations in a Secret Police File*. Durham: Duke University Press.

Viola, Lynne. 1990. The Peasant Nightmare: Visions of Apocalypse in the Soviet Countryside. *Journal of Modern History* 62 (4): 747–70.

Wynot, Jennifer Jean. 2004. *Keeping the Faith: Russian Orthodox Monasticism in the Soviet Union, 1917–1939*. College Station, Texas: Texas A&M University Press.

Yashchenko, Viacheslav G. 2008. *The Anti-Bolshevik Insurgency in the Low Volga and the Middle Don Regions in 1918–1923* [*Antibol'shevistskoe povstanchestvo v Nizhnem Povolzh'e i na Srednem Donu 1918–1923*]. Moscow: "Librokom".

Zimina, Nina P. 2010. "On the Ioannite Movement within the Russian Orthodox Church and the Origin of the Catacomb Movement of "Archbishop" Agafangel (Sadovskov)" ["K voprosu ob ioanitskom dvizhenii v Russkoi Pravoslavnoi Tserkvi i vozniknovenii v kontse 1920-kh gg. katakombnogo techeniia "arkhiepiskopa" Agafangela (Sadovskova)"]. *Vestnik PSTGU. II: Istoriia. Istoriia Russkoi Pravoslavnoi Tserkvi* 37 (4): 28–54.

3 The legal context of religious activities in Hungary between 1945 and 1989/90

Szilvia Köbel

Introduction

This study presents the legal framework within which religious activities took place during the socialist era in Hungary. First of all, I briefly draft the administrative and political conditions according to which churches were legitimized by the state; including the communist church policy and the official institutions that carried out the state's "anticlerical" policies. After that I focus on the situation of the different categories of religious groups pursued by the regime. In my conclusion, I focus on the remission of these actions in the late 1980s as the socialist system slowly faded and came under international pressure.

The administrative and the political conditions of legitimization of churches by the state

Since the Marxist and Leninist ideology of the state, which declared the Worker's Party "the leading force of society,"[1] was in direct contradiction to the churches' mission in society, the religious organizations and their respective ideology became an enemy, or more precisely, the enemy of the state as it was strongly believed that they represented the capitalist culture. This resulted in a "hostile" separation model between state and church (XX. Act of 1949) in Hungary.[2] It was hostile because despite the use of the term "separation," religious organizations were far from able to act autonomously. Stalin's church administration model was adopted by the Hungarian regime, thus the State Office of Church Affairs (referred to as ÁEH in the following)[3] was created and Church Affairs Secretaries were placed in every county (Köbel 2002a) of Hungary to achieve total supervision and surveillance (Köbel 2000, Köbel 2001a, Soós 2014). In addition to the activities of the ÁEH, the political police used undercover agents in this ideological war. Their main tasks were surveillance, deconstruction and overall manipulation which was achieved with a network of collaborators inside the churches, who were enrolled mostly through the use of extortion (Köbel 2002b).

The "political police" is actually an umbrella term for the various Hungarian state security or secret services that operated between 1945 and 1989. The task of the state security services was initially to execute the policies of the communist party and then later in the one-party-system – after the fusion of the left (1948) – those of the Hungarian Workers's Party (MDP) until 1956 and after the revolution of 1956, those of the Hungarian Socialist Worker's Party (MSZMP). Thus, it truly became the "political police."

In 1946 the Budapest Police Headquarters' Political Department (PRO) transformed into the first unified, central state administrative service, the State Defence Department (ÁVO). The ÁVO then – supervised by the Ministry of Home Affairs and after January 1, 1950 supervised by the Government – transformed into the State Defence Authority (ÁVH) and worked as an autonomous organ. The Government assigned the Minister of Home Affairs to be its head supervisor. At the same time, the Political Department of the ÁVH got tacked on to the party headquarters and its cooperation was assured. In the restructuring process that took place during 1952–53, the Central Head Departments were created in the ÁVH, one of which was Head Department I, tasked with the deflection of reactionary movements within the country. In 1953 the ÁVH was unified with the Ministry of Home Affairs.

In the wake of the revolution of 1956, in January of 1957, the ÁVH inside the Ministry of Home Affairs was disbanded and the responsibility of criminal investigation regarding interior as well as exterior security was passed down to the regular police. In 1962 – during the process of consolidation – through a decree by the party's (MSZMP) Political Commission (PB), a new form of the state security was created in the organ of the Ministry of Home Affairs, which – despite some amendments – remained in place until 1989/1990. The former system of Head Departments was replaced in favour of a system of Major Divisions and (Sub) Divisions. In this system, Major Division III oversaw the handling of all the various interior security affairs. Within Major Division III resided the (in)famous Division III (Division III/III) which was responsible for averting reactionary movements.

Within Division III, Department 1 was responsible for clerical reactionary movements and worked closely together with Division III/I – the central intelligence group – in their actions against clerical emigration to Israel and the Vatican. Averting clerical reactionary movements included all the tasks done by the state security within sects, various churches and groups of former religious orders. Later, the tasks of Department 1 were categorized according to the various churches. In the countryside, these tasks were the responsibility of the political department of the respective county's police headquarters.

The actions of state security were based on the party's manifesto, which declared that the "clerical reaction is political reaction painted in the colour of religion, and thus the fight against it is political in nature." The state security's task was twofold: uncovering and prosecution of illegal clerical activity, and constantly observing the legal actions of the church through surveillance and notifying the party and state services.

What did all this mean in practical terms? In essence, the state security services adapted their methodology of prevention to fit the unique circumstances of the clerical field. Their goals were the following:

- surveillance and removal of the headquarters of the Hungarian clerical reactionary movement
- infiltration of the illegal channels of the domestic reactionary movements and that of the Vatican via collaborators
- destruction of the church's reputation
- surveillance of hostile activities within the seminaries, and infiltration by agents both on the student and teacher's side
- surveillance of priests that intended to leave their profession

The following methods were used by the political police:

- arrests
- disruption (investigation, amplification – and if needed – creation of conflicts within the church)
- disciplinary procedures against church persons (the disciplinary punishment of priests by the State Office of Church Affairs through the proxy of collaborating bishops)
- admonition by police, by universities or bosses in workplaces (warnings by bosses or expulsion from the university was an effective method against non-clerical church members)
- police supervision (this was used less frequently by the sixties)
- displacement of clerics through the State Office of Church Affairs
- collaborators (this was the most important)

The political police was at its most effective and efficient with the use of collaborators. Agent candidates were clerics who – through personality traits and their ability for acquiring intelligence – were capable of winning the trust of the "enemy." By the first half of the fifties the agent network consisting of clerics had been established. These clerical agents infiltrated every organizational and functional aspect of the Church: church leadership, the episcopacy, the faculty and student body of clerical theology, church owned high schools, press, functioning religious orders dedicated to teaching – Piarists, Benedictines, Franciscans or the Svetits' female order that operated in Debrecen – as well as the already disbanded religious orders. A number of methods were used in the recruitment process of the agents: compromising or incriminating information (this was the most expedient method), human weakness (material needs of wealth or otherwise), amplifying the process of compromising the moral integrity of clerical personnel by integrating female agents that had a past of bad morals, and lastly, a long and gradual recruitment process appealing to the "patriotism" of its subjects (Köbel 2005).

The legal status of churches between 1947 and 1990 in Hungary was based on the *XLIII. Act of 1895 on free exercise of religion*'s *7. §, 8. §, 18. §* and on the *XXXIII. Act of 1947 on the abolition of disadvantages between established and acknowledged churches*.[4] As a result of the latter, the privileges of the established churches (Catholic, Calvinist, Lutheran, Unitarian, Greek Orthodox,[5] Jewish[6]) (see Fazekas, this volume) ceased, furthermore the act kept the rules regarding the foundation of churches declared by the XLIII. Act of 1895. This included the structuring of at least one congregation, religious education in public schools, and the baseline regulations regarding these organizations, which were the following: it cannot be against the state, the nation and it cannot be unlawful; it cannot have nationalist or racist characteristics; it cannot offend other churches.[7] In addition to the above-mentioned established churches, the Baptist church gained legal acknowledgement in 1905[8] and the Methodist church in 1947,[9] and also the Islamic religion (not as church) was acknowledged with a special law in 1916.[10]

In reality, however, with legal acknowledgement in many cases political conditions were decisive rather than legal ones. Ergo in return for loyalty towards the socialist state legal acknowledgement was granted. The already established churches were not excluded from this process, thus agreements were made between them and the state from 1948 to 1950. These were technically contracts but served as political accords. Complete loyalty and political support was demanded from the religious leadership in exchange for their legality. In these agreements, the extent of a church's freedom to operate in the socialist system was beginning to show its true nature.[11]

Religious groups pursued by the regime – categories from a legal standpoint[12]

There were, however, those who were actively pursued by the state. For the purposes of this study, I have categorized these into four major groups:

1. Resisting groups within state-approved churches (a minority within a so-called majority church, pursued by both the state and their own church)
2. Unapproved religious communities (illegal churches, "sects")
3. Religious communities who gained legality during socialism
4. Semi-legal religious groups with expanded possibilities and publicity, following the continuous change of church policy in the 1980s

Resisting groups within state-approved churches (minority in a so-called majority church, pursued both by the state and by the leaders of their own church)

The baseline for these pursuits was that every church or religion is an enemy of the socialist system. On July 1st, 1950, the Hungarian Workers's Party (MDP)[13] made a decision regarding the *fight against the clerical reaction*.

According to this resolution, the "clerical reaction is the fifth column of the imperialists in Hungary" and "its intrigues are directed to undermine the unity of the working people." The resolution also created some concrete tasks, such as: The state's right to intervene in the appointment of bishops was to be enforced, church associations were to be subject to official inspection; "the financial support of instigant priests harmful to the Hungarian People's Republic must cease," at the same time the priests "cooperating with the people" must be guaranteed an "adequate living subsidy"; "Action must be taken against reactionary trends in Protestant and Jewish churches, as well as against the sects and freemason lodge controlled by the American imperialism."[14]

Later, however, this changed and the resolutions of the Political Committee of the Hungarian Socialist Worker's Party (MSZMP)[15] of 1958 declared that the cooperation between the socialist state and state-approved churches is not only possible, but is also necessary as it "eliminates clerical reaction." This so-called "clerical reaction" was officially defined as

The actions of anti-popular elements under the guise of the church, whose goal is the toppling of democracy, and the restoration of the old and oppressive system of capitalist landowners – including the political and economic might of reactionary high priests [...] (MNL OL-M-KS-288-5/82)

In short, any ideological opposition to the system and to cooperation between state and church. This clerical reaction was to be fought within the church as well. Loyal church members could get into leadership positions but were required to step up politically against the "reactionary" and exclude them from financially beneficial positions as well as request their removal from within the church so its leadership may act according to state and internal church laws. Furthermore, the political agenda of the Priest Peace Movement[16] was to be placed in the hands of the party in the form of regular political education for clerics. The church's connection to the youth was also to be limited to religious lessons in schools, first communion (Catholic) and confirmation (Protestant), everything else (sports, choirs and so on) was deemed "unacceptable." The leadership of the churches were transformed into "consociates" and the cooperation of church members accelerated. The only choice was submission as the cooperation between approved churches and the state grew stronger with each year (MNL OL-M-KS-288-5/82, 85).

In the 1970s, a political softening occurred internationally which was also noticeable in the policies of the Hungarian People's Republic towards the churches. Some necessary decisions were taken in order that the illusion of religious freedom could be held up in the international eye. The party (MSZMP) declared in 1973, that "in the last 15 years, the churches have found their place in the socialist society," they accept the domestic and international objectives and join the "political programme for the construction a complete socialism." It reached the point where, in the party resolution of 1973, "church allies" and "progressive church individuals" were declared "allies of the regime" through "the exposure, political and ethical disgracing and isolation of the clerical reactionary forces" (MNL OL-M-KS-288-5/625). An example would be the oversight of religious education, which was passed to church leaders on the "basis of trust" (MNL OL-M-KS-288-5/625). Kádár János, General Secretary of Hungarian Socialist Workers' Party, stated: [...] we have to clearly say, that the supervisory right of the state is untouchable, now however as a sign of trust it will be passed on to the episcopacy. They must also be immediately told, that if the experiences are bad, the direct supervision of the state will be reinstated. (MNL OL-M-KS-288-5/625)

When the Political Committee of the Hungarian Socialist Worker's Party released their resolution regarding religious separatist (nonconformist) groups in 1982, the original course of action was once again reinstated. In this resolution, the name "clerical nonconformists" was given to those, who opposed the official clerical leadership. The resolution declared them "socially dangerous" as they interfered in the "orderly relationship between state and the churches." The action against the nonconformist groups was declared an internal matter and was ordered to be "resolved by their religious leaders according to their own laws." The Political Committee ordained that "the state and social organizations must aid the legal clerical leadership with political tools" and strengthen their "political safety." In case the church fails to deal with its internal matters, the Political Committee prescribed the use of "coordinated administrative instruments" (MNL OL-M-KS-288-5/846). If interference was deemed necessary, criminal lawsuits were to be instituted against those in aforementioned *socially dangerous* category, who were often accused of conspiracy against the state.

During the socialist period, every church had an opposing, nonconformist layer. Some examples would be the so-called Bulányist Group in the Catholic Church who refused military service for reasons of conscience (ÁBTL 3.1.9. V-140907/1–4); the Bethanist group within the Calvinist church; the Lawsuits against ex KIE (Christian Youth Association) members in 1967 (e.g. Károly Dobos, Bálint Kovács Calvinist pastors) (ÁBTL 3.1.9. V-155460/4; ÁBTL 3.1.5. O-13142/1–3). In the Lutheran church, pastor Ferenc Sréter separated himself from the main organization and took most of the members of the Budavár congregation with him (ÁBTL 3.1.5 O-9390/1–3). Pastor Zoltán Dóka engaged in opposition to the regime too, but he eventually remained a member of the Lutheran church (ÁBTL 2.7.1. NOIJ; ÁBTL 3.1.5. O-13599/1).

More extreme cases of these kinds of divisions were present in the Methodist church, where an actual split happened with the nonconformists acknowledged by the state in 1981 (ÁBTL 3.1.2. M-40918/4, 6, 8–11; ÁBTL 3.1.5. O-9045; ÁBTL 3. 1.5. O-19764/1; Lakatos 2011; Heinz et al. 2013). A similar division also took place in the Seventh Day Adventist church but the nonconformist group was pursued by the state and operated illegally during the remainder of the socialist system, after which their legal status was acknowledged (ÁBTL 3.1.2. M-40918/1–11; Á BTL 3.1.5. O-19856/1–2; Á BTL 3.1.5. O-14916; Holló 2012). Despite declaring such divisions within churches as an internal matter, the state built a network of informants inside the churches to fight against these groups.

Catholic orders constitute a somewhat unique case. In 1950, their right to legally operate was revoked and with the exception of some teaching orders, they were forced into illegality. The estates of the disbanded orders, with the exception of churches and buildings housing religious personnel, were nationalized by the state.[17]

Unapproved religious communities (illegal churches or so-called "sects")

The unapproved religious communities – Nazarenes, Adventists, Seventh-day Sabbatarians, Jehovah's Witnesses, Church of God, Ancient Christians and Pentecostals – were mostly churches that were "tolerated" before their ban in 1939[18] and were reinstated in 1945 by the Minister of Home Affairs and the Prime Minister (BMKI 250.105/1945. VI. 3),[19] however, they didn't achieve state-approved status. The above-mentioned 1947 church-equality act with the "established churches" (Catholic, Reformed, Lutheran, Unitarian, Greek Orthodox, Israelite together with the uniquely designated "Islamic religion") was only applied to the churches that had been acknowledged up until 1947, namely the Baptist and Methodist churches. The other communities were referred to as "sects" as they were not recognized by the state and a distinction had to be drawn between them and the acknowledged churches. An example of this category would be the Jehovah's Witnesses Church, which was banned during the socialist era (Petrás 2017).[20]

In the eyes of the political police, there was a difference between sects and free churches. According to a 1980 internal dictionary of the State Security, "free churches" were "smaller, legally permitted religious groups which do not get financial aid from the state." The dictionary defined the "Council of Free Churches" as such: "according to the contract made with the Hungarian People's Republic, ten so-called 'small churches' operate legally, such as: Adventist, Baptist, Pentecostalists, etc." Next to "sects" the following was stated: "Some 15-20, middle-sized sect groups operate illegally in our country, such as Jehovah's Witnesses, etc. These fall outside of the so called small churches" (Gergely 1980). From this, one can see that the categorization of religious groups by the state security underwent changes through the decades depending on whether they gained acknowledgement by the state or not.

The option of obtaining legal status was available but it meant merging with other small communities in the Council of Free Churches (e.g. with the Pentecostal Church). Existing as an independent community as an "association" was not strictly speaking an option according to the law, however, the legal literature acknowledged from the 1970s on that their legal status could be determined by the general laws of association and assembly.[21] Up until January 1952, the supervision of "sects" was handled by the Association Division of the Ministry of Home Affairs,[22] later, however, the Protestant Division of ÁEH handled the "sects." In 1960, ÁEH stated that they were "our ideological enemies," "they are more dangerous than the historical Churches, because they don't have a definitive dogma but instead talk about whatever they want to" (MNL OL XIX-A-21-d-0021-1, 2, 3/1960). In 1973 however, the president of ÁEH, Miklós Imre, remarking a "positive" result, said: "The communities existing in the Council of Free Churches have continuously developed and strengthened the assembly of the progressive clerical forces" (MNL OL XIX-A-21-c-6/17).

Religious communities that achieved state-approved church status during socialism

After Hungary joined the UN in 1955, a closer eye was kept on the regime and its actions especially regarding basic human rights, such as religious freedom. Because of this international pressure, some of the aforementioned banned churches or "sects" gained approved status during the socialist era due to these changed external political conditions.

In 1957, the Seventh Day Adventist Church achieved a legally acknowledged status, however, in the 1970s, those who protested against the loyal church leadership were excluded. This happened because acknowledgement of the Adventist church was important for UN membership after the revolution of 1956 (Köbel 2012). The case of the Nazarene Church in 1977 was even blunter, because the 8th Enactment of 1976 proclaimed the International Covenant on Civil and Political Rights,[23] it had to be demonstrated that religious freedom existed in Hungary (Köbel 2001b). A few years later in 1981, a group excluded from the Methodist Church, called the Hungarian Evangelical Fellowship (MET), was legally acknowledged after quite heavy international pressure involving the Archbishop of Canterbury who addressed the matter in the British parliament (Köbel 2001b). At this time, the Cold War was beginning to fade and as a result, at the end phase of the system, cases like these started to accelerate. In 1986 permission was given to the Hungarian Patroness (Patrona Hungariae) caritative female convent;[24] in 1988 legal acknowledgement of the Mormon Church followed as it brought numerous wealthy American investors (Köbel 2013); in 1988 legal acknowledgement of the Islamic Centre was granted mainly for economic reasons in relation to contacts with Saudi-Arabia (Köbel 2017a). All of these cases had ulterior – mostly economic and political – motives designed to prop up a rapidly failing system.

Semi-legal religious groups following the continuous change of church policy in the 1980s

The fourth category were religious groups that were semi-legal but were given more and more opportunities following the continuous change of church policy in the 1980s. The liberalization of the Association Act[25] provided aid for not yet acknowledged groups and granted a legal framework for diverse clerical activities of churches such as religious youth organizations (Köbel

2017b). Small co-operatives were also formed, for example, the Hare Krishnas, as a result of the liberalization of the economic laws (Köbel 2017b). In 1989 the functioning of Catholic orders was reinstated.[26] In the same, and also final year of the socialist system, several religious communities gained legal acknowledgement. In the last days of the ÁEH, for example, the Jehovah's Witnesses and the Faith Church were both recognized. After the ÁEH ceased to exist in June 30, 1989, the Ministry of Education took over and more and more communities gained legal status (Köbel 2013).

Conclusion – remission of pursuit in the 1980s

During the period of regime change, the pursuit of these groups progressively ceased. The name *clerical reaction* was changed to *clerical opposition* resulting in the disappearance of illegal religious activity. The activity of the political police and their methods changed during the end phases and they were no longer regarded as the absolute enemy. With the IV. Act of 1990 a new law for freedom of religious conscience was prepared and the pursuit of church groups was over (Köbel 2005, Köbel 2017c).

Ultimately, we can conclude that the clarification and transparency of the legal status of both acknowledged, not acknowledged and pursued churches (as categorized above) could have been resolved with a comprehensive law regarding religious affairs. However, the socialist regime was satisfied with its approach of "backstage legislation" and "flexible praxis" in making political decisions. There was a great difference between declaratory laws and "backstage legislation." The lower level, mostly inaccessible orders and instructions ("backstage legislation") visualized the hostile church policy of the party, which were carried out with the dictatorial tools of the ÁEH and the political police ("flexible praxis"). Legal guarantees were missing and unless the state had a political agenda tied to it, obtaining legal acknowledgement for a new denomination was impossible. The situation of pursued churches with a pending status was beginning to be resolved in the second part of the 1980s, as legal guarantees for civil rights were becoming more and more important. The unclear and chaotic way of obtaining legality as a denomination was slowly being exposed not only in legal literature, but also in the everyday press. The laws regarding the establishment of a church and their legal status were eventually settled after the regime change by the IV. Act of 1990 (Köbel 2005).

Notes

1 The I. Act of 1972 concerning the Constitution of the Hungarian People's Republic and the modification of the XX. Act of 1949 codified the state's ideological commitment which had virtually been in effect since: "3. § The Marxist-Leninist party of the working class is the leading force of society."

2 The XX. Act of 1949 concerning the Constitution of the Hungarian People's Republic originally contained: "54. § (1) The Hungarian People's Republic ensures

freedom of conscience and the free practice of religion for its citizens. (2) In order to ensure freedom of conscience the Hungarian People's Republic will separate state from church."

3 The Hungarian appellation for this office: Állami Egyházügyi Hivatal, short: ÁEH.

4 The law was promulgated on December 23, 1947 in the Országos Törvénytár [Law Report].

5 See XX. Act of 1848 regarding religion.

6 See XLII. Act of 1895 regarding the Israelite Religion.

7 According to the law, religious communities that wished to be legally acknowledged church had to meet two fundamental conditions. On one hand, they had to establish at least one congregation and the school education of children belonging to their denominations must be ensured. On the other hand, they had to present their bylaws for approval to the Minister of Religion and Public Education (after 1951 to the president of the ÁEH). These bylaws had to contain every aspect regarding the daily religious life especially the doctrine, the moral codes, the service itself and other religious ceremonies, as well as disciplinary rules regarding officials and other servants. In some instances, the approval could be denied. These instances were: (1) the ideology of the religious group that wished to be formed was against the state or nation; (2) the conditions regarding the congregation and public education were not met; (3) the doctrines, the service, other religious ceremonies or the planned organization went against existing laws and the common good, as well as having little to no difference to those of other, established churches; (4) the denomination of the church group that wished to be formed was of racial or national character or insulted other, established churches.

8 See the 77.092. VKM Act of 1905 regarding the acknowledgement of the Baptist Church. In *Rendeletek Tára* [Collection of Decrees of Hungary], November 2, 1905.

9 See the 120.000/1947. II. VKM Act regarding the legal acknowledgement of the Methodist Church. In *Magyar Közlöny* [Hungarian Official Gazette], 1947/55. November 9, 1947.

10 See the XVII. Act of 1916 regarding the Islam religion. See also Stipta 2017.

11 In 1948, the Hungarian government made an agreement with the Calvinist, Lutheran, Unitarian and Israelite churches which were published in the *Magyar Közlöny* (Number: 1948/227, 1948/271, 1948/276) during 1948. The agreement with the Catholic Church was made in 1950 and unlike the others – because of its unclear legal nature – was never published in the Magyar Közlöny only in *Szabad Nép* (August 30, 1950) and *Kis Újság* (September 1, 1950), both daily newspapers. The reason for the delay and the form of publication was, that according to Catholic canon law, the Hungarian bishopric was not entitled to conclude a high-level agreement with the state, which was solely the prerogative of the Apostolic See.

12 The categories presented in this study were not codified legal categories, but rather a personal categorization from a legal standpoint as a result of extensive research of various legal documents as well as party resolutions.

13 In Hungarian: Magyar Dolgozók Pártja (MDP).

14 See Anonymous, 1951, 163–71.

15 In Hungarian: Magyar Szocialista Munkáspárt (MSZMP), the successor to MDP from 1956.

16 The so-called "Priest Peace Movement" was established on August 1, 1950 with the support of the party. The keyword of the Peace Movement was "world peace".

The goal of the party, however, was to turn the lower clergy against the hierarchy and use the 'peace priests' as a form of propaganda. See Köbel 2005, 119–20.

17 34th Legislative Decree of 1950; See also Geréb (1968).

18 The 363.500. Act of 1939 by the Hungarian Royal Minister of Internal Affairs regarding the cessation of sects threatening homeland security.

19 See also Government Regulation nr. 6270/1946. ME. regarding the repeal of the official instructions about the dissolution of select religious denominations and financial matters of said action. See Köbel (2005, 24).

20 See also: ÁBTL 3.1.9. V–139674/1-2, penal file of Hubicsák Zoltán; ÁBTL 3.1.9. 146708/1-2, penal file of Konrád János and associates; ÁBTL 3.1.9. V–149948/1-4, penal file of Konrád János and associates.

21 See the documentary material of the ÁEH MNL OL-XIX-21-b-420. box., document nr. ad 45.045/1984. The legal expertise states the following:

> It has to be established right now, that if an organisation continues to operate following refusal of their acknowledgement, then we cannot act against it based on the sanctions of a non-existent religious law. If, however we regard them as associations – and I believe it to be the only option – we can, according to the association law, act not only against the leadership of the organization, but also its members. I must point out however, that this is a rather far-fetched interpretation of the law, but I do not see any alternatives. Regrettably, there was no example of this during the bourgeois era, or if it did occur, it was dealt with by force. That is not on the table, however, if there are no denominations, then there are only associations.
>
> Cited by Köbel (2001b)

22 See container MNL OL-XIX-A-21-c/6/3-142. ÁEH memo, July 7, 1955 "Szabadegyházak Szövetsége, Szekták helyzete" [The position of Sects and the Council of Free Churches]. The document is worthy of quoting:

> Our job with the sects was on one hand to talk with their leaders about supporting the tasks of the state and to make them report on their activities and their results, on the other hand, we sent the more cardinal doctrines to the county secretary in order to aid the political actions against them. Besides the police, other state institutions didn't really bother with the actions of sects. If the actions of a preacher were markedly harmful, they were simply sent to internment. The introduction of certificates, which came with regular check-ups from the police turned out to be quite the tool in the inspection of sect activities. The only downside was, that this supervision was limited to those who had a certificate. Those without a certificate could operate uninterruptedly, direct action could only be taken if someone reported them and could prove criminal offence against the state. Thus, in a lot of cases, cooperative sect preacher found themselves in a disadvantageous position. The actions of wild sects, despite their number being irrelevant, remained unreconnoitered and we can do next to nothing. This question still causes problems to this day in our work.

23 International Covenant on Civil and Political Rights adopted and opened for signature, ratification and accession by General Assembly resolution 2200A (XXI) of 16 December 1966 entry into force 23 March 1976, in accordance with Article 49.

24 See ÁEH resolution Nr. 1/1986. (XII. 3.) regarding the legal operation of the "Magyarok Nagyasszonya Társaság" [Society of Patrona Hungariae].

25 See II. Act of 1989 regarding the right of association.

26 See the 17th Legislative Decree of 1989.

Archival sources

BMKI – Belügyminisztérium Közigazgatási Államtitkári Hivatal Irattári Osztály [Archive Department of the Administrative Office of Ministry of Interior's State Secretary]

ÁBTL – Állambiztonsági Szolgálatok Történeti Levéltára [Historical Archives of the Hungarian State Security]

MNL OL – Magyar Nemzeti Levéltár Országos Levéltára [National Archives of Hungary]

References

Anonymous. 1951. *The Important Resolutions of the Central Leadership, Political Committee and Organizing Committee of the Hungarian Labourer's Party* [*A Magyar Dolgozók Pártja Központi Vezetőségének, Politikai Bizottságának és Szervező Bizottságának fontosabb határozatai*]. Budapest: Szikra Kiadó.

Geréb, Sándor. 1968. *The Observation of the Operative Inspection of Illegal Convents [Az illegális szerzetesrendek operatív ellenőrzésének tapasztalatai]*. Budapest: BM Tanulmányi és Kiképzési Csoportfőnökség.

Gergely, Attila. 1980. *State Security Dictionary* [*Állambiztonsági Értelmező Kéziszótár]*. Budapest: BM Könyvkiadó.

Heinz, Daniel, Zoltán Rajki, and Ervin Simon (eds.). 2013. *Free Churches, Religious Minorities and Dictatorships in Europe during the 20th Century* [*Szabadegyházak, vallási kisebbségek és a diktatúrák Európában a 20. században*]. Budapest and Friedensau: Gondolat Kiadó – Historisches Archiv der Siebenten-Tags-Adventisten in Europa – Kisegyház-kutató Egyesület.

Holló, Péter. ed. 2012. Background: State Security Documents from the Hungarian History of the Seventh Day Adventist Church [Háttér: Állambiztonsági dokumentumok a H. N. Adventista Egyház magyarországi történetéből]. Budapest: Spalding Alapítvány.

Köbel, Szilvia. 2000. "The Operation of the State Office of Church Affairs in the 50s 1951–1959" ["Az Állami Egyházügyi Hivatal működése az 50-es években. 1951–1959"]. *Magyar Közigazgatás* 50 (8): 504–12.

Köbel, Szilvia. 2001a. "The Operation of the State Office of Church Affairs from its Re-Organization to its Cessation 1959–1989" ["Az Állami Egyházügyi Hivatal működése az újjászervezéstől a megszűnésig. 1959–1989"]. *Magyar Közigazgatás* 51 (10): 608–18.

Köbel, Szilvia. 2001b. "The Legal Acknowledgement of Denominations during the Kádár-Period" ["Vallásfelekezetek törvényes elismerése a Kádár-korszakban"]. *Jogtudományi Közlöny* 56 (6): 287–97.

Köbel, Szilvia. 2002a. "Active Atheist Propaganda: Political Police and Church Policy" ["Aktív ateista propaganda: Politikai rendőrség és egyházpolitika"]. *Beszélő* 7 (9–10): 66–74.

Köbel, Szilvia. 2002b. "Three Glasses of Mass Wine: Conversation between Ex-Secretary of Church Affairs István Horváth and Szilvia Köbel" ["Három pohár misebor: Horváth István volt egyházügyi titkárral Köbel Szilvia beszélget"]. Beszélő 7 (9–10): 75–8.

Köbel, Szilvia. 2005. "Divide and Rule!" The Political, Legal and Administrative Relationship of the State and the Churches in Hungary, 1945–1989 ["Oszd meg és uralkodj!" Az állam és az egyházak politikai, jogi és igazgatási kapcsolatai Magyarországon, 1945–1989]. Budapest: Rejtjel Kiadó.

Köbel, Szilvia. 2012. "The Relationship of the Hungarian Seventh Day Adventist Church and the State Security" ["A Magyarországi H.N. Adventista Egyház és az állambiztonság kapcsolata"]. In: *Background: State Security Documents from the Hungarian History of the Seventh Day Adventist Church* [*Háttér: Állambiztonsági dokumentumok a H. N. Adventista Egyház magyarországi történetéből*], edited by Péter Holló. Budapest: Spalding Alapítvány, 31–56.

Köbel, Szilvia. 2013. "Legal Recognition of Churches and Religious Denominations in Hungary after 1945" ["Egyházak, vallásfelekezetek törvényes elismerése 1945 után Magyarországon"]. In: Free Churches, Religious Minorities and Dictatorships in Europe in the 20th Century [Szabadegyházak, vallási kisebbségek és a diktatúrák Európában a 20. században], edited by Daniel Heinz, Zoltán Rajki and Ervin Simon. Budapest and Friedensau: Gondolat Kiadó – Historisches Archiv der Siebenten-Tags-Adventisten in Europa – Kisegyház-kutató Egyesület, 136–82.

Köbel, Szilvia. 2017a. "Islam and the State Party – In Light of State Security Documents" ["Az iszlám és a pártállam – állambiztonsági iratok tükrében"]. In: The Hungarian Islamic law is 100 years od [100 éves a magyar iszlámtörvény], edited by Szilvia Köbel, and Zoltán Tóth. J., 100. Budapest: Károli Gáspár Református Egyetem, Állam- és Jogtudományi Kar.

Köbel, Szilvia. 2017b. "'Establishing a Rule of Law is a Process': 1989 – The Changing of the Political System in Hungary, Focusing on Freedom of Expression and the Activities of the Political Police." In: 1989. Year of Change: Anthology of the International Scientific Conference, Bratislava 4–5 November 2014 [1989. Rok zmeny: zborník z medzinárodnej vedeckej konferencie, Bratislava 4.-5. novembra 2014], edited by Peter Jašek, 98–152. Bratislava: Ústav Pamäti Národa.

Köbel, Szilvia. 2017c. "Prosperity Instead of Backlash? Additions to the Cessation of Office of Church Affairs Based on the Reports about the Meetings of Commanding Officers of State Security" ["Visszaszorítás helyett felvirágoztatás? Adalékok az Állami Egyházügyi Hivatal megszüntetéséhez az állambiztonsági parancsnoki értekezletek jegyzőkönyvei alapján"]. *Magyar Jog* 64 (9): 560–6.

Lakatos, Judit. 2011. The Policy of the Communist States Towards the Free Churches after 1945 in Hungary with Special Regards to the Metodist Church Occasional Papers on Religion in Eastern Europe. *Occasional Papers on Religion in Eastern Europe* 31(2): 30–41. http://digitalcommons.georgefox.edu/cgi/viewcontent.cgi?article=1145&context=ree (downloaded February 2, 2018)

Petrás, Éva. 2017. "The Story of Jehovah's Witnesses between 1945 and 1989" ["Jehova Tanúi története 1945 és 1989 között"]. In: *The History of the Hungarian Jehovah's Witnesses' Church from the Beginning to the Present Day* [*A Magyarországi Jehova Tanúi Egyház története a kezdetektől napjainkig*], edited by Csaba Fazekas, Attila Jakab, Éva Petrás, and Szabolcs Szita, 203–69. Budapest: Gondolat Kiadó.

Soós, Viktor Attila. 2014. *The Archontology of the State Office of Church Affairs. The Structure, International Connections and Career Path of Employees in the ÁEH* [*Az Állami Egyházügyi Hivatal archontológiája. Az ÁEH szervezeti felépítése, nemzetközi kapcsolatai és dolgozóinak hivatali pályaképe*]. (PhD dissertation). Budapest: ELTE BTK. http://doktori.btk.elte.hu/hist/soosviktorattila/diss.pdf (downloaded February 1, 2018)

Stipta, István. 2017. *"The Creation and Legal Dogmatic of the XVII. Act of 1916 Regarding the Recognition of the Islamic Religion in Hungary"* ["Az iszlám vallás hazai elismeréséről szóló 1916. évi XVII. tc. létrejötte és jogdogmatikai elemzése"]. In: *The Hungarian Islamic Law is 100 Years Old* [*100 éves a magyar iszlámtörvény*], edited by Szilvia Köbel, and Zoltán J. Tóth, 23–37. Budapest: Károli Gáspár Református Egyetem, Állam- és Jogtudományi Kar.

4 Turning religious practices into political guilt

Jehovah's Witnesses in the narratives of the Securitate files

Corneliu Pintilescu

Introduction

This study analyzes the narratives of the Securitate files on Jehovah's Witnesses by focusing on how this religious minority was perceived by the Securitate and how the institutions legitimized the repressive measures taken against it. The first part of this chapter will deal with perception of the Jehovah's Witnesses within the bureaucratic discourse of the Securitate based on the study of several files archived by the Securitate in the so-called Bucharest Documentary Fonds (*Fond Documentar București* in Romanian) concerning the issue entitled "Sects" (*secte* in Romanian). These fonds reflect how the headquarters of the Securitate conceived, planned and implemented policies at a national level dealing with various areas of activity such as: collectivization of the agriculture, annihilating the political opposition, combating sabotage in industry or, as in this case, containing the religious groups labelled as "sects." The second part of the article will deal with a specific aspect of the narratives of the Securitate files: the discourse aimed at legitimizing the legal repressive measures taken against those Jehovah's Witnesses sent to military courts to be convicted according to the criminal laws of that period.

At a general level (and perfectly illustrated by the files of the Bucharest Documentary Fonds of the Securitate), the narratives of the documents reflect the practices of this institution which combined collecting and analysing information about a category of people with implementing policies on them. For example, the policies of the repressive institution concerning a so-called "issue" (*problemă* in Romanian, which was, in fact, a field of activity) combined the activity of gathering information about a social group with actions that aimed at influencing it by using both coercive and non-coercive tools. In this respect, Florin Poenaru rightly points out that the Securitate practices of "producing knowledge" about social groups were intertwined with practices aimed at transforming society (Poenaru 2013, 113).

From a conceptual point of view, my research draws also on the distinctions Sabrina Ramet (1991) makes between different modes of state-church relations, which provide adequate conceptual tools for understanding the perspective of both state institutions and churches. According to Ramet, "when social institutions subscribing to divergent programmatic theories (or theologies) come into contact, the result is apt to be some mixture of conflict and accommodation" (Ramet 1991, 80–3). Ramet proposes two modes of state-church relations: the "confrontational mode" and the "accommodative mode." The "confrontational mode" is defined by disagreement between church and state regarding "the premis for their mutual relations" which causes a lack of a "*modus vivendi*" (Ramet 1991, 80). In this situation, "neither side makes serious compromises," and the "hostility" of state institutions "towards religion is overt" (Ramet 1991, 83). On the contrary, "the accommodative mode [...] involves compromise on both sides – sometimes mostly on the Church's side," and at other times "on the part of both Church and state" (Ramet 1991, 83).

In the case of Jehovah's Witnesses, there is a clear lack of *modus vivendi*, reflected in the endeavours of the Securitate to repress the religious group and contain its expansion. This tense relationship was caused by several issues over which the Jehovah's Witnesses and the communist regime entered into conflict: 1. the subordination of the Jehovah's Witnesses to an external religious centre from a Western country; 2. the active presence in the public space of Jehovah's Witnesses, especially through proselytism conducted by members of the religious community; 3. the rejection of any state interference into its internal affairs; 4. the Jehovah's Witnesses's attitude towards political co-optation and performing citizen's duties in a communist state, especially the obligation of military service.

Historical context

The history of Jehovah's Witnesses in Romania is characterized by a troubled relationship with the various political regimes that succeeded one another during twentieth century. Due to the negative perception, in part, caused by their attitudes towards state institutions, Jehovah's Witnesses were kept under close surveillance and became the target of intense repressive measures during the dictatorships of King Carol II (February 1938 to September 1940), National Legionary State (September 1940 to January 1941) and Antonescu (January 1941 to August 1944). These regimes carried out policies of ethnic and cultural homogenization that intensified the hostility of state institutions towards Jehovah's Witnesses that already had manifested before 1938 (see, Solonari 2010, i–xv). After the Second Word War, the Romanian state legalized some religious groups as "associations," including the Jehovah's Witnesses (Tismăneanu, Dobrincu and Vasile 2007, 282). Thus, from July 1945 to August 1949, Jehovah's Witnesses enjoyed a period of relative toleration from the state institutions. As a result of the Jehovah's Witnesses refusal to accept the communist regime's policies towards religion, which required all official denominations to accept state interference in church internal issues the hostility of the state institutions was again aroused. Besides, their external subordination to a religious centre in the United States and their active proselytism antagonized even more the communist authorities.

Consequently, the communist regime dissolved and confiscated the patrimony of "the religious association Jehovah's Witnesses" by issuing the order no. 86,310 of the Ministry of Justice from August 8, 1949 (Ioniţă 2008, 216). Jehovah's Witnesses became one of the religious denominations placed under close surveillance and subjected to violent treatment in communist Romania. They were a target of the repressive policies of the communist regime not only during the period 1948–64, as were many other religious groups, but also after 1968, when the predominance of repressive methods was replaced with more complex and diffuse surveillance practices by the state institutions. As a result, the Securitate, produced an impressive quantity of files on Jehovah's Witnesses, in relation to their percentage of the total population, taking into account that the number of Jehovah's Witnesses was estimated at only around 15,000 in 1949 from a total population of approx. 16 million (*Jehovah's Witnesses Yearbook* 2006, 90; Ioniţă 2008, 215–16). The attention paid to Jehovah's Witnesses by repressive institutions has attracted the interest of several historians who have tackled the issue of state policies towards Jehovah's Witnesses in Romania (Neagoe-Pleşa and Pleşa 2005; Spânu 2005; Petcu 2005; Ioniţă 2008; Jánosi 2015; Pintilescu and Fătu-Tutoveanu 2011; Pintilescu 2015).

Perceptions and policies of the Securitate towards Jehovah's Witnesses during 1950s

The discourse of the state institutions in communist Romania divided religious groups into three main categories: "official denominations," "sects" and "anarchist groups." Aside from the so-called "historical churches"[1] (Muntean 2005, 92), that had already been recognized as official denominations, in 1948 the communist regime granted the status of official or legal denomination to four religious denominations that previously had been considered "sects": the Baptist Christian Church, the 7th Day Adventist Church, the Christian Evangelical Church of Romania (*Cultul Creştin după Evanghelie din România*), and the Pentecostal Church. Other religious groups that were officially not recognized continued to be labelled as "sects" or "anarchist groups" (Tismăneanu, Dobrincu, and Vasile 2007, 282). The latter category included factions or radical movements that emerged from within some of the official denominations such as the "The Lord's Army" (*Oastea Domnului*) within the Romanian Orthodox Church, or the "Bethanists" (*Betaniştii*) within the Reformed Church. Those considered to be "sects" or "anarchist groups" were outlawed (Tismăneanu, Dobrincu, and Vasile 2007, 282). Although the outlawed religious groups suffered heavily from the repressive measures of the communist authorities, the official denominations were also not exempted from this broader repressive policy that aimed at containing religion in society and intimidating those groups considered hostile by the communist regime. Taking into account the tense relationship with the communist authorities on the aforementioned issues, Jehovah's Witnesses were included by the state institutions within the category labelled as "sects." Although used in the narratives of communist state institutions in a different ideological context, this concept was borrowed from the official discourse in interwar Romania, when the term was used by both state authorities and the Romanian Orthodox Church.

The narratives of the Securitate files assert that Jehovah's Witnesses regularly transmitted to their "Brooklyn headquarters," as the institution labelled the religious centre in the United States, reports that contained information with "an espionage character and slanderous data meant to compromise our regime" (Petcu 2005, 149). Due to this supposed subordination to a Western entity, Jehovah's Witnesses were very often labelled in the Securitate files as an "imperialist spy organization." The communist authorities were worried that Jehovah's Witnesses were able collect information from their communities from inside the country, send them to West, and even transfer published materials across the Iron Curtain. Jehovah's Witnesses were not a singular case in this respect. All denominations that were subordinated to a religious centre in a Western country were perceived similarly, including Roman Catholics and the Greek Catholics. In the case of the latter, the harsh repression that targeted them after 1948 was partially legitimized by the fact that their priests carried out espionage activities because they gathered and sent information to the Vatican (Vasile 2003).

All denominations that carried out intense proselytism were perceived as dangerous by the communist authorities because they represented a competitor in the public space in shaping social values and mobilizing people. As Cristian Vasile rightly pointed, the communist regime in Romania tried to move religion "out of the public space" and reduce its social visibility as much as possible (Vasile 2003, 187). Thus, the proselytism carried out by Jehovah's Witnesses intensified the hostility of the repressive institutions that were alarmed by their increase in number. Taking into account the strict subordination to the centre in the United States and their negative view on state institutions based on their specific interpretations of passages from the Bible (such as Romans 13:1–2), Jehovah's Witnesses not only rejected all possible state interference in their activity, but also displayed a defiant anti-state discourse. According to the translation provided by "New International Version" of the Bible in Romans 13:1–2, Paul the Apostle states:

> Let everyone be subject to the governing authorities, for there is no authority except that which God has established. The authorities that exist have been established by God. Consequently, whoever rebels against the authority is rebelling against what God has instituted, and those who do so will bring judgment on themselves.

During the leadership of Charles Taze Russell (1874–1916), the founder of the denomination, the higher authorities mentioned in Romans 13 were considered to be the state authorities and Russell "taught that one should obey the law of the land, except where it conflicts with God's law" (Chryssides 2009, 72). The presidency of Joseph Franklin Rutherford (1917–42) represented a "radical break" concerning many theological and organizational aspects of the Watch Tower Bible and Tract Society (Knox 2018, 37), including the attitude towards state institutions. While initially C.T. Russell "advised Bible Students to avoid involvement in political affairs whenever possible but to ultimately obey superior authorities" (Knox 2018, 64), Rutherford turned the doctrine of Jehovah's Witnesses towards a more radical anti-state attitude. After 1929, the higher powers "were no longer to be understood as secular rulers, but rather as Jehovah God and Christ Jesus" (Penton 2015, 210). This new interpretation led Jehovah's Witnesses into an open conflict not only with various dictatorial regimes, but also with liberal democracies (Knox 2018; Besier, Stokłosa 2016; Penton 2004). This last interpretation of Romans 13:1–2 was in force until 1962, when the leadership of the Watch Tower Bible and Tract Society returned to a "doctrinal stance on the matter very similar to that expounded by C.T. Russell" (Penton 2015, 211), which significantly improved their relations with government authorities from various parts of the word.

Thus, in the Soviet Bloc, including Romania, Jehovah's Witnesses were discouraged by their leadership from performing citizen's duties, such as participation to political life. This anti-state attitude was very intense especially before 1962, and more moderate after this date. Beside this aspect, the Jehovah's Witnesses were conscientious objectors to military service, which had also been the main cause of the repressive measures by the far right dictatorships in Romania from 1938 to 1944.

Because the "historical churches" had well-defined hierarchies and distinctions between the priesthood and the flock, state institutions in communist Romania were able to develop effective strategies for infiltrating and putting their leadership under close surveillance. The more diffuse character of Jehovah's Witnesses' inner structure, however, caused difficulties for the state institutions in adjusting their policies to their distinct characteristics.

The discourse of the communist authorities that presented Jehovah's Witnesses as a state enemy was initially framed by the plenary meeting of the Central Committee of the Romanian Workers' Party from June 1948. In order to legitimate the future repressive actions against the Jehovah's Witnesses, the religious group was accused of "having served as an instrument of the Fascist, Iron Guard elements" (Petcu 2005, 149). Their assimilation with fascism was a discursive strategy of the communist regime of labelling all its enemies as fascists or their collaborators. Thus, the communist regime legitimated the repressive actions against those considered to be its enemies by including them in the measures taken in post-war Europe against the perpetrators and collaborators of far-right dictatorships. This assertion was in contradiction to the attitudes of the Iron Guard towards Jehovah's Witnesses. From September

1940 to January 1941, the period when the Romanian fascist movement ruled the country alongside Antonescu, the Iron Guard took part in the repression of the Jehovah's Witnesses.

The discourse of the political leadership from the late 1940s was transferred into the narratives of the repressive institutions. For example, an internal memo of the Securitate issued on September 30, 1949 labelled the Jehovah's Witnesses as "the most hostile and harmful" for the communist regime amongst other religious groups included in the category of "sects" (Petcu 2005, 147). Consequently, Jehovah's Witnesses were to receive "special attention" because, as the aforementioned memo stated, their activity was "imbued with hatred towards our popular democratic regime" and their leaders "consciously took part in a spy network" (Petcu 2005, 182).

Although, Jehovah's Witnesses received special attention in the period from 1949 to 1958, several internal reports and plans of the General Directorate of the Securitate (its headquarters) from 1958 show that their policies of placing the religious group under strict surveillance and pursuing harsh repressive measures did not limit their expansion in number. In July 1958, a document issued by the Securitate's headquarters contained some instructions to the regional directorates of the Securitate to categorize all Jehovah's Witnesses and issue either surveillance files or personal sheets according to their level of dangerousness for the communist regime's security (ACNSAS, FDB, File no. 009486, vol. 3, 133–4). The Securitate recognized in this document the ineffectiveness of the Securitate's activity by emphasizing the fact that despite the repressive measures taken against them, Jehovah's Witnesses "are currently reorganizing and expanding numerically." The document also highlighted the danger of Jehovah's Witness activity for the regime's security because "they proved conscious instruments of foreign imperialists and to be domestic class enemies in the course of their activity" (ACNSAS, FDB, File no. 009486, vol. 3, 133–4).

This document illustrates in a suggestive manner the practices of gathering information about persons and their networks, and conducting policies that aimed at transforming these networks. It stated that "in order to put an end" to their activity against the security of the state and to "facilitate the compilation of strong evidence against the Jehovah's Witnesses," the regional directorates of the Securitate were asked to identify all Jehovah's Witnesses and classify them by using three categories: 1. "those with intense activity, those who continued their activity despite suffering imprisonment"; 2. "those with lower activity, poor members, those who renounced their activity after suffering imprisonment"; 3. "those with low activity, individuals who fall under the influence of Jehovah's Witnesses" (ACNSAS, FDB, File no. 009486, vol. 3, 133–4). These categories functioned as instruments of organizing the field of work. The key criterion was evaluating the danger they posed for the regime's security by invoking various degrees. Through this document, the headquarters asked the regional directorates of the Securitate to pay special attention to the networks developed by Jehovah's Witnesses within the communities. The agents of the local directorates of the Securitate had to “focus on spotting messengers, couriers and liaisons to the higher echelons” and to “know the location of Jehovah’s Witnesses at any moment” (ACNSAS, FDB, File no. 009486, vol. 3, 133–4). These practices illustrate how the Securitate combined surveillance activity, that of penetrating the community with informers, with influencing its members or groups. As Katherine Verdery rightly observed while studying her own Securitate file, the institution perceived individuals within their social network (Verdery 2014, 187). Their dangerousness or usefulness according to the Securitate was evaluated by the analysis of their social milieu. The information was gathered and organized according to the danger that the persons represented for the state security. In this respect, the activity of gathering information was shaped from the very beginning in order to produce evidence in order to legitimate future repressive measures. Information was gathered with the definition of the offences regarding state security from the Criminal Code in mind. Here, as Poenaru noticed, there was an inner contradiction in the Securitate practices between the activity of producing knowledge about persons and groups for the Party leadership and producing evidence for legitimizing repressive acts (Poenaru 2013, 117). These inner contradictions also produced contradictory statements within the narrative of the Securitate files. For example, the Securitate emphasized within its discourse that the Jehovah’s Witnesses carried out subversive activities against the regime “under the guise of religion” (ACNSAS, FP, P 1000, vol. 2, 29). On the one hand, by the frequent use of the expression “under the guise of religion,” the Securitate asserted implicitly that Jehovah’s Witnesses were not, in fact, a religious denomination, but a “subversive organization” that aimed at undermining the “state security.” On the other hand, the Securitate’s files frequently mention the fanatical character of their religious beliefs, which contradicted the argument that the religious activities were only a veil.

Turning religious practices into political guilt

In order to justify their repressive actions according to the prevailing legal framework, the institutions involved in the implementation of the Romanian communist regime’s repressive policies, namely the Securitate, the Prosecutor’s Office and military courts, issued documents that interpreted the targeted religious practices as political activities against the regime. Thus, in the case of Jehovah’s Witnesses, the three aforementioned institutions gave political meanings to their religious practices, such as meetings organized in the homes of certain members, fundraising, printing and distribution of publications, and proselytism. By promoting a narrative that combined the regime’s anti-religious rhetoric (which became aggressive in the case of certain denominations that were not officially recognized but successful in recruiting new followers) with the legal discourse, these institutions legitimized the regime’s repressive actions. In 1950s Romania, these actions meant that a person could be sent to prison following a court sentence or to a labour camp following an administrative decision by the Ministry of Internal Affairs. Giving political meanings to everyday acts was not only used in the case of legitimizing the repression against various forms of religious practices. Constructing political guilt by giving political meanings to everyday acts was, in fact, the main discursive strategy of these institutions to legitimize repressive acts against those whom the communist regime perceived as hindering progress towards socialism.

The discourse that legitimized the sentences passed by military courts was elaborated in three stages that reflect the involvement of each key-institution in the process: the Securitate, the Prosecutor's Office and military courts. In the first stage, the Securitate collected information on Jehovah's Witnesses and assessed their danger for the regime's security according to the intensity of their activity. The conclusions of the inquiry were based on the minutes taken during the interrogation of suspects and witnesses. Subsequently, the Military Prosecutor's Office determined under which Section(s) and Article(s) in the Criminal Code the offences mentioned in the inquiry's conclusions were indictable, and then legally argued for the indictment. Finally, the most important piece of this legal puzzle was the sentence which legitimized the repressive actions of the regime.

Beginning in 2005, files pertaining to cases in which the Securitate carried out the investigation were released to the National Council for the Study of the Securitate Archives (*Consiliului Național pentru Studierea Arhivelor Securității*), and currently make up the so-called Criminal Fonds (*Fondul Penal*). The files of the Criminal Fonds contain documents issued by the Securitate, the Prosecutor's Office and the military courts, declarations of those under criminal investigation and witnesses, legal evidence, documents from the period of the execution of the sentence etc. The "criminal files" (*dosare penale*) or "investigation files" (*dosare de anchetă*), alongside the "surveillance files" (*dosare de urmărire informativă*) (focused on those under surveillance) and network files (*dosare de rețea*) (that were focused on the Securitate informers activity), represent the main categories of file produced by the Securitate (Vățulescu 2010, 36).

The Criminal Files (and sometimes the Documentary Files) include in their final section various materials confiscated by the Securitate from those under criminal investigation such as: printed documents, correspondence, photos reflecting religious practices. Taking into account that under communism many Jehovah's Witnesses destroyed such kind of documents either to avoid repressive acts of the state institutions or due to modifications of theological dogma they contained, the Securitate archives have become ironically a repository of cultural and religious heritage. For example, the criminal file of R.H.,[2] who was sentenced in 1955 by the Oradea Military Court, included several issues of the *Watchtower* magazine from the 1940s, the main periodical of the Jehovah's Witnesses (ACNSAS, FP, P 1000, vol. 2–3). In other cases, the files included not only publications, but also photos taken during the search of the domicile or the so-called "re-enactment," a police method of documenting how a crime took place (ACNSAS, FDB, File no. 9486, vol. 3; ACNSAS, FDB, File no. 11245, ff. 71–5). During the "re-enactment," those under investigation were asked to play their roles in the narrative of the Securitate at the place where the "crime" and the Securitate officers took pictures with them in order to illustrate how the events took place. In these cases, the Securitate photographed the books and periodicals in those places where the Jehovah Witnesses under investigation had hidden them.

When dealing with these materials, one should keep in mind the main reason why these documents were archived in these files: in order to support the accusations. Thus, from a broad variety of materials that were usually found and confiscated by the Securitate during the home searches, only those supporting the accusations have been selected to be archived in these files.

The central theme of the discourse of the repressive institutions regarding the convicted Jehovah's Witnesses was that they were not members of a religious group but rather of a conspiratorial group intent on subverting the regime that was controlled directly from the United States, the centre of the capitalist world. The evidence presented in this respect was not hard to find given that, after the denomination had been banned, its members met, organized fundraising events, and distributed printed materials secretly. Some of the terms that the Securitate employed to describe the organization and the activity of Jehovah's Witnesses were taken from the Securitate's internal terminology in order to suggest that they were gathering intelligence for capitalist countries. Thus, the new members were "recruited" similar to Securitate informers, they had "code names" in the same way as Securitate informers, used "passwords," received "tasks to recruit new members," organized "conspiratorial meetings," used "safe houses," and issued "activity reports" (ACNSAS, FP, Cluj SRI 200, vol. 1, 27; FP, P 1000, vol. 2, 138; Jánosi 2015).

For example, an investigation report drafted by the Military Prosecutor's Office in Târgu-Mureş on the suspect G.L. on August 27, 1959 includes the following interpretation of his activity based on the description provided by the Securitate in the investigation file:

> In order to make the hostile activity and clandestine connections of ministerial servants more conspiratorial, he recruited P.A. from the township of Culpiu in the organisation, then appointed him a safe house host and courier, and then organised clandestine meetings with ministerial servants.
>
> (ANR, MCB, FPMT, 1954–1965, Indictment regarding file 123/1959 of 27 August 1959, 127–8).[3]

The indictment brought by the Military Prosecutor's Office in Târgu-Mureş against A.S. On July 12, 1961 highlight his activity from 1959–61:

> he turned A.S.'s home, situated in the township of Praid, in the Mureş-Autonomous Hungarian Region, into a safe house for the purpose of printing propaganda materials that smeared the democratic people's

> regime in the R.P.R. [...] he organised a secret meeting in the town of Câmpia Turzii, at which non-arrested leading elements participated and decided to continue and further intensify their hostile endeavours, and took steps to increase the conspiratorial character of clandestine activities.
>
> (ANR, MCB, FPMT, 1954–1965, 803/1960, 219)

The same intention to emphasize the conspiratorial character of the activities of Jehovah's Witnesses is also revealed by the frequently mentioned assertion that they carried them out "under the guise of religion" (ACNSAS, FP, P 1000, vol. 2, 29).

The conspiratorial character of their activities also implied that their goals were subversive. By pointing out what repressive institutions considered to be anti-regime actions, the activity of Jehovah's Witnesses acquired political meanings. For example, the introduction of the indictment of August 27, 1959 against G.L. underlined that:

> for a long time, hostile elements from among the sects have been carrying out, under the hypocritical guise of the bible, clandestine activities against our people's democratic state. By combining anti-popular activity with activity under the guise of the bible, they exploit the religious feelings, gullibility and credulity of backward elements and seek to instigate hostile activities against the people's democratic regime. [...] Such a group is the clandestine organisation the Jehovah's Witnesses that carries out an intense hostile activity against the people's democratic state across the entire country.
>
> (ANR, MCB, FPMT, 1954–1965, 617/1959, 125–6)

The discourse of the repressive institutions pointed to the subversive character of Jehovah's Witnesses by emphasizing that they refused to perform military service, thus weakening the country's defence capabilities, and that they refused to participate in the country's political life. The threat that this denomination posed to the security of the state was the main argument brought by the prosecution during the sentencing phase of a trial. For example, in sentence no. 44/1955, the Military Court in Oradea imposed the maximum penalty (between 5 and 8 years in a correctional facility) for "public incitement" (Codul Penal 1959, art. 327, *§* 3) on members of a group of Jehovah's Witnesses. The Court argued that, in view of their activities, they "posed a threat to national security" and "[did] not regret their deeds," hence it found no mitigating circumstances (ACNSAS, FP, P 1000, vol. 2, 138, 140–1).

Their conscientious objection to military service was a reason why many Jehovah's Witnesses were persecuted during the far right dictatorships that succeeded each other in Romania from 1938 to 1944. From this perspective, the discourse promoted by courts in the communist era was not much different from that promoted before 1944. In addition, during the 1970s and 80s, when overall repression was much less intense in comparison with the period 1949–62, courts continued to convict Jehovah's Witnesses in great numbers due to their refusal to perform military service. In the 1950s, this refusal was highly politicized and presented as part of their anti-regime propaganda. For example, the indictment against the aforementioned R.H. criticized him that "under the guise of religion, he knowingly instigated and carried out agitation among the citizens in order to turn them away from the special political life of the state, [...] agitation that can pose a threat to national security" (ACNSAS, FP, P 1000, vol. 2, 29). The refusal to perform military service antagonized a political regime that was in an almost permanent state of mobilization in the context of the Cold War.

The Securitate interpreted their proselytism and involvement in the denomination's organizational structures as the expansion and reactivation of an espionage network. Thus, the indictment brought by the Military Prosecutor's Office against A.S. on July 12, 1961 mentions that he managed to "reactivate the groups and clandestine circuits in the Mureș-Autonomous Hungarian Region and in the Banat" (ANR, MCB, FPMT, 1954–1965, 803/1960, 217–18). In addition, the indictment brought by the same institution against M.K. on October 12, 1960 emphasizes in a language specific to espionage activities that: "he carried out intense religious propaganda with a view to recruiting new members, established contacts with the leadership in order to receive instructions with a view to intensifying his activity and sending coded reports" (ANR, MCB, FPMT, 1954–1965, 802/1959, 83). In their discourse, repressive institutions also perceived proselytism as "counter-revolutionary propaganda." The regime was prepared to tolerate the activity of denominations in the public space so long as they observed the limits imposed by it. Any attempt to go beyond these limits automatically triggered reprisals. The regime perceived the discourse of Churches as a rival discourse meant to undermine the values that it wanted to instil in members of society.

In order for a denomination to be active in the public sphere, it had to make a compromise with the regime, or else it could not be recognized officially. Given that the Jehovah's Witnesses were not officially recognized as a denomination and were unwilling to reach a compromise with the authorities, the latter's discourse regarding their proselytism and the measures taken against them were violent. Therefore, the documents issued by the Securitate, the Prosecutor's Offices and military courts described their endeavours to recruit new members as "hostile and bellicose propaganda against the regime" (ACNSAS, FP, P 1000, vol. 1, 223–5). The investigation report of the Military Prosecutor's Office in Cluj, which justified the indictment of B.S., a peasant from the region and one of the Witnesses sentenced by the Military Court in Cluj on December 18, 1951, emphasized that "he carried out activities hostile to our regime by means of inflammatory religious propaganda [...]" and "disseminated various brochures with an inflammatory content among citizens with the obvious aim of undermining the people's democratic regime" (ACNSAS, FP, Cluj SRI 200, vol. 1, 27, 34). The discourse of repressive institutions argued that, in fact, this subversive "propaganda" was directed against "performing military service," "the socialist transformation of agriculture," and participation in "elections" or other "social-political activities" (ANR, MCB, FPMT, 1954–1965, 802/1959, 126).

The most invoked articles of the Criminal Code were Art. 209 referring to the offence of "plotting against the social order," Art. 325 referring to the "dissemination of banned publications," and Art. 327 referring to "public incitement." The repressive institutions used Article 209 most often because it covered a wide spectrum of organized "counter-revolutionary" activities and, unlike the other two aforementioned articles, it provided the opportunity to pass harsher sentences. The structure and practices of the Jehovah's Witnesses provided the authorities with sufficient pretext to interpret them as "subversive," one example in this sense being the indictment brought by the Military Prosecutor's Office in Târgu Mureş against a group of 20 Witnesses on October 12, 1960:

> The following deeds of the defendants [...] belonging to the counter-revolutionary organisation "Jehovah's Witnesses" and carrying out an intensely hostile activity by organising secret meetings, new member recruitments, [...] carrying out public agitation and incitement to break the laws of the state, writing coded reports on the activities and financial contributions to subsidize the organisation, detaining and disseminating counter-revolutionary propaganda materials constitute the offence of plotting against state order.
>
> (ANR, MCB, FPMT, 1954–1965, 617/1959, 148)

As Florin Poenaru noted with respect to documents issued by the secret police agencies in Eastern Europe, "in the Soviet system, the individual is never guilty as such, as an isolated human being, but always part of a 'guilty' wider set of social relations" (Poenaru 2013, 132). In other words, the individual's assessment from the perspective of his/her political guilt was conducted according to the Securitate's logic, that is, by assessing his/her social network and relationships. The investigations it conducted with regard to Jehovah's Witnesses are among the most illustrative in this respect. The perception of these networks as subversive organizations made the process of constructing individuals' political guilt easier, sometimes by simply invoking their membership in a "counter-revolutionary organisation," which simplified bureaucratic procedures because, instead of compiling individual criminal investigation files, they compiled group files.

Conclusions

Jehovah's Witnesses were among those denominations outlawed by the communist regime in Romania. They were put under close surveillance and become a target of repressive measures. This reaction was caused by the way the communist regime perceived Jehovah's Witnesses' everyday religious practices and their close relationship with the religious centre in the United States. In order to legitimize their repressive measures, the Securitate created a discourse in which the Jehovah's Witnesses' religious practices were turned into political guilt by ascribing them political meanings. The narratives of the repressive institutions in communist Romania presented Jehovah's Witnesses as a subversive organization which, in order to undermine the regime, worked intensely to set up a conspiratorial network by recruiting new members, rejected military service, and eschewed participation in the social and political life of the new communist society. These narratives constructed by the Securitate, the Prosecutor's Office and military courts legitimized the punishment of Witnesses under several articles in the Criminal Code, which concerned state security. In the narratives of the Securitate, the everyday religious practices of Jehovah's Witnesses were mainly perceived as plotting against the social order. Thus, they were repressed through convictions issued by the military courts on charges of "conspiracy against social order," "public instigation," "dissemination of forbidden publications," as well as of refusing to enrol for military service.

In relation to their proportion of the total population in Romania, the Securitate produced an impressive quantity of files about Jehovah's Witnesses. Although so numerous, Securitate's files are not of much help when trying to reconstruct precise aspects of the history of this denomination in communist Romania. These files are rich sources when studying the Securitate's narratives or "rhetoric" (Vățulescu 2010, 12–13), but less for studying the social milieus that the Securitate targeted. In this respect, they are very helpful in understanding how the Securitate gathered, organized and gave meaning to information according to its own categories, and produced its own "truth" about the "enemies" of the regime. They give us insights into the inner logic of the Securitate's bureaucratic apparatus and help us to understand the motivation behind gathering information, issuing documents, or collecting artefacts. Concerning the final aspect, by collecting and archiving cultural artefacts produced by those under investigation in order to prove their political guilt, the Securitate became a repository for a valuable cultural heritage that illustrates the diversity of religious practices in communist Romania. These documents also illustrate which religious practices were acceptable or tolerable by the communist regime in a certain period and which were not.

Acknowledgement: Results incorporated in this study received funding from the European Union's Horizon 2020 research and innovation programme under grant agreement No 692919.

Notes

1 This is how denominations such as the Romanian Orthodox Church, the Roman Catholic Church or the Protestant Churches presented themselves by highlighting their longer tradition in the country in contradistinction to denominations that only

became established in Romania at the end of the 19th century and beginning of the 20th century.
2 In order to protect the private life of those mentioned in the Securitate documents cited here I refer to individuals only by their initials.
3 I would like to thank Csongor Jánosi for facilitating my access to the investigation reports drafted by the Military Prosecutor's Office in Târgu-Mureş, which I mention in this study.

Archival sources

Arhiva Consiliului Naţional pentru Studierea Arhivelor Securităţii [National Council for the Study of the Securitate Archives] (ACNSAS), Fond Documentar Bucureşti (FDB).
Arhiva Consiliului Naţional pentru Studierea Arhivelor Securităţii [National Council for the Study of the Securitate Archives] (ACNSAS), Fond Penal (FP).
Arhivele Naţionale ale României [National Archives of Romania] (ANR), Mureş County Branch (MCB), Fond Procuratura Militară Tg. Mureş (FPMT), 1954–1965.

References

Besier, Gerhard and Stokłosa, Katarzyna. eds. 2016. *Jehovah's Witnesses in Europe: Past and Present*, vol. 1. Newcastle upon Tyne: Cambridge Scholars Publishing.
Biblica. 2016. "New International Version." Accessed on 5 June 2018. www.biblica.com/bible/niv/romans/13/
Chryssides, George D. 2009. *The A to Z of Jehovah's Witnesses*. Lanham, Maryland: Scarecrow Press.
Ioniţă, Nicolae. 2008. "The Jehovah`s Witnesses' in the Archives of the Securitate – the Problem of the Toleration of Activity of Religions" ["Martorii lui Iehova" în Arhivele Securităţii Române – Problema tolerării activităţii cultului"]. *Caietele CNSAS* 1 (2): 199–236.
Jánosi, Csongor. 2015. "Rumänien gegen Jehovas Zeugen in der Autonomen Ungarischen Region: die Strafverfahren gegen die Beklagtengruppen um Ungvári, Fülöp und Kovács". In: *Jehovas Zeugen in Europa – Geschichte und Gegenwart. Band 2. Baltikum, Großbritannien, Irland, Rumänien, Skandinavien und UdSSR/GUS*, edited by G. Besier and L. Stoklosa, 435–75. Berlin, LIT Verlag.
[The] *Jehovah`s Witnesses Yearbook* 2006 [*2006 Anuarul Martorilor lui Iehova*]. 2006. New York: Watchtower Bible and Tract Society of New York, Inc.
Knox, Zoe. 2018. *Jehovah's Witnesses and the Secular World: From the 1870s to the Present*. London: Palgrave Macmillan.
Muntean, Aurelian. 2005. "Church-State Relations in Romania: Problems and Perspectives of Interdenominational Cooperation at the Level of Church-based NGOs." *Journal for the Study of Religions and Ideologies* 4 (12): 84–100.
Neagoe-Pleşa, Elis and Pleşa, Liviu. 2005. "The Neo-protestant Denominations in Romania during 1975–1989" ["Cultele neoprotestante din România în perioada 1975–1989"]. In: *The Party, the "Securitate" and the Religious Denominations* [*Partidul, Securitatea şi cultele*], edited by Adrian N. Petcu, 363–64. Bucharest: Nemira.
Penton, M. James. 2004. *Jehovah's Witnesses and the Third Reich: Sectarian Politics Under Persecution*. Toronto: University of Toronto Press.

Penton, M. James. 2015. *Apocalypse Delayed: The Story of Jehovah's Witnesses.* Toronto: University of Toronto Press [First edition 1985].

Petcu, Adrian. N. 2005. "The "Securitate" and the Churches in 1949" ["Securitatea şi Cultele în 1949"]. In: *The Party, the "Securitate" and Religious Denominations* [*Partidul, Securitatea şi cultele*], edited by Adrian N. Petcu, 189–92. Bucharest: Nemira.

Pintilescu, Corneliu. 2015. "Jehovas Zeugen im 20. Jahrhundert in Rumänien – zwischen Toleranz und Repression." In: *Jehovas Zeugen in Europa – Geschichte und Gegenwart, vol. 2: Baltikum, Großbritannien, Irland, Rumänien, Skandinavien, UdSSR/GUS,* edited by G. Besier and K. Stoklosa, 407–34. Berlin: LIT Verlag.

Pintilescu, Corneliu and Fătu-Tutoveanu, Andrada. 2011. "Jehovah's Witnesses in Post-Communist Romania: The Relationship between the Religious Minority and the State (1989–2010)". *Journal for the Study of Religions and Ideologies.* 10 (30): 102–26.

Poenaru, Florin 2013. *Contesting Illusions: History and Intellectual Class Struggle in Post- communist Romania.* PhD thesis submitted to Central European University, Budapest, Department of Sociology and Social Anthropology.

Ramet, Sabrina. P. 1991. "Politics and Religion in Eastern Europe and the Soviet Union." In: *Politics and Religion in the Modern World*, edited by G. Moyser, 67–96. London: Routledge.

[The] Romanian Criminal Code with modifications until June 1, 1959 [*Codul Penal (cu modificările făcute până la 1 iunie 1959)*]. 1959. Bucharest: Editura Ştiinţifică.

Spânu, Alexandru. A. 2005. "The Sects reflected in the Reports of the Intelligence Service of the Romanian Army." ["Sectele religioase în rapoartele Serviciului de Informaţii al Armatei"]. In: *The Party, the "Securitate" and Religious Denominations* [*Partidul, Securitatea şi cultele*], edited by Adrian N. Petcu, 117–23. Bucureşti: Nemira.

Solonari, Vladimir. 2010. *Purifying the Nation: Population Exchange and Ethnic Cleansing in Nazi Allied Romania.* Baltimore: The Johns Hopkins University Press.

Taylor, Pauline. B. 1965. "Sectarians in Soviet Courts." *Russian Review* 24 (3): 278–88.

Tismăneanu, Vladimir, Dobrincu, Dorin and Vasile Cristian. (eds.) 2007. *The Presidential Commission for the Analysis of the Communist Dictatorship in Romania. Final Report* [*Comisia Prezidenţială pentru Analiza Dictaturii Comuniste din România. Raport final*]. Bucureşti: Humanitas.

Vasile, Cristian. 2003. *History of the Romanian Greek-Catholic Church under Communism. Documents and Testimonies* [*Istoria Bisericii Greco-catolice sub regimul comunist (1945–1989). Documente şi mărturii*]. Iaşi: Polirom.

Văţulescu, Cristina. 2010. *Police Aesthetics: Literature, Film, and the Secret Police in Soviet Times.* Stanford: Stanford University Press.

Verdery, Katherine. 2014. *Secrets and Truths. Ethnography in the Archive of Romania's Secret Police.* Budapest: CEU Press.

5 A coercive political environment as place of testimony

Jehovah's Witnesses in the era of state socialism in Hungary, 1948–89

Éva Petrás

Introduction: Jehovah's Witnesses in Hungary

Jehovah's Witnesses, as a small religious entity, have been present in Hungary for more than a 100 years. Worldwide the Jehovah's Witnesses have more than 8.1 million members[1] and today, according to national surveys, there are more than 31,000 Jehovah's Witnesses in Hungary (Csordás 2014, 90).[2] They form a legally acknowledged and recognized so-called "small church." But this was not the case for most of their history. In fact, apart from a couple of years after World War II, Hungarian Jehovah's Witnesses suffered the consequences of being an illegal and persecuted religious entity. Their legal status was settled only in 1989 after many years of negotiation with the state authorities.[3]

In this study, I first trace the history of the Jehovah's Witnesses in Hungary to introduce their spread and settlement in the country and show some problematic issues that arose when they encountered the church, social and state administrative actors before World War II. Then I describe the historical context of post-World War Hungary in the political and church political milieu. A situation that fundamentally defined and limited the possible scope of action of the Jehovah's Witnesses' communities as they were rendered amongst religious underground movements during the decades of state socialism. My intention is to show the historical trajectory of a small religious entity leading from persecution to at least partial accommodation, then to final recognition among East-Central European historical circumstances. To achieve this goal I used two types of historical sources: written sources of legislative, press and state security materials, which can be found in the National Archives of Hungary and in the Historical Archives of the Hungarian State Security, and the written and oral historical sources of Jehovah's Witnesses, which are in the possession of the Hungarian Jehovah's Witnesses' Archives, or are based on the interviews I made among them during my research. By juxtaposing sources from an external, mainly oppressive power actor with insider sources of the Jehovah's Witnesses own experiences, my aim is to shed light on the strategies and practices of survival of coercive historical situations. This study examines some of these strategies and practices, which are closely knit with that specific type of religiosity and devotion shared by Jehovah's Witnesses and which enabled them to become one of the most resistant religious communities to the atheistic fervor of communist ideology.

History of the Jehovah's Witnesses before 1945

The first communities of Jehovah's Witnesses appeared in Hungary at the beginning of the twentieth century. Hungarian guest workers and immigrants in the United States and Canada took up the new religion and brought home their new faith. Their communities first spread in the Northern and Eastern parts of the country (the first congregations were settled in Hajdúböszörmény, Balmazújváros, Nagyvisnyó, Marosvásárhely (now Târgu Mureş, Romania) and Kolozsvár (now Cluj, Romania)) (Jehova Tanúi Évkönyve 1996, 68–9).[4] Watchtower, the world-wide publication of the "Bible students," as the Jehovah's Witnesses were called at that time, has been printed in Hungarian since 1913.

Since the new members of the Jehovah's Witnesses were recruited from other denominations, their first encounters with the Hungarian religious environment brought them into serious conflict with the representatives of the major historical churches, those of the Roman Catholic, the Reformed (Calvinist) and Lutheran churches. But some teachings of the Witnesses also brought them to the attention of the state authorities: preaching about the end of this world was understood as a revolutionary message against the political *status quo* and the method of evangelization, the personal persuasion moving from one individual to the next and from door to door, was understood as a propaganda against the political establishment. On the basis of these elements, a narrative of having "communist" ideas was constructed in the interwar period, which finally resulted in a ban on their work in 1939 by the Minister of the Interior. The decree forbade the activity of the Nazarenes, the Seventh-day Adventists and the Witnesses of Jehovah and "other millenarians" (Belügyi Közlöny 1939, 1647). The official ban was followed by different kinds of police proceedings: there were home raids, interrogations and detentions. In the shadow of the war, the refusal of military service was considered the most dangerous practice of the Jehovah's Witnesses, which resulted in the arrest of hundreds of them. Similar to Hungarian Jews, about 160 Jehovah's Witnesses were taken to the labour camps of Bor in Serbia to work in the copper mines. Some Witnesses were also taken to concentration camps in Auschwitz-Birkenau, Dachau, Buchenwald and Bergen-Belsen. As the military situation worsened and morale decayed in Hungary, four young Jehovah's Witnesses were even executed publicly to demonstrate what could happen to those refusing military service. During the war, not only men, but also women Jehovah's Witnesses were arrested. They were incarcerated in the prison of Márianosztra (North Hungary) for preaching their message (Szita 2017, 165–202).

Jehovah's Witnesses between 1945 and 1948

In the turmoil of the twentieth century, Hungary experienced nine political system changes, or at least attempted changes. Three of them took place in the period under discussion: 1945, 1948 and 1956 all represent significant turning points in Hungarian history. The so-called "coalition era" between 1945 and 1948 was followed by the infamous Rákosi regime, which ended in the revolution and freedom fight of 1956, followed by the Kádár era. These decades were not homogeneous in the life of the churches (Gyarmati 2007, 20–39). Apart from having their own internal historical processes, their history was also influenced by the state's church policy. The major historical churches encountered restrictions on their activities very soon, while small churches and religious entities experienced for the first couple of years after World War II a long-wished for, and in some cases for the first time, a period of freedom of activity. Therefore, their perception of these years was quite different from those of the major historical churches.[5] Nevertheless, after the communist seizure of power in 1948, repression also reached the small churches, albeit with different periods of intensity, and lasted until the change of system in 1989.

After the war, people returned from prisons and camps and the congregations of the Jehovah's Witnesses were reorganized. Some small churches had already formed the Alliance of Hungarian Free Churches (later called: The Council of Free Churches) in October 1944 but the Jehovah's Witnesses did not join. The legislation concerning the activity of the previously banned small churches and religious entities also changed as the war came to an end. The new, Interim Hungarian Government assured freedom of thought and religion (Nemzetgyűlési Napló 1944, 23). In 1946 the republic was proclaimed and Act I/1946 on the republican form of government declared the free exercise of religion as an inalienable right. As a consequence, the former ban on the activity of the small churches was abolished by a decree (1000 év törvényei No. 6270/1946). However, the status of the previously not recognized denominations did not change automatically. Therefore, in 1947 a law was passed, which revoked the legal differences between the denominations (Act XXXIII/1947). Although the decree making religious education optional in schools was already a step towards restricting the influence and work of the churches in general, it still had positive side effects for children coming from small churches because for them it meant that they were no longer obliged to take part in the forms of religious education determined by the major historical churches as had been the practice before World War II.

As a consequence of the positive changes to the legal framework, the work of the Jehovah's Witnesses became legal and the situation became more advantageous for their activity. A general assembly was convoked for July 28, 1946, where in the presence of 322 church members, the Association of Hungarian Jehovah's Witnesses was established. János Konrád was elected as the branch office leader, or "country servant," as in the vocabulary of the Jehovah's Witnesses the national leader was called. They bought a building for the branch office in Budapest and started their mission. Since the Jehovah's Witnesses had to make a yearly written report of their achievements, we know that by the end of 1945, 590 members submitted reports. This number increased to 837 in 1946. They were also able to organize public events. The biggest of them took place in Budapest Sports Hall in August 1947, which was attended by 1,200 participants (Jehova Tanúi Évkönyve 1996, 95–6). In the short period between 1945 and 1948, it was also a positive development that the press avoided the use of the expression "sect" with regards to the Jehovah's Witnesses. Mostly they were called a "religious entity" instead (Gergely 2012, 94–107). Sometimes even positive articles were published about them, for example, about the "theocratic congress" in 1947.

In Hungarian political life, however, the elections in August 1947 set the stage for the crisis of the parliamentary democracy and for the advancement of the communists, which finally resulted in the total seizure of power of the Hungarian Communist Party, or, as it was called after the union of the two workers' parties (the communists and the Social Democrats) in 1948: the Hungarian Workers' Party (Magyar Dolgozók Pártja, or MDP). It soon became clear that Hungary would follow the Soviet pattern and that the state's church policy would change accordingly. For the Jehovah's Witnesses the dramatic turn happened in 1949 when Hungary, in the atmosphere of the Cold War and already as an ally of the Soviet Union, took a stand against the United States. From that time on, the Jehovah's Witnesses were regarded as the agents of the Americans and as supporters of American imperialistic interests. It is interesting to note that before World War II they were accused of being communists and yet just a couple of years later in the media and in public discourse they were constructed as American spies. Together with other small churches they began to be mentioned as destructive sects again.[6]

Paradoxically the Hungarian Workers' Party finally defined the struggle against the small churches as a part of its struggle against "clerical reaction," a term which had basically been used for combatting the Roman Catholic Church. József Révai, the chief ideologist of the party settled the question this way:

> We have to carry on the struggle against the sects, too. The leaders of the Adventists, the Jehovists [as they were called during the decades of state socialism], the Baptists and other sects are in most cases in the service of American imperialism. These sects are no more than propaganda organs of imperialism.
>
> (Szabad Nép 1950, 3)

This speech determined the future of these small churches. However, the history of the Jehovah's Witnesses and that of the other small churches divered from this point forward. Those of them that joined the Alliance of Hungarian Free Churches, were controlled by the State Office for Church Affairs (Állami Egyházügyi Hivatal, ÁEH) following its establishment in 1951. The State Office for Church Affairs as an authority became the most important executive body of the communist state's church policy during the whole era (Köbel 2005, 60). It played a decisive role, for example, in accomplishing bilateral agreements with the great historical churches and supervised their work afterwards. It also had crucial tasks regarding the small churches. According to a discussion with the representatives of the Ministry of the Interior on August 8, 1951, however, ÁEH refused to take up the matters of those religious entities, which did not join the Alliance of Free Churches. Only the member churches of the alliance were recognized as legal, while illegal minorities such as the Jehovah's Witnesses and some other Neo-Protestant communities, were assigned to the authority of the Ministry of the Interior (MNL OL M-Ks-276/54 item 155). Their activities were considered against the constitution of the People's Republic of Hungary, since they refused the only assigned legal route for their activity: joining the state-controlled work of the Alliance of Hungarian Free Churches. From that time on, the Ministry of the Interior treated their cases as a police matter and with the active involvement of the state security a large number of operations and legal proceedings were carried out.

The 1950s in the life of the Jehovah's Witnesses

Similar to other communist countries, at the beginning of the 1950s the Jehovah's Witnesses were also targeted in Hungary.[7] On November 9, 1950 the State Security Authority (Államvédelmi Hatóság, ÁVH) arrested the branch office leader, János Konrád, the main translator András Bartha and other elders of the community. During their interrogation, the political police learned the data of the 10 districts of the Hungarian Jehovah's Witnesses and the names of their leaders. This data formed the basis of the first show trial of the Hungarian Jehovah's Witnesses (ÁBTL 3.1.9. V-71056, 15–19). During the home raids lots of printed material and educational devices were confiscated. In the brochures the authorities found statements, which could easily be considered as criminal. During the legal proceedings some of these statements were cut from their original context and were re-contextualized in order to make them usable as evidence for treason and provocation against the people's democracy. For example, they summarized the findings like this:

> It is an often used phrase of the Jehovists [sic!] to call our form of government as the "realm of the Satan." For example this was the case with the brochure with the title "The truth will make you free," in which there are plenty of anti-democratic statements. The propagandists are educated

also illegally. They start their "speech" with this sentence: "This world is condemned and its days are counted!"

(ÁBTL 3.1.9. V-71056, 30)

We can see from this quotation that the eschatological character of the speech was not recognized by the authorities. Instead, they understood the message politically in order to criminalize it. Thus, it could be transformed into an argument and used as evidence in the show trial. The Jehovah's Witnesses could be presented as the enemies of the country who, it is seen, literally jeopardize the people's democracy.

In the first trial, János Konrád was sentenced for ten years imprisonment, András Bartha got nine years and the other accused Witnesses each received 5 to 8 years (ÁBTL 3.1.9. V-149948/4, 2–15). The court suppressed the brochures and banned the meetings of the Jehovah's Witnesses as well. While János Konrád and his fellows were in prison, a new, clandestine leadership stepped up. Elek Nemes became branch office leader and his work was supported by László Bussányi, László Papp and other elders. However, they were also arrested in 1953 and in the second show trial of the Jehovah's Witnesses they also received severe penalties: Elek Nemes and László Bussányi were put in prison for 10 years, the other accused persons got 5 to 9 years for "active participation in an organization trying to subvert the people's republic," as it was stated (ÁBTL 3.1.9. V-111784/1, 259–62). The convicts were taken to the prison of Márianosztra, where, after a short period, they were interrogated again. This time the authorities asked about the Western contacts of the Jehovah's Witnesses, how they had managed to maintain contact with the international centre and if they had sent any information abroad. These questions introduced a new direction in the accusations because in the meantime the ÁVH had learned that the Jehovah's Witnesses kept in contact with their Eastern European centre in Switzerland and they gathered proof for next round of arrests.

One of the imprisoned Witnesses, József Csobán, terrified by the ordeal, finally gave his approval to become a collaborator (ÁBTL 3.1.1. B-87058, 1–11). He gave information mainly about the foreign contacts of the Hungarian Jehovah's Witnesses and specifically about his fellow Witness, Mihály Paulinyi, who was the contact person between the Swiss centre and Hungary and commuted between the two countries, taking the reports of the Hungarian Jehovah's Witnesses regularly to Bern. Partly on the basis of information given by Csobán, a new circle of leaders was arrested in 1954, including Paulinyi. Their case was put to the courts of justice in 1955. In this third show trial, besides the "usual" charges of endangering people's democracy the arrested Jehovah's Witnesses were accused of espionage. The sentences were shocking: Zoltán Hubicsák, the new branch office leader was committed to 13 years in prison, Paulinyi got 12 years and the others received sentences of 5 to 13 years, which they spent in the prison of Vác, where many other political prisoners were incarcerated (ÁBTL 3.1.9. V-149948/4, 19–32).

Underground religious life and the state security

Since the activity of the Jehovah's Witnesses was banned, religious life became restricted to home gatherings and meetings in the forests, but these too were often disturbed by the police. Nevertheless, the authorities were not able to prevent the work of the Jehovah's Witnesses altogether. They could reach people living in remote farms by bicycle and could meet for studying the Bible in meadows (see Figure 5.1). Since for Jehovah's Witnesses devotional life was not bound to a church building, total state control of their activities was not feasible. The State Security many times confiscated printed material in home raids and sometimes they even found the typewriters on which these educational materials were multiplied. But religious life in set terms, as was the case with most churches, was difficult to uncover. The confiscated devotional material (Bibles, copies of Watchtower and other educational materials) (see Figure 5.2), typewriters, or printing machines were therefore regularly used to prove the forbidden religious activity of the Jehovah's Witnesses, but sometimes even such indirect methods failed to be used effectively in a legal proceeding. Or rather the real meaning and significance of the confiscated material escaped the attention of the state security.

Figure 5.1 Jehovah's Witnesses at a bicycle meeting (MJTEA). ©Hungarian Jehovah's Witnesses' Archives.

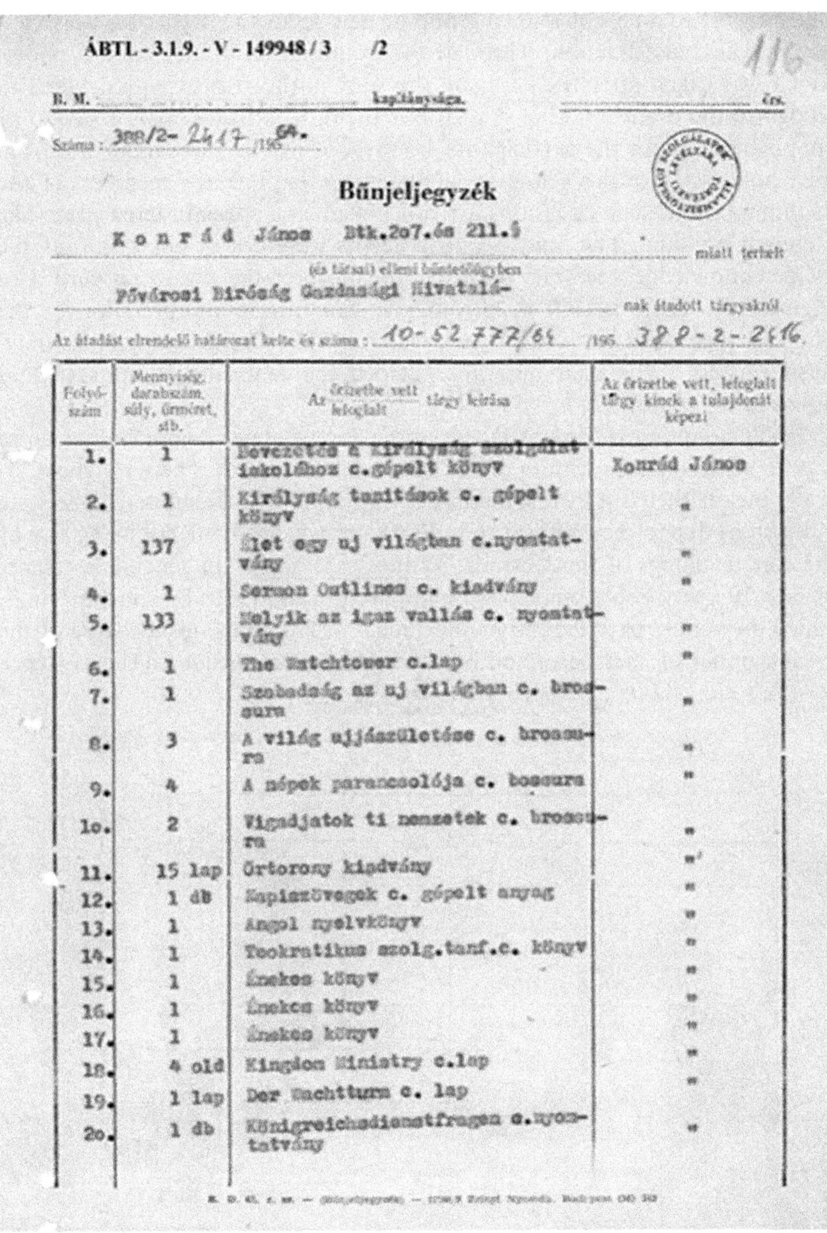

ÁBTL - 3.1.9. - V - 149948 / 3 /2

116

B. M. .... kapitánysága. .... őrs.

Száma : 388/2- 2417 /1964.

Bűnjeljegyzék

K o n r á d János Btk.2o7.és 211.§ miatt terhelt

(és társai) elleni bűnügyben

Fővárosi Bíróság Gazdasági Hivatalá- nak átadott tárgyakról

Az átadást elrendelő határozat kelte és száma : 10-52 777/64 /196. 388-2-2416.

Folyó-szám	Mennyiség, darabszám, súly, űrméret, stb.	Az őrizetbe vett / lefoglalt tárgy leírása	Az őrizetbe vett, lefoglalt tárgy kinek a tulajdonát képezi
1.	1	Bevezetés a Királyság szolgálat iskolához c.gépelt könyv	Konrád János
2.	1	Királyság tanitások c. gépelt könyv	"
3.	137	Élet egy uj világban c.nyomtatvány	"
4.	1	Sermon Outlines c. kiadvány	"
5.	133	Melyik az igaz vallás c. nyomtatvány	"
6.	1	The Watchtower c.lap	"
7.	1	Szabadság az uj világban c. brosura	"
8.	3	A világ ujjászületése c. brosura	"
9.	4	A népek parancsolója c. bosura	"
1o.	2	Vigadjatok ti nemzetek c. brosura	"
11.	15 lap	Őrtorony kiadvány	"
12.	1 db	Napiszövegek c. gépelt anyag	"
13.	1	Angol nyelvkönyv	"
14.	1	Teokratikus szolg.tanf.c. könyv	"
15.	1	Énekes könyv	"
16.	1	Énekes könyv	"
17.	1	Énekes könyv	"
18.	4 old	Kingdom Ministry c.lap	"
19.	1 lap	Der Wachtturm c. lap	"
2o.	1 db	Königreichsdienstfragen c.nyomtatvány	"

Figure 5.2 List of confiscated education material (ÁBTL 3.1.9. V-149948/3/2, 116). ©Historical Archives of the Hungarian State Security.

This happened, for example, in the case of a confiscated photo from 1954, which recorded an event when a group of new Jehovah's Witnesses were (re)-baptized in Lake Balaton. Through the examination of the tableau photo, which was taken after the baptism, the state authorities attention failed to recognize the event for what it was. For them, it indicated only a group of people bathing, for the participants, however, it was no mere momento from their holiday. Jehovah's Witnesses baptize or re-baptize new members of the community and such occasions are not linked to a special sacred place like a church building. The State Security agents were not in possession of the insider knowledge necessary in order to interpret the photo properly (see Figure 5.3). There is shift in meaning, a semantic re-interpretation of the photo if spectators know the ritual, which in this case the authorities obviously missed. Thus their ignorance helped the Jehovah's Witnesses avoid police interrogation.

Easily adapting to circumstances and using whatever opportunities arose was an advantageous feature of the Jehovah's Witnesses. These practices literally meant their survival sometimes. Many of them encountered the state authorities due to their refusal of military service, non-violence being one of the core teachings of the Jehovah's Witnesses. For this, in general, sentences of 8 to 10 years imprisonment were imposed in the 1950s by court martials, which they could partly spend in internment or labour camps. Because of the great number of such cases and because the regime considered the existence

Figure 5.3 Baptism at Lake Balaton (MJTEA). ©Hungarian Jehovah's Witnesses' Archives.

of the Jehovah's Witnesses as a danger to society, the refusal of military service proved to be a structural problem. The court martial dealt with these cases *en masse*. As an eye-witness later told:

> The proceedings were like on a conveyor belt. It happened that five brothers were called in at the same time and after five minutes the whole proceeding was over: they all got ten years one by one, so altogether they got fifty years.
>
> (MJTEA, personal witnessing of Ferenc Nagy)

We don't know the exact number of convictions, but in the Archives of the Hungarian Jehovah's Witnesses there is a list, which counted those who, after refusing military service and being convicted, spent their penalty, or a part of it, in a labour camp in North-Eastern Hungary. According to this list, 265 men were deported to Tólápa labour camp, where they were forced to work in the coalmines of Ladánytáró in the Bükk Mountains. It was a general practice in the 1950s that prisoners were forced to work and thus they had to contribute to "the building of Socialism." Such camps were regularly built in desolate places and convicts usually worked in mines or on large industrial projects.

In Tólápa and in other camps Jehovah's Witnesses came together and established Bible study circles. In their memoirs they emphasize the significance of these because the community provided a kind of insulation against the circumstances. They even eulogized their experiences as illustrated by the case of a devotional song originating from this period in the labour camps.

The poem below is a precious remnant of religious devotion and spirituality of the labour camps that was written by Elemér Rakmányi who was a prisoner in Tólápa. His poem was recited even into the 1960s when copies of it were confiscated by the state security (see Figure 5.4). The poem has a dozen stanzas and was written in a Hungarian verse form using 12 syllables in each lines, every two lines rhyming, as was generally used by Hungarian Romantic poets in the nineteenth century. It is culturally interesting to note after nearly 100 years, this verse form influenced a Jehovah's Witnesses devotional song written in the 1950s.

SONG FROM THE MINE PIT OF LADÁNYTÁRÓ
Have you heard of the deep coalmine?
Of dark pits below with no sunshine?
Where long tunnels wind under the hills,
Muffling the noise of pickaxe and drills.
Pale-faced miners held behind that gate,
Fighting for faith, bound by their fate.
Come by for a moment, you who dwell in sunshine,
I'll be your guide in that deep coalmine,
Where the mouth of a dark pit opens,

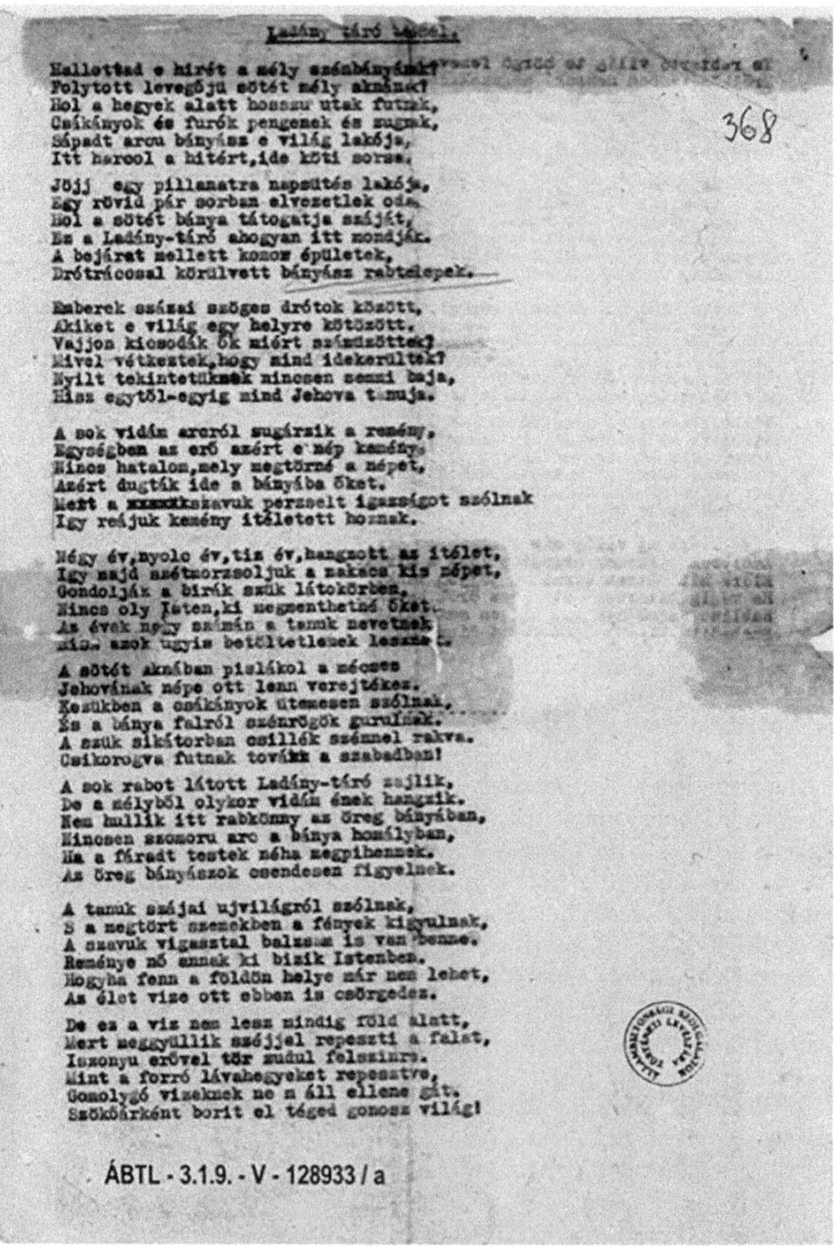

Ladány táró [illegible].

368

Hallottad e hirét a mély szénbányának?
Folytott levegőjü sötét mély aknának?
Hol a hegyek alatt hosszu utak futnak,
Csákányok és furók pengenek és zugnak,
Sápadt arcu bányász e világ lakója,
Itt harcol a hitért, ide köti sorsa.

Jöjj egy pillanatra napsütés lakója,
Egy rövid pár sorban elvezetlek oda,
Hol a sötét bánya tátogatja száját,
Es a Ladány-táró ahogyan itt mondják.
A bejárat mellett komor épületek,
Drótráccsal körülvett bányász rabtelepek.

Emberek százai szöges drótok között,
Akiket e világ egy helyre kötözött.
Vajjon kicsodák ők miért száműzötték?
Mivel vétkeztek, hogy mind idekerültek?
Nyilt tekintetüknek nincsen semmi baja,
Hisz egytől-egyig mind Jehova tanuja.

A sok vidám arcról sugárzik a remény,
Egységben az erő azért e nép kemény,
Nincs hatalom, mely megtörné a népet,
Azért dugták ide a bányába őket.
Mert a xxxxxkszavuk perzselt igazságot szólnak
Igy reájuk kemény itéletett hoznak.

Négy év, nyolc év, tiz év, hangzott az itélet,
Igy majd szétmorzsoljuk a makacs kis népet,
Gondolják a birák szük látokörben,
Nincs oly Isten, ki megmenthetné őket.
Az évek nagy számán a tanuk nevetnek
Mig azok ugyis betöltetlenek lesznek.

A sötét aknában pislákol a mécses
Jehovának népe ott lenn verejtékes.
Kezükben a csákányok ütemesen szólnak,
És a bánya falról szénrögök gurulnak.
A szük sikátorban csillék szénnel rakva.
Csikorogva futnak tovább a szabadban!

A sok rabot látott Ladány-táró zajlik,
De a mélyből olykor vidám ének hangzik.
Nem hullik itt rabkönny az öreg bányában,
Nincsen szomoru arc a bánya homályban,
Ha a fáradt testek néha megpihennek.
Az öreg bányászok csendesen figyelnek.

A tanuk szájai ujvilágról szólnak,
S a megtört szemekben a fények kigyulnak,
A szavuk vigasztal balzsam is van benne.
Reménye nő annak ki bizik Istenben.
Hogyha fenn a földön helye már nem lehet,
Az élet vize ott ebben is csörgedez.

De ez a viz nem lesz mindig föld alatt,
Mert megagyülik szétjjel repeszti a falat,
Iszonyu erővel tör zudul felszinre.
Mint a forró lávahegyeket repesztve,
Gomolygó vizeknek ne m áll ellene gát.
Szökőárként borit el téged gonosz világ!

ÁBTL - 3.1.9. - V - 128933 / a

Figure 5.4 Song from the minepit of Ladánytáró (ÁBTL 3.1.9. V-128933/a). ©Historical Archives of the Hungarian State Security.

That's the coalmine, wire fenced.
Gloomy buildings by the entrance,
Barbed wire 'round a prisoner camp.
Hundreds behind those wire fences,
Locked up in there with shattered chances.
Who are they? Why were they expelled?
What's their crime, the charges upheld?
Nothing wrong with these well-faced men,
Jehovah's Witnesses – so they call 'em.
Hope is in their happy eyes,
Unity makes strength, and solid spines.
No power can break their spirit,
Hence they've been put in this pit.
They spoke the truth that some hated to hear,
Harsh verdicts threw them down here.
"Four years", "eight years", "ten years" – so the verdicts went,
with narrow-minded judges thinking:
"It will make their backbones bent",
"No god could save them" they believed,
But the Witnesses only laughed at those years,
None of the threats could bring them to tears.
[…]
The pit has seen countless prisoners,
But cheerful singing is heard from deep below,
No tears are shed, all faces glow.
The mine is gloomy, but no sadness there.
When tired workers are asleep,
Old miners guard their sleep […]

(ÁBTL 3.1.9. V-128933/a, 368–9;
translation: Zoltán Farkas)

The persecution also left its stamp on religious visual arts. Lajos Gerencsér, who also spent years at Tólápa labour camp having been convicted for refusing military service, left Hungary in 1956 as a refugee. He settled in Austria and became a painter. Among other themes he painted rural landscapes. Open skies are one of his recurring motifs of his work and he is referred to as "the painter of the skies" by art historians.[8] Sky symbolizes freedom in his paintings and represents a direct connection with his experiences in the coalmines as a prisoner of faith (see Figure 5.5).[9]

Jehovah's Witnesses in the Kádár era

1956 signifies a turning point in the history of the Hungarian Jehovah's Witnesses. During the revolution their leaders were set free at least temporarily and the labour camps were also closed during that year. The revolutionary

Figure 5.5 Ludwig L. Gerencsér: Bächlein. ©Ludwig L. Gerencsér.

times, however, represented only a short pause in the persecution: at the beginning of 1957 the leaders were again incarcerated to continue their sentences and new military summons were delivered to those having refused military service earlier.

After the revolution of 1956, the Kádár regime restored the previous situation with regards to the state's church policy. The bilateral agreements with the major historical churches were renewed and the state authorities started to measure the real extent of the small churches as well. The ultimate aim remained the same: gradually eroding away the churches and finally putting an end to their social influence. As a party resolution put it: "We have to count with the fact that the churches will still exist under Socialist circumstances for a long time. That's why the cooperation between the state and the churches will be a necessity in the meantime" (Fundamental Issues 2005, 1003–4). To reach this aim, however, a new strategy was implemented. They intended to broaden the loyalty of the churches to the state by using those church leaders and members who would collaborate with the authorities either due to open or secret pressure, or in the hope of gaining certain advantages.

"Divide and rule" became the chief motive. Regarding those denominations, which did not join the Council of Free Churches, the primary aim was to achieve their participation. This way these entities could be controlled and influenced. The State Office for Church Affairs took up this task.

Despite avoiding the harsh measures that were typical of the 1950s, in regards to the Jehovah's Witnesses the administrative steps were still in use even in the first half of the 1960s. János Konrád, the branch office leader, after having finished his prison sentence, was released but after a couple of months he was arrested again together with other elders of the community in August 1961. After their detention, home raids were carried out at the homes of a number of Jehovah's Witnesses. Brochures, Bibles and other printed materials were confiscated. According to the scenario set up by the state security, common members of the Jehovah's Witnesses were to be led to believe that their leaders had given their addresses to the police (ÁBTL 3.1.9. V-146708/2, 186–97). Of course, this was not the case: the state security gathered information about them well before Konrád was arrested. Konrád and his fellows' cases were not put before the court this time, and they were released after a couple of weeks. The aim of the police at this time seems to have been to spread uncertainty and distrust within the community.

In the meantime, the Jehovah's Witnesses were continuously sentenced to prison because of refusing military service. The sentences were lenient compared to those of the 1950s. However, the presence of the Jehovah's Witnesses in court martials and in prisons caused lots of problems for the Ministry of Defence and for the Ministry of the Interior, which urged the State Office for Church Affairs to find a solution to this problematic situation.[10] Consequently, the State Office prepared an "itinerary" in 1964 for the community of the Jehovah's Witnesses in order to settle their legal status. The plan of the State Office was "to split the loyal and reactionary segments within the sect. (…) We have to offer legal recognition to the loyal wing and make them join the Council of Free Churches" (MNL OL XIX-A-21-d-0037-9/1964, 1–4). Accordingly, János Konrád, the branch office leader was arrested again in 1964 and was forced to elaborate on a possible agreement with the state. He was only "urged" to make a draft of what he saw as indispensable from the perspective of the Hungarian Jehovah's Witnesses to their legal recognition. After being released, Konrád made his draft, which was the basis of his negotiations with the representatives of the State Office for Church Affairs. According to the documentation about the negotiations, Konrád made two versions of his drafts: one in April and one in October 1965, but finally agreement could not be achieved. Konrád stuck to the position of not joining the Council of Free Churches and not giving data about the Jehovah's Witnesses to the state authorities. He also took a firm stand on questions concerning military service (MNL OL XIX-A-21-c-60/5/1965, 164). Imre Miklós, at that time the deputy director of the State Office for Church Affairs, bitterly communicated the failure of the negotiations to the Minister of the Interior:

> I inform you that the denomination, which calls itself the Jehovah's Witnesses in Hungary did not ask for the legalization of their status. Therefore they cannot be regarded as such. Consequently their activity or

> the control of it remains in the authority of the Ministry of the Interior. Hereby we (the State Office for Church Affairs) give back their case.
> (ÁBTL 3.1.9. V-149948/3, 103)

With the lack of an agreement, the activity of the Jehovah's Witnesses remained illegal even after 1965. Home raids were carried out at the homes of a number of Jehovah's Witnesses. Brochures, Bibles and other printed materials were often confiscated. It was the aim of the state authorities to keep the community in a state of panic and spread the suspicion that Konrád might have betrayed them.

Conclusion

The case of the Jehovah's Witnesses remained unsolved until the downfall of the communist regime. Although attempts at state control and persecution reduced in the 1970s and 1980s, there was still need of a decade-long negotiation with the authorities until their status was finally settled in 1989. This, however, happened already in the political milieu of the change of system, which pushed both sides in the direction of an agreement. Their case was and has remained an absolute test for the practice of religious freedom in Hungary.

The study attempted to shed light on certain turning points of the history of the Jehovah's Witnesses in Hungary, with a special emphasis on their history in the era of state socialism. Jehovah's Witnesses as a forbidden and persecuted religious entity could survive these decades by using their community specific social, cultural and devotional practices, which on the one hand demanded a personal public commitment that risked even individual freedom when making testimonies, promoting religious community life, or denying military service. On the other hand, their devotional life was enriched and deepened by the persecution. The case of the Jehovah's Witnesses' represents an uncompromising resistance to political influence and a steadfast reluctance to accommodate in a basically hostile political milieu. The flourishing spirituality of the Jehovah's Witnesses drew strength from difficulties by interpreting persecution on an eschatological level. This was the key to their activity and survival during these decades. This chapter study explored the parallel the legislative, press and state security sources and their counterparts in Jehovah's Witnesses' own archival documentation. Through this juxtaposition, it is possible to demonstrate the religious interpretation of historical events. Examples of devotional songs that were composed in labour camps, paintings that were inspired by the historical experience of the 1950s and photos that played a role in the survival of the community show the process how certain specific historical experiences could be transcended and became part of this small religious group's communities identity construction, and in exchange how this group could stand firmly amidst the changing, but essentially coercive, historical circumstances.

Notes

1 According to their own statistics, in 2016 there were approximately 8.13 million active members. In: *2017 Yearbook of Jehovah's Witnesses* 2017, 176.
2 National surveys that contain information on religion were carried out in 2011 in Hungary. According to it, 31,727 people declared themselves Jehovah's Witnesses.
3 Jehovah's Witnesses were acknowledged as a legally recognized "small church" on 27 June 1989 by resolution 4/1989. (VI. 30.) of the State Office for Church Affairs (Állami Egyházügyi Hivatal).
4 The first recognized preacher was a Hungarian lady, returning from USA in 1908. A certain Andrásné Benedek later established a congregation in Hajdúböszörmény, in Eastern Hungary. Károly Szabó from Marosvásárhely (Târgu Mureş, Romania) and Károly Kiss from Abar (Oborín, Slovakia) also became leaders in their local congregations.
5 The Land Reform of March 1945 was already considered to have shaken the financial basis of the Roman Catholic Church. Education was also placed on the agenda in 1945 and generated years of fierce political and church political debate on schooling that concluded in the total nationalization of education in 1948.
6 The party newspaper of the Hungarian Workers' Party, *Szabad Nép* devoted several articles to combat the Jehovah's Witnesses, e.g. 9 May 1950, 7., 21 May 1950, 11., 26 May 1950, 2., 1 June 1950, 5 and 3 June 1950, 7.
7 For the history of persecution of the Jehovah's Witnesses see: Dirksen (2002, 229–38).
8 Lajos Gerencsér. In: www.volksgruppen.orf.at (Downloaded: 17 December 2017)
9 Oral history interview with Lajos Gerencsér. Eisenberg (Austria), 21 June 2016, made by Éva Petrás.
10 Seventh-day Adventist and Nazarenes also had similar commitment to nonviolence and took a stand against military service. From 1977, however, an agreement made it possible for the members of the small churches to choose a nonviolent service when making their compulsory defence service. See Dirksen (2013, 72–81).

Archival sources

ÁBTL – Állambiztonsági Szolgálatok Történeti Levéltára [Historical Archives of the Hungarian State Security]
MNL OL – Magyar Nemzeti Levéltár Országos Levéltára [National Archives of Hungary]
MJTEA – Magyarországi Jehova Tanúi Egyház Archívuma [Hungarian Jehovah's Witnesses' Archives]

Press

2017 *Yearbook of Jehovah's Witnesses*
1996 *Jehova Tanúi Évkönyve [Yearbook of Jehovah's Witnesses]*
1000 év törvényei [*Laws of 1000 Years*], 1000ev.hu (Downloaded: 10 December 2017)
Belügyi Közlöny [*Home Affairs Bulletin*], 1939
Nemzetgyűlési Napló [*National Assembly Almanacs*], 1944
Szabad Nép [*Free Folk*], 1950

References

Csordás, Gábor. ed. 2014. *Népszámlálás, 2011. 10. Vallás, felekezet*. Budapest: Központi Statisztikai Hivatal.

Dirksen, Annegret. 2013. “Denying Military Service: Developments in Hungary and in GDR” [“A katonai szolgálat megtagadása: fejlődések Magyarországon és Németországban”]. In: *Free Churches, Religious Minorities and Dictatorships in Europe in the 20th Century* [*Szabadegyházak, vallási kisebbségek és a diktatúrák Európában a 20. században*], edited by Daniel Heinz, Zoltán Rajki and Ervin Simon, 72–81. Budapest and Friedensau: Gondolat Kiadó – Historisches Archiv der Siebenten-Tags-Adventisten in Europa – Kisegyház-kutató Egyesület.

Dirksen, Hans Hermann. 2002. “Jehovah’s Witnesses under Communist Regimes.” *Religion, State & Society* (3): 229–38.

“The Fundamental Issues of the Cooperation of the State and the Churches, 10 June 1958” [“Az állam és az egyházak közötti együttműködés elvi alapjai]. 10 June 1958.”]. 2005. In: *State, Churches and Religious Practices in Hungary, 1790–2005* Vol. 1–2. [*Állam, egyházak, vallásgyakorlás Magyarországon, 1790–2005 vol. 1–2*], edited by Margit Balogh and Jenő Gergely, 1003–4. Budapest: História.

Gergely, Ferenc. 2012. “The Relationship of the Community of Jehovah’s Witnesses and the Party State, 1950–1970” [“A Jehova Tanúi közösség és a pártállam viszonya (1950–1970)”]. *Egyháztörténeti Szemle* 13 (3): 94–107.

Gyarmati, György. 2007. “Church, Many Systems and the Historical Time from the Perspective of 20th Century Hungarian Church History” [“Egyház, sok rendszer és a történelmi idő a 20. századi magyar egyháztörténet nézőpontjából”]. In: *New Approaches to the Hungarian Catholic Church History after World War II* [*Az 1945 utáni magyar katolikus egyháztörténet új megközelítései*], edited by Szabolcs Varga and Lázár Vértesi, 20–39. Pécs: PHF Pécsi Egyháztörténeti Intézet.

Köbel, Szilvia. 2005. *“Divide and Rule!” The Political, Legal and Administrative Relationship of the State and the Churches in Hungary, 1945–1989* [*“Oszd meg és uralkodj!” Az állam és az egyházak politikai, jogi és igazgatási kapcsolatai Magyarországon, 1945–1989*]. Budapest: Rejtjel Kiadó.

Szita, Szabolcs. 2017. “The Jehovah’s Witnesses’ Church during World War II” [“A Jehova Tanúi Egyház a második világháború idején (1939–1945)”]. In: *The History of the Hungarian Jehovah’s Witnesses’ Church from the Beginning to the Present Day* [*A Magyarországi Jehova Tanúi Egyház története a kezdetektől napjainkig*], edited by Csaba Fazekas, Attila Jakab, Éva Petrás, and Szabolcs Szita, 165–201. Budapest: Gondolat Kiadó.

Part II

Anti-religious operations

6 Soviet state security and the Cold War

Repression and agent infiltration of the Jehovah's Witnesses in the Moldavian SSR, 1944 to late 1950s

Igor Caşu

Introduction

The Soviet state although it perceived all religions as competing ideologies and a threat to the success of the Soviet project, in reality it promoted a differentiated policy towards various religious groups. While Eastern Orthodox Christians were also widely persecuted, in comparison with other denominations they were treated much more favourably. The Orthodox Church seemed less likely to embrace a radical stance against the regime as historically it had been more inclined to collaborate and cohabit with the political authorities. In contrast, denominations such as the Jehovah Witnesses (hereafter JWs), which were considered worldwide to be a radical religious group, had a history of defying political regimes and power. For the Soviets, their principled non-participation in social and political life and their rejection of military service were among the most disturbing and unacceptable aspects of the religion. Another reason JWs were particularly targeted, especially in the early 1950s – but not in 1939–41 – pertained to the new international situation, i.e. the Cold War. The JWs in the Soviet Union were part of an international network based in the United States (Brooklyn, New York), the main enemy of the post-war Soviet Union until its demise in 1991 (see also Pintilescu and Petrás, this volume). For these reasons, JWs were amongst the most repressed and were the only religious group subject to mass deportations to the Gulag. This chapter, however, based on newly available archival material, highlights another aspect of the repression of the JWs. Starting before the mass deportation in the early 1950s and continuing up to late the 1950s, after their return from Gulag (and later, but that is beyond the scope of this chapter), JWs in Soviet Moldavia were subject to heavy infiltration of their networks by state security organs. This strategy of infiltration resembles in some ways the methods used by Soviet security organs against armed anti-Soviet insurgents in regions such as Western Ukraine and the Baltics. Although JW's resistance to the Soviet regime was very determined and radical, it did not entail armed resistance. In some cases, there is evidence that JWs owned guns and were sentenced for that (ASISRM-KGB, 825, 33) but JWs did not embark on violent resistance instead pursuing peaceful methods. At the same time, as I will argue, apparently paradoxically, the JW's staunch resistance to Communism as an ideology and to the political regime was paralleled by a sense of resignation and passivity, and sometimes with a pragmatism well suited to Cold War realities. Structural factors played a key role in the unleashing of repression against groups perceived as a threat in the new international context after WWII but the way in which the JWs responded to state terror reveals important aspects of their agency during this period.

Religion and the state in Bessarabia before 1940

From the second half of the fourteenth century until early 1812, when it was annexed by the Russian Empire, Bessarabia constituted the eastern part of the Moldavian Principality. The majority population was Romanian and belonged to the Eastern Orthodox Church. From the mid-fifteenth century, Moldavia was a vassal of the Ottoman Empire, however, unlike the territories to the south of the Danube which was under direct Ottoman rule, the Turks did not have the right to build mosques on the territory of Moldavia (or the other Romanian Principality, Wallachia). Only in some directly controlled areas, called *rayas*, where the Turks set up military garrisons, such as at Cetatea Albă (Akkerman), Bender (Tighina) and Hotin, were Muslim religious buildings erected. Otherwise, especially in the ethnically diverse urban areas, the other religious communities in the Principality of Moldavia consisted of Roman Catholics, Gregorian Armenians, and the Mosaic Jews.

From the late eighteenth century, the Russian Empire claimed the status of protector of the Orthodox Christian peoples under Ottoman rule and the annexation of Bessarabia by Russia in 1812 was justified on this basis. Bessarabia, especially the southern part which was inhabited prior to the annexation by Crimean Tartars, was heavily colonized with Protestant Germans and Orthodox Gagauz (Turkish-speaking Orthodox Christians) and Bulgarians from the Balkans brought in by the Russians. According to the first imperial census of 1897, the main religious groups in Tsarist Bessarabia were Orthodox (82.7%; almost all of whom were Romanians, Ukrainians, Russians, Gagauz and Bulgarians), followed by Mosaic Jews (11.8%), Protestant Germans (2.8%), Old Believers (1.47%, Russians), Gregorian Armenians (0.12%) and Catholic Armenians (0.01%) (Berg 1923, 11).

In the interwar period, when Bessarabia was part of Romanian Kingdom, the religious composition of the local population remained almost the same as in the late Tsarist period except for the arrival of a number of new religious communities, amongst them the Jehovah's Witnesses. Before 1917, when they were known as Bible Students, and they had expanded into Bessarabia and other Western Tsarist gubernias. Their leader, Charles Taze Russell visited Chișinău (then known as Kishinev) in 1891 and concluded that there was "no opening or readiness for the truth in Russia." This proved to be the case even after 1905 when Tsar Nicholas II granted legal status to many religious denominations (Baran 2014, 15–16).

In interwar Bessarabia, as in the whole of Romania, the Orthodox Church enjoyed a favoured status in relation to other Christian and non-Christian denominations. Moreover, some mainstream intellectuals such as Nae Ionescu and Nichifor Crainic propagated the idea that an authentic ethnic Romanian should belong to the Orthodox faith (Volovici, 1991). In other words, religion was equated with ethno-national identity and belonging. Romania was not alone in this respect in this period as many other European nations adopted similar ideological positions. For example, in countries such as Poland, Spain, and Ireland, Catholicism was considered the cornerstone of their national identity and received special constitutional status. "Orthodox equals Romanian" thus became the ideological underpinning of the toleration of the other beliefs and religions, and sometimes resulted in the adoption of fierce measures against them.

Perhaps partly as a consequence of the growing dissatisfaction in the new Romanian provinces with the activity of the Romanian Orthodox Church and the new heavily centralized state system that was being introduced on the French model, the religious message spread by JWs in Romania seemed to have more appeal in the Eastern provinces of Bessarabia and Bukovina and later in Transylvania. In the 1936 annual report on the activities of Jehovah's Witnesses worldwide, it was mentioned that "in no part of the earth do the brethren work with greater difficulties than in Romania" (Baran 2014, 24; see also Pintilescu, this volume), although in Poland their fate was not better either, perhaps even worse. In 1933 alone, roughly 100 incidents of state interference in preaching works were reported and 41 cases of mob violence. Intolerance towards other religions in Romania intensified in the late 1930s as King Carol II instituted his personal dictatorship. Prior to 1938, the year when the royal dictatorship was established, there had been discrimination and repressions employed against a range of groups but especially JWs and Inochentists (see Kapaló 2019), an autochthonous Orthodox Christian dissent movement born during the Tsarist Empire among the Romanian speaking population. The same was true for Orthodox Christians who refused to accept the reform of the religious calendar instituted by the state (ANRM, 738, 1, 6835, 6836, 6577, 6802). However, from 1938 Christian denominations perceived as a threat to the national Orthodox community were entirely prohibited. The Jehovah's Witnesses office in Bucharest was shut down and their leaders were arrested (Baran 2014, 23–4). During the Second World War, the persecution of various evangelical denominations as well as JWs and Inochentists expanded as many of them refused the military draft. In several instances, members of the so-called neo-protestant groups received harsh sentences of up to 25 years in prison of labour camps (see Kapaló 2019, 189–210). For the wartime regime of Marshall Antonescu, Romania's wartime dictator, issues of religion and national identity also became closely linked to national security (ACNSAS, P122087, I, 41–41 verso).

Religion in Soviet Moldavia, 1940–41 and 1944–49

Bessarabia was occupied by the Red Army on June 28, 1940. In the first year of the Soviet occupation, the policy towards religion was rather ambiguous. The majority of the Orthodox Churches were allowed to continue to function on condition that their priests agreed to pay a special tax for religious services. The Chişinău Cathedral, for instance, paid an annual tax of 240,000 rubles, an exorbitant sum for that period. The liturgy in Old Slavonic was reintroduced to Orthodox Churches as was the old Church calendar, which had been changed by the Romanian Orthodox Church and was prohibited in the interwar period by the Romanian authorities (see Kapaló, this volume). Of the 1090 Orthodox churches and 28 monasteries existing in June 1940, only 898 were found by the Romanian administration in a relatively normal state in summer 1941 when Romanian forces reoccupied Bessarabia, while 27 had been converted into warehouses or other activities (Caşu 2000, 35).

During the Second World War, the German authorities reopened thousands of churches that had been closed by the Bolshevik regime in the previous two decades. The Nazis tried thus to capitalize on the deep discontent existing in the USSR among Russians and non-Russians alike in regard to religion and other unpopular policies. In turn, Stalin decided to relax the restrictions towards the functioning of the Orthodox churches in the unoccupied areas and tried to instrumentalize religion and other Russian national symbols (such as Tsarist military commanders like Kutuzov and Suvorov) in order to mobilize the people for the war effort. In 1943, the Russian Orthodox Patriarchate was reestablished. Amongst the population, there was hope that after the war the Soviet state would relax even more its religious policy and even disband the kolkhozes. These hopes were reflected in the meetings of the representatives of the Communist Party of Moldavia with Bessarabian draftees in the summer of 1944. They complained to the new authorities, amongst other things, about not being allowed to pray and asked for newspapers and books in their mother tongue, Romanian, while serving in the Red Army (AOSPRM, F. 51, inv. 2, d. 217, ff. 34–5.). There is no evidence that these requests were met, but these details give us a window on the perceptions and expectations of ordinary Bessarabians who believed they were entitled to religious rights.

Reports of the party institutions and state security organs show that in 1944 and immediately after the war the Soviet authorities were particularly aware of religious allegiance of Bessarabians, no matter the denomination. If in the other territories the Soviets seemed to favor Orthodox believers, in Bessarabia the Orthodox Church was suspected of collaboration with the Romanian wartime authorities and their linguistic Romanianization drive. This suspicion and hatred spread to all Christian denominations regardless of whether they had been persecuted by Romanian authorities previously. This attitude represented an exception because usually the Soviets automatically considered groups that had suffered injustices or repression on the part of their political enemies to be potential allies. The Soviets were especially suspicious of religious groups that had created and maintained clandestine networks during Romanian rule, which was the case with regards to the Inochentists (see Kapaló 2019). Even though they had been repressed in the interwar and during the war by the Romanian authorities, the Inochentists were perceived as one of the most important threats to the regime. Without any evidence, the NKVD and NKGB suspected the Inochentists of being collaborators with the German and Romanian secret services and that they were acting as anti-Soviet agents (ASISRM-KGB, Fond Delo s direktivami za 1944, inv. 6, d. 1, ff. 61–3). At this point in 1944, the Jehovah's Witnesses were not yet on the radar of the Soviet security organs, but in a short while, they too would be included in the list of priority threats to be dealt with.

We can first trace the JWs in the archival record of the state security organs in 1946. A report sent on October 23 of that year by Iosif Mordovets, the minister of State Security (MGB) of Moldavian SSR, to Fyodor Butov, the chief of the Bureau of the All-Union Central Committee of the Communist (Bolshevik) Party in Moldavia, contains an important section related to the main religious groups operating in the immediate post-war years on the historical territory of Bessarabia, including the so-called "sects." Among the officially registered sects, he lists the Baptists (500 believers, 88 presbyters, and 88 praying houses); the Adventists (500 believers, 9 presbyters) and the Molokans (500 believers and 5 presbyters). But not all believers were officially registered. Among those that did not have legal status were the Jehovah's Witnesses and the Inochentists (Pasat 2009, 199–200). In the subsequent years, the activity of all Christian and non-Christian denominations would be substantially curtailed using legal, semi-legal and illegal methods. But only in regard to the Jehovah's Witnesses did the Soviet state resort to the dramatic wholesale deportation of a religious group. The Inochentists, who were also perceived as a high threat, were not subjected to the same treatment for reasons that remain unclear.

The structure of Soviet state security apparatus in Moldavian SSR

The state security organs of the Soviet Union that carried out the mass repression of JWs have a complex institutional history having changed several times not only in name, but also in structure. Soon after the Soviet takeover of Bessarabia, now named the Moldavian SSR, in March 1946, the NKGB[1] (Narodnyi kommissariat gossudarstvennoj bezopasnosti) was renamed MGB (Ministerstvo gosudarstvennoy bezopasnosti), as part of the renaming of all the *narkomats* in ministries. Under the name MGB it functioned until 1953 – the main period covered in this chapter – so it would be useful to give a short overview of the structure of MGB of Moldavian SSR in order to understand better how repression and agent infiltration were organized against the JWs.

As of March 1946, when it was created, the MGB of MSSR had several departments (*otdely*) which were divided in units (*otdeleniia*). The first department dealt with gathering intelligence (*razvedyvatel'nyi otdel*) and was divided in three units, the first one specializing on Romania, the second one on Moldavian and Jewish emigration abroad and the third one was responsible for communication (*otdel svyazy*). The second department focused on counterintelligence and was divided in three units as follows: Great Britain, USA, Europe and Asia; former Nazi allies; the third unit dealt with counterintelligence among repatriated Soviet citizens – most of whom had been repatriated forcefully – after the WWII. The fourth department had as part of its responsibilities the task of carrying out investigations, one unit dealing with agents sent by the intelligence services of foreign countries and by the anti-Soviet organizations of the émigrés circles and the second one with traitors to the Fatherland, active German and Romanian collaborators as well as state criminals escaped from prisons and camps. The fifth department, the operational one, dealt directly with one of the main issues of this chapter: agent infiltration (first unit), but in the spring of 1946 it had only one person in the unit, Piotr Iosifovich Mordovets, the son of the minister of MGB of MSSR, Iosif Lavrentievich Mordovets. Other duties covered by the fifth department were external surveillance (second unit), verification of signals and suspected persons (third unit) and verification of persons having access to state secrets and countering foreign agents from penetrating institutions of importance for state security (forth unit); and identification of authors of anti-Soviet leaflets and documents (fifth unit) (ASISRM-KGB, Sovershenno sekretnye prikazy NKGB-MGB MSSR za 1946 g., 166–71). The next department in the official structure of the MGB of MSSR was department "O" dealing with religious groups, namely with priests (*tserkovniki*) of legally accepted religious denominations (first unit), mostly Orthodox Christian; and anti-Soviet elements amongst sectants, Jewish spiritual leaders (*dukhovenstvo*) and Zionists (second unit) (ASISRM-KGB, Sovershenno sekretnye prikazy NKGB-MGB MSSR za 1946 g., 172–94).[2] According to the names, the absolute majority of the cadres of the MGB of MSSR were Russians, Ukrainians and Jews. Out of 610 members of the cadres, only 15 have Moldavian/Romanian names, but one can assume the majority of them are from the interwar MASSR, a part of Ukraine until 1940, i.e., were not fluent in Romanian since the national elites or those speaking in Moldavian/Romanian were executed during the Great Terror of 1937–38 (Caşu 2015, 95–107). The structure of the MGB at the All-Union level of the USSR was only slightly different (Directorates or *Upravlenie* instead of departments) but covered more types of activity, like counter-terrorism (department "T"); fabrication and expertise of documents (department "D"); diversions and intelligence (department "DR") (Kokurin & Petrov 1997, 34–40).

Deportation of Jehovah's Witnesses (1951)

The mass deportations of social and ethnic categories to Siberia and other inhospitable areas of the Soviet Union was a ubiquitous element of Sovietization in the Western newly re-annexed territories after 1944 ('Ribbentrop-Molotov areas' to use Timothy Snyder's terminology). In Western Ukraine and the Baltic States where the anti-Soviet resistance was more pronounced, Moscow organized several deportations in 1948–49. In the Moldavian SSR, where armed resistance was much less evident, the regime organized only one mass deportation. The deportation of July 1949, comprising of 35,796 persons in total, was aimed at the elimination of all actual or potential opponents of the collectivization of agriculture. It thus only included a limited number of categories other than kulaks, i.e. the supposed well-to-do peasants. The deportation of specific religious groups was not a target of that mass operation. Two years later, however, in 1951, it organized a mass deportation aimed solely at the Jehovah's Witnesses.

As already mentioned, all religious organizations were viewed as a threat to Soviet power, with Jehovah's Witnesses being considered as the most dangerous. This was partly because their headquarters were in the United States and as such their activities were considered completely opposed to the Socialist way of life and therefore, involved security threats. According to a document dated March 10, 1951, signed by Lieutenant Colonel Mochyalov, the head of the fifth section of the Soviet MGB, who had come to Chişinău on a special mission, Jehovah's Witnesses were labelled as highly dangerous for the Soviet regime because they a) "were spreading provocative fabrication about the inevitable death of Soviet power and the establishment of theocratic rule"; b) "refusal to comply with state duties connected to the defense of the country"; c) "anti-Soviet agitation against the collectivization of the agriculture"; d) "refusal to participate in the elections of the representatives of the power and agitation among the youth against joining social-political organizations." Mochyalov's report also mentions the fact that Jehovah's Witnesses were organizing hostile activities such as the organization of illegal meetings and the mass distribution of hand-written leaflets and literature of American origin (ASISRM–KGB, *Delo po operatsii Sever*, ff. 1–4). Based on these perceived threats, one can say that the decision to deport Jehovah Witnesses through a special mass operation was reached based on a combination of internal and external factors. With regards to the most pressing internal factor, they were the most vocal opponents of the collectivization of agriculture recently completed (1949–50), which formed the central element of the Sovietization of the countryside and thus could not be put into question, criticized or undone. As to the external factor, the deportation of the Jehovah's Witnesses is circumscribed in the Cold War context when all things connected with the West, and especially America, were perceived as a threat to state security. In some way, the deportation of the Jehovah's Witnesses was anticipated by the campaign against Western influence in literature, arts, and science launched in 1946–47 by Andrei Zhdanov (thus known as Zhdanovshchina). In reality, we now know that this campaign was initiated by Stalin himself and targeted especially Soviet Jews, perceived as American underlings after the creation of the state of Israel (Gorlizki & Khlevniuk 2004, 31–8).

The deportation of Jehovah's Witnesses from the Moldavian SSR was part of a larger-scale operation, which targeted the same religious group in several western regions, in particular, all the territories occupied by the USSR under the secret additional Protocol to the Ribbentrop-Molotov Pact of August 23, 1939: Bessarabia, Northern Bucovina, Western Ukraine, Western Belarus, Estonia, Latvia and Lithuania.[3] The head of the Soviet MGB, Viktor Abakumov, launched the deportation idea in a letter sent to Stalin on February 19, 1950. The operation was set for March–April 1951. Initially, it was planned to deport 8,576 people from 5 Union Republics, including 1,675 people or 670 families from the MSSR. Subsequently, the number of people due to be deported from the MSSR amounted to 2,480 or 700 families (Pasat 1994, 613; ASISRM–KGB, *Delo po operatsii Sever*, ff. 1–4).

The deportation operation started at 4 am on April 1, 1951 and ended officially on the same day at 8 pm. The organization of the deportation followed the previous Soviet model: representatives of the Soviet MGB were sent to coordinate the development of the deportation operation; 546 field officers and 1,127 officers and servicemen of the Moldavian MGB, 275 MVD (civil police or militia) officers and servicemen and 750 party and Soviet activists were mobilized (Pasat 1994, 641). Just as in the 1949 operation, some people included in the list learned about the deportation and managed to hide. Presently, we know of seven such people as they have been identified by historian Nicolae Fuştei on the basis of files of the Moldavian Interior Ministry (Fuştei 2013, 73–4). As in the previous mass deportations of mid-June 1941 and early July 1949, deportees were subjected to inhuman treatment, the more so as there were 106 people aged less than one-year, old people aged about 90 and gravely ill people. Despite the tragedy, members of the deported families displayed solidarity. For certain reasons, some members of the JWs were on the list whereas others were not and the latter demanded that they too are deported to Siberia together with their loved ones. This was the case of Natalia Curtis, for instance, from Lipcani district, who insisted on being allowed to leave together with her sister Olga Balan who was gravely ill. The wife of Iacov Cislinschi, Claudia, followed her husband too (Fuştei 2013, 75).

According to some data of the Moldavian State Security Ministry, 723 families or 2,617 people self-identifying as Jehovah's Witnesses were arrested and deported during Operation North (Pasat 1994, 635). Yet, data from the archive of the Moldavian Interior Ministry shows that the number of those deported on 1–2 April 1951 was higher, reaching 2,724 people, 93 people more than the State Security Agency reported (Fuştei 2013, 77). A total of 16,255 people were deported on those days from all the regions that the USSR annexed after 1944 – the Baltic States, Western Ukraine, Western Belarus, Northern Bucovina and the ex-Bessarabian part of the MSSR (Tsarevskaia-Dyakina, 2004, vol. 5, 665). Repressions against neo-protestants, mainly Jehovah's Witnesses continued in the following years, including after Stalin's death (Caşu 2011).

The legal basis of mass deportation of Jehovah's Witnesses vs. individual sentencing

The deportation of Jehovah's Witnesses in 1951 from former Ribbentrop-Molotov territories, including Moldavian SSR, had the same legal basis as other mass deportations in the post-1944 period. The initiative came formally from Viktor Abakumov, the All-Union minister of State Security (MGB) who sent a memo to Stalin on February 19, 1951. It mentioned that since 1947, the Soviet political police had identified and liquidated several anti-Soviet organizations and groups of illegal religious denomination (labelled "sect" in the document) of Jehovah's Witnesses that were very active in Western areas of Ukraine, Belorussia, Moldavia, and the Baltic republics. In this period, 1048 leaders and active members of Jehovah's Witnesses were arrested, five clandestine printing presses were closed, as well as 35 leaflets, brochures, journals and other JW's literature being confiscated. Nevertheless, as noted already above, Abakumov argued that this religious group had intensified its proselytism and anti-Soviet activities, agitating against the collectivization of agriculture, military service and preaching the coming of theocratic rule. Thus, he suggested the deportation of 8576 persons (making 3048 families) as follows: from Ukrainian SSR – 6140 persons (2020 families); from Belorussian SSR – 394 persons (153 families); from Moldavian SSR – 1675 persons (670 families); Latvian SSR – 52 persons (27 families); Lithuanian SSR – 76 persons (48 families) and from Estonian SSR – 250 persons (130 families). Abakumov informed Stalin that the first secretaries of these six republics were consulted in this regard and all of them, including Leonid Brezhnev, the party boss in Soviet Moldavia and future Secretary General of CPSU, agreed to the deportation of Jehovah's Witnesses (Pasat 1994, 612–13).

On the basis of Abakumov's memo, the Council of Ministers of the USSR issued a special decision the same month (the document has no exact date, but the month and year are mentioned as February 1951). The Council of Ministers, in turn, ordered the MGB to formalize the deportation through the decision of the Special Board (*Osoboe Soveshchanie*) of the MGB (Pasat 1994, 614–15). The later, along with the infamous Troika, was the supreme extrajudicial organ of the Soviet political police that sent to deportation or death thousands of Soviet citizens based on loosely defined political crimes (Shearer 2009, 320–70). Thus, the deportation of Jehovah's Witnesses was illegal according to the Soviet legislation in force at that time.

In comparison, the condemnation of individual members of the Jehovah's Witnesses to various terms in prison or in special labor correction camps before and after the deportation of 1951 was made according to the Criminal Code of the Soviet republics. Before 1953, members of Jehovah's Witnesses were condemned to up to 25 years in prison according to article 54-10 part 2 and 54-11 of the Criminal Code of the Ukrainian SSR (the Moldavian SSR did not have its own Criminal Code until 1961). The first part of the 54-10 article referred to "propaganda and agitation containing an appeal to overthrow or weaken Soviet power" as well as "distributing and manufacturing and storing literature of the same content." The second part of article 54-10 instead referred to the same crime but in a mass setting: "the same actions that lead to mass disturbances or with the use of religious or national prejudices of the masses, or in a military setting, or in areas declared martial law, entail – social protection measures," i.e. execution or imprisonment of at least 3 years. The social protection measures were used largely in the 1930s and especially during the Great Terror (or Great Purges) of 1937–38, but the concept was pre-Soviet and Western in origin (Hoffmann 2011, 176). Article 54-11, in turn, referred to the same crimes but involving participation in an organization that aimed at overthrowing the Soviet regime (ASISRM-KGB, file 017732, 257–258; file 020201, 292–8).

Agent infiltration of Jehovah's Witnesses organizations

One of the least known episodes connected to the mass deportation of Jehovah's Witnesses in 1951, and to the individual condemnations before and after that year, is related to the role that agents of the state security organs played in these operations. As mentioned above, Operation North involved the mass deportation of 723 families or 2,617 people. For reasons we do not know exactly, numerous other members of the Jehovah's Witnesses remained in the Moldavian SSR. A year after the April 1, 1951, deportation, a report of the MGB of the Moldavian SSR from April 10, 1952, mentioned that there were at that time 1053 persons or 643 families of Jehovah's Witnesses living especially in the northern district of the Republic. At the same time, the report mentioned the existence of at least 34 agents recruited from among the Jehovah's Witnesses while another 114 persons were in the process of being recruited (ASISRM-KGB, file 825, 7–8). This data was not previously known, as access to these secret files has only recently been granted. For understandable reasons, I cannot disclose the names of the agents. What is significant about this new information is that it adds to our understanding of the context and the way in which the Soviet political police tried to infiltrate and undermine the Jehovah's Witnesses clandestine networks in Soviet Moldavia.

The agents were deployed by the MGB several weeks before Operation North. The aim was to find out about the *état d'esprit* of JWs and if they knew or suspected about their coming fate. According to the reports sent to MGB by the agents infiltrated in the JWs circles, some of them suspected that something was going on that could lead to their deportation. On March 16, 1951, about two weeks before the actual deportation, the agent "Sedoy" reported that in the village of Volodeni, Edineţ district a meeting was organized of the leaders of the JWs. Among other issues discussed was the participation of local Soviet activists and agitators at a meeting in the neighbouring village of Brânzeni, together with others from several villages. This made many leaders JWs suspect that something was going on and an imminent deportation like the one in 1949 was about to happen. The reason for believing in the repetition of 1949, according to the same report, was the fact that before the previous mass deportation the activists and agitators also met late in the night to get instruction how to proceed. Even though the deportation did not follow the same night, a lot of JWs thought that it would happen soon and started to prepare for. A certain Parascovia Turic, for instance, a member of JWs, decided to sell her house for 5,000 rubles to a local resident Cevaciuc Andrei, while another JW intended to sell her cow. The later was not succeesful, reported agent "Sedoy," but she did not give up, adding that "even if they will deport us, at least I will have some money [to live on for a while]" (ASISRM–KGB, *Delo po operatsii Sever*, f. 26). The same source informed the Soviet political police that as the rumors about the coming deportation were not confirmed immediately, there were no more discussions about it (ASISRM–KGB, *Delo po operatsii Sever*, f. 26). In other words, as of March 25, 1951, when the report was signed, the local members of JWs did not think the deportation was imminent, which in itself could be counted as a success of the disinformation campaign led by the MGB. As in previous mass operations, the unpreparedness of the victims was among the main guarantees of a successful deportation.

In order to have credible information, the MGB recruited informers to report on the same "objects." Agent "Vladimir" informed the Soviet political police on the state of mind of JWs residents of Volodeni in the same timeframe. According to him, the local members of the JWs expected the deportation to take place in the night of 16th to 17th of March as well. But in contrast to what agent "Sedoy" reported, "Vladimir" insisted on the fact that JWs are prepared for the deportation to take place soon. The later seemed to be more informed as he succeeded in being trusted by the local JW community to the degree that he was allowed to attend their clandestine meetings. One of the leaders of the JWs in Volodeni, Vasile Adamciuc, declared at one of these meetings held on March 22, 1951, that the MGB will arrest the older members of their religious group and thus the younger ones should prepare to take the lead. Adamciuc added also that later on the younger leaders will be identified by "Satana" and their arrest will be imminent too, but meanwhile they should do their duty in spreading the Word of God. One can notice a level of resignation in these declarations, but a sort of pragmatism as well. According to agent "Vladimir," another leader of the local JWs said that the deportation is not only expected, but it is also desired because a war will break out soon and the deportees will not be recruited into the Soviet Army. Consequently, members of JW will have more chance of survival in the Gulag if a war is going to come. Another important detail from agent Vladimir's report is that he succeeded in uncovering who the source was in the local Soviet institutions who informed the JWs. Isai Rotari, the deputy chairman of the village Soviet, was the one who pointed to the fact of the meeting of activists and agitators from several villages that took place in Brânzeni on March 16 late in the night (ASISRM–KGB, *Delo po operatsii Sever*, 27).

The infiltration of the agents after 1951 was not a new practice used by the Soviet political police in regard to the Jehovah's Witnesses and other so-called dangerous religious and political groups (AOSPRM, F. 51, inv. 13, d. 349, f. 14–16, 38). After WWII, however, the practice of infiltration by agents inside these real or perceived anti-Soviet elements is used on a much larger scale. This explains, if only partially, why more than 1,000 members of the Jehovah's Witnesses may have been left in Moldavia after the deportation. Those remaining were to be controlled through the same method used mainly in the fight against the armed anti-Soviet resistance groups in Western Ukraine and the Baltic States, especially Lithuania, namely agent infiltration (Statiev 2010, 233–8; Tannberg 2010, 63–80; Anušauskas 2006, 23–45, 63–70). The aim of this kind of operation was not to destroy the whole organization but to bring it under the control of the state security organs. Instead of deportation and reeducation through hard labour in Siberia, it seems to have been considered more appropriate to use softer methods on the spot in order to convince members of this radical religious group to moderate their beliefs, participate in elections, and engage in other day-to-day aspects of social and political life as well as accepting military service in the Soviet Army.

At the same time, the documents show that the MGB was observing closely the correspondence between JWs forcefully removed to Siberia and those remaining in Moldavian SSR. The practice was already in place at least one year before the mass deportation of JWs to Siberia. This is because prior to (and following) Operation North in April 1951 there had been individual removals of JWs members to the Gulag. The correspondence intercepted by the authorities was thus another source of information about the state of mind of members of JWs, how they perceived their fate and their attitude towards the Soviet regime (ASISRM-KGB, file 825, f. 25, 27–8). Soviet monitoring and control of the correspondence resembles the Tsarist-era practice of perlustration, but in comparison it looks less systematic and professional (Daly 2004, 4, 73, 104; Ruud & Stepanov 1999, 71–9). This is true at least in relation to the way the Soviet political police handled the letters sent by members of the Moldavian community of JWs back and forth.

In several letters sent from Siberia to the JW center in the Moldavian SSR, the deported members of the community asked for "spiritual food," implying religious literature. Initially the language of the literature asked for was Romanian (called Moldavian by the Soviet officials), but later on the leaders of Moldavian JWs settled in Tyumen and Tomsk regions of Russia were calling for religious literature in Russian, but also in Lithuanian. These details imply that Moldavian members of the JW community were targeting in their proselytism the local Russian population and were eager to help their religious brethren from Lithuania to get "spiritual food" in their mother tongue. In order to keep a close eye on the JWs in the cold territories of resettlement, the Soviet political police also used the strategy of agent infiltration strategy there too (ASISRM-KGB, file 825, f. 33–4, 36). It is not clear if the agents were insiders in the JWs community or recruited specifically to penetrate into their ranks. Whichever it was, employing agents within the JWs community in Siberia, the Soviet political police were able to find out details that could not be uncovered in the correspondence sent through the official post. Being aware of the perlustration practice, the letters written by members of the JWs community tended to use more and more a sophisticated codified language that created headaches for the Soviet authorities when trying to decipher it (ASISRM-KGB, file 825, f. 25–7).

In mid-1950s, as part of the broader, but limited, process of so-called De-Stalinization, the majority of the deported persons in USSR as a whole and from Moldavian SSR in particular started to return to their homelands. By 1960, it was reported that about 80 per cent of the former deportees had returned from Gulag and special settlements. In many cases however they could not resettle again in their home localities due to the fact their properties, including houses, were nationalized and distributed to the new Soviet elites, both locals and those sent from other parts of the Soviet Union. The prohibition of return to their original domiciles was conceived to avoid conflicts over property rights, but also as a form of punishment. Moreover, it was legally binding and the decrees of release from places of deportation did not stipulate the right of the returnees to reside in their former villages and cities (Cașu 2015, 194). These circumstances were prone to create complications for the regime and thus the most dangerous groups of Gulag returnees among them the JWs were to be observed closely. One way to do that, if not the main one, was to keep existing agents within JWs ranks and increase their numbers. In time, this new policy started to show results. In Soviet Moldavia, for instance, 200 members of the Jehovah's Witnesses took part in the 1959 election to the Supreme Soviet of the Republic (Pasat, 1994, 655). It is also important to note that by infiltrating agents in the Soviet branches of the JW's organization the MGB, and after 1954 the KGB, also attempted to infiltrate the European and American centers. At a certain moment, such attempts were made through the German and Finish organizations of the Jehovah's Witnesses (ASISRM-KGB, file 825, 59). This latter detail suggests that the policy of not totally pacifying or liquidating the influence of JW's, and instead infiltrating massively its ranks, was not only an alternative to the brutal deportation, but also a strategy aimed at adapting to the context of the Cold War and the reality that if the external influence and threat could not be eliminated, it should, and could, be controlled instead. This was certainly more the case after the death of Stalin and the condemnation of mass terror campaigns perpetrated by his regime which had lasted three decades (and had been initiated by his predecessor and teacher, Lenin). Due to these policy changes in the mid-1950s, the state security experts in Moscow were obliged to modify and modernize their methods while pursuing the same goal and ideological commandments. Otherwise, fighting against the JWs with traditional methods would not bring the desired results: by deporting their most active members to Siberia the organization had, in fact, became stronger and had started to spread its beliefs in areas where they had not been known previously (Fuștei 2013, 78).

Conclusion

The JW's activities in Bessarabia started in the mid-1920s when the region was a part of the Greater Romania. In interwar Romania, the position of the Orthodox Church was supported openly by the state and by mainstream intellectuals. Moreover, Orthodoxy was considered synonymous with Romanian identity (a rather totalitarian understanding of national identity). In 1938 when Carol II established his royal dictatorship, JW's activity was forbidden. But the JWs not only survived in Bessarabia through the WWII, but also their activity had even intensified after the second takeover of the province by the Soviets in 1944. The reports of the Soviet political police and security organs in the immediate post-war years single out the Inochentists (see Lisnic and Kapaló, this volume) and JW's as the most dangerous religious groups because of their highly clandestine *modus operandi*. Acting in this way was enough of a motive for the Soviet regime to suspect these groups of being under foreign and hostile influence and thus posing a threat to the stability of the regime. Recent scholarship suggests that the members of the communist party in the Soviet Union under Lenin and Stalin could be understood better if they are considered as "millenarian sectarians preparing for the apocalypse" (Slezkine, 2017, XII). This idea is not new (Voegelin 1938) but it could help us understand better the intolerance and determination with which the Soviet regime fought against religious groups that shared a very strong sense of identity and fanaticism.

At the end of the day, the JW were the only religious denomination, a small minority in comparison with other religious groups, that were deported *en masse* to Siberia (to the Tomsk and Irkutsk regions), in 1951. The decision to deport JW's from Soviet Moldavia and other Ribbentrop-Molotov territories can be explained by several factors: the Soviet regime perceived JW as a threat as they were very critical and extremely vocal in attacking the main pillars of the regime: the collectivization of the agriculture, service in the Soviet Army and participation in social-political organizations. Besides, they considered the state as a whole, and the Soviet system in particular, as a creation of Satan and thus doomed to disappear soon. The Soviets interpreted these millennial beliefs as a confirmation that the JWs were acting as agents of "imperialistic" America and in case of a nuclear war between East and West, they would sympathize with the enemy. Thus, the JWs were deported to Siberia. The decision to deport them was, however, technically illegal even according to Soviet legislation at that time as it was operated by an extra-judiciary organ within the Ministry of State Security (MGB).

In contrast to the illegal character of the mass operations, the individual condemnation of members of the JW organization was made in conformity with the Criminal Code (various parts of the article 54 in Ukrainian SSR corresponding to the article 58 of the RSFSR). What makes the case of the JWs very interesting, even after the unique move to deport them in 1951, was the Soviet regime's attempt to extend the tactics already used in the fight against armed anti-Soviet guerilla groups in Western Ukraine and the Baltic States, to this religious organization. The strategy of agent infiltration on a massive scale in order to undermine and disintegrate the religious networks from inside has only now come to light. As time has shown, this proved a more realistic and appropriate way of controlling and using the JWs. By infiltrating agents inside the Soviet JWs – including the higher levels of the organization – the Soviet political police and security organs also gained the possibility, as a second stage, to infiltrate their foreign centers. Last but not least, I argue here that state ideology played an important role in the repression against the so-called anti-Soviet elements, including religious groups, but that an appreciation of the local context and agency of religious groups is important as well. At the same time, Soviet concepts and practices of repression were predated by other political regimes including, to a certain extent, Tsarist Russia and interwar Romania.

Notes

1 Prior to this, between 1917 and 1934 state security police functioned as a separate institution under the name of CheKa until 1922 and then OGPU. In 1934, the later merged with the militia (civil or regular police) to create one institution, the infamous NKVD. In the wake of the German–Soviet war, in April 1941 the state security was recreated again as a separate institution under the name of NKGB. In July 1941, the unified NKVD has been reestablished for the next two years when in April 1943 Stalin decided to divide again political police from the civil one.

2 Other departments within the MGB of MSSR after the WWII and the begining of the Cold War were: investigation department; cadres' department; economic department; financial department; department "A" (archive, including maintaining a database of arrests and agents); department " B" (interception of phone conversations); department of military censorship; the so-called group " PK" (*proverka korrespondentsii* or perlustration); department of direction-finding stations (*pelengator*) and prison department (see ASISRM- KGB, Sovershenno sekretnye prikazy NKGB- MGB MSSR za 1946 g., 172–94)

3 Initially, Lithuania was not in the sphere of Soviet influence, but it was annexed to the USSR following an agreement between Moscow and Berlin on 28 September 1939.

Archival sources

Arhiva Consiliului Naţional pentru Studierea Ahivelor Securităţii [The Archives of the National Council for the Research of the Archives of Securitate] (ACNSAS), P122087

Arhiva Organizaţiilor Social-Politice a Republicii Moldova [Archive of the Social Political Organizations of the Republic of Moldova, Chişinău, Moldova] (AOSPRM), fond. 51

Arhiva Serviciului de Informaţii şi Securitate al Republicii Moldova, fostul KGB al RSSM [Archive of the Service for Information and Security of the Republic of Moldova, former KGB of MSSR] (ASISRM-KGB), *Delo po operatsii Sever* [Case of Operation North]; Fond Delo s direktivami za 1944 [Fond dealing with directives for 1944]; Sovershenno sekretnye prikazy NKGB-MGB MSSR za 1946 g. [Top Secret Orders of the NKGB-MGB MSSR for 1946]; file 825; file 017732; file 020201

Arhiva Naţională a Republicii Moldova [The Archive of the National Republic of Moldova] (ANRM); 738-1-6835; 738-1-6836; 738-1-6577; 738-1-6802

References

Anušauskas, Arvydas. 2006. *The Anti-Soviet Resistance in the Baltic States*. Vilnius: The Genocide and Resistance Museum.

Baran, Emily. 2014. *Dissent On the Margins: How Soviet Jehovah's Witnesses Defied Communism and Lived to Preach about it*. Oxford: Oxford University Press.

Berg, Lev. 1923. *Bessarabiia. Strana, Liudi, Khoziaystvo*, Petrograd: OGNI.

Caşu, Igor. 2000. "Nationalities Policy" In: Soviet Moldavia [*"Politica naţională" în Moldova Sovietică, 1940–1989*]. Chişinău: Cartdidact.

Caşu, Igor. 2011. "Soviet Power, the Power of Satan" ["Puterea sovietică – puterea Satanei"], in the Moldovan issue of the newspaper *Adevărul*, 3 November.

Caşu, Igor. 2015. "The Fate of Stalinist Victims in Moldavia after 1953: Amnesty, Pardon and the Long Road to Rehabilitation". In: *De-Stalinising Eastern Europe: The rehabilitation of Stalin's Victims after 1953*, edited by Kevin McDermott, Matthew Stibbe, 186–203. Houndmills, Basingstoke: Palgrave MacMillan.

Daly, Jonathan. 2004. *The Watchful State. Security Police and Opposition in Russia, 1905–1917*. DeKalb: Northern Illinois University Press.

Fuştei, Nicolae. 2013. *The Persecution of Religious Organization Jehovah's Witnesses: Operation "North" (1951) in Moldavian SSR* [*Persecutarea organizaţiei religioase "Martorii lui Iehova". Operaţia "Sever" (1951) în RSS Moldovenească*]. Chişinău: Cuvântul-ABC.

Gorlizki, Yoram & Khlevniuk, Oleg 2004. *Cold Peace. Stalin and the Soviet ruling Circle, 1945–1953*. Oxford: Oxford University Press.

Hoffmann, David L. 2011. *Cultivating the Masses. Modern State and Soviet Socialism, 1914–1939*. Ithaca and London: Cornell University Press.

Kapaló, James. 2019. *Inochentism and Orthodox Christianity: Religious Dissent in the Russian and Romanian Borderlands*. Abingdon and New York: Routledge.

Kokurin, Aleksandr I. & Nikita Petrov, eds. 1997. *Lubeanka. VChK-OGPU-NKVD-NKGB-MGB-MVD-KGB, 1917–1960*, Moscow: Fond Demokratiia.

Pasat, Valeriu (ed.). 1994. *Difficult Pages from the History of Moldova, 1940–1950* [*Trudnye stranitsy istorii Moldovy, 1940–1950-e gody*]. Moscow: Terra.

Pasat, Valeriu (ed.). 2009–2012. *Eastern Christianity in Moldavia: Power, Church, Believers, 1940–1991*, vols. 1–4 [*Pravoslavie v Moldavii. Vlast', Tserkov', Veruiushchie, 1940–1991*]. Moscow: ROSSPEN.

Ruud, Charles A. & Stepanov, Sergei A. 1999. *Fontanka* 16. *The Tsars' Secret Police*. Montreal: McGill-Queen's University Press.

Shearer, David R. 2009. *Policing Stalin's Socialism. Repression and Social Order in Soviet Union, 1924–1953*. New Haven: Yale University Press.

Slezkine, Yuri. 2017. *The House of Government: A Saga of the Russian Revolution*. Princeton, and Oxford: Princeton University Press.

Statiev, Alexander. 2010. *The Soviet Counterinsurgency in the Western Borderlands* Cambridge: Cambridge University Press.

Tannberg, Tõnu. 2010. *Politika Moskvy v Respublikakh Baltii v poslevoennye gody (1944–1956). Issledovaniia i dokymenty*. Moscow: ROSSPEN.

Tsarevskaia-Dyakina, Tatiana V. ed. 2004. *The History of Stalin's Gulag Vol. 5: Mass Repression* [*Istoria Stalinskogo Gulaga. Vol. 5: Massovye repressii*]. Moscow: ROSSPEN.

Voegelin, Eric. 1938. *Die politischen Religionen*. Stockholm: Bermann Fisher.

Volovici, Leon. 1991. *Nationalist Ideology and Antisemitism: The case of Romanian Intellectuals in the 1930's*. Oxford: Pergamon Press.

7 The secret police and the Marian apparition

Actions of the Polish Security Service against the miracle of Zabłudów in 1965

Maciej Krzywosz

Introduction

Although the communist system was imposed on Poland after World War II, various miraculous phenomena such as Marian apparitions and weeping images and the like continued to appear. This situation was a challenge for the atheist authorities, who tried to eliminate them as quickly as possible. Thus, they confiscated texts related to miracles, arrested their supporters and blocked roads to prevent pilgrims from reaching the sites of religious revelations. The secret police played an important role in these activities. This chapter describes the measures taken by the secret police to dismiss the 1965 Marian miracle of Zabłudów, a small town in the Podlasie region situated in north-eastern Poland. The miracle took place on the day of the communist parliamentary election, which was the cause of especially strong reactions from the then authorities. The secret police operation, which was given various codenames at the time, included the surveillance of pilgrims arriving at the site of the Marian apparition, a propaganda press campaign and direct violent intervention. These actions were effective as they managed to put an end to the pilgrimage movement and ridiculed the miracle of Zabłudów by associating it with ignorance and backwardness. As a result, it was forgotten and only after the collapse of the communist system were actions taken again by the local community to commemorate the events of 1965.

In the first part of the article, I briefly outline the general socio-historical context of miraculous phenomena in the Polish People's Republic, I then go on to describe the site of the Marian apparition of Zabłudów and the course of the related events. In the third part of this chapter, I describe the activities of the secret police leading to the dismissing of the miracle. Much of my account is drawn directly from the reports of the state security police, which included surveillance and informers' reports containing photos, which are based on direct observation, operational plans, dispatches sent to the headquarters in Warsaw and other similar documents. Despite the destruction a number of the secret police documents in the end of communist rule, materials related to the miracle of Zabłudów survived and can be used not only to study the secret police activity, but also to do research on pilgrims' behaviour or the attitude of religious institutions towards the miracle. Furthermore, this study used additional existing sources such as minutes of local authorities' meetings, contemporary press articles and unprinted eye-witness account. In my research I treat the miraculous phenomena as social facts, not as theological phenomena; the question of their divine nature lies completely beyond the scope of my study.

Miraculous phenomena in the Polish People's Republic

After World War II, Poland, like many other Eastern European countries, came under the Soviet sphere of influence. This was of great significance for the religiosity of Poles because the communist system that was imposed on them was, by definition, atheistic and began combating religious life and institutions soon after coming to power. This hostility on the part of the authorities also applied to miraculous events that continued to occur throughout the entire period of communist rule in Poland (1944–1989). This is not surprising because Polish religiosity, even today, is primarily of a so-called folk nature and involves a strong Marian cult (Królikowska 2014).

In my book dedicated to miracles from this period, I have estimated that there were about 50 miraculous events of social significance at that time (Krzywosz 2016a, 12). However, subsequent archival research and studies indicate that there were, in fact, many more. The problem faced by researchers, and which has resulted in a small number of scientific publications on this subject, is that these events often took place in provincial areas, in the proverbial middle of nowhere, and information about them has survived primarily in the memories of locals and in secret police materials. It was the secret police who mostly dealt with miracles, limited the dissemination of information about them and persecuted visionaries. In Poland, the function of the secret police was served by the Security Service from 1956.[1] In 1967, one of the internal Security Service training departments developed a "guide" for combating miraculous phenomena entitled "Niektóre problemy pracy polityczno-operacyjnej związanej z występowaniem rzekomych cudów" (Some Problems of Political and Operational Work Related to the Occurrence of Alleged Miracles) (see Figure 7.1).

Between 1944 and 1948, in the initial period of the establishment of the communist state, the degree of repression against miraculous phenomena was limited (Bączek 2014, 281). However, the communists quite quickly came to the conclusion that miracles were being deliberately caused by the Catholic clergy. This understanding influenced the type and scale of repression used. Numerous supporters of the first famous post-war miracle that took place in Lublin Cathedral in 1949 (Krzywosz 2016b, 46–8) were sentenced to imprisonment for many years. It was the beginning of Stalinism in Poland and hence

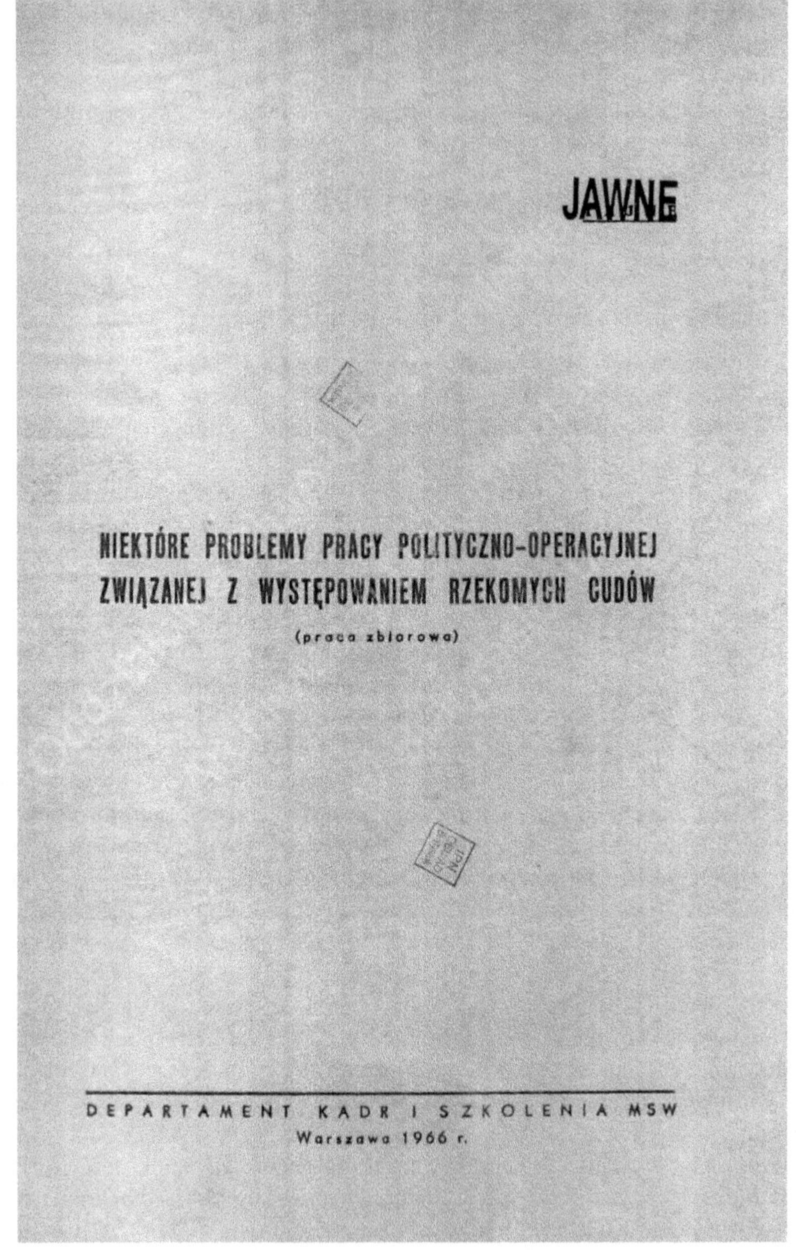

JAWNE

NIEKTÓRE PROBLEMY PRACY POLITYCZNO-OPERACYJNEJ ZWIĄZANEJ Z WYSTĘPOWANIEM RZEKOMYCH CUDÓW

(praca zbiorowa)

DEPARTAMENT KADR I SZKOLENIA MSW

Warszawa 1966 r.

Figure 7.1 The title page of the book serving as a "guide" to combat miraculous phenomena in communist Poland (AIPN Bi 067/44, 3). ©Archives of the Institute of National Remembrance in Białystok.

the repression was very severe. Due to fear of the communist authorities, the miraculous phenomena that emerged at that time were not widely propagated for obvious reasons and therefore, lasted for a very short time.

However, with the political thaw of 1956 and the increasing awareness on the part of the authorities that miracles were natural socio-religious phenomena, the level of repression decreased significantly. Consequently, they returned to the public space, as exemplified by the miracle of Nowolipki which took place in Warsaw in 1958 (Kaliski 2017). In the following decade, the most famous case was the Marian apparition of Zabłudów, to which this article is devoted.

The miracles and revelations that took place in the 1980s, when communism was coming to an end, were allowed to function fairly freely. During this period, some visionaries even tried to build their "own" sacred buildings, and the voice of the Roman Catholic Church had become decisive in determining the fate of miraculous sites. For example, repression of the pilgrims heading for Oława, the location of the activity of the visionary Kazimierz Domański, began only after the Episcopate issued a statement in 1986 in which the Catholic bishops stated that this phenomenon was purely natural and told the faithful not to go to the place of the apparitions (Biuro Prasowe Episkopatu Polski 1998). The collapse of the communist system in 1989 brought freedom to this form of religious life and adherents of miraculous phenomena could now publish texts devoted to this subject and establish contacts with visionaries from other countries without any obstacles.

The characteristics of the site of the Marian apparition of Zabłudów and the course of the event

The miracle of Zabłudów in 1965 was one of the most famous miracles in communist Poland.[2] It took place in the small town of Zabłudów, 18 kilometres from Białystok, the largest city in the Podlasie region and the capital of the then Białystok Province. At that time, Zabłudów had 1,580 residents (Rocznik statystyczny województwa białostockiego 1965–1966, 30). Despite having the formal status of a town, it was actually a large village, which was influenced by various factors. One of them was the post-war influx of local people who brought their rural lifestyle to the town. Most of the residents were farmers and workers commuting to work in Białystok.

Both the Catholic and Orthodox Churches played an important role in the social life of Zabłudów and the surrounding area as Zabłudów is located on a Catholic-Orthodox confessional border. The religiosity of the residents of Zabłudów and the surrounding area can be best characterized, regardless of denomination, using terms associated with the phenomenon of Polish folk religiosity. Certain behaviours and attitudes originating in traditional folk culture and folk religiosity, however, underwent some changes during the communist period. Paradoxically, communism itself contributed to this by "freezing" the traditional form of religiosity. For various reasons, the Catholic

Church itself adopted a strategy which supported folk religion (Piwowarski 2000). This form of religiosity had a range of characteristics: the dominance of rites and rituals over doctrinal and ethical elements; an emphasis on emotional and experiential aspects of religion; a greater role played by women than men in its social functioning; strong worship of the Mother of God; expressing intentions not only through prayers and gestures, but also through objects (votive offerings, medallions); a tendency towards sensualist and visionary understandings of religious phenomena (cult of images and revelations); personal religiosity less significant; an enhanced role of the priest who is ascribed more authority than his pastoral functions normally entail, despite not always being the sole and final authority in religious matters (Czarnowski 1982).

May: a month of the Blessed Virgin Mary

The first Marian apparition took place at sunset on May 13, 1965, in a meadow about one kilometre from Zabłudów when a 14-year-old girl Jadwiga Jakubowska (see Figure 7.2) saw the Virgin Mary. The message she heard did not differ much from many other messages of this kind: Namely, the Mother of God ordered people to pray, convert and threatened that her Son would otherwise punish them. She also assured the girl that her sickly mother would recover. Terrified by the incident, Jadwiga fled home where she told her mother Maria Jakubowska about the event (Ambroziewicz 1968, 86).

The next morning, Maria Jakubowska stated that all her physical ailments subsided and thus she was the first to believe her daughter's words and decided to inform the priest Jan Skarżyński about what had happened. The priest did not show much interest in the apparition and ordered that the whole matter be kept secret (Ambroziewicz 1968, 86). Zabłudów was a small town so it can be assumed that the news of the Marian apparition and the miraculous healing spread among its residents fairly quickly through word of mouth. Moreover, the Jakubowski family did not obey the priest's request and talked a lot about what had happened to their daughter.

At one of the subsequent apparitions, about 100 people appeared in the meadow. These people sang Marian songs, said the Rosary and prayed. At sunset, the Jakubowski family appeared with their daughter who saw the Mother of God again. She foretold hard times ahead unless people prayed and promised to appear in a week's time, on Sunday May 30. Although other people present there did not see the Blessed Virgin Mary, they clearly felt Her presence, and their arrival was rewarded with a miracle of the dancing sun, often depicted in the literature devoted to Marian apparitions. Zygmunt Jakubowski, Jadwiga's father, described this event as follows:

> My daughter knelt down and said to people: "People, kneel down, the Mother of God has come." At that time, I saw that the sun began to

Figure 7.2 Photos of Jadwiga Jakubowska from a special album created by the secret police in 1965 (AIPN Bi 012/1337, 55). ©Archives of the Institute of National Remembrance in Białystok.

> spin and drew closer to us. It was obscured by a blue veil, surrounded by cherry colours from below and by yellow colours from the side.
>
> (Ambroziewicz 1968, 78)

Even though only some of the witnesses experienced something extraordinary, the Marian apparition was considered true and according to the state security police news of the event began to spread rapidly throughout the entire Białystok province (AIPN Bi 0037/42, 35). In line with the logic of this type of story, repeated mouth to mouth, the story of the apparition began to transform into a myth of a bedridden mother, her holy daughter and miraculous healing.

Although no information about the events in Zabłudów appeared in the press, many residents of the Podlasie region eagerly awaited the apparition announced to take place on the following Sunday. The local communist authorities also eagerly waited for the event that day, but for a completely different reason. Namely, the parliamentary election planned for that day. Elections in the Polish People's Republic were primarily aimed at demonstrating social unity and support for those in power, and thus primarily served a propaganda function. For this reason, the announced Marian apparition alarmed local decision-makers. At a meeting of the Provincial Committee of the Polish United Workers' Party in Białystok,[3] two days before the election, the first secretary Arkadiusz Łaszewicz stated:

> The initiation of the "miracle" in Zabłudów is an unpleasant dissonance in the face of the active attitude of Białystok society in supporting the electoral programme of candidates for deputies and national councils. Appropriate steps have already been taken.
>
> (APB KW PZPR 380, 212)

Łaszewicz was probably referring to the measures taken by the secret police at the beginning of the third week of May (AIPN Bi 0037/42, 70). These consisted of warning talks with people interested in subsequent apparitions. More overt actions were taken by the Citizens' Militia[4] which deployed patrols of the Motorized Reserves of the Citizens' Militia[5] on roads accessing Zabłudów, at the site of the apparition and at the Jakubowski family's house on May 27 (AIPN Bi 047/1309, 1–4). This did not escape the attention of the local population and, paradoxically, contributed to the popularization of the miracle. As one of the residents of the Podlasie region put it: "I don't believe it but there must be something in it as even the militia became interested" (Pawluczuk 1965, 1–2). At that time, the appearance of the miraculous meadow began to change: aesthetically arranged stones and bottles with flowers began to appear and black cherry branches were planted. Children gathered during the day and women in the evening (AIPN Bi 0037/46, 40), demonstrating the social expectation of another Marian apparition.

Election Sunday

On May 30th, on the day of the announced Marian apparition and of the parliamentary election, thousands of people went to Zabłudów despite a rainy day and lack of any publicly available information about the miracle. The communist authorities organized numerous roadblocks, trying to prevent pilgrims from reaching the site of the apparition. The Motorized Reserves of the Citizens' Militia from Białystok were also sent there and officers of the Citizens' Militia stood at the Jakubowski family's house (AIPN Bi 0037/43, 141). Despite the aforementioned roadblocks, people continued to arrive in Zabłudów, and by 4.20 pm there were already about 2,000 pilgrims near the miraculous meadow. While some of them prayed and sang religious songs, others waited passively for developments. As usual in such situations, various rumours circulated among those waiting, for example, about the arrest of Jadwiga Jakubowska (AIPN Bi 0037/45, 29). This only heated the already tense atmosphere.

Around 4.25 pm, the gathered crowd clashed with the Motorized Reserves of the Citizens' Militia, stationed at the site of the Marian apparition. The pilgrims were empowered by the presence of Jadwiga Jakubowska, who was forced out of her house around 4.00 pm by a crowd of 200 people. In the meadow, the militia used clubs, firecrackers, tear gas and live ammunition to disperse the crowd. The people did not remain passive, throwing back firecrackers and destroying militia cars with stones. The atmosphere of a regular battle is best reflected in the statement made by one of the participants:

> The communists went crazy, it just seemed like hell was on fire. They threw firecrackers, fired ... and so on! ... And people and men, and children, and women; there was a huge pile of stones so they hit them with stones. They overturned the cars, broke car windows. And they (militia officers) threw firecrackers, so they caught these firecrackers and threw them back at them.
>
> (Busłowska 1999, 12)

Around 5.00 pm, the Motorized Reserves of the Citizens' Militia withdrew from the meadow, leaving only the civilian patrols of the Citizens' Militia in Zabłudów (AIPN Bi 0037/42, 44). Ultimately, the fight was won by pilgrims, which in itself was considered a new miracle. The event was a breakthrough in the history of Marian apparitions and made Zabłudów famous throughout Poland. An estimated 5,000 people gathered in the meadow at 5.30 pm. The weather changed and the sun came out. When the announced apparition took place, the Mother of God said: "Pray and convert." The girl repeated her words to her mother who said this to the people around her (Ambroziewicz 1968, 87–8). Moreover, Jadwiga Jakubowska said: "Do not be angry that the militia beat you. Everyone will see a miracle at home, and whoever is ill will recover" (AIPN Bi 0037/43, 142). Just like before, only the girl saw the Blessed Virgin Mary, although some pilgrims claimed that they also experienced miraculous events (AIPN Bi 012/1337, 133). However, it seems that the miraculous events on that day were rather limited, given the size of the crowd of thousands of pilgrims.

Our Lady of Zabłudów

Due to the clash with the Motorized Reserves of the Citizens' Militia, the extraordinary atmosphere became heightened in line with the processes related to crowd psychology. The very fact of the victory over significant militia forces was perceived in a symbolic way (e.g. the defence of the Blessed Virgin Mary from ungodly communism) and treated as another miracle. As a result, the next day, according to the secret police, a small wooden cross was put at the site of the apparition (AIPN Bi 0037/42, 82) previously, no such religious objects had appeared there and some pilgrims began to treat Jadwiga as a saint asking her for blessing and touching the sick (AIPN Bi 0037/42, 136).

Although no successive Marian apparitions were announced, crowds of pilgrims, who were more and more numerous each day, came to Zabłudów, not only from the Białystok province, but also from other parts of the country. The pilgrimage usually consisted of two elements: seeing the miraculous meadow and visiting, or at least seeing, Jadwiga Jakubowska. In the following days, the site of the apparition was covered with stones and subsequent pilgrims brought new crosses (AIPN Bi 0037/42, 131), including Orthodox crosses.[6] In the meadow, pilgrims prayed, sang religious songs, left different votive offerings, such as rosaries, ceremonial towels[7] and money, as well as collected water (a spring appeared, or was actually dug) and soil, which were considered to have miraculous curative properties (see Figure 7.3). The phrase "Our Lady of Zabłudów" appeared in litanies (AIPN Bi 0037/42, 133).

Initially, information about the events that happened on May 30 and earlier circulated around Poland primarily through private letters and individual conversations because the first mention of the Marian apparition in Zabłudów appeared in the press as late as June 19 (Tak rodzą się mity 1965, 3) and was described in terms of ignorance and backwardness.

With the start of warmer days and nights, more and more people came to Zabłudów. The miraculous meadow was alive not only during the day, but also at night because some pilgrims slept there. It can be said that the site of the apparition served people 24 hours a day. The lack of subsequent apparitions was compensated for by other miraculous events. In addition to extraordinary healings, some saw Our Lady of Sorrows in a tree knot in one of the wooden crosses (AIPN Bi 0037/43, 86). We gain a sense of atmosphere in the meadow from the undercover surveillance photographs taken by the secret police (see Figure 7.4).

Figure 7.3 The site of the Marian apparition with Catholic and Orthodox religious votive offerings (AIPN Bi 012/1336/4, 163). ©Archives of the Institute of National Remembrance in Białystok.

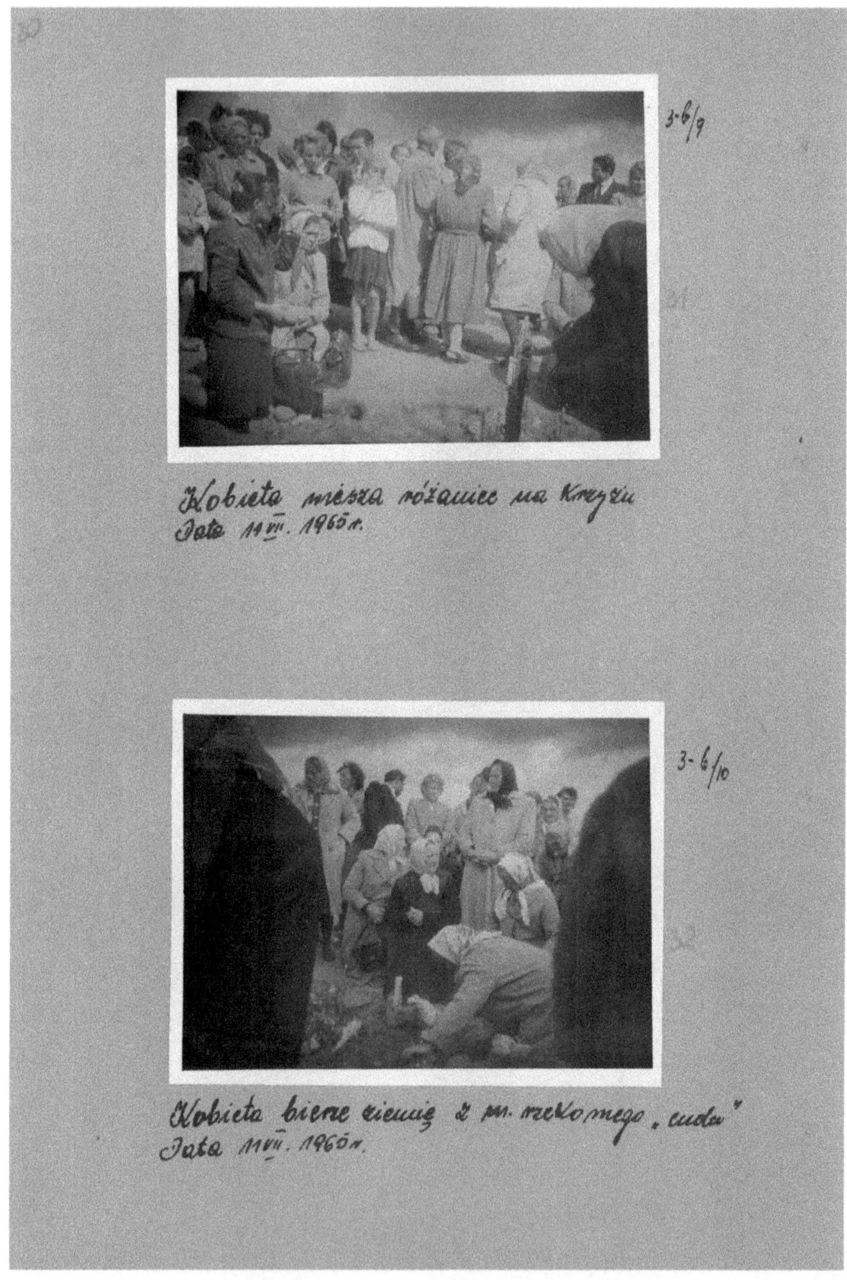

Figure 7.4 A page from the Security Service's album with surveillance photographs showing the behaviour of pilgrims at the site of the Marian apparition: hanging rosaries and collecting soil (AIPN Bi 012/1337, 30). ©Archives of the Institute of National Remembrance in Białystok.

Most pilgrims arrived on Thursday, June 17, the Catholic feast of Corpus Christi, and Sunday June 20. The secret police reported that in the afternoon of the 17th, there were an estimated 4,000 people at the site of the apparition (AIPN Bi 0037/46, 147), and on the Sunday, there were 5,000 pilgrims in the meadow (AIPN Bi 0037/42, 215), more or less the same number as on the Sunday of the election. This huge pilgrimage movement caused many unforeseen consequences. Among them were new apparitions outside of Zabłudów. Having returned home, the faithful who religiously experienced their stay in the miraculous meadow began to experience various visions or interpret events in a supernatural way. New Marian apparitions took place in Sokoły and Stare Krzewo, among other places (AIPN Bi 0037/42, 127, 129).

With the decrease in the number of pilgrims in the third week of June, the authorities began to take specific actions against individuals associated with the Marian apparition. On June 23, Jadwiga Jakubowska's parents were called to the provincial prosecutor's office. The day before, a Catholic bishop Adam Sawicki had met with Stefan Żmijko, chairman of the Presidium of the Provincial National Council in Białystok.[8] The effect of the meeting was a statement issued by the Białystok curia about the events in Zabłudów, telling the faithful to stay calm. In the following days, it was read in Catholic churches throughout the diocese (AIPN Bi 0037/42, 210). On Monday June 28, "The Local Sanitary Inspector's Warning" (1965, 2) appeared in the local press, in which people were warned against using water from the miraculous meadow because the level of pollution found in it classified it as sewage (Figure 7.5).

Figure 7.5 A general view of the miraculous meadow in June 1965 (AIPN Bi 012/1336/4, 278). ©Archives of the Institute of National Remembrance in Białystok.

At the beginning of July, there was a clear drop in the number of people coming to Zabłudów. In the first week of July, the Security Service estimated that there were 20 to 40 people in the meadow in the morning and 40 to 50 pilgrims in the evening (AIPN Bi 0037/42, 215). This changed situation influenced the attitude of the communist authorities, who began to take offensive measures at the beginning of the second decade to definitively end the Marian apparition in Zabłudów.

The quarantine of Zabłudów

On the night of July 11–12, 1965, uniformed officers of the Motorized Reserves of the Citizens' Militia came to the site of the apparition and removed people arriving there. The same happened to those who tried to get to place "C" as the secret police referred to the forbidden area.[9] It was the first such explicit and decisive action of the authorities since election Sunday. The meadow was blocked and the quarantine of Zabłudów began. The entire adjacent area was controlled round the clock by the Citizens' Militia and the Motorized Reserves of the Citizens' Militia. The constantly arriving pilgrims were sent home (AIPN Bi 0037/42, 229). On the first day, about 100 people were sent back before 8.00 am (AIPN Bi 0037/45, 175).

The residents of the Podlasie region who started a new day by reading the press could read in "The Statement of the State Sanitary Inspectorate for the Białystok District" (1965, 1) that local residents and all those coming to Zabłudów were obliged to take protective vaccination. At 1.40 pm, employees of the Provincial National Council from Białystok took crosses with devotional items from the site of the apparition and at 3.00 pm, the team of the district sanitary and epidemiological station began disinfection (AIPN Bi 0037/46, 162).

The measures taken by the authorities clearly limited the pilgrimage movement. Access to the miraculous meadow was forbidden, and those who tried to break through to the site of the apparition were punished with a typhoid vaccination and a fine. If this did not deter the pilgrims and they still would not give up their desire to reach the meadow, they were taken to a hospital of infectious diseases for quarantine (AIPN Bi 0037/42, 237). The Zabłudów Miracular Movement founded by a group of local residents who were actively involved in the Marian apparition, was subjected to similar repressive measures.[10] On July 21, three participants of this movement: Nadzieja Kalinowska, Albina Drewnowska and Marianna Minkiewicz, were isolated in a hospital for infectious diseases in Bielsk Podlaski for a week's observation (AIPN Bi 0037/42, 241).

Pilgrims' reactions to the blockade were mostly negative. Policemen were often asked by pilgrims for permission to reach the site of the apparition or to collect water from the miraculous meadow. The actions taken by the authorities were a disaster for all those who were convinced that the miracle of Zabłudów could solve their life's misfortunes (most often of a health nature). An example of a failed trip was the pilgrimage of Maria Woźna and her seven-year-old mute son, among other people, from the Bielsk Podlaski district. In his report, Captain Józef Dragonek, who served in the Zabłudów area on July 13, stated:

> Woźna Maria brought her dumb son hoping that he would be healed. After explaining why we would not let them reach their destination … Woźna Maria began to cry softly claiming that "her son's last resort is gone." Everyone was poorly dressed, poorly fed; we had the impression that the costs associated with travel would seriously affect their home budget. They left the place very peacefully.
>
> (AIPN Bi 0037/46, 153)

On July 24, the last article devoted to the Marian apparition entitled "Reflections on Zabłudów" (WIT 1965) was published in the local press. Signed under a pseudonym, the author claimed that the "the miracle" was over (WIT 1965, 3). The next day, on Sunday evening, as if confirming his opinion, the Białystok Security Service sent their last report to the headquarters in Warsaw with the following content:

> On 25 July 1965, there were no gatherings at the place of the event in Zabłudów. During the day, 14 people tried to reach the place, including four from Warsaw province, two from Olsztyn province and four from Lublin province. All of the above were vaccinated and fined.
>
> (AIPN Bi 0037/42, 245)

It can, therefore, be argued that by the end of July, the Marian apparition ceased to be a problem for the Ministry of the Interior in Warsaw, where reports were sent daily. However, what seemed to be over from the capital city's perspective looked completely different from the position of Białystok. Checkpoints established on the July 12 remained there until mid-September, and secret police officers, despite the dismissal of the mass pilgrimage movement, continued to visit Zabłudów. Their activities were aimed at people associated with the Zabłudów Miracular Movement and the Jakubowski family. September 1967 can be considered the date of the ultimate end of the miracle as Jadwiga Jakubowska left for Częstochowa and joined one of the convents there.

Actions taken by the secret police in relation to the Marian apparition in Zabłudów

Officially, the actions of the secret police fighting the miracle of Zabłudów were led and coordinated by the Fourth Department of the Provincial Citizens' Militia Headquarters in Białystok, headed by Lieutenant Colonel Józef Bzdela.[11] This department primarily dealt with the fight against the Roman Catholic Church, surveillance of the clergy of all denominations (legal and illegal) in Poland, as well as religious issues in a broad sense, including miraculous phenomena.

The actions of the Security Service regarding the Marian apparition of Zabłudów lasted two years, from May 1965 until September 1967. They were given various codenames, such as: "Ada" "Zjawa" [Apparition], "Cud" [Miracle], "Rodzina" [Family] and "Obłudnicy" [Hypocrites], depending on who was the subject of interest. The activity of the secret police was crucial in the elimination of the miracle of Zabłudów. The information obtained by the state security agency, was the foundation on which all of the open repressive actions of the authorities were based. Prosecutors' actions were initiated based on official notes of the Security Service. It was the secret police, not the Sanitary-Epidemiological Station, which planned the sanitary quarantine of the meadow. It was also the Security Service officers who conducted the numerous warning talks limiting the pilgrimage movement to Zabłudów. Some press articles were also based on secret police materials and were even commissioned by them (Lulewicz 2012). Above all, however, the Security Service was the brain that planned the successive moves of the authorities as it was its officers who made plans to eliminate the miracle. These plans were then either accepted or rejected by the coordination team of the Provincial Committee of the Polish United Workers' Party.

Based on the analysis of the actions taken by the secret police in relation to the Marian apparition in Zabłudów, three levels of activity can be distinguished:

a) information gathering;
b) creating and disseminating fake news;
c) intimidating, threatening and causing a state of emergency.

Collecting information was the primary but not the only task of the Security Service. The secret police in communist Poland often interfered in social life through various types of provocations aimed at setting the course of events in the direction desired by the communist authorities. Informants created and disseminated fake news and misinformation related to the Marian apparition and the Zabłudów Miracular Movement.

As for intimidation, it is difficult to say to what extent it was the conscious behaviour of the authorities or of the subjective state of people involved in propagating the miraculous phenomena. The fact is that secret police officers visited Zabłudów so often that some of them could still be identified by local residents by site even after some time had passed. The communist apparatus of repression functioning in the authoritarian state aroused, above all, fear in citizens, and the more extensive the secret the police actions, the greater the fear.

Collecting information

Information gathering was the primary task of the secret police. The activities related to this revolved around three main themes. Firstly, they concerned the intentions and plans of the Jakubowski family and later participants of the Zabłudów Miracular Movement and their relations with the rest of Zabłudów's residents, and with the local clergy in particular. Secondly, the secret police were interested in the popular mood and opinions in various environments about the miracle across the entire Białystok province. Thirdly, they collected information about the situation at the site of the Marian apparition and at the Jakubowski family's house, including the number of pilgrims, their opinions and places of origin.

Information from Zabłudów

The method of collecting information was standard and did not differ from other routine activities of the Security Service. First of all, informers – a network of secret collaborators,[12] civil contacts[13] and business contacts[14] – were used. The secret police managed to obtain informers in all the environments in which they were interested. Initially, the lack of an informer in Jadwiga Jakubowska's family was a big problem. However, as part of the operational work, they managed to obtain such a person with the pseudonym "Rak" and received information directly from the Jakubowski family (AIPN Bi 0037/44, 306–7). With the formation of the Zabłudów Miracular Movement, an informer who had access to its active participants was also needed. The secret police managed to recruit an agent called "Lech" to cooperate. At the first meeting, Captain Tomkiel ordered him to:

> [M]aintain friendly relations with … residents of Zabłudów who are interested in maintaining and disseminating news about the alleged "miracle" of Zabłudów. Moreover, to identify all persons who contact the Jakubowski family on a regular basis and provide more detailed information on these persons.
>
> (AIPN Bi 0037/44, 185)

There were few secret collaborators in Zabłudów but they provided a lot of useful information. Father Bronisław Poźniak, who had the pseudonym "Janek" was certainly the most valuable source of information (Leończuk 2012, 118). He informed about the situation in the presbytery and the attitude of other priests to the miracle. Moreover, he provided the Security Service with information that clergymen received from their parishioners (AIPN Bi 0037/44, 262). "Czesław" was another secret collaborator who reported on the mood among the clergy in Zabłudów. Another priest, Czesław Czerwiński, hid under this pseudonym (Leończuk 2012, 118). He seemed to be less active in undercover activity than Father Poźniak yet his information was also valuable and used to verify "Janek's" denunciations.

Moreover, "Ekonomista" and "Adam" employed in a local dairy, reported on the mood in Zabłudów. Former secret collaborators who had the pseudonyms "Kwiecień", "Kiczkajło" and "Łana" were also engaged in undercover work. The latter was important because he often wrote petitions for the cancellation of compulsory deliveries to the authorities, among other issues, on behalf of farmers from Zabłudów (AIPN Bi 0037/52, 645) and he therefore had a large network of contacts.

What is more, other residents of Zabłudów, referred to as civil contacts in documents, also informed the Security Service about the mood and plans of the Jakubowski family, as well as the situation in the town. Based on their information, the secret police had a full picture of the married life, family and social relations of the Jakubowski family at their disposal. Later, the network of civil contacts was also used to obtain information about the intentions of participants of the Zabłudów Miracular Movement. Here is an excerpt from a secret police officer's note prepared after a visit to Zabłudów and meetings with informants:

> On 17 June 1965 in Zabłudów, I talked with a number of civil contacts. M. G. said that her daughter, who was in the 7th grade, said she felt disgust when listening to the pious songs that were sung at the site of the "miracle" about Our Lady of Zabłudów and about Jadzia [Jadzia is a diminutive of Jadwiga] of Zabłudów. M.G.'s daughter even sang these songs. Therefore, I asked her to write the lyrics down and give them to me at our next meeting. She promised to do this by Sunday 20 June 1965. These songs are sung by fanatics from Zabłudów at the site of the "miracle".
>
> (AIPN Bi 0037/46, 378)

It should also be added that, along with the repressive actions of the authorities, particularly the high fines, some of the participants of the Zabłudów Miracular Movement radically changed their attitude and were ready to cooperate with the secret police. For example, on April 28, 1966, Nadzieja Kalinowska – an active figure in the Zabłudów Miracular Movement, against whom an investigation took place in 1965 – offered to cooperate with the Security Service. Captain Tomkiel wrote:

> Kalinowska emphasized keeping her statements secret and that under this condition she could inform about the Jakubowski family's intentions regarding the "miracle". She did not want to submit testimonies in writing because she had been often slandered by various people from Zabłudów since 1965. She invited me to visit her in her flat where she could talk freely.
>
> (AIPN Bi 0037/44, 314)

Moreover, information provided by persons holding managerial functions in various institutions and thus obliged to cooperate with the secret police was used. For example, on June 10, comrade[15] Zygmunt Pankiewicz, director of Dairy Cooperatives in Białystok, met with the Colonel of the Security Service Leon Sobczyk, to talk about Zygmunt Jakubowski.[16] Pankiewicz suggested taking him back to work in the dairy in Zabłudów so that comrade Malinowski, the head of the dairy, could influence his views (AIPN Bi 0037/46, 357). The secret police accepted the plan and Zygmunt Jakubowski returned to work on June 28. A few days earlier, Major Kalinowski of the Security Service met with comrade Malinowski to give him instructions related to Zygmunt Jakubowski's work. Major Kalinowski wrote:

> I agreed with comrade Malinowski that after employing Jakubowski, he would observe his behaviour and statements on the plant's premises. Moreover, with the help of trusted employees, he would skilfully try to discredit and ridicule him in connection with his statements about the alleged "miracle". At the same time, I instructed comrade Malinowski to ridicule Jakubowski in a very skilful manner.
>
> (AIPN Bi 0037/46, 401)

Moreover, the Security Service officers came to the primary school in Zabłudów to obtain information from the head of the school, Czesław Nurczewski, about the progress of Jadwiga Jakubowska's education and her school attendance (AIPN Bi 0037/46, 252, 264). As for technical activities, the secret police planned to set up a room wiretap at Jakubowski's house. On May 31, Colonel Leon Sobczyk submitted an application to the Ministry of the Interior in Warsaw (AIPN Bi 0037/46, 309), which the Ministry rejected (AIPN Bi 0037/46, 309). However, there were no problems with recording sermons in the church in Zabłudów with a mini-phone[17] (AIPN Bi 0037/45, 198).

The secret police department "W" dealing with perlustration of correspondence, also began mass control of letters sent from Zabłudów, Białystok and other towns of the Podlasie region. This was done for at least two reasons. The first was to examine the public mood and attitudes towards the Marian apparition. The second was the desire to limit the spread of news about the miracle, which is why some letters were destroyed and did not reach the addressees (AIPN Bi 0037/45, 249). The first letter to be checked was sent from Zabłudów on the May 20 and the last one, also from Zabłudów, on July 30. In total, the archives of the Institute of National Remembrance contain materials describing the contents of 462 letters related to the miracle of Zabłudów (AIPN Bi 0037/45, 204–63).

The Security Service officers who devoted the most time and energy to the situation in Zabłudów were operational officers: Lieutenant Michał Uściłowicz, Captain Wacław Tomkiel and Corporal Aleksy Iwaniuk. They received the information they needed by working with informers. The surviving documents show that in June and July they were at the site of the events several times a week and had already been identified by Zabłudów residents as secret police officers (AIPN Bi 0037/44, 126). It seems that Uściłowicz was most personally involved in combating the miracle and he sometimes even expressed an emotional attitude to the events. For example, on the June 1, when booking two Warsaw students at Jakubowski's house and asked why he did it, he replied:

> For the purposes of our statistics, to analyse how many fools we have in Poland who believe in miracles. … If they want to know the details [about the miracle], I can … tell them exactly and told them. I added that if they do not believe me, let them ask wise people … and not listen to such authorities as the two hysterics and stupid women, in whose family there were mentally abnormal people. I said that they should be ashamed of their behaviour and advised them to properly describe the actual state of affairs after returning home, that there was no miracle here.
>
> (AIPN Bi 0037/43, 19)

A month later, Lieutenant Uściłowicz behaved in a non-standard way again because he was "invited" by the Jakubowski family to their home. Below is a fragment of his *Operational Note*:

> On 6 July 1965 … I saw Jadwiga Jakubowska riding a bicycle. I asked her how she was doing and whether she was promoted to the next grade level and the like. … I asked her how her family was doing. As we were talking close to the Jakubowski family's house, the girl asked me to enter the yard.
>
> I came in, talking with her. No one was in the yard. The little one called her mother who was at home, saying that there was a gentleman with her and he might want to talk to her. The old woman came out of the house and seemed surprised. I started a conversation with her asking her how she felt after the miraculous healing, how they were doing and so on. Mr Jakubowski entered the yard, … A conversation began with the entire family. Mrs Jakubowska began to complain that the authorities pick on them, that they backbite them, have described them in newspapers, etc. … She began to swear that she had not hurt anyone in her life and that they had insulted her. … I told Jakubowska that apparently people saw this and they didn't talk about this in vain. And if they said something about her, it was her fault. …
>
> In turn, the old Jakubowska said that the worst thing was when someone moved from the village to the city and then forgot about those who remained in the countryside. I said that indeed I came from a village, I didn't deny it, and I told everyone that I knew that I was a son of a peasant. …
>
> The daughter, in turn, said that they knew everything, that I did them a lot of damage and that I contributed a lot to what they wrote in the newspapers.
>
> Stop wishing us wrong because it really isn't nice.
>
> If something was nice or not nice, this was theirs and nobody else's fault, and with these comments I left the Jakubowski family's farm.
>
> (AIPN Bi 0037/44, 63–4)

Information from the Podlasie region

Secret police actions outside Zabłudów were carried out in various environments. Above all, they were interested in the clergy but they also paid attention to other professional groups. For example, workers from large industrial plants (Cotton Industry Factory in Białystok "Fasty", Instruments and Handles Plant "Bison-Bial") (AIPN Bi 0037/45, 113), journalists from the local Polish Radio station and newspaper *Gazeta Białostocka* (AIPN Bi 0037/45, 17), doctors (AIPN Bi 0037/45, 172) and intelligentsia meeting in local cafes (AIPN Bi 0037/45, 95–6). In the initial phase of the miracle, the focus was on determining the data of the people coming to Zabłudów and their opinions of the events. Below is an excerpt from *The Official Note* about the mood in the environment of the Białystok media:

> On 31 May 1965, the administrative staff of the *Gazeta Białostocka* Editorial Office commented on the miracle of Zabłudów. Active publishers included accountant Zofia Muzyka and cashier of the editorial office Halina Orzechowska, both nonpartisan believers and practitioners. They talked about this miracle in a provocative manner, also pointing out, having been reprimanded, that many non-believing employees of the editorial office would convert. The editor-in-chief Kazimierz Nowak was informed about the behaviour of both employees.
>
> (AIPN Bi 0037/45, 17)

Among the church agents, the activity of the secret collaborator "Szczery" is noteworthy. On June 29, he ate dinner with Bishop Adam Sawicki from Białystok, during which they talked about the Marian apparition of Zabłudów. The bishop spoke about the attitude to the miracle, the communist authorities' actions and those taken by the Church, and "Szczery" reported on it all to the secret police (AIPN Bi 0037/43, 156–7).

Intelligence officers in the meadow

In addition to obtaining information by working with a network of informants and checking correspondence, the Security Service engaged intelligence officers of Department "B", who collected information primarily through observation and tracking. In June and July, employees of Department "B" stayed in key places in Zabłudów, such as the Jakubowski family's property and in the meadow, usually from 1.00 pm to 9.00 pm. Five intelligence agents usually worked a four-hour shift (AIPN Bi 012/1335/1, 20). In addition to observing, recording car registration numbers, eavesdropping on conversations, recording sermons, counting the number of arriving people and so on, they took pictures with a hidden camera, which were then put in a special album (AIPN Bi 012/1337). Thanks to this, today we know what the

Figure 7.6 Women singing a religious song at the site of the Marian apparition identified by the Security Service (AIPN Bi 012/1337, 64). ©Archives of the Institute of National Remembrance in Białystok.

miraculous meadow looked like and how the arriving pilgrims behaved (see Figure 7.6).

The intelligence officers had to report every hour from a car set up in Zabłudów, equipped with a radio, with the help of which they were connected to the Headquarters (AIPN Bi 012/1335/1, 20). Below is an excerpt of a report from June 13 from Department "B":

> – At 1.15 pm, there were about 100 people at the Jakubowski family's place of residence. Everyone wanted to see little Jakubowska. At around 12.55, the girl appeared in the window, and all the gathered people, particularly men, took off their hats.
>
> – At 2.30 pm, there were about 60–70 people at the Jakubowski family's place of residence. The girl stood in the window with her mother. There was a tight squeeze around the window. The gathered people gave the girl money, even as much as 20 [Polish] złoty, which she in turn gave to her mother. The mother also took the money.
>
> (AIPN Bi 0037/46, 367)

The intelligence agents were given special tasks on June 5 and 6, when the riots of May 30 were expected to be repeated. On these days, 28 agents were mobilized, including some directed from the neighbouring Olsztyn province.

Working in pairs, they were supposed to identify potential leaders in the crowd, urge hooligan behaviour, and take pictures of "people who behave actively in this environment and look like intellectuals in the way they behave, speak and dress" (AIPN Bi 012/1335/1, 58). If violence was used, the security slogan protecting the intelligence agent from a police truncheon would be the phrase "Z-6" (AIPN Bi 012/1335/1, 58).

Department "B" sent a letter to the Fourth Department of the Provincial Citizens' Militia Headquarters in Białystok asking them to assess the actions regarding the miracle of Zabłudów. The letter summarized the observations of Department "B" and contained statistical data. The intelligence staff managed to identify "67 civil contacts, 748 cars and 513 motorcycles" (AIPN Bi 0037/52, 652) and take over 300 photos. The actions taken by Department "B" officers were positively evaluated by the Fourth Department. Captain Jerzy Porowski wrote:

> The work of Department "B" on the alleged "miracle" of Zabłudów was organized duly and properly. ... On behalf of the Department's management, I express my appreciation for the contribution of the intelligence agents to this matter.
>
> (AIPN Bi 0037/52, 653)

Manipulative and compromising measures

The primary purpose of the secret police was to collect and store data. However, they sometimes engaged in reverse activity, namely, the dissemination of untrue or compromising information among the public through a network of informers or the media. Actions such as plots or provocations also occurred during the miracle of Zabłudów. Throughout its duration, the Security Service informers, whenever they could and avoiding the risk of exposure, were required to demonstrate the falsity of and ridicule the Marian apparition. For example, point 8 of *The Direction Plan* of the May 30 recommended "spreading misinformation" (AIPN Bi 0037/42, 37). Such activities did not necessarily arouse suspicion because a significant part of the society of the Podlasie region and the residents of Zabłudów were sceptical of the miracle of Zabłudów from the very beginning. When new Marian apparitions occurred in Podlasie, the Security Service from Wysokie Mazowieckie, not wanting to allow pilgrims to concentrate in Sokoły, deliberately spread the rumour about the new miracles they made up in Waniewo and Pietkowo (AIPN Bi 0037/43, 227).

Another activity of the secret police was to discredit the participants of the Zabłudów Miracular Movement in the local environment. Based on the report of a secret collaborator "Łana" saying that there were statements from Zabłudów accusing Nadzieja Kalinowska of testifying against the local priest Jan Skarżyński, on the basis of which he had been fined as a punishment, the Security Service recommended that this false information be further promoted through a network of informers. The goal was clear – to compromise the local community of Nadzieja Kalinowska, an active participant of the Zabłudów Miracular Movement (AIPN Bi 0037/44, 130).

In autumn 1965, the secret police also prepared a plot using agent "Janek" which was a pseudonym of Father Bronisław Poźniak. He was instructed to describe the Jakubowski family's attitude towards his visit to their house in a negative light when reporting to priest Jan Skarżyński. This plot was to deepen (according to the Security Services) the negative attitude of the priest to the Jakubowski family and, consequently, lead to their public condemnation (AIPN Bi 0037/52, 576). The secret police were also interested in the health condition of Maria Jakubowska, who considered herself a wonderfully healed person. The secret collaborator "Jan" reported on November 8, 1966 that she was bedridden, showing that she had not been completely healed. Therefore, the Security Service officer who read this report instructed Corporal Iwaniuk: "To develop a plan to disseminate information on Maria Jakubowska's disease and further discredit her in public" (AIPN Bi 0037/44, 357).

Intimidating actions

The actions taken by the Security Service to intimidate the Jakubowski family and participants of the Zabłudów Miracular Movement were certainly not the most important aspect of the activities of the secret police. The frequent visits of Lieutenant Uściłowicz and Captain Tomkiel to Zabłudów were the result primarily of the requirements of their operational work, and not from their direct desire to intimidate those involved in the Marian apparition. The fact is, however, that this may have created a sense of danger. According to the preserved documents, the Security Service officers came to the Jakubowski family without any formal reason, not even a search warrant. One can imagine how the family living in the communist, authoritarian state felt when exposed to such unannounced visits. For example, on the June 2, Lieutenant Uściłowicz wrote:

> At 6.30, on 1st June 1965, at Maria Jakubowska's house, I found two individuals who talked with mother Maria and daughter Jadwiga. I check these individuals' identity cards.
>
> (AIPN Bi 0037/43, 19)

Corporal Iwaniuk had already talked to Jadwiga Jakubowska twice in her apartment by the June 4 (AIPN Bi 0037/44, 10). However, it seems that as the network of informers developed, this kind of activity was abandoned. Nevertheless, secret police officers also threatened the Jakubowski family. For example, Jadwiga Jakubowska mentioned that she was threatened with deportation to Siberia if she did not refute the information about the miracle (Szczesiak 1998, 186). After the quarantine was initiated, attempts were made to influence other people in a similar way. On the first day of its founding,

Lieutenant Uściłowicz met Nadzieja Kalinowska from the Zabłudów Miracular Movement in the market square in Zabłudów who was heading towards the pilgrims waiting at the bus stop, and told her:

> [N]ot to hang around among strangers. Then Kalinowska started shouting loudly that she did not know what we wanted from her and asked me not to scare her because we would not be able to do her anything, and she would continue to do what she wanted and so on.
>
> I told her again not to hang around with strangers there, to stop shouting otherwise, we would calm her down in a different way.
>
> (AIPN Bi 0037/44, 93)

Conclusions

My aim in this article was to describe the range of measures taken by the secret police to effectively eliminate the miracle of Zabłudów in 1965. Their activity can be analysed from various points of view including from the perspective of effectiveness of these actions or from an ethical perspective. It can be said that Security Service officers performed their tasks effectively. This is evidenced by that the fact the Jakubowski family and other persons involved in the miracle were completely entangled by a network of informers. This is confirmed by the notes of the secret police containing the comments of interrogated persons. For example, Albin Morawski, a participant in the Zabłudów Miracular Movement, who was arrested for his positive statements about the Marian apparition, warned a friend:

> [N]ot to speak to anyone about the "miracle" because there are a lot of people in Zabłudów who help barbarians and report to the secret militia on who says what and does what.
>
> (AIPN Bi 0037/44, 416)

It should be added here that this friend of Albin Morawski was the secret collaborator "Janek". Thus, the Security Service knew almost everything that happened with the Jakubowski family, among the participants of the Zabłudów Miracular Movement and in the presbytery. The secret police's successes were influenced by some objective circumstances, which made their work easier. Zabłudów was a small town and, in such communities, people know a lot about each other and it was virtually impossible to hide anything from neighbours. What facilitated the operation of the Security Service was the fact that there was a clear division in the local community as regards the attitude towards the Marian apparition. Some people believed in the miracle and others did not. It was from this latter group that those collaborating with the secret police quite often came. Moreover, the persons against whom the Security Service took actions were elderly or middle-aged individuals with low education, which certainly facilitated operational activities.

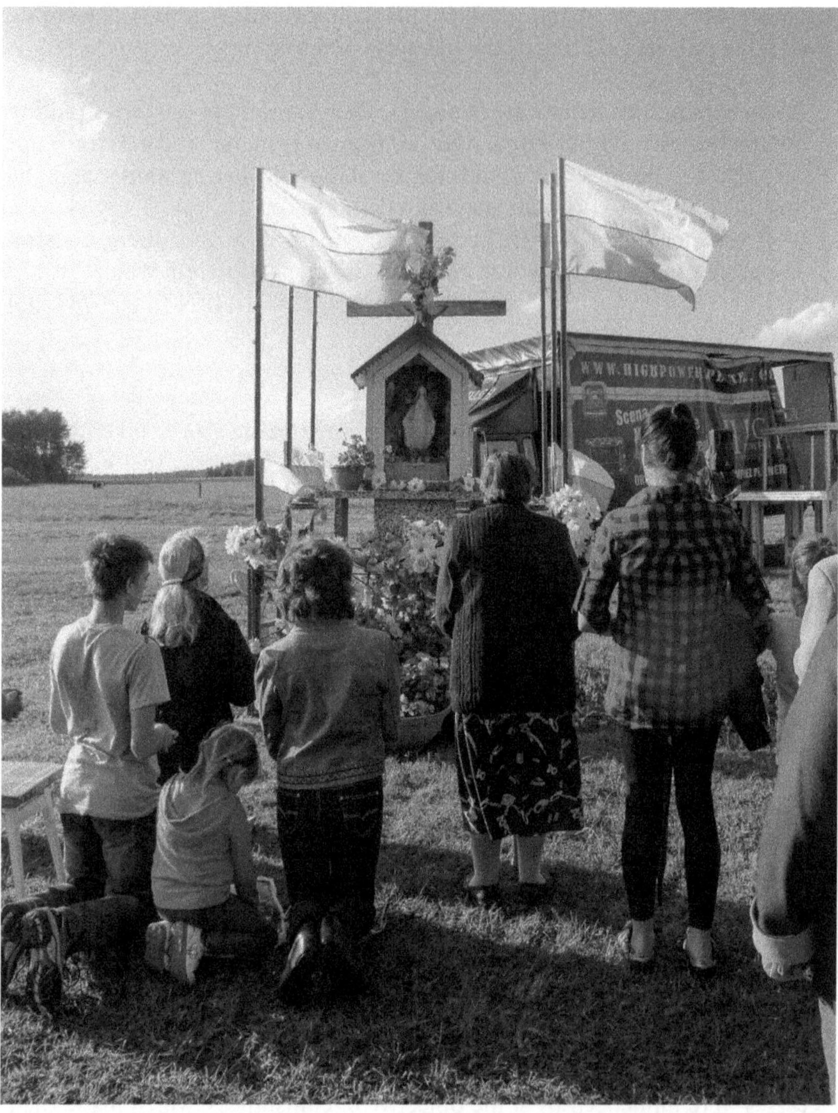

Figure 7.7 Religious ceremonies in the meadow on the 50th anniversary of the miracle of Zabłudów. © Photo by Małgorzata Kasperowcz.

Assessing the ethical activity of the secret police functioning in the authoritarian communist state, it is clear how consciously they not only fought against the manifestations of religious life, such as miraculous phenomena, but also attempted for ideological reasons to destroy the lives of specific people or the bonds that held the Zabłudów community together. However, the 1965 success was not complete. The memory of those events has survived in the local community. This can be demonstrated by a neat, glass chapel standing in the miraculous meadow with a statue of the Virgin Mary, a crucifix and fine votive offerings. In front of it, on the 50th anniversary of the miracle on the May 30, 2015, local people took part in a solemn mass celebrated in remembrance of those days (see Figure 7.7).

Notes

1 The Polish Security Service were secret police whose purpose was to protect the communist political system. It primarily fought against the political opposition and the Roman Catholic Church. It was dissolved in 1990, and the documents it produced were forwarded to the Archives of the Institute of National Remembrance.

2 In the following part of this article, I use fragments of chapters 5 and 7 of my book (Krzywosz 2016a).

3 The Polish United Workers' Party was the main political party that exercised power in communist Poland between 1948 and 1989. It implemented the principles of Marxism-Leninism, as a result of which it pursued a conscious policy of secularization.

4 The Citizens' Militia was a public, state organization of a police nature, whose declared goal was to ensure public order and security. In fact, like the Security Service, it was often used by the communist powers to control society.

5 The Motorized Reserves of the Citizens' Militia were special units of the Citizens' Militia intended to suppress social unrest and riots.

6 For the attitude of the Orthodox population to the Marian apparition experienced by the Catholic girl, see Krzywosz (2003).

7 Ceremonial towels are a characteristic object of the local folk Orthodox religiosity. They serve aesthetic and votive functions.

8 The Provincial National Council was a provincial body of state administration in communist Poland. In practice, it pursued the political goals of the Polish United Workers' Party.

9 Other terms were also used, including: a place of ghosts, a place of miracle or a place of alleged miracle.

10 The Zabłudów Miracular Movement refers to a group of people connected with the Jakubowski family, who aimed to sponsor and encourage further public Marian apparitions or at least to commemorate those that had already taken place.

11 The Fourth Department of the Provincial Citizens' Militia Headquarters should not mislead us because in the Polish People's Republic, local branches of the Security Service were located at the headquarters of the Citizens' Militia, which guaranteed them some form of discretion.

12 In the nomenclature of the Security Service, a secret collaborator was a person who signed a formal declaration of cooperation with the secret police and assumed a pseudonym. A supervising officer would then ordered him or her to perform various tasks, the most common of which was to collect information.

13 In the nomenclature of the Security Service, a civil contact was an ordinary citizen who cooperated with it. His or her help was used in reconnaissance and preliminary activities. This cooperation was informal so he or she did not sign any declaration and was not registered in the files.

14 A business contact was a person who, due to his or her professional and social functions, was obliged to cooperate with the secret police and inform about any matters that might interest them. Business contacts were mostly people who held administrative positions.

15 The term "comrade" was used in communist Poland in relation to members of the Polish United Workers' Party.

16 Zygmunt Jakubowski was dismissed from his job as dairy keeper in Zabłudów on the 31st May, the day after election Sunday. It was one of many repressions that the Jakubowski family experienced in connection with the Marian apparition.

17 A mini-phone was a small recording device placed in the clothes of a secret police officer, with a small microphone attached to outerwear.

Archival sources

Archiwum Instytutu Pamięci Narodowej w Białymstoku [Archives of the Institute of National Remembrance in Białystok] (AIPN Bi) – AIPN Bi 0037/42. (1965); AIPN Bi 0037/43. (1965); AIPN Bi 0037/44. (1965–1967); AIPN Bi 0037/45. (1965); AIPN Bi 0037/46. (1965); AIPN Bi 0037/52. (1965); AIPN Bi 012/1335/1. (1965); AIPN Bi 012/1336/4. (1965–1979); AIPN Bi 012/1337. (1965); AIPN Bi 047/1309. (1965); AIPN Bi 067/44. (1966).

Archiwum Pracowni Badań i Dokumentacji Zjawisk Mirakularnych w Polsce, Instytut Socjologii, Uniwersytet w Białymstoku [Archives of the Laboratory of Research and Documentation of Miraculous Phenomena in Poland, Institute of Sociology at the University of Białystok] – Pawluczuk, Włodzimierz. 1965. *Sprawozdanie z wydarzeń dnia 30 V 1965 w Zabłudowie. Niepublikowana relacja z zabłudowskiej niedzieli wyborczej spisana 31 maja 1965 przez świadka wydarzeń* [*Report on the Events of 30 May 1965 in Zabłudów: An Unpublished Account of the Election Sunday in Zabłudów Written on 31 May 1965 by a Witness to the Events*].

Archiwum Państwowe w Białymstoku [State Archives in Białystok] (APB) – APB KW PZPR 380. (1965) [Documents on the Provincial Committee of the Polish United Workers' Party in Białystok].

References

Ambroziewicz, Jerzy. 1968. *The Apocalypse* [*Apokalipsa*]. Warszawa: Książka i Wiedza.

Bączek, Piotr. 2014. "Activities of Communist Security Structures in Response to the Events Considered Miracles in the Years 1946–1953" ["Działania komunistycznego apartu bezpieczeństwa w odpowiedzi na wydarzenia uznawane za cuda w latch 1946–1953"]. *Saeculum Christianum* XXI: 279–90.

Biuro Prasowe Episkopatu Polski [Press Office of the Polish Episcopate]. 1998. "Information from the Press Office of the Polish Episcopate of 17 January 1986" ["Informacja Biura Prasowego Episkopatu Polski z 17.1.1986"]. In: *Do Not Despise Prophecies, But Test Everything: Private Revelations in the Light of God's Word* [*Proroctwa nie lekceważcie, wszystko badajcie: Objawienia prywatne w świetle Słowa Bożego*] edited by R. Pindel, 160–1. Kraków: Wydawnictwo M.

Busłowska, Anna. 1999. "The Miracle of Zabłudów" ["Zabłudowski Cud"]. *Z Zabłudowskiej Ziemi*, (44): 7–13.

Czarnowski, Stefan. 1982. "The Religious Culture of the Rural Polish People" ["Kultura religijna wiejskiego ludu polskiego"]. In: *A Selection of Sociological Works* [*Wybór pism socjologicznych*] edited by Stefan Czarnowski, 366–401. Warszawa: Książka i Wiedza.

Kaliski, Bartosz. 2017. "Nowolipki AD 1959, or Miracle in Communist Warsaw" ["Nowolipki AD 1959, czyli cud w komunistycznej Warszawie"]. *Pamięć i Sprawiedliwość* 29: 25–49.

Królikowska, Anna M. 2014. "'Folk' Elements in the Contemporary Religiosity?" ["Elementy 'ludowe' w religijności współczesnej?"]. *Opuscula Sociologica* 4: 5–16.

Krzywosz, Maciej. 2003. "Folk Religion on the Catholic-Orthodox Borderland from the Perspective of Private Marian Apparition" ["Religijność ludowa na pograniczu katolicko-prawosławnym w perspektywie prywatnego objawienia maryjnego"]. *Pogranicze. Studia społeczne* 11: 107–14.

Krzywosz, Maciej. 2016a. *Miracles in the Polish People's Republic: Case Study of the Private Marian Apparition in Zabłudów* [*Cuda w Polsce Ludowej: Studium przypadku prywatnego objawienia maryjnego w Zabłudowie*]. Białystok: Instytut Pamięci Narodowej Oddział w Białymstoku.

Krzywosz, Maciej. 2016b. "Sociological Aspect of Miracles and Apparitions in Contemporary Poland." *Przegląd Religioznawczy – The Religious Studies Review* 4: 43–56.

Leończuk, Antoni Ł. 2012. "'The Miracle of Zabłudów' in the Light of Materials Collected in the Białystok Branch of the Institute of National Remembrance" ["'Cud w Zabłudowie' w świetle materiałów zgromadzonych w Białostockim Oddziale Instytutu Pamięci Narodowej"]. *Rocznik Zabłudowski* 6: 102–41.

"Local Sanitary Inspector's Warning" ["Ostrzeżenie Wojewódzkiego Inspektora Sanitarnego"]. 1965. *Gazeta Białostocka*, 28 June, 2.

Lulewicz, Sylwiusz I. 2012. "The Role of the Media in the Liquidation of the So-called Miracle of Zabłudów" ["Rola mediów w likwidacji tzw. cudu zabłudowskiego"]. *Rocznik Zabłudowski* 6: 68–101.

Piwowarski, Władysław. 2000. "From 'the National Church' to 'the Optional Church'" ["Od 'Kościoła ludu' do 'Kościoła wyboru'"]. In: *Sociology of Religion* [*Socjologia Religii*], edited by Władysław Piwowarski, 265–71. Lublin: Redakcja Wydawnictw Katolickiego Uniwersytetu Lubelskiego.

Statistical Yearbook of the Białystok Province 1965 [*Rocznik statystyczny województwa białostockiego 1965*]. 1966. Białystok: Wojewódzka Rada Narodowa.

"Statement of the State Sanitary Inspectorate for the Białystok District" ["Komunikat Państwowego Inspektoratu Sanitarnego dla pow. Białostockiego"]. 1965. *Gazeta Białostocka*, 12 July, 1.

Szczesiak, Edmund. 1998. *The Heal* [*Oni uzdrawiają*]. Gdańsk, Oficyna Pomorska.

"That Is How Myths Are Born" ["Tak rodzą się mity"]. 1965. *Gazeta Białostocka*, 19–20 June, 3.

WIT. 1965. "Reflections on Zabłudów" ["Zabłudowskie refleksje"]. (1965). *Gazeta Białostocka*, 24–25 July, 3.

8 Acting in the underground

Life as a Hare Krishna devotee in the Soviet Republic of Lithuania (1979–1989)

Rasa Pranskevičiūtė-Amoson

Introduction

This chapter presents research on the formation of International Society for Krishna Consciousness (ISKCON) and its underground existence in the Lithuanian Soviet Republic up to its official registration in 1989. The aim of this work is to reveal the situation of ISKCON in Lithuania under the Soviet regime, focusing on the approach and strategies of Soviet authorities towards alternative religions, interactions of the KGB[1] with the Krishna community, the life of the community under KGB surveillance and its impact on the members of ISKCON. The material in the chapter comes from the previously secret documents of the State Security Committee of the Lithuanian SSR (KGB) on Lithuanian Hare Krishnas, which are now preserved in the Lithuanian Special Archives (LSA), as well as, from the Lithuanian ISKCON archives. The chapter covers a wide range of questions related to the phenomena of alternative religiosities in the Soviet Union and their attendant fields of influence: the politics and strategy of the regime towards alternative religiosities; restrictions, repressions, survival strategies and resistance of representatives of alternative religiosities; the milieu of alternative religiosity as a space of resistance; the formation and transfer of religious and spiritual ideas within the Soviet Union and from the outside; and methodological problems in research on alternative religiosities within the Soviet Union.

ISKCON is based on a Hindu tradition of Gaudiya Vaishnavism, which considers God Vishnu and his incarnations, primarily Krishna, as an ultimate reality. The founder of ISKCON was Srila Bhaktivedanta Swami Prabhupada (1896–1977). ISKCON today is the largest active organization in the West representing the Indian Vedic philosophy and religion, and its headquarters are in Mayapur (India, West Bengal). The ideas of Krishna Consciousness came to Lithuania via Moscow (Russia) through Tallinn (Estonia) and Riga (Latvia) in 1979 and spread among students in Šiauliai who were interested in yoga and soon also spread to similar circles in Kaunas and Vilnius. The community developed underground with the threat of KGB repression until the beginning of the Sąjūdis,[2] when public activities became possible, such as public programs, book distribution and the founding of official temples. ISKCON existed in Lithuania without any organizational structure until 1989 when, with the collapse of the Soviet Union, official registrations of religious communities started. The Lithuanian ISKCON community played a significant role in the development of ISKCON throughout the Soviet Union, because after the imprisonment of Armenian activists, Lithuanian members organized the secret printing and distribution of ISKCON literature throughout the Soviet region (Pranskevičiūtė and Juras 2014).

The circumstances in Soviet times were not favorable for the existence of socio-cultural alternatives or religious communities, as religious and spiritual activities were considered to conflict with the officially established ideology of atheism. In general, the religious policy under the Soviet regime (as well as in communist Central and Eastern Europe more broadly) up until late 1980s comprised three main elements: 1) a socialization process aimed at the formation of the new Soviet (atheist) man; 2) the administrative and legislative regulation of religious bodies with the apparent intention of ultimately extinguishing them; 3) coping with the responses of believers to official policies, if necessary by repressive means (Anderson 1994, 3). Due to Soviet control, most socio-cultural alternatives existed underground, and religious communities could survive only if they acted in secret. During the 1970s and 1980s in the Soviet Union (including Lithuania), a small number of alternative religious movements were active in the underground. Examples are ISKCON (Pranskevičiūtė and Juras 2014), Tibetan Buddhist groups (Pranskevičiūtė 2014b, 100), Paganism (Pranskevičiūtė 2013, Stasulane and Ozoliņš 2017), the movement of Tolstoyism (Gordeeva 2017), Astral Karate (Panin 2017), diverse circles orientated towards Theosophy, parapsychology (Peškaitis and Glodenis 2000, 133) and various practices of yoga.

Generally, the attitude of Soviet authorities towards religions was negative, based on the officially established ideology of Atheism. Talking about Soviet Hare Krishnas, it was claimed in secret KGB documents that

> the dogmatics of the 'society' (ISKCON – *R. P.-A.*) represent reactionary, ideologically harmful, anti-materialistic teaching, based on religious-mystic conceptions, which declare full abandonment from materialism, an ascetic lifestyle, education of the masses in a spirit of mysticism, pessimism and submission to exploitive classes.
>
> (LSA K-1-46-215, 1)

ISKCON was considered to be one of the widely spread international threats to the Soviet socio-political *status quo* which "by denying the communist ideology and the socialist state and by struggling with them seeks to withdraw its followers from participation in political and labor activities drawing them towards mysticism" (*Kommersant. Vlast'* 2009, 49).[3] For example, it was claimed that Robert Campagnola (Harikesha Swami)[4] was a CIA (Central Intelligence Agency) agent who had infiltrated the organization, specializing in ideological diversions, including subversive activities of imperialism against the socialist system and that he was sent with the mission to "destroy the country from the inside" (Kassis and Kolosov 1983; Sarvabhavana das (Buniatyan) 2007, 71).[5]

The Soviet authorities considered "uncompromising fight with ideological diversions and diversionists" as one of the crucial tasks, and subsequently their task activities affected the lives of the Soviet devotees (Kassis and Kolosov 1983; LSA K-1-46-215, 1–2; LSA K-18-1-540, 8–9; LSA 1771-260-68, 2–6; LSA K-18-1-184, 84–104; LSA K-18-1-206, 91–8; LSA K-18-1-262, 1–15; LSA K-18-1-315, 15–22; LSA 1-46-242, 43–4). In this socio-cultural context, the activity of Lithuanian Hare Krishnas could be interpreted as a form of resistance against the Soviet regime.

> It did not emerge as an open opposition to the communist ideology, but its actions appeared more as an attempt to exist in a suppressive socio-cultural environment. Almost every initiative of the believers eventuated in interference by the Soviet apparatus: arrests of participants and subsequent interrogations at KGB headquarters, processes in Komsomol meetings and exclusion from educational institutions, work, etc.
>
> (Pranskevičiūtė and Juras 2014, 4)

Methods and the scope of data

The past events of the movement have mainly been recorded by devotees themselves using typewritten *samizdat* magazines such as *The Hare Krishna Chronicle of the Krishna Consciousness in the USSR*, published by the Moscow devotee I. Matushkin (Indradyumna) since 1988 (CFSHK 1988, 3); bulletins of ISKCON such as information bulletin from the Committee to Free Soviet Hare Krishnas (CFSHK): *The Persecution of the Hare Krishna Movement in the USSR* (CFSHK 1986), *Psychiatric Abuse of Hare Krishna Devotees in the U.S.S.R.* (CFSHK 1987) and *Hare Krishna in the USSR* (CFSHK 1988). There were also foreign magazines such as *Express Chronicle* (CFSHK 1988, 3) and *Religion in the Communist Land* (Anderson 1986). Recently an anthology has been published *Dvizhenie soznaniya Krishny v SSSR. Ocherki istorii 1971–1989 godov* [*The Movement of Krishna Consciousness in USSR. Essays of History of 1971–1989*] by V. A. Piskarev (Vidjitatma das – the so-called ISKCON historian) on the history of ISKCON in USSR (Piskarev 2017). The anthology covers various topics, including the particularities of the beginning and the second generation of the Hare Krishna movement, the Hare Krishna movement in Soviet Russia, Caucasus, Ukraine, Latvia, and Lithuania.

The presence of ISKCON (and other alternative religions) in Soviet Lithuania, as well as in the rest of the USSR, has not been widely researched by scholars to date. Previous research on religion in communist regime countries has been mostly focused on restrictions on traditional religions and their survival strategies, while research on alternative religiosities under these regimes is only recently gaining more scholarly attention (Rosenthal 1997; Menzel, Hagemeister and Rosenthal 2012; Pranskevičiūtė and Aleknaitė 2017). The only scholarly work on ISKCON in the Soviet Union is by R. Pranskevičiūtė and T. Juras (2014), this work has contributed to the historical reconstruction of the ISKCON movement in Lithuania and the USSR, revealing ideas that have influenced the formation, spread of sociocultural alternatives, and rise of religious groups. Equal emphasis is given to the archival materials and to the perspectives of the Lithuanian Hare Krishna believers themselves, as well as to the changes that took place in Soviet society.

The study drew on the previously secret documents of the State Security Committee of the Lithuanian SSR (KGB) on Lithuanian Hare Krishnas, which are now preserved in the Lithuanian Special Archives (LSA), a part of the State Archives.[6] For this article, mostly documents of the KGB 5th Service related to the Hare Krishna movement in Lithuania were used. Established in 1979, the KGB 5th Service (former KGB 5th Department) aimed at "fighting against ideological subversion," which was perceived as the fight against "nationalism and anti-Soviet activities." The 5th Service consisted of three departments which

> analyzed processes taking place among the creative, scientific and pedagogical intelligentsia, and young people, and did everything to stop anti-Soviet and nationalist manifestations, while also taking care of the security of members of the Party and the bureaucratic apparatus. It searched for the writers of anonymous anti-Soviet documents and leaflets and checked information about possible terrorist acts and intentions to acquire illegal firearms. Its functions included counterintelligence work among former public figures of independent Lithuania, Latvia and Estonia, former partisans, deportees, prisoners, and national organizations, and the fight against the anti-Soviet activities of émigrés and the influence they had. The 3rd Department was in charge of the work of the Catholic Church and other religious communities.[7]

However, the archive of the KGB 5th Service did not contain much information on Lithuanian Hare Krishnas. It is also important to mention several problems related with the KGB documents which render them insufficient on their own as sources for an accurate analysis of deep sociocultural processes, in this case of the success of ISKCON in Soviet Lithuania. The documents often only indicate accepted decisions, but do not reveal their motivation and it is not always possible to deconstruct the ideological coding used in the documents. Documents that were especially secret were generally destroyed, so there is much information lacking in the remaining documents of Soviet archives (Streikus 2009, 82). KGB documents have a certain specific style of writing and presentation of information, which was determined by the particularity of the KGB's activities. The content of KGB documents is typically abstract and do not provide comprehensive information on presented events, persons etc., as only general instructions or instructions to perform one or another task are given. The documents often lack detail, they are templated (especially, reports and plans), and there is little representation of the real activities of the KGB. Information in KGB documents needs to be interpreted carefully, paying attention to form and context. Initial preconceptions, the ideological evaluations of the activities of targets of the KGB and imitation of activity sometimes distort the truth for the reader, leading to false conclusions; therefore, it is necessary to check facts with other sources (Burinskaitė 2011, 23). For these reasons the material in this chapter not only comes from KGB files, but also from interviews: for the most part they were acquired from a personal archive of the ISKCON historian in Lithuania, David Strashunskij (Bhavananda), plus two interviews that were conducted by Tadas Juras.

The Lithuanian Special Archives (LSA): access to KGB files in Lithuania and the legal rules that govern their use for researchers

After the restoration of Lithuanian independence and right after after the KGB stopped its activity in 1991, the government of the Lithuanian Republic immediately took control of the KGB archives. On August 24, 1991, the Supreme Council of the Lithuanian Republic decided to examine the activity of the SSRS KGB in Lithuania. Later, SSRS KGB documents were declared to be the possession of Lithuanian Republic regardless of their actual location. On December 5, 1995, a special part of the state archives was marked out in the *Law on Documents and Archives of the Republic of Lithuania*:[8]

> The archives of former Lithuanian SSR division of the Committee for State Security (KGB) and other SSRS security and intelligence services, which operated in Lithuania, as well as of the former Ministry of Interior of the Lithuanian SSR and of the Communist Party of Lithuania, the archives of former first divisions of LSSR institutions constitute a special part of state archives – the Lithuanian Special Archives.

The KGB archives (the files are mainly in Lithuanian and Russian) are generally open to individual researchers, and access to files is regulated by law: the *Law on Legal Protection of Personal Data of the Republic of Lithuania* regulates protection of the right of individual privacy with regard to the processing of personal data,[9] and the *Law on Documents and Archives of the Republic of Lithuania* determines the rules on closed periods of access that are applied to structured sets of personal data.[10] Personal data may be processed for scientific research, statistical and historical purposes if the data subject has given his or her consent.[11]

There are two general types of cases when access to KGB files is restricted, but there is still a possibility to get permission to access these files. First, in the case of files that contain information regarding individuals admitting to secret collaboration with the intelligence agencies of the USSR, who appear on the record of the persons who have confessed – access to these can be requested by applying to the Lithuanian Special Archive. Second, when a person who was a target of the intelligence agencies of the USSR has expressed his or her will that material pertaining to him or her should be restriction until his or her death – access to these files can be obtained with written consent from the person in question.

Hare Krishna movement in the Soviet Lithuania

In the late-Soviet period, underground activities, including access to alternative spiritual and esoteric ideas and practices, generally existed in parallel, or even jointly, with the official culture and institutions (Komaromi 2007, 626; Menzel 2013). Besides the officially established Soviet culture, connected with the communist party's aim to control all aspects of the public sphere, there was an unofficial cultural field that was very receptive to the arrival, formation, spread and expression of diverse alternative religiosities and spiritualities. Hare Krishna philosophy and ideas arrived and were integrated naturally into this existing unofficial cultural field. According to Komaromi, this "unofficial culture emerged as an autonomous field from inside Soviet society as a result of its own tensions" (2007, 610). The disappointment with the existing narrowness of the official communist ideology and the loss of the absolute allegiance to it led to the formation and rise of unofficial sociocultural alternatives within the system (Pranskevičiūtė 2014a, 31–2). Various forms of spiritual seekership emerged in the Soviet youth cultural underground especially in the late-Soviet period in the 1970s–1980s (Pranskevičiūtė and Juras 2014; Gordeeva 2017; Panin 2017). Interestingly, in Lithuania, the communist party, in trying to decrease the influence of the Catholic Church and to promote its atheist ideology, widely increased the amount of information available about non-Christian religions. This information was provided as part of atheist indoctrination of the youth through atheist education and the grounding of atheist propaganda with a scientific foundation during 1975–1988 (Streikus 2003). At the same time, from the mid-1970s, the pace of proliferation of all kinds of unofficial religious activities began to accelerate, particularly in the major cities and among educated young people. The change may be related to the continuing search for spiritual values as well as the defense of religious and human rights, an area of activity that received a boost when the Soviet Union signed the Helsinki Final Act in 1975 (Ramet 1993, 27).

Atheist propaganda, KGB and ISKCON

The repressive structures of the KGB were one of the main supports of the communist regime. Communist party ideology influenced the implementation of KGB functions, which were supposed to guarantee the dominance of the communist ideology and one-party rule. Besides the general negative KGB approach towards religion, new campaigns were launched against diverse religions in the Soviet Union in the 1980s. In 1982, after the death of Leonid Brezhnev, the KGB chairperson Yuri Andropov became the leader of Soviet Union (he influenced Soviet political life in the last years of Brezhnev's rule). Andropov's attitude towards religion was very negative and this complicated the lives of registered religious institutions (Catholics), religious minorities (Jehovah's Witnesses, Pentecostals, Adventists) and alternative religious communities (White Brotherhood, krishnaites). In 1980, Andropov wrote about ISKCON, mentioning that followers of the organization had started forming groups in Estonia, Latvia, Lithuania, Ukraine, Moscow and Leningrad and other cities. According to him, they organized meetings in private apartments in order to study literature and to participate in "the teaching" of rituals. Andropov believed that they also organized events in premises belonging to public organizations, without the owners knowing. Here they showed foreign films and held reading lectures in order to implement missions. "Such facts were recorded in Moscow, Kiev, Vilnius, Riga. Up to 100 individuals participated in such activities," therefore the KGB was involved in the activity of "dismantling groups of followers of ancient Eastern religious-philosophical trends by preventing their missionary activities in the country" (*Kommersant. Vlast'* 2009, 47).

The situation of ISKCON changed at this time when atheist propaganda again intensified in 1983 after the easing at the end of the Brezhnev's rule. During 1983–1988, the last attempts to revitalize atheist propaganda in Lithuania started. The most important emphasis on the ideological front during the years of Andropov was the plenum of the Soviet Union Communist Party Central Committee[12] in June 1983 dedicated to questions of ideological performance. In his main speech, Konstantin Chernenko talked about foreign ideological centers, which seek to use religious feelings for anti-Soviet aims. He emphasized the necessity of undertaking additional measures to educate a "new man" (Streikus 2003, 14). The increased negative approach and intensified persecution against Soviet Hare Krishnas was also partly related to the struggle against Western influence in the Soviet Union in the beginning of 1980s, when the political tensions of the Cold War increased. At the end of 1982, the Central Committee office of the Lithuanian communist party, duplicating an analogous Central Committee of the Communist Party of the Soviet Union decision, adopted a resolution "Regarding the Response Against Diverse Propagandist USA Actions and the Activation of Subsequent Propagandist Work in the Republic" (LSA 1771-260–8, 2–6).

Persecutions of KGB: strategy and actions

In the *Plan of Means of Lithuanian SSR KGB to Protect Intelligentsia from Ideological Diversion and the Report on How this Plan was Accomplished*, presented by the KGB 5th Service on December 30, 1982, one paragraph was dedicated to the operations against Lithuanian Hare Krishnas (LSA K-18-1-184, 84–104). Here, the stated aim was

> to implement agent-operative means arranged in a separate plan by localizing and stopping the activity of an ideologically harmful ISKCON, inspired by the West ISKCON, which aims to spread pseudo philosophical and sectarian conceptions in the environment of youth, creative and scientific intelligentsia.

The main focus was on revealing ISKCON channels of communication with Krishna Consciousness followers in the USSR to continue

> deepening the fragmentation among "krishnaites" and distracting ordinary members of mystical-sectarian groups from the influence of the authorities, to document specific enemy actions of the circle leaders (former students Brunza and Kruopis of Kaunas Technical School of Applied Art, as well as temporarily unemployed Gabrėnas and Galadauskas) in the republic.

This was to be done in order to prevent the formation of more organized activities by Lithuanian Hare Krishnas. The other focus was trying to stop individuals becoming involved in the teaching of Hare Krishna ideas, by applying "administrative legal and preventive warning measures with the help of society," as well as by disclosing publicly "in the press of the republic the ideologically harmful essence of krishnaism." In order to achieve these tasks, it was decided to "implement agent-operational means through the agents 'Krianklis', 'Genys', 'Janonis' in further demoralizing 'Krishna teaching' followers in the Lithuanian SSR, as well as by maintaining made up operational ties with the authorities of krishnaites, objects of the case of operative observation – [names and occupations of two individuals are given – *R. P.-A.*]." The KGB 5th Service divisions in the cities Kaunas, Šiauliai and Panevėžys and other Lithuanian SSR KGB divisions in cities and regions were responsible for this task.

Most of the devotees (10–15 devotees from Lithuania) first became acquainted with the KGB in September of 1980 in Riga, during the public lecture of Harikesha Swami in the House of Pioneers (Anderson 1986, 316; CFSHK 1986, 9–10). The people that were arrested there were taken to the militia (Soviet police) offices and were registered. Later on, persecution started in their places of residence. After the arrest, the spiritual teacher and his helper, Kirtiraj, were deported from the Soviet Union as *personas non gratas* (they were forbidden from re-entering the country for 10 years). During this visit to Moscow, Harikesha planned to initiate about 40 devotees from the Soviet republics, including five individuals from Lithuania. Due to the deportation, initiations were postponed and were instead granted from a distance. Two *Brahmins* in Moscow and Riga performed the initiation rituals, and the spiritual names were sent by mail. The other mass arrests took place in Kaunas in 1981, at the home of Shrutadeva and Yogamaya during a program where about 20 devotees participated (Bhavananda). Meetings became rare after this event and the number of participants significantly decreased to around three or four individuals, whereas earlier the meetings often included 20 devotees. Many devotees who had just joined the community were blacklisted by the KGB and were frequently interrogated and reprimanded for conducting sectarian activities in Soviet higher educational institutions (Dhruvananda).

Almost all active devotees from Šiauliai were expelled from the Pedagogical Institute. In the report, dated May 26, 1982, Lithuanian SSR KGB Šiauliai city commander P. Čiudas informed the First Secretary of the Lithuanian communist party of Šiauliai city, J. Lukauskas, on the progress of the case of four devotees (three males and one female), who were studying at the institute (LSA K-18-1-540, 8–9). In this report, it was mentioned that in April 1982, a preventive talk by institute staff and the *Komsomol* of the institute was carried out with the students, who "surrendered the influence of ideologically harmful, anti-materialistic 'teaching' of 'International Society of Krishna Consciousness'" (LSA K-18-1-540, 8). In this meeting, male students were reprimanded for their activity which was "not deserving of the role of representatives of *Komsomol*," but despite such punishment they continued their involvement in the Krishna teaching practices. Very soon after the preventive talk, on May 18, referring to the case against the leaders of krishnaites raised by SSSR Prosecutor, a KGB operation was conducted in the apartment of one devotee called Mayapura. During the raid, the KGB took 24 audio cassettes with the recordings of Krishna teachings, 125 slides, 10 photo rolls, 12 international books translated to Russian, various paintings, posters with religious mystical thematic, and paraphernalia. The report on the confiscated material was later presented to the Rector of the pedagogical institute. At the end of the KGB report, there was the following conclusion: "we consider that there is no reason to present a possibility for a pedagogical activity for [names of devotees are given – *R. P.-A.*] in the future" (LSA K-18-1-540, 9).

In another report of the KGB department of Kaunas regarding the city's creative intelligentsia dated November 11, 1985, information was included on the Hare Krishna community in Kaunas. During the operation for the suppression of the "illegal" gathering of krishnaites at the museum of B. Dauguvietis in the Biržai region, which took place on the night of September 7 to September 8 in 1985 (LSA K-18-1-206, 95–6), 28 individuals were arrested, nine of them were krishnaites from Kaunas. One of members of the group of active krishnaites mentioned was Mayapura – the former student of Šiauliai pedagogical school, who was expelled in 1982 and who lived in Kaunas at the time. In the report, it was suggested that a case be opened against him (LSA K-18-1-206, 96).

In 1986, a significant KGB operation was performed during which many sweeps of the community were made in various locations all over the Republic. On August 25, a KGB perquisition operation was conducted in the apartments of devotees in Kaunas and Vilnius. At this time, the KGB seized a huge amount of newly printed underground literature plus various paraphernalia and personal belongings from the Kaunas temple in Aleksotas. Following this, proceedings were initiated against several *bhaktas* or devotees.

Almost all devotees who shared their memories with the author about these days mentioned that the KGB was looking for information about other group members in order to be able to convict them. The devotees tried to speak without mentioning names and tried to evade such questions. Moreover, all devotees who had to deal with the KGB were forced into cooperation with them. The wide spectrum of intimidations (threats to expel them from an institute or work, false fraud or crime allegations) were usually followed by incentives to cooperate. In all cases, all interviewees (Sanatana, Anirudha, Ramabhadra, Ratiprada) mentioned that they avoided agreeing to cooperate in written form at any cost and refused to sign any documents. It should be noted that the intimidation was not a bluff and almost all original devotees had to quit educational institutions, and some of them lost their jobs.

The KGB justified its campaign against the Hare Krishna organization ISKCON by claiming that it was harmful to health and antisocial in character (LSA K-1-46-215, 1–2; LSA K-18-1-540, 8–9; LSA 1771-260-68, 2–6; LSA K-18-1-184, 84–104; LSA K-18-1-206, 91–8; LSA K-18-1-262, 1–15; LSA K-18-1-315, 15–22; LSA 1-46-242, 43–4). According to the early members, the KGB wanted to besmirch worshipers of Krishna, presenting them to society as antisocial people who used various drugs, organized orgies, and so on. For instance, four devotees (two men and two women) were forcibly hospitalized after an encounter with the militia. The official report stating that "they were found naked in ecstasy of an orgy" (Ramabhadra) was sent to their workplaces and educational institutions. At least one of them was expelled from her job and her institute (Ratiprada). During interrogations, the KGB staff used to tell the devotees that they are trying to protect the members of the Hare Krishna community from the harmfulness of religious activities (*mantra*, as it supposedly damages the brain, was considered by the KGB staff to be a threat to health) (Bhavananda). However, the KGB was mainly worried about gatherings and organized activities.

The consequences of the KGB repressions to the members of the community

The majority of the community were students and thus the KGB tried to frighten members and to constrain their activities through educational institutions. A devotee who was taken by the KGB and who refused to cooperate was processed by the board of the *Komsomol.*[13] If this board decided (in fact, its decisions were formal, it merely declared the judgment that was passed down by the KGB) to exclude a person from the list of the *Komsomol*, this person was in practice withdrawn from the institute. Officially, he or she would be expelled because of the violation of the status of a student

(Anirudha). Moreover, males expelled from a higher educational institution could be drafted to the Soviet Army, or in cases such as this they would be made to serve in a KGB reeducation project.

As far as it is known, none of the first generation of devotees in Kaunas who studied in the Art Institute of Stepas Žukas completed their studies and most of the devotees in Šiauliai Institute of Pedagogy also failed to graduate (Pranskevičiūtė and Juras 2014, 13). The latter had been given an opportunity to choose between abandoning their current lifestyle or leaving the Institute:

> They had me understand that I would be expelled from the Institute if I didn't reform my attitudes. They asked me if I was going to reform myself. I said that I did not see reasons why I should reform myself, I did not do anything wrong.[…] I had an inner barrier, and I could not pass it – to betray my own beliefs and say that ok, I would try to be different. And such a thing happened to all of us.
>
> (Ramabhadra)

Most of the devotees who joined the community later succeeded in finishing their studies, but they also got strict reprimands from *Komsomol*.

The KGB was particularly interested in the leaders of the community whom they aimed to convict and put in jail or in psychiatric hospitals as had been done in Russia and Armenia (CFSHK 1987; 1988, 8–28). In Lithuania – as in other Soviet republics – more resolute KGB actions began in 1983. Lakshmuvan, accused of being a leader of the Kaunas group, was directly brought from his home to a psychiatric hospital. The instruction that was given to a senior doctor was that he was to be given "Full treatment," which meant intensive use of psychotropic drugs (Bhavananda). He was treated like this for two months, and if it had not been for the benevolence of the senior doctor, these procedures could have continued for an unlimited time.

> The senior doctor tried to help, but the nurses were recruited by the KGB. They injected drugs without even asking the senior doctor. "They'll make a vegetable from you, if I don't help. They'll damage your brain and health." Finally, the doctor wrote that the course was finished, but the next day the nurses injected again. "He wrote that the course is over; I don't need anymore!" "We don't care what he has written," – they said. "You'll get what you have to get," – and again, drugs were injected, and he felt terrible pains …
>
> (Bhavananda)

Another three members of the community who were hospitalized in these types of institutions – the "diagnosis" of psychic illness was often termed "pathologic development of personality" (LSA K-18-1-315, 18) – did not endure such extreme treatment. Sanaka Kumara spent six months in a psychiatric hospital where the staff treated him relatively gently and he just had to spit the psychotropic tablets into the toilet. Sanatana Dharma and Ramabhadra were both hospitalized in 1988 because they refused to join the Soviet Army.[14] Sanatana Dharma also got a benevolent doctor who did not prescribe him any medication and allowed other devotees visit him frequently.

The KGB in Lithuania ruined the future of many devotees, took away their career possibilities and exhausted them with constant pressure and interrogations. Nevertheless, the KGB repression in Lithuania was moderate when compared to other Soviet Republics. Usually, the KGB just interfered with the registration of members and had a small talk with them (Anirudha).[15]

Conclusion

In Soviet Lithuania (as in the rest of the Soviet Union), the Krishna community existed under the threat of the repressive structures of the KGB. The KGB applied operational means and conducted surveillance of individuals involved in Hare Krishna activities. Almost every initiative of the Lithuanian believers eventuated in the interference by the Soviet apparatus including home searches, the arrests of participant and subsequent interrogations in the KGB headquarters, processes at *Komsomol* meetings, exclusion from educational institutions and work, or sometimes confinement in psychiatric hospitals. The Krishna group activities were a form of resistance against the Soviet regime and the communist ideology which were constantly suppressed from 1980 until 1989. It did not emerge in open opposition towards the communist ideology but its actions appeared more as an attempt to exist in a suppressive sociocultural environment. Although the KGB persecutions were not as severe as in some other Soviet republics such as Russia, Armenia and Georgia, at least 10 community members were expelled from higher educational institutions in the period 1980–1989. Many of them met with difficulties at their jobs or were even fired, and a few members were forcibly hospitalized in psychiatric hospitals.

Notes

1 KGB – the Committee for State Security (*Russ.:* Komitet gosudarstvennoy bezopasnosti).
2 Sąjūdis (the Reform Movement of Lithuania) – the political organization that sought the return of independence for Lithuania in the late 1980s and early 1990s.
3 Mysticism was often understood as distracting a man from real life (Kassis and Kolosov 1983).
4 The ISKCON *guru*, responsible for the region to which Eastern Europe and the USSR belonged.
5 Actually, the government of the Soviet Union gave this report to the United States (R. Campagnola was its citizen) government, and accused it of espionage (Squarcini and Fizzotti 2004, 19).
6 The general information on preserved documents in LSA is presented on: www.archyvai.lt/en/archives/specialarchives.html Retrieved 10 February 2019.

7 *KGB in the Baltic States: Documents and Researches. The KGB 5th Service* www.kgbdocuments.eu/index.php?4049663882 Retrieved 10 February 2019.
8 *Law on Documents and Archives of the Republic of Lithuania* www.e-tar.lt/portal/en/legalAct/TAR.1FEF229DA7C6/icGHUxVcMD.
9 *Law on Legal Protection of Personal Data of the Republic of* Lithuania www.e-tar.lt/portal/lt/legalAct/TAR.5368B592234C.
10 Information on access to data, data protection, legal framework basis of data preserved in LSA can be found on: www.archyvai.lt/en/legislation.html.
11 More on access and services in LSA: www.archyvai.lt/en/accessandservice.html.
12 The Soviet Union Communist Party Central Committee (*Russ.:* Tsentralniy Komitet Kommunistitcheskoi Partii Sovetskogo Soyuza – TsK KPSS) – the highest body of the Communist Party of the Soviet Union (CPSU) between Party Congresses.
13 *Komsomol* – youth division of the Communist Party of the Soviet Union. In Lithuania, the local term Komjaunimas was used.
14 Generally, all male devotees who were expelled from higher educational institutions and who had no military rank, had to choose between a psychiatric hospital and the Army.
15 On the life of *vaishnavas* and KGB repression in other Soviet republics (especially in Russia, Armenia and Georgia) refer to Anderson 1986, 316–7; CFSHK 1986; 1987; 1988, 13–27; Sarvabhavana das (Buniatyan) 2007.

Interviews

Archival sources

Archive of David Strashunskij (Interviews were conducted between 2006 and 2009. The interviewees at that time were about 40–50 years old. Interviews are stored in a private author's archive):

Anirudha, male (Kaunas, Lithuania, 2007; joined the movement in 1979). Interviewed by D. Strashunskij.

Dhruvananda, male (b. 1960), (Kaunas, Lithuania, 2007, 2008; joined the movement in 1981). Interviewed by D. Strashunskij.

Ramabhadra, male (Vilnius, Lithuania, 2008; joined the movement in 1980). Interviewed by D. Strashunskij.

Ratiprada, female (Kaunas, Lithuania, 2008; joined the movement in 1981). Interviewed by D. Strashunskij.

Sanatana Dharma, male (b. 1961), (Kaunas, Lithuania, 2006, 2008; joined the movement in 1981). Interviewed by D. Strashunskij.

Lietuvos Ypatingasis Archyvas [Lithuanian Special Archives], (LSA), fond 1, fond K-1; fond K-18; fond 1771.

Bhavananda, male (b. 1961), (Kaunas, Lithuania, 24 April 2010, 7 July 2010; joined the movement in 1981). Interviewed by T. Juras; stored in a private author's archive.

Sanatana Dharma, male (b. 1961), (Kaunas, Lithuania, 5, 7 August 2009; joined the movement in 1981). Interviewed by T. Juras; stored in a private author's archive.

References

Anderson, John. 1986. "The Hare Krishna Movement in the USSR". *Religion in Communist Lands* 14 (3): 316–17.

Anderson, John. 1994. *Religion, State and Politics in the Soviet Union and Successor States.* Cambridge: Cambridge University Press.

Burinskaitė, Kristina. 2011. *The Ideological and Political Aspects of Lithuanian SSR KGB Activity in 1954–1990* [*LSSR KGB veiklos ideologiniai ir politiniai aspektai 1954–1990 m.*]. Doctoral dissertation, Humanities, History (05 H), Vilnius University.

Gordeeva, Irina. 2017. "Tolstoyism in the Late-Socialist Cultural Underground: Soviet Youth in Search of Religion, Individual Autonomy and Nonviolence in the 1970s–1980s." Open Theology Topical Issue "Alternative Religiosities in the Soviet Union and the Communist East-Central Europe: Formations, Resistances and Manifestations", 3 (1): 494–516.

KGB in the Baltic States: Documents and Researches www.kgbdocuments.eu/index.php?4049663882 [date of retrieval 2019 February 10].

Komaromi, Ann. 2007. "The Unofficial Field of Late Soviet Culture." Slavic Review, 66: 4 (Winter): 605–29.

Menzel, Birgit, Hagemeister, Michael and Rosenthal, Bernice. G. (eds.). 2012. *The New Age of Russia.* Munich: Verlag Otto Sagner.

Menzel, Birgit. 2013. "The Occult Underground of Late Soviet Russia." *Aries.* 13 (2): 269–88.

Panin, Stanislav. 2017. "Astral Karate as a Phenomenon of Late-Soviet Esoteric Underground." *Open Theology.* Topical Issue "Alternative Religiosities in the Soviet Union and the Communist East-Central Europe: Formations, Resistances and Manifestations", 3 (1): 408–16.

Peškaitis, Artūras and Glodenis, Donatas. 2000. *Contemporary Religiosity* [*Šiuolaikinis religingumas*]. Vilnius: Vaga.

Pranskevičiūtė, Rasa. 2013. "Contemporary Paganism in Lithuanian Context: Principal Beliefs and Practices of Romuva." In: *Modern Pagan and Native Faith Movements in Central and Eastern Europe*, ed. by Aitamurto, Kaarina and Simpson, Scott, 77–94. Durham: Acumen.

Pranskevičiūtė, Rasa. 2014a. "Manifestation of Alternative Religiosity in Post-Soviet Societies: New Religious, New Age and Nature-Based Spirituality Movements" ["Alternatyvaus religingumo raiška pokomunistinėse visuomenėse: naujieji religiniai judėjimai, Naujojo amžiaus ir dvasingumo judėjimai"]. *Culture and Society* 5 (1): 25–44.

Pranskevičiūtė, Rasa. 2014b. "The variety of Buddhism in Lithuania: Zen and Tibetan Buddhism Communities" ["Budizmo įvairovė Lietuvoje: *Zen* ir Tibeto budizmo bendruomenės"]. In: *The Acknowledgement of Religious Diversity in Lithuania: The Forms of Alternative Religiosity* [*Religinės įvairovės pažinimas Lietuvoje: alternatyvaus religingumo formos*], edited by M. Ališauskienė, 100–10. Kaunas: Vytautas Magnus University. http://religija.lt/sites/default/files/religiju_ivairove-2014-optimizuotas.pdf.

Pranskevičiūtė, Rasa. 2017. "Editorial." Topical Issue "Alternative Religiosities in the Soviet Union and the Communist East-Central Europe: Formations, Resistances and Manifestations". *Open Theology.* 3 (1): 665–7.

Pranskevičiūtė, Rasa and Juras, Tadas. 2014. "Acting in the Underground: Life as a Hare Krishna Devotee in the Soviet Republic of Lithuania." *Religion and Society in Central and Eastern Europe,* 7 (1): 3–22.

Ramet, Sabrina. P. 1993. *Religious Policy in the Soviet Union.* New York: Cambridge University Press.

Rosenthal, Bernice. G. ed. 1997. *The Occult in Russian and Soviet Culture.* Ithaca: Cornell University Press.

Squarcini, Federico and Fizzotti, Eugenio. 2004. *Hare Krishna.* Salt Lake City: Signature Books in cooperation with CESNUR.

Stasulane, Anita and Ozoliņš, Gatis. 2017. "Transformations of Neopaganism in Latvia: From Survival to Revival." Topical Issue "Alternative Religiosities in the Soviet Union and the Communist East-Central Europe: Formations, Resistances and Manifestations". *Open Theology* 3 (1): 235–48.

Streikus, Arūnas. 2003. "The Character of Atheist Propaganda in Lithuania in 1975–1988" ["Ateistinės propagandos pobūdis Lietuvoje 1975–1988 m."]. *Genocidas ir rezistencija* 1(13): 7–21.

Streikus, Arūnas. 2008. Vakarų kultūrinės įtakos ribojimas Sovietų Lietuvoje 1965–1986 m. [*Restrictions Placed on Western Culture in Soviet Lithuania in 1965–1986*]. *Genocidas ir rezistencija.* 1(23): 7–23.

Streikus, Arūnas. 2009. "Historical Investigations of Cultural and Religious Life in Soviet Lithuania: Problems with the Sources" ["Kultūrinio ir religinio gyvenimo sovietų Lietuvoje istoriniai tyrimai. Šaltinių keliamos problemos"]. *Darbai ir dienos* 52: 75–83.

Documents of the researched group and mass media

Bhaktivedanta Swami Prabhupada and Abhay, Charanavinda. 1990. Bhagavad-gyta, kokia ji yra [Bhagavad-Gita as It is]. Bhaktivedanta Book Trust: Minskas.

Bhaktivedanta Swami Prabhupada and Abhay, Charanavinda. 1994. Šrimad Bhagavatam. Pirmoji giesmė. 1 dalis. [Srimad-Bhagavatam. First Canto. Part 1]. Bhaktivedanta Book Trust: Minskas.

The Information Bulletin from the Committee to Free Soviet Hare Krishnas (CFSHK). 1986. "The Persecution of the Hare Krishna Movement in the USSR". Almviks Gård, Sweden: CFSHK.

The Information Bulletin from the Committee to Free Soviet Hare Krishnas (CFSHK). 1987. "Psychiatric Abuse of Hare Krishna Devotees in the U.S.S.R.". Almviks Gård, Sweden: CFSHK www.hkussr.com/doc/hkdoc02p1.htm [date of retrieval 2020 August 25].

The Information Bulletin from the Committee to Free Soviet Hare Krishnas (CFSHK). 1988 (December). "Hare Krishna in the USSR". Almviks Gård, Sweden: CFSHK.

Kasiss, Vadim and Kolosov, Leonid. 1983. "Prikryvayas' tsvetuschim lotosom" [Under Cover of Blossoming Lotus]. Nedelya 22: 10. 2009 (10 August).

Pamyatnye poslaniya. Iz zapiski predsedatelja KGB Y. V. Andropova v CK KPSS 1980 g. [Commemorative Messages. From Notes of KGB Chairman Y. V. Andropov in the Central Committee of the Soviet Union Communist Party in 1980]. *Kommersant. Vlast'* 31 (835): 47. www.kommersant.ru/doc/1218354 [date of retrieval 2020 August 25].

Piskarev, Vladimir A. (Vidjitatma Das). 2017. *Dvizhenie soznanija Krishny v SSSR. Ocherki istorii 1971–1989 godov* [The Movement of Krishna Consciousness in USSR. Essays of History of 1971–1989]. Moskva: The Bhaktivedanta Book Trust (Fond "Bhaktivedanta").

Sarvabhavana Das (Buniatyan, Gagik). 2007. *Salted Bread: a True Story as Told To His Son*. New Delhi, India: Torchlight Publishing Inc.

9 Between simplification and absurdity

The Czech protestant milieu, "New Orientation" and the secret police

Ondřej Matějka

From the very beginning of its activity inside the biggest Czech Protestant church, (*Českobratrská církev evangelická* – ČCE – Evangelical Church of Czech Brethern) at the turn of the 1940s and 1950s, the Czechoslovak secret police (*Státní bezpečnost* – StB – State Security) encountered numerous difficulties in dealing with a complex and highly socially and theologically differentiated institution with a presbyterial structure. Furthermore, StB officers were confused by influential Protestant actors who, on the one hand, sincerely supported the communist regime and "socialist re-construction" of Czech society and, on the other hand and at the same time, dared to criticize not only the anti-religious campaigns of the communist party, but also certain political stances of the regime. For this reason, representatives of the church department of the secret police gladly instrumentalized the appearance of a group of similarly formed and theologically and politically oriented co-evals inside the Czech Protestant church. This group, which had an overall positive, yet systematically critical attitude towards the repressive and dictatorial practices of socialist state, labelled themselves the "New Orientation" (NO) in the early 1960s.

From, roughly, 1966 on, StB officers became almost obsessed with the group NO that progressively became a general label for every "enemy" inside the Czech protestant milieu (the frequency of the use of this category can be illustrated by the early appearance of the abbreviation "NO" in StB files). Historians of the Czechoslovak communist regime who based their interpretations directly on StB archives or documents of secret police transmitted to the leadership of the Communist Party of Czechoslovakia (*Komunistická strana Československa* – KSČ) have perpetuated this perspective even after 1989. Hence, in Karel Kaplan's thick syntheses on Czechoslovakia in the 1960s, NO constitutes the central element of passages dealing with Czech Protestantism (Kaplan 2008, 133–9). This narrative almost becomes a caricature in the study by Slovak historian Peter Dinuš who published his dissertation entitled *Českobratrská církev evangelická v agenturním rozpracování StB* (Evangelical Church of Czech Brethern under StB surveillance) in 2004 and mentioned NO on almost every page. It is possible to find in total 231 occurrences of the "New Orientation" (more than any other name or concept) in this book of 130 pages.

This chapter, which is based on secret police archives, state archives[1], church archives and personal testimonies, aims to offer a better understanding of the (mis)uses of this label by the secret police between the 1960s and 1980s and the historiographical consequences of this phenomenon. In doing so, I will make more explicit some of the risks of too heavy reliance on secret police archives in the study of religion during communism. This chapter proceeds chronologically, contrasting the development of this particular theological group inside the Protestant milieu based on diverse sources contrasted with the view produced by the StB which reflected the agendas and operational patterns of the Czechoslovak secret police.

"The situation remains very unsatisfactory": StB and Czech protestants in the 1950s

Whether judged from a social, political or theological point of view, the largest Czech Protestant church entered the era of the construction of the communist dictatorship as a complex and internally diversified entity. The internal cleavages within the church were the result of the tumultuous history of modern Czech Protestantism. After officially re-entering Bohemian public space in 1781 (The Act of Tolerance issued by Austrian emperor Joseph II), Protestants began to progressively and laboriously assert themselves in the predominantly Catholic context. They never constituted more than 3% of the population of the Bohemian lands and until the end of the nineteenth century they remained a predominantly rural, uneducated and socially and culturally marginal community dependent on help from Western Protestant countries.

This started to change with the rise of the Czech nationalist movement that forged a particular (anti-Habsburg and anti-German) narrative of Czech history centered around non- or anti-Catholic episodes (mainly the Hussite movement and its aftermath in the fourteenth century). The thus far peripheral Czech Protestants began to acquire a particular position of discursive centrality in the construction of the Czech nation from the 1850s on. This fact contributed to facilitating their access to the newly arising strata of the educated middle and upper middle classes of Czech society at the turn of the nineteenth and twentieth centuries.

At the moment of the creation of an independent Czechoslovak state in 1918, they were already represented by a growing group of well-situated urban Protestant élites. These élites succeeded in integrating influential circles of the First Czechoslovak Republic close to President Masaryk and proposed the image of Protestantism as the embodiment of "democratic Czech spirit." This stance undeniably attracted thousands of newcomers and converts in the 1920s who gladly identified with this mildly nationalist and theologically liberal version of Protestantism and soon came to outnumber the surviving stratum of rural conservative Protestantism (Matějka 2009).

Since the mid-1920s, these versions of mainstream Czech Protestantism came under strong attack from young Protestant theologians led by Josef Lukl Hromádka (1889–1969). In close interaction with the Swiss professor Karl Barth (1886–1968), Hromádka developed the so-called dialectical theology which, at least in its Czech version, contained a strong anti-nationalist accent as well as political sympathies for socialism. These dimensions only strengthened in the 1930s in the context of the anti-Nazi struggle: after 1936 Hromádka and his allies formed a coalition with the left wing Czech social democrats and also a part of the Czech communists. Together, they also collaborated in resistance activities when the Third Reich occupied the Bohemian lands in 1939. At the same time, Hromádka's circle profited from the rising influence of Barth in Western Protestantism and Hromádka himself, but also his students, became intensely involved in various ecumenical initiatives leading to the establishment of the World Council of Churches (WCC) in its provisional form in 1938 and definitively in 1948 (Matějka 2012).

By the second half of the 1930s, at the latest, Hromádka had become the main figure of identification for the majority of young Czech Protestant élites who followed him both theologically and politically. As a result, in 1945 an important part of these élites adopted a positive attitude towards the communist party and its efforts to transform Czechoslovakia into a socialist state. They remained loyal to the communist dictatorship even after the February coup-d'Etat in 1948 – which contrasted dramatically with the attitude of the Catholic Church. Czechoslovak bishops (supported and instructed from the Vatican) did not hide their anti-communism and suffered severe repression and criminalization by the communist state administration which actively engaged the StB in its anti-Catholic operations. Moreover, several highly placed communists did not forget their old bonds forged in the 1930s to the Protestant milieu and they placed a protective umbrella above their protégés even in the context of the (discursively) atheist dictatorship. Last but not least, Hromádka was elected to the Central (and later also Executive) Committee of the WCC where he (and his Czechoslovak colleagues) defended the Eastern bloc's interests and served as one of the, at times, rare bridges between Czechoslovakia and the West.

Consequently, in the early phase of the establishment of the regime (1948–56), the ČCE remained outside the primary sphere of interest of the Czechoslovak political police. There are several reasons for this attitude. In the first place, in the sphere of church politics the StB invested a great deal of time, money and personnel into the struggle with the disobedient Catholic hierarchy. State security officials, when they dared to formulate the dangers linked to the "bourgeois character" and potentially susceptible Western connections of Czech Protestantism, also rapidly understood that the influential protectors of Czech protestants constituted an obstacle too great to fight.[2] Furthermore, the StB itself went through a protracted process of internal organization and re-organization. For all those reasons, it seems that ČCE did not constitute a relevant object for sustained StB's attention until the late 1950s (Dinuš 2005).

This is confirmed by the very scarce documentation accessible in the archives from that era. Peter Dinuš, who has meticulously assembled StB files related to ČCE, found the first explicit passages related to StB perspectives on the largest Protestant church only in general reports from 1958 and 1959. If we read these documents carefully, we can clearly sense a sort of helplessness on the part of the mighty police agency vis-à-vis the Protestant milieu:

> even though we got some new collaborators in ČCE this year, the situation in the church remains very unsatisfactory because we do not have such an actor on the ground who would be able to penetrate the reactionary elements of the church.
>
> (Report 1958 quoted in Dinuš 2005, 364)

This 1958 report points at the same time to a new accent in the presentation of the ČCE. The secret police explicitly asserted the existence of "reactionary elements" in the church – which had been until then presented as a "very progressive church" by the state apparatus (Matějka 2007). This discursive shift was related to important changes in the general attitude of the Czechoslovak communist leadership towards religion. In the context of a stabilized regime, the Czechoslovak leaders decided to accelerate the construction of "a socialist society" – which left less and less space for "the remnants of religious backwardness."[3] The late 1950s thus became the moment of an intense anti-church offensive which, for the first time in the existence of the Czechoslovak communist dictatorship, also systematically struck the Czech protestants as well as Catholics who were, nevertheless, already used to communist repression. The StB was to play an important part in this phase – but with little success in the beginning. This is confirmed, for instance, by the 1961 report where we can find statements similar to embarrassed observations from the late 1950s: "it is very difficult to infiltrate the leadership of the ČCE with our agents" (Report 1961 quoted in Dinuš 2005, 364).

Locating the "hostile center" inside the ČCE – the 1960s

Nevertheless, only a few years later, the level of urgency in the StB's rhetoric on Protestants was elevated to a totally new level with the rather scarce and vague remarks being replaced by regular reports emphasizing the danger since the mid-1960s of certain representatives of the Protestant milieu. From the StB perspective, ČCE began to constitute a genuine "security issue" (Kosová 1980, 80; Štícha 1980, 36; Křišťál 1985, 102) and acquired the status (in the StB's lenses) of "the most reactionary of all churches" (Radikovský 1980, 31; Tuček 1983, 58). The change is directly connected to the StB appropriation of the appearance of a group of young pastors and laymen inside the ČCE that had labelled themselves as the "New Orientation" around 1962. In the following years this label became omnipresent in StB reports on the ČCE but also when analyzing wider security threats. It began to serve as the axis along which the StB could organize the (until then) too complex and, to a certain extent, impenetrable Czech Protestant world: StB officers created an easily accessible and applicable system of binary oppositions (supporters vs opponents of the NO considered as the "hostile center" inside ČCE).

This particular historical moment illustrates the dynamic interplay between several actors resulting in a different (and aggressively antagonistic) approach of the StB towards the ČCE with lasting consequences in following decades.

In order to understand how this unfolded, it is necessary to introduce the "New Orientation" as it emerged as a historical reality (Pfann 1998). While this group put itself firmly on the Czech Protestant map only at the end of the 1950s when it emphasized its fundamental theological and generational specificities in rigorously formulated programmatic texts, its homogeneity and readiness for action was based on long-lasting friendships forged in the early post-war years mainly inside the Czech branch of the student YMCA (*Akademická YMCA*). This institution transmitted to young Czechs a peculiar mixture of ideas and opportunities including an openness to socialist ideas, dialectical theology, the possibility to learn Western languages (German but also English), an appetite for political debating and also direct engagement in domestic but also international affairs (Matějka 2019b).

Alfréd Kocáb (1925–2018), Jaroslav Pfann (1924–1998), Jan Šimsa (1929–2016), Jakub Trojan (born 1927) and others, many of whom first got to know each other in the YMCA, then deepened their personal and intellectual affinity at the Comenius Protestant theological faculty where they all studied in the early 1950s and were substantially influenced by Josef Lukl Hromádka. This team of pastors was completed by several laymen with similar trajectories – namely Ladislav Hejdánek (born 1927) and Jaroslav Procházka (1926–2010). The New orientation thus appears, above all, as a group of friends and coevals (predominantly pastors), formed by identical influences in an important socializing setting and at an important juncture in their lives.[4]

For that matter, it is significant that the "Theses of the New Orientation" designed to present the programme of the group to the ČCE, and later perceived by the StB as "the battle call" against socialist state (Kosová 1980, 58–61), were debated, formulated and prepared for publication by the above-mentioned members in July 1962 while on holiday together with their families in the woods of Western Bohemia: "we discussed, we swam in the nearby pond [...], we organized Olympic games for our children, we picked blueberries, we read, we sent a protest telegram to Moscow and we drew up the theses of New Orientation" (Trojan 2010, 290).

Pastor Trojan's account could certainly stand for a rather typical picture of Czech pastoral holidays in the 1960s, reflecting how their modest social standing limited the available options for vacation. Complementing blueberries and swimming with international politics represented, however, a New

Orientation specificity, clarified explicitly in the conclusion of the product of their summer debates. The 7th thesis of the New Orientation programme stated: "The Gospel leads us to take responsibility for the economic, political and cultural situation in our country and in the whole world" (Pfann 1998, 17–23). In this regard, Trojan, Vébr, Šimsa and their colleagues faithfully developed positions of their much admired professor Hromádka, claiming to be his only "genuine interpreters" (Šimsa 2007). Their "genuiness" was undeniably mixed with a great ambition, both theological and socio-political, related to rising reformatory ferment in Czechoslovak society in the early 1960s. These young men updated on one hand Hromádka's "engaged theology" (confirming its unambiguous pro-socialist orientation) and acted out concretely the public dimension of Christian social responsibility. At the same time, on the other hand, they re-actualized his peace commitment by focusing on the domestic arena and by balancing disproportions in Hromádka's one-sided criticism of Western imperialism.

For this reason, in 1958 the New Orientation initiated the establishment of a special "Peace Department" inside the Union of the ČCE Clergy (Trojan 2010, 209–11). Representatives of the New Orientation used this Peace Department (as well as other ČCE platforms) to repeatedly issue calls to both super-powers to stop the arms race, to end the testing of nuclear weapons and to start negotiations on complete disarmament. For instance, during the Cuban missile crisis they wrote a message to Khrushchev asking him to withdraw the Soviet nuclear installations. In 1964, they did not hesitate to address even Chinese leaders entering the nuclear club. In the beginning of the 1960s they also engaged in correspondence with Martin Luther King and Albert Schweitzer, whom they considered the most striking examples of "concrete peace work" (Trojan 2010, 223–31). A summer telegram to Moscow from a New Orientation camp hence constituted a standard practice in the repertory of the engaged pastors like Trojan, Kocáb, Veber and their friends – but also a source of strangeness inside the Protestant milieu where they were perceived as "bizarre" (Šimsa 2007).

If we consider their public activity and sincere support of fundamental socialist ideas and the respect for KSČ,[5] it is understandable that, at first, they attracted the attention of the state administration as potential allies. In 1959, Jiří Veber was noticed for "influencing the believers in a progressive way" in his parish in Domažlice.[6] In 1964 the ministry reporter at the annual meeting of the Union of the ČCE Clergy brought Čapek, Balabán, Trojan and Šimsa to the fore: "Their knowledge of Soviet literature is amazing! It is fundamental to bring them on our side!"[7] With such publicity, the principal representatives of the New Orientation were invited on two occasions, in 1964 and again in 1965, to discuss their opinions with the Church Department of the Ministry of Education and Culture. These encounters indicated, however, substantial difficulties in "bringing them on our side": after a lively debate centred mainly on the relationship between science and faith and on anti-religious discrimination practices in schools, state officers responsible for church policy led by a conservative apparatchik Karel Hrůza (with close connections to the StB) realized that the New Orientation support for socialist principles was incompatible with their ideas on the necessary ghettoization of the church and its progressive disappearance in the process of the construction of socialist society.[8]

A potential ally thus rapidly transformed not only into an opponent but, due to its effective mobilization strategies inside ČCE, also into a dangerous threat for the defenders of the *status quo* in the Czech ecclesiastical field. What were the mobilization strategies of the New Orientation? First of all, members of the group were in permanent contact. Not only did they regularly meet, but they also conducted intense correspondence (which later offered a great source of data for StB surveillance) and in 1964 they launched an internal newsletter called "Problems and tasks." All these semi-private forums served to clarify and fine-tune positions that they then presented, defended and advanced inside the ČCE. The church reviews (*Kostnické jiskry*, *Český bratr*, *Křesťanská revue*) represented their principal platforms. They became indeed a consistent pressure group establishing lists of important articles to write and distributing them among themselves with deadlines included (and mostly respected) (Šimsa 2008). But this hyper-activity inspired also an important dose of criticism inside the church: hence, even though Šimsa, Trojan, Veber and their close allies were very visible and audible inside the church, they never succeeded in getting elected to the supreme executive body of the ČCE – the Synodal Council and they irritated many influential church figures who complained about "wild and disorderly synod sessions" where NO delegates "indeed did not stop interrupting."[9]

These ambitious pastors full of youthful energy further developed and radicalized their engaged theology and practices and soon began to focus more consistently on issues outside the narrow church frame. They followed and participated in the reformist movement in the entire Czech society: "It is absolutely imperative that we take part in the struggle for the spiritual, cultural and moral orientation of our society," proclaimed the New Orientation in 1964 (Trojan 2010, 258–62). One of younger pastors even warned the ČCE would deservedly "suffer God's judgement for its silence and conformity" should it stay aloof from current debates and controversies by concentrating instead on the "building up the walls around our parishes."[10]

It seems plausible, however, that despite this hectic activity the StB would not have perceived them as the principal "hostile centre" inside the Protestant milieu and a "national security threat" from the late 1960s on without taking into consideration two additional (and fundamental) factors. First of all, it is important to underline that the NO representatives directly engaged with the StB when they publicly challenged its recruitment methods.[11] In fact, in the summer of 1966 in the course of the always dynamic debates during the Union of the ČCE Clergy plenary sessions, pastor Šimsa (well known for his quick temper) decided to "settle a very old score" in front of the assembly of more than 100 pastors and emissaries of the state administration. In an improvised speech, he shared with the frozen audience his story from February 1952 when he was kidnapped by Security officials and pressured during an interrogation lasting several hours to become a secret collaborator of the StB. He testified that the StB had offered him a position of teaching assistant at the Comenius faculty in exchange for submitting regular reports on teachers and students of the faculty, namely professor Hromádka. Should he refuse, the StB threatened that Šimsa's mother would lose her pension and his brother would be expelled from the KSČ. Šimsa resisted this attempt to blackmail him and declined the Security's proposition.[12]

The ČCE pastors reacted to this revelation in different ways. While some of older pastors almost "shitted in their pants" (Pfann et al. 2001) according to accessible testimonies, several of Šimsa's colleagues (most of them members of the NO) picked up the gauntlet and made public the same type of experience – altogether seven of them. Even the extremely cautious synodal senior Viktor Hájek contributed to the debate and his statement startled his usual young staunch opponents. In "the most glorious moment of his mandate" (according to Šimsa), Hájek confirmed that during the last decade many pastors had come to him for advice when facing the same situation as Šimsa. Hájek systematically recommended that they refuse offers from the StB for such contracts as they were "compatible neither with faith nor with pastoral office."[13] This dramatic 1966 discussion had a profoundly liberating effect according to the participants: "we felt like a bad spell had just broken."[14]

StB archives prove the ensuing shock of this powerful agency: the Protestant clergy was indeed the first to dare to publicly criticize StB methods in recruiting its secret agents (Dinuš 2005, 370). The follow-up investigation of the seven pastors did not bring any concrete results, "methods of psychological coercion" criticized by the pastors remained unpunished but, at the same time, the Protestant complainers' boldness or "insolence" led to no sanctions against them or their church (Pfann et al. 2001, 523–4). Šimsa himself concluded his 1966 interview with security officials "by interpreting their encounter as a good sign of the progress of democratization [...] inviting even the StB to self-reflection" which filled Šimsa with "confidence into the future of socialism."[15] Repressive proposals from the Church Department of the Ministry of Education and Culture to the Central Committee also achieved nothing (Kaplan 2008, 135).

It seems, however, that it was after this public criticism of StB practices that the institution began to focus closely on the main proponents of the New Orientation and from 1966 we can find regular mentions of the NO in StB general reports on the Czechoslovak security situation. StB officers did not hide their frustration caused by "NO perseverance in coming again and again with new excessive claims, by NO efforts to influence and participate in political life of our society" (Reports from 1966 and 1967 quoted in Dinuš 2005, 368).

In February 1968, the StB presented NO as "completely unified" with "wide support" inside the Czech protestant milieu and, furthermore, closely collaborating with "dangerous revisionists" among the reformist communist intelligentsia.[16] For instance, New Orientation activists were in close contact with influential journalists like Ludvík Vaculík and, as the security files document, pushed soon and hard for a clear ČCE welcome of the new KSČ course. This only amplified in the following weeks and the attitudes and activities of pastors of the NO during the months of the Prague spring brought enough proof for the StB to justify and fix its conception of the entire ČCE as "the most reactionary" of all churches in socialist Czechoslovakia (Radikovský 1980, 31). In fact, during the meeting of the Union of Clergy in February 1968, pastor Šimsa, Trojan and others, impressed by the January changes in the KSČ leadership, carried through a motion sent to the presidium of the National Assembly proposing an encounter with the Assembly leadership to "discuss ecclesiastical problems."[17] Understandably, NO enthusiastically welcomed changes in the management of the recently created "Secretariat for Church Affairs" where reform communists and revisionist theoreticians open to Christian-Marxist dialogue such as Erika Kadlecová took the lead in March 1968 and replaced apparatchiks with close links to StB like Karel Hrůza.

Soon after the demise of censorship, NO representatives found their way onto the pages of the national media. In the summer months of 1968 Jakub Trojan, Milan Balabán and Jan Šimsa published extensive articles in *Literární listy*, one of the principal platforms of radical reformists of the Prague spring (Balabán 1968, Šimsa 1968, Trojan 1968). They showed in their texts, on one hand, the capacity of the proponents of the New Orientation to present to their contemporaries notions like "sin" or "grace" in a civil, understandable and even humorous way, and on the other, their firm will to claim responsibility for their society, to move from imposed civil margins to the centre.

However, the time proved to be short: the most ambitious autonomous and explicitly political NO initiative during the Prague spring, which in the end did not produce any outcome, consisted in proposing pastor Kocáb as a candidate for the elections to the National Assembly (planned in autumn 1968 but postponed until 1971). NO also participated in initiatives indicating the waking up of Czech civil society: its leaders were explicitly solicited to cooperate with two other important civil initiatives, namely KAN (Club of Politically Engaged Non-Partisans) and K231 (Club of ex-political prisoners), but with no concrete consequences because NO representatives preferred to continue their collaboration with reformist communists.[18]

Faithfulness to their reform communist allies constituted the most visible manifestation of NO consistency throughout the period 1968–69. According to testimonies of Kadlecová and her deputy secretary Ladislav Prokůpek, they could "always rely" on their Protestant (mainly NO) counterparts who formed with them a stable coalition against regional and district, often conservative and anti-reformist, ecclesiastical secretaries (Kadlecová 2008, Prokůpek 2008). Prokůpek remembered that "negotiations with the Catholics were much more complicated, they most often had to wait for instructions from the Vatican, and they did not trust us" (Prokůpek 2008; Cuhra 1999,

13–14). The ČCE on the contrary continued to express full loyalty if not admiration to these reformists at various public occasions even after the invasion of the Warsaw pact armies in August 1968 (Matějka 2019a).

It is important to note that despite unlimited access to the church and the public sphere during the months of Prague spring, the New Orientation did not succeed in electing its representatives to high positions in the church at the first completely free synod during the communist dictatorship in 1969.[19] Nevertheless, after the definitive demise of reformists and the successful installation of the process of "normalization" in the second half of 1969, the NO became the main target for the StB that began to systematically repress it with the willing cooperation of other parts of the state apparatus (namely Karel Hrůza who returned to the head of the Secretariat of Church Affairs).

"We have to join the NO, all of us" – 1970s

In the 1970s, the NO label acquired a new signification encompassing every Protestant with a critical attitude towards post-1968 "real socialism" and a soon after, NO started to serve as a kind of pedagogical tool in StB discourse and education. As we have already seen, since the mid-1960s, the secret police representatives re-appropriated NO as a formidable instrument for simplifying the complex ČCE landscape. But it was only at the turn of the 1960s and 1970s (the beginning of "normalization") that StB officers began to use the label intensively and extensively for branding every person they perceived as problematic inside the Protestant milieu as "an exponent of the NO." This generalization had various consequences. Protestants themselves first perceived this phenomenon as proof of the StB's incompetence. Pastor Jan Šimsa talked, for instance, about "those idiots" who "stupidly" took over a sociologist's tentative definition of the NO as "the group of thirty to forty young theologians following the line of J. L. Hromádka,"[20] and "could not stop looking for those fateful forty brave men until they found them" (Šimsa 2004, 2008). In an even more paradoxical way, some students of Protestant theology and young pastors active in dissent in the 1970s were, at first, almost offended by being subsumed under this label. In fact, they did not feel much in common with their older brothers who never stopped praising their mentor Hromádka; while for this younger generation he was just a "collaborationist" or "socialist fellow traveller" occasionally stopping in Prague between two ridiculous "peace congresses" somewhere in communist countries (Karásek 1998, 49, 61–2).

But the indiscriminate repression that hit all of these actors in the 1970s succeeded in producing a new sense of loyalty and cohesiveness among Protestant opponents of the regime. This resulted, ironically, in the stabilization of solidarities over theological and generational cleavages inside ČCE. According to pastor Miloš Rejchrt (born in 1946), "they [StB] *gleichschalted* us so effectively by putting us all under the New Orientation brand that in the end we really got much closer in every regard" (Rejchrt 2002, 102;

Karásek 1998, 190). One of the most critical voices towards Hromádka and his NO admirers – the very popular pastor Svatopluk Karásek (born in 1942), who signed the Charter 77 and later was forced to emigrate to Switzerland, proclaimed in the early 1970s: "We have always been against the New Orientation. However now, when the StB is after them, we have to join the NO, all of us. They cannot put us all in jail" (quoted in Keřkovský 2017). This inner rapprochement was confirmed by numerous interviews with (then) young students of theology who tolerated more easily different theological and political (always basically pro-socialist) perspectives of their older colleagues when they found themselves summoned together for interrogation by the StB (Hudcová 2010). In this regard, the StB that looked so feverishly for "a unified hostile headquarters" and firmly believed in the existence of "a second power centre" (Kosová 1980, 66; Štícha 1980, 42; Křišťál 1985, 44) inside the ČCE, *in fine* succeeded (at least partly) in creating it.

This creation was so persuasive that it became a pedagogical resource for students of the StB faculty of the Police University (*Vysoká škola SNB*). We can observe this particular instrumentalization of the NO in seven master theses that were prepared and defended at the Police University in the first half of the 1980s. These master theses constitute an interesting source in several respects. The one that we will not develop here is their scientific quality – for a university teacher in 2021 they open the window to another world where a very primitive sort of plagiarism was obviously a part of everyday "academic" practice: in the seven theses we can find long passages copied and pasted from one another (without any referencing, of course). For this reason, they (taken as a whole) constitute a unified narrative showing various uses of the NO (and Czech protestant milieu in general) by the StB. They can serve as an illustration of the fact that the StB, in a way, co-constructed the NO because it needed it as a tool in the struggle for its own recognition and legitimation, a need that became more acute in occasional tensions with other state agencies (Trusina 2015). We can observe manifestations of this phenomenon in three "topoi" that form the argumentative skeleton of these theses.

The first "topos" traceable in all of the analysed theses relates to the essential role of the StB as the "keeper" not only of state security in material affairs, but also of the fidelity to fundamental ideological principles; the authors repeatedly emphasize their allegiance to "true Leninist principles" (Štícha 1980, 48). In fact, the theses are based on an identical argumentative pattern (often copied and pasted with slight variants from one thesis to another) which presents the "false progressivism" as the basic line of the history of modern Czech Protestantism and the role of the StB in uncovering this line and its ability to draw adequate conclusions from it (Štícha 1980, 5). In a determined opposition to "revisionist uses" of early Marx's writings by Czech reform communists (such as the above-mentioned Kadlecová and others) and their dialogical encounters with Protestant intellectuals in the 1960s (Matějka 2017), StB officers underline in the introductory passages of their studies again and again that it is imperative not to forget the basic Leninist principle in dealing with religious institutions: every communist is an atheist and has to be aware of the ongoing "strenuous struggle" between the Party and churches; a struggle which is to lead to the establishment of a religion-free society (Tuček 1983, 8). They further argue that the difficulty (and the risk) of dealing with Czech protestants is their proximity to some of the "most progressive" traditions of Czech history (namely the Hussite movement) – which differentiates them from "reactionary Catholics" (Radikovský 1980, 9–10; Křišťál 1985, 2). In their argumentation, the StB officers bring numerous proofs of the "falsity" and "danger" of relying on those external impressions – some even use the image of "ingenious hypocrisy" (Křišťál 1985, 25). In Czech contemporary history, they underline the closeness of Protestants to Masaryk which made them into one of the keystones of the "dominance of bourgeoisie" and into "proponents of Western capitalism" (specifically connected to local Protestant-led associations YMCA and YWCA) during the interwar First Republic. In a typical version of this narrative, sergeant major Radikovský observes that after a "surface acceptance" of the post-1948 changes, "Czech Protestantism proved its insurmountable existential connection to the bourgeois order" in the "crisis years" around 1968 (Radikovský 1980, 15).

The StB "researchers" then all develop the image of their agency as a victim of NO aggressiveness in the mid-1960s – which is, of course, rather surprising from today's perception of the power of this agency. This presentation then results in the topoi of the StB as a last rampart of socialism and a sort of brave yet threatened fighter against the "anti-socialist wave" of the Czechoslovak reform movement culminating in spring 1968. In fact, according to the StB master theses, the NO was a precursor in "untrue" attacks on the StB during Prague spring (Šmarda 1984, 37). This refers to the 1966 incident at the meeting of the Union of the ČCE clergy. From the StB perspective, at that occasion NO representatives set the tone for "pressure actions" and "seditious campaign" (Křišťál 1985, 44) against the StB in wider Czech society. State security officers also accused NO of acting in a cowardly way with these "anonymous attacks" and, in summary, of paving the way "for counter-revolution" (Radikovský 1980, 37; Šticha 1980, 30).

This version of a long-term epic struggle between the StB and NO led young StB elites to conclude their theses with an ambivalent message. There, they combined expressions of their pride related to successes in "containing NO subversive activities," with the omnipresent call for vigilance (Křišťál 1985, 108). Each of the authors of the analysed theses did not forget to mention that he or she based his/her reflections on personal experiences "from the field" (all of them had to prove their capacity and reliability as rank-and-file agents of the StB before being admitted to the Police University). Logically then, they presented their achievements in the recruitment of new secret informers from the church milieu in a particular region or at the Prague Protestant Theological Faculty. Each of the theses proudly mentions the elections of a new synodal council in 1977 including StB agent(s) and also the continuing "process of isolation" of NO "exponents" inside the Protestant milieu (Tuček 1983, 61). Nevertheless, all the authors further state that their dealings and research on NO in particular and the Protestant milieu, in general, confirm their assertion that the "danger of NO cannot be underestimated" (Radikovský 1980, 49). In this regard, they remind their readers of the global context of "mounting tensions between imperialism and socialism" (Tuček 1983, 66) but also of the not-so-distant experience with the NO during the Prague spring when, according to StB, it succeeded "to mobilize supporters in times of crises" of the regime – a capacity labelled as extremely dangerous (Kosová 1980, 98).

The above observations confirm the interpretation that these theses also functioned as a particular kind of self-legitimation: they provided arguments explaining the ongoing importance of the StB which was endangered, as any other government agency, due to budget cuts brought on by economic difficulties in late socialist Czechoslovakia (Kosová 1980, 99). Furthermore, from the mid-1980s, the StB (as a symbol of the hard power policies of dictatorship) had to justify more and more its relevance and raison-d'être in the context of *perestroika* and *glasnost*.

Conclusion

After 1989, it seemed, at first that the words and deeds of the StB would inevitably and rapidly be erased from history. Nevertheless, the heritage of the StB discourse on the NO proved to be much more durable and have continued to influence the Czech Protestant milieu. In this chapter, we observed the conditions of the appearance of this discourse: from the original confusion and helplessness of the StB vis-à-vis complexities of Protestant milieu in the 1950s through its progressive activization against (and thus with the help of) a clearly contoured critical challenger inside the Protestant milieu towards the, sometimes absurd, generalizing use of the label NO in the 1970s and 1980s. The StB in this way co-created a power constellation and a discursive pattern that has remained noticeable in the life of the contemporary Protestant milieu. In fact, immediately after 1989, this StB instrumentalization of the NO (as a particularly dangerous and powerful opponent of the regime) brought an important amount of symbolic capital to the principal representatives of NO. Understandably, they then acquired the prestigious status of being beyond doubt inside the Protestant milieu – which was, of course, also linked to their personal qualities, such as courage, intelligence and charisma. Trojan, Hejdánek and Balabán became important professors (and identification figures for young Protestant élites) at the Prague Protestant Theological Faculty whilst others returned to their pastoral profession.

Yet the story has not ended with the formidable use of renewed professional opportunities by NO representatives legitimized (among other things) by the history of their epic struggle with the StB. The influence of the StB version of the inner functioning of the Protestant milieu has also continued to shape the ČCE in other ways. With the progressive opening and wider utilization of StB archives and, more noticeably, in 2004 after the publication of Peter Dinuš's thesis (that had the aura of an academic work but was in reality only an uncritical compilation of StB documents) which was sent to every ČCE parish by the synodal council to help Czech Protestants come to terms with their past, the wide dissemination of the StB simplified version of a bipolar ČCE (dangerous opponents NO vs loyal constructors of socialism) proved extremely divisive. And so, even though StB officers Kosová, Štícha, Radikovský and others sank into oblivion, their interpretation of the trajectory of Czech Protestants between 1948 and 1989 has not stopped producing painful conflicts inside the Church milieu to this very day. In 2019, for instance, it was still possible to observe this phenomenon in the latest publication of the ČCE Commission on contemporary history which terminated its work in bitterness and conflict palpable on the pages of the booklet *Cesta církve IX* (The Journey of the Church). Some of the older eminent members of the commission (accepting the StB perspective on ČCE as the most reliable version of what was going on between 1948 and 1989) could not tolerate the efforts of their younger colleagues – PhD students of history who tried to offer more differentiated interpretations of Czech Protestant history during the communist dictatorship based on critical work and utilizing a vast array of sources (without exclusive preference for StB files). For example, pastor Pavel Hlaváč (born in 1939) expressed his "sorrow and surprise" over the work of these young historians who are "unable to understand" that the emphasis on a critical and circumspect attitude towards secret police production is only the result of a continuous "demagogical campaign" orchestrated by still active StB agents and another attempt to prevent the recognition of "what really happened" (Hlaváč 2019, 60).

Acknowledgement

I am thankful for the support of the PROGRES Q18 research funding scheme ("Social Sciences: From Multidisciplinarity to Interdisciplinarity," Cahrles University, Prague).

Notes

1 In the studied period the state institutional infrastructure for surveillance of the churches changed several times: the State Bureau for Church Affairs created in 1949 was transformed into the Church Department at the Ministry of Culture and Education in 1956. After another reorganization this department was renamed the Secretariat for Church Affairs in 1967.

2 Report 3 March 1951, folder H-153, Security Services Archives (SSA), Prague (*Archiv bezpečnostních složek*) Historical fond of the Ministry of Interior (*Historický fond MV*).

3 Usnesení XI. Sjezdu, *Rudé právo*, 23 July 1958, 1.

4 In the 1970s, under strong political pressure this group evolved, according to one of its key proponents, into a "charismatic community" (Trojan 1977).

5 Jan Šimsa confessed for instance during the synod debates in 1966: "I like KSČ very much! My brother and my mother are both members of the Party!" (National Archives Prague, fond MEC, MŠK 47 IV, ČCE, A 1, box 45, 15th Synod 1966, Minutes of the debate). Trojan explained their position on socialism as "a legitimate attempt at constructing a new society" (Trojan 2010, 266–9).
6 NA Prague, fond MEC, MŠK 47 IV, ČCE, A 2a, box 46, Union of the ECCB Clergy 1959–1966, Report on the meeting with the Union representatives, 30 June 1959.
7 NA Prague, fond MEC, MŠK 47 IV, ČCE, A 2a, box 46, Union of the ECCB Clergy 1959–1966, Report on the plenary session of the Union, 30 August 1966.
8 NA Prague, fond MEC, MŠK 47 IV, ČCE, A 2a, box 46, Report on talks with the board of the Union of the ECCB Clergy, 14 January 1964.
9 NA Prague, fond MEC, MŠK 47 IV, ČCE, A 1, box 45, 15th Synod 1966, Notes on the discussion; Evaluation of the synod at the meeting of the Comenius faculty council 8 March 1966.
10 CA ECCB Prague, fond SC, Synods, I/15, 16th Synod 1969, Minutes of the debates.
11 NA Prague, fond MEC, MŠK 47 IV, ČCE, A 2a, box 46, Union of the ECCB Clergy, Information on the summer theological workshop of the Union of the ECCB Clergy (29 August – 2 September 1966).
12 Letter of Jan Šimsa, 20 December 1966, edited in *Soudobé dějiny* 8, 2–3 (2001): 552–3.
13 NA Prague, fond MEC, MŠK 47 IV, ČCE, A 2a, box 46, Union of the ECCB Clergy, Report on the workshop in August 1966, manuscript by Vl. Polák.
14 Letter of Jan Dus, 7 August 1978, published in *Svědectví* 61 (1979): 79.
15 Letter of Šimsa (1966), *Soudobé dějiny*, 557.
16 Daily summary 33, 12 February 1968, StB online archives, accessible at www.ustrcr.cz/data/pdf/svodky/ds-hs033-1968.pdf.
17 Ibid.
18 NA Prague, fond 1261/0/5 (Presidium of the CC of the CPC 1966–1971), f. 126, a.u. 203, point 4, Information on the current political situation in churches in Czechoslovak Socialist Republic, 14 April 1970.
19 It means that the Synod was not disturbed by any intervention or previous "preparation" from the side of the state administration.
20 This definition comes from a short article by a Czech sociologist (Hranička 1970, 37).

Archival sources

Archiv bezpečnostních složek [Security Services Archives (SSA), Prague] – Historický fond MV – Historical fond of the Ministry of Interior,

Národní archiv v Praze [National Archives, Prague], fond MEC [Ministry of Education and Culture], MŠK 47 IV, ČCE,

Národní archiv v Praze [National Archives, Prague], fond 1261/0/5

Ústřední církevní archiv ČCE [Central Archives of the ECCB], fond SC

Interviews

Erika Kadlecová, (2008) Interviewed by Ondřej Matějka.

Ladislav Prokůpek, (2008) Interviewed by Ondřej Matějka.

Jan Šimsa, (2007) Interviewed by Ondřej Matějka.
Jan Šimsa, (2008) Interviewed by Ondřej Matějka.

References

Balabán, Milan. 1968. "A Struggle with Bogeymen. On Irreplaceability of Christians" ["Zápas se strašidly. O nezastupitelnosti křesťana"]. *Literární listy.*" 17 (1): 7.

Cuhra, Jaroslav. 1999. *The Church Policy of the CPC and State from 1969 until 1972* [*Církevní politika KSČ a státu v letech 1969–1972*]. Praha: Ústav pro soudobé dějiny AV ČR.

Dinuš, Peter. 2004. *The Evangelical Church of Czech Brethren and the State Security* [*Českobratrská církev evangelická v agenturním rozpracování STB*]. Praha: Úřad dokumentace a vyšetřování zločinů komunismu.

Dinuš, Peter. 2005. "The Evangelical Church of Czech Brethren and the State Security from 1957 until 1967" ["Českobratrská církev evangelická a StB v letech 1957–1967"]. *Securitas Imperii.* 12: 363–71.

Hlaváč, Pavel. 2019. "The Evangelical Church of Czech Brethren and the State Security" ["Českobratrská církev evangelická a Státní tajná bezpečnost"]. In: *Cesta církve IX*, edited by Pavel Hlaváč and Pavel Keřkovský, 51–62. Praha: ČCE

Hranička, Josef. 1970. "Churches" ["Církve"]. In: *Small Dictionary of Sociology* [*Malý sociologický slovník*], edited by Josef Turek, 36–7. Praha: Svoboda.

Hudcová, Eliska. 2010. "A Wonderful Class. The Life of Protestant Students of Theology and of Pastors in the Era of Normalization in Contemporary Accounts" [Báječný ročník: život evangelických bohoslovců a farářů v období normalizace v jejich dnešních vyprávěních] Master Thesis, Charles University, Prague.

Kaplan, Karel. 2008. *The Chronicle of Communist Czechoslovakia. The Roots of Reforms 1956–1968. Society and Power* [*Kronika komunistického Československa. Kořeny reformy 1956–1968*]. *Společnost a moc.* Brno: Barrister & Principal.

Karásek, Svatopluk. 1998. *Your Excellent Wine: Interviews* [*Víno tvé výborné: Rozhovory*]. Praha: Kalich.

Keřkovský, Pavel. 2017. "Life in Totalitarianism – Soft Terror and Normalized Church" ["Život v totalitě – měkký teror a normalizovaná církev"]. *Protestant* 9.(online: https://protestant.evangnet.cz/zivot-v-totalite-mekky-teror-normalizovana-cirkev)

Kosová, Vlasta. 1980. The Fight of the StB with Anti-socialist Tendencies Inside the Evangelical Church of Czech Brethern [Boj orgánů StB s antisocialistickými tendencemi v Českobratrské církvi evangelické]. Master Thesis, Vysoká škola SNB, Fakulta StB, Praha.

Křišťál, Miroslav. 1985. The Contribution of the StB towards the Limitation of Enemy Activities Inside the Evangelical Church of Czech Brethern and Their Abuse by Political and Church Opposition in Czechoslovakia and by Foreign Opponents ["Podíl orgánů StB na zamezování nepřátelské činnosti v Českobratrské církvi evangelické a na jejím zneužívání politickou i církevní opozicí v ČSSR, jakož i zahraničním protivníkem"]. Master Thesis, Vysoká škola SNB, Fakulta StB, Praha.

Matějka, Ondrej. 2007. "They Are Stubborn as Rams But We Can Use Them. Czech Protestants and the Communist regime 1948–1956" ["Jsou to berani, ale můžeme je využít. Čeští evangelíci a komunistický režim 1948–1956"]. *Soudobé dějiny* 2–3: 305–40.

Matějka, Ondrej. 2009. Die tschechischen protestantischen Kirchen. In: *Handbuch der Religions- und Kirchengeschichte der bohmischen Lander und Tschechiens im 20. Jahrhundert*, edited by M. Schulze Wessel, 147–65. München: Oldenbourg.

Matějka, Ondrej. 2012. "A Generation? A School? A Fraternity? An Army? Understanding the Roots of Josef Lukl Hromádka's Influence in the Czech Protestant Milieu 1920–1948." *Communio Viatorum. A theological journal* LIV/ 3: 307–20.

Matějka, Ondrej. 2017. "Dialogues on Religion in a 'Socialist Society' under Construction: Marxist Social Scientists and Czech Protestants, 1940s–60s." In: *Reconstructing Communities in Europe, 1918–68*, edited by Stefan Couperus and Harm Kaal, 238–59. London: Routledge.

Matějka, Ondrej. 2019a. "A Long Evangelical Spring? The Czech Protestant Milieu and Communist Reformers between 1963 and 1977. In: *The Prague Spring as a Laboratory*, edited by M. Schulze Wessel, 143–62. Göttingen: Vandenhoeck & Ruprecht.

Matějka, Ondrej. 2019b. "Un mur contre le bolchevisme? La Young Men's Christian Association (YMCA) dans la Tchécoslovaquie de l'entre-deux-guerres." *Le mouvement social* 267: 25–46.

Pfann, Miroslav. 1998. The New Orientation in the Evangelical Church of Czech Brethren from 1959 until 1968. A Concise History of a Movement of Protestant Christians Written on the Basis of Archival Materials [*Nová orientace v Českobratrské církvi evangelické v letech 1959–1968. Malá historie jednoho hnutí evangelických křesťanů podle archivních dokumentů*]. Středokluky: Zdeněk Susa.

Pfann, Miroslav, Šimsová, Milena, Šimša, Jan. 2001. "Public Debate On the Activity of the State Security during the 1966 Meeting of the Union of the ECCB Clergy" ["Veřejná diskuse o činnosti Státní bezpečnosti v roce 1966 na půdě Svazu českobratrského evangelického duchovenstva"]. *Soudobé dějiny* 8 (2–3): 521–66.

Radikovský, Zdeněk. 1980. "The Fight of the StB with Anti-socialist Tendencies Inside the Evangelical Church of Czech Brethern in Poděbrady Church District" ["Boj orgánů StB s antisocialistickými tendencemi v Českobratrské církvi evangelické církevního seniorátu Poděbrady"]. Master Thesis, Vysoká škola SNB, Fakulta StB, Praha.

Rejchrt, Miloš. 2002. *A Little More Free: Interviews* [*O něco svobodnější: rozhovory*]. Praha, Kalich.

Šimsa, Jan. 1968. "Hot News from Catechism" ["Aktuální z katechismu"]. *Literární listy* 1 (17): 6.

Šimsa, Jan. 2004. "New Orientation as Seen by the State Security" ["Nová orientace filtrem Státní bezpečnosti"]. *Protestant* 7. (online https://protestant.evangnet.cz/nova-orientace-filtrem-statni-bezpecnosti)

Šmarda, Bedřich. 1984. The Fight of the StB with Anti-socialist Tendencies Manifested at Protestant Theological Faculties ["Boj orgánů StB s antisocialistickými tendencemi projevujícími se na protestantských bohosloveckých fakultách"]. Master Thesis, Vysoká škola SNB, Fakulta StB, Praha.

Štícha, František. 1980. The Fight of the State Security with Anti-socialist Tendencies Inside the Evangelical Church of Czech Brethern in the Region of Central Bohemia and in Prague ["Boj orgánů Státní bezpečnosti s antisocialistickými tendencemi v Českobratrské církvi evangelické na teritoriu Středočeského kraje a hlavního města Prahy"]. Master Thesis, Vysoká škola SNB, Fakulta StB, Praha.

Trojan, Jakub. 1968. "The Only Necessary" ["Jedno potřebné"]. Literární listy. 1 (17): 6.

Trojan, Jakub. 1977. "Christian Existence in Socialist Society or the Theology of Trouble Making" ["Křesťanská existence v socialistické společnosti aneb teologie průšvihu"]. *Studie.* 49 (1): 67–86.

Trojan, Jakub. 2010. *Dialogues with the Memory I* [*Rozhovory s pamětí I.*]. Středokluky: Zdeněk Susa.

Trusina, Šimon. 2015. "A Member of Counter-Intelligence Service in the Direction of the Secretariat for Church Affairs" ["Příslušník kontrarozvědky do vedení Sekretariátu pro věci církevní"]. *Sborník Archivu bezpečnostních složek.* 13: 197–212.

Tuček, Karel. 1983. "The Process of Building and Formation of Agency Inside Protestant Churches" ["Proces budování a formování vlivové agentury k působení v protestantských církvích"]. Master Thesis, Vysoká škola SNB, Fakulta StB, Praha.

Part III

Methodological approaches to religions in the secret police archives

10 Secret police informer files as sources for the study of vernacular religion under communism

Ágnes Hesz

Religion during communism has typically been studied from a top-down perspective, focusing on the regime's church policy, the entanglement of churches with state authorities, the pursuit of religious groups and especially their leaders, and the directives and methods of religious persecution. Certain churches and denominations have been at the forefront of research, depending on their relationship with the state and the level of their dissent from the regime. Not much is known, however, about how everyday religious believers experienced this period and what it meant to live a religious life in an environment where the expectations of the state about what a proper citizen should feel, think and do often conflicted with religious norms or the inner drives of a religious person.

The vernacular religion approach was conceived as a means to study religious practice from a bottom-up, practice-oriented perspective. Formulated by the folklorist Leonard Primiano, vernacular religion emerged as one of several alternatives to the terms "folk religion" or "popular religion," which in the last decades came under harsh criticism for defining the religion of the "masses" in distinction from the religion of the elite, and thus implying that it is somehow a less up-to-date, less correct or incomplete reproduction of religion proper. Critics, including Primiano, also argued that religion is much more than institutional dogma and practice.[1] According to Primiano vernacular religion is "religion as it is lived: as human beings encounter, understand, interpret and practice it" (Primiano 1995, 44). It is an on-going creative process during which individual believers constantly negotiate their religious ideas and practices while interacting with their environment. Thus to understand vernacular religion, argues Primiano, research should pay attention to "the processes of religious belief, the verbal, behavioural, and material expressions of religious belief, and the ultimate object of religious belief" (Primiano 1995, 44–5). Thus, the vernacular religious approach has the benefit of drawing our attention to aspects of religion and religious practice that formerly have been overlooked or less de-emphasized. By focusing on the religious practitioner and understanding religiosity as an on-going interpretative process, this approach presents individual believers as having creative agency in shaping their religion, instead of simply being passive receptors of official doctrine. By stressing the intersubjective and interactive nature of this process, this approach also helps us to grasp the complex power relations behind religious practice. And finally, by pointing out the versatility of expressions of belief, it broadens our perception of what makes religion.[2]

Since the vernacular religious approach is primarily inductive in the sense that it focuses on the believers and their practices, vernacular religion has mostly been researched through ethnographic fieldwork methods. In this paper, however, I argue for the value of secret police files as one of the rare sources for research on vernacular religion under communism.[3] My arguments are mainly based on my research in the Historical Archives of the Hungarian State Security (ÁBTL), where I consulted materials concerning clandestine religious movements (mostly Roman Catholic), members of abolished monastic orders or unrecognized religions, and village priests and to a lesser extent on my experience in the National Council for the Study of the Securitate Archives (CNSAS) where my research focused on various religious minority groups in Transylvania.[4]

Reading secret police files

The source value of secret police files has been the subject of much discussion ever since they became accessible for the public and researchers. As many have pointed out, most readers who came across secret police files, historians among them, read these documents as though there was a referential relationship between their content and the realities of the past (Vățulescu 2010, 13; Takács 2014, 110; Laczó 2009). The main task of historians was thus to investigate the nature of this relationship: are particular statements in the files correct or incorrect, did informers, agents or secret police officers lie when they reported about what their targets had said and done (Takács 2014, 110; Verdery 2014, 62 – citing Poenaru 2013, 219) or did they record things truthfully. This factual approach in the search for "truths" has been criticized for failing to reflect on the fact that these documents were produced according to the logic of the state security agencies (Takács 2014, 110).[5] Subordinated to the task of identifying and controlling the enemies of the regime, these files, it can be argued, are more of an ideological construct than a credible reproduction of what informers, witnesses or the targets themselves experienced.

This discursive critical approach has led to a re-evaluation of secret police files as source materials. It has been argued by several researchers working on secret police materials from different countries that instead of telling us about the reality of the past, secret police archives first and foremost provide us with information on the inner workings of the secret police (Farkas 2006, 154; Verdery 2014, 39–40; Rainer 2008, 18) and on "the values, apprehensions and fantasies" they entertained (Vățulescu 2010, 13). Understood in this way, the files reveal how state security services perceived and presented society and therefore, as Katherine Verdery has put it, secret police archives are "less useful as a source of knowledge than as a form of it" (Verdery 2014, 159).

It has also been pointed out, however, that the textual reality constructed in the files had actual and tangible influence on reality in many ways – in other words, the files had (and still have) performative power (Vățulescu 2010, Verdery 2014, 60–73; Luehrman 2015, 42–3). Therefore, the right questions to ask about secret police files according to this approach should focus on how they were produced and what they did to their subjects and to society: how their existence and the activities that produced them influenced personal identities, interpersonal relationships, social norms, arts etc. (Verdery 2014, 63; Verdery 2018; Vățulescu 2010).

Conversely, the extent to which information in secret police files could be fabricated has also been debated. Krisztián Ungváry has pointed out that there was a limit as to how far the information provided by informers could diverge from reality in the course of this passage through the secret police system, since, at the end of the day, the secret services' goal was to "learn what the citizens really thought," and they had a complex system of cross-checking the data they worked with (Ungváry 2014, 92–3). An essay written by an anonymous informer in 1958 seems to support this argument with the author claiming that the best advice he was given early on by one of his case officers was to refrain from blowing up things:

> it is not for us to enhance the effect and it is not for us to distort the size of danger, because with that we would undermine our credit. [...] From this I knew that we were responsible for every word we write down and every opinion we make.

This essay was written – along with three others – on the request of the Hungarian secret service for methodological purposes (ÁBTL 4.1. A–3253 – published in Takács 2013, 104–22). While there is evidence that secret police files sometimes do contain fabricated information (see, for example, Takács 2014, 122–5), several researchers have argued that despite their factual unreliability regarding the lives and deeds of targeted individuals, secret police files may provide valid insights into broader social-historical issues (Kula 2004, 203 – quoted by Gieseke 2010, 5; Farkas 2006: 154; Luehrman 2015, 22; Verdery 2018, 212). In order to move beyond the textual reality of the files, it is argued, researchers have to "read between the lines" applying a narratological approach that takes into account the position and aim of their authors and the logic and discursive frames in which these documents were produced (Luehrman 2015, 40; Rainer M. 2008; Takács 2014). In the following pages, I will try to show how, in applying this approach, secret police files can shed light on several aspects of religious life during communism.

In the secret police archives, there are several file types that include information on religion and religious practice. The richest sources from a vernacular religion perspective are informer's files and documentary files of particular religious communities, but penal files of religious leaders or religious activists may also sometimes contain valuable data. Those charged with reporting on religious matters constituted a diverse group. Some were recruited with the aim of informing on a particular target religious group of which they may often have been members or had close connections to (see Caşu, Chapter 6 and Kapaló, Chapter 12, this volume).[6] Others were assigned to work in local communities on various groups such as ethnic minorities, kulaks, former army officers, gendarmes, doctors, lawyers or teachers. These informers were often instructed to report on local priests and the religious activity of the local community as well. Priests and pastors were also represented amongst the rank of informers with the primary task of reporting on fellow clerics and on internal affairs of their churches (see Cindrea-Nagy, Chapter 16, this volume).

With the exception of informer's files, which collect all the reports given by a single informer, secret police files generally comprise various document types from informer's reports to analytic reports or case summaries written by higher rank officers, evaluations, action plans, hand written or transcribed confessions, interrogation minutes, transcripts of tapped conversations, reports on shadowing, surveillance photos, and confiscated materials (letters, books, pamphlets, images, photos of confiscated objects). All these "genres" were produced with a particular aim and follow various discursive schemes that have to be discerned for a correct or satisfactory understanding of their meaning. Secret police files are also polyphonic or, as Katherine Verdery has argued, heteroglossic in that they reflect the voices of informers, case officers, their superiors as well as the voice of the people under surveillance, who all use a variety of linguistic conventions (Verdery 2014, 51). Although in the context of the files these voices are subjected to one dominant interpretation which presents the surveilled people as enemies (Verdery 2014, 52), critical reading can help their re-contextualization and open them up to other possible interpretations. Therefore, to see what secret police files can really tell us about vernacular religious practice, we should first understand how the documents they contain were produced.

Of all the document types, informer's reports have received by far the most scholarly attention – which is not surprising if we think about the central role they had in the workings of the secret police and their significance after the fall of communism in lustration processes and political debates around it. In the discussions about what can and cannot be learned from these documents, many researchers have stressed that these texts were collective products of multiple authors and demonstrated how the secret services, through their working procedures influenced and determined their contents (see Farkas 2006, 148–149; Rainer 2008, 16–17; Verdery 2014; Pihurik 2011; Takács 2013; Gyarmati 2014, 69). Informer's reports are, therefore, selective, manipulated (and as a result, manipulative) representations of their subjects – even if they seem to be truthful, and often lively accounts, of what informers had seen and heard.

The distortive influence of the secret service was already at work before the actual surveillance had started. Informers operated under the close guidance of their case officers from whom they received well-defined assignments at their regular meetings. The detail of the instructions they were given before completing a task is a good indication for how close this guidance was. In 1960, for example, a parish priest in Hungary reporting under the cover name "Szirmai Béla" was ordered to gain the confidence of a theology student, through whom he could gather information about a clandestine Catholic youth movement. In order to succeed, his case officer told "Szirmai" to invite the student to his home, offer him coffee and watch television together with him. He also instructed him to adopt an "ecclesial manner" during these visits (ÁBTL, 3.1.2. M–23166, 286). In another case an informer, a projectionist with the task of reporting on a village priest to whom he was distantly related, was instructed to "deepen" their relationship by paying him occasional visits, talking about common relatives and asking advice on beekeeping. Since he was a party member, his case officer noted in his action plan from 1967 that

> the agent's behaviour pattern has to be specified as different from [the target's] doctrinal and political approach in terms of economic and political issues. This in turn could facilitate debates [between the two], and by properly guiding and educating the agent, the overall attitude of [the priest] could be revealed.
>
> (ÁBTL, 3.1.2. M–28356/1, 64–5)

By telling the informers what to look for and how to behave, the secret police directed their gaze and predefined what they saw (Farkas 2006, 148).

The instructions of the case officer also defined how informers wrote their reports. These texts were produced following different practices (see Gyarmati 2014, 69). In the Hungarian case, most informers submitted handwritten reports to their case officers, which they wrote either prior to their meetings or at the meetings under the supervision of the case officer. Handwritten reports were then often typed up by assistant staff, which gave room for modification, especially if the typewritten version contained only selected segments of the original. In some cases informers reported only orally to their case officers who made a written summary later, in which case we can talk about actual co-authorship.[7] In any case, the reports constitute selective "secondary" accounts of the informer's experiences, composed according to the goals of the secret services.[8] Whether reporting orally or in writing, the informer's "ideal reader" was of course always the secret police (Takács 2013, 23) and it was in her or his best interest to fulfil the expectations placed upon her or him. Most informers did more than just recount what they had seen and heard – they were already interpreting their experiences and did so from the perspective of what they understood to be the secret police aims or agenda, deploying learned linguistic clichés (Farkas 2006, 149).

How and what informers reported also depended on their relationship with their case officers (Rainer 2008, 17). Reports were followed by three sections: an *evaluation* stating if the report was operatively valuable, a *note* containing additional information on the case and commenting on the informer's work or attitude, and a *list of assignments* the informer had to carry out until the next meeting. When read together with the reports, these sections reveal the dynamics of the informer–case officer relationship. In this respect, informer's files containing the reports of an informer in a roughly chronological order are especially revealing: they show us how much informers were influenced by the evaluations they got from their case officers and how their approach to their jobs changed during the course of time.

A particularly good example comes from the file of informer "Bátori," a teacher living and working in a small town in the east of Hungary. His task was to report on the local intelligentsia, but he also had a series of assignments concerning local religious life. In December 1958, he was ordered to explore the extent to which the Church distracted people from "productive work." He carried out his task diligently and concluded in his report that none of the three local churches (Roman Catholic, Greek Catholic and Reformed) prevented people from carrying out their daily jobs, and supported his argument by giving a detailed account of service schedules and reporting that catechism classes were often cancelled in each of the denominations. "Bátori" did suggest, however, that workdays in December should start at 6 in the morning and end earlier than usual to prevent people from attending early morning church services during Advent season. No matter how hard he tried, his report was not received well by his officer, who scolded him for failing to report on the methods local churches used for recruiting believers and for "activating the masses." He was ordered to do the same assignment again, but there is no proof in his file that he ever did so. However, he clearly tried to please his superiors when around Christmas of the same year he was instructed to find out what "the church taught through its ideal [sic!], religious teachings against Marxist education and whether it agitated against collectivisation." Since he couldn't visit religious education classes because of the winter break and because he was advised against talking directly to priests or students, he attended three Roman Catholic masses. In his neatly written account, the informer recalled some elements of the sermons and interpreted them as being hostile against the regime. His readings are so far-fetched that some of them deserve verbatim quotation.

On 21 December 1958 the young Roman Catholic priest said the following:

> What could we expect from Jesus at Christmas? Everything. God owns everything on earth and in heaven. If we give something, we only give back something that belongs to God. (Meaning: nothing belongs to the state. The material world does not exist.) [...]
>
> What did the three wise men of the East bring with them? And what showed them the way? The eastern star.
>
> (The church thus propagates the star of God instead of the star of the international proletariat.)

He also said about the last line of a religious song, "Because this is the king of heaven and earth" that "this is how the church keeps the conception of the monarchy alive for the believers." In fact, his interpretations are so preposterous that one cannot help but wonder if he was trying to be sarcastic after being scolded. His case officer nevertheless found his efforts moderately interesting by dryly remarking in his evaluation that "the agent claimed that the church aims to agitate against our social system during masses," but was seemingly more interested in the fact that the Reformed pastor boasted about receiving church taxes from all local party members – a piece of extra information provided by "Bátori" (ÁBTL 3.1.2. M–15468, 211–14).

How informers reported on certain people was also influenced by the relationship they had with them. Although the anonymous agent quoted above was warned against acting out of revenge (Takács 2013, 104), it is clear from the files that informers were more inclined to give unfavourable or incriminating accounts when they were reporting on someone they did not like. Although never writing in too friendly a manner about religion and religious people, "Bátori" gave an especially malicious report when he had a clash with the Reformed pastor over conflicting festival schedules. Their conflict started when, according to "Bátori," the priest threatened to report him to the authorities for keeping his students away from religious education classes by scheduling the Mother's Day chorus rehearsals at this time. In turn "Bátori" accused the pastor in his report for deliberately putting the confirmation ceremony to the exact date of the school's Mother's Day celebration, by which – writes "Bátori" – "he prevented a party member's daughter from participating at the ceremony" (ÁBTL 3.1.2. M–15468, 261). The opposite is also true; informers often gave neutral or favourable descriptions of surveilled individuals, downplaying the danger they might pose for the regime, or refrained from reporting at all (Farkas 2006, 153). There are, for example, numerous reports where informers depicted priests as leading a reclusive, apolitical life (even if other sources proved the opposite – see for example: ÁBTL 3.1.2. M–26516/1, 140) or denied that the sects they had to surveil were politically active. Informers, it seems, did not always try to serve the goals of the secret services and they did not always try to identify the "enemy."[9]

Informers' work has been compared to doing ethnography – most notably by Katherine Verdery (2014, 6–8), but also by other anthropologists (see Horváth 2009). As Verdery puts it, surveillance was a "different way of doing ethnography"; like anthropologists, informers made "close examinations of everyday behaviour and interpret[ed] what they found."[10] They did so with similar investigative strategies: they were encouraged by their superiors to note down everything that could possibly be interesting and to contextualize the information they have gathered.[11] Some informers were indeed "good ethnographers" in the sense that they provided detailed reports with subtle observations about their environments. They also resembled anthropologists in that very often they did not just record what they had experienced but also interpreted what they saw – or thought they had seen. An informer called "Marika," a member of a Catholic youth group, wrote in one of her detailed reports from the summer of 1959 about her group's visit to Pannonhalma, a Benedictine abbey and one of the few remaining church-run secondary schools in Hungary. Here she wrote about a young boy, who – according to her observation – was deeply impressed when hearing that the abbot and headmaster of the school, along with four other Benedictine monks, was studying in the same school as he did. "He was also very much moved by the fact," continues "Marika,"

> that a figure on one of the school chapel's relief bore a surprising resemblance to him. This little boy returned home with very deep impressions. I don't want to go too far with my conclusions, but according to my opinion, this visit to Pannonhalma has brought [him] closer to the priesthood and the Benedictine order.
>
> (ÁBTL, 3.1.2. M–22846/1, 62)

Although not written without a pinch of malice, this excerpt, with all its details, clearly could not be wholly fabricated and thus invites us to see it as a rare glimpse into the vernacular religious process: the power of personal experience in deepening one's devotion to religion.

In this report, "Marika's" gaze was clearly driven by the secret police's agenda, since she was meant to inform about how the Catholic Church (and illegal or semi-legal groups on its periphery) influenced young people. Informers, however, often went beyond the somewhat narrowly defined focus of their actual tasks, and provided "snapshots" capturing the tidbits of everyday life – either because they thought their superiors would be interested or because they did not have anything else to report on, but nevertheless had to "do their homework." A case in point is a report by the movie projectionist already mentioned above, whose main task included reporting on local people of German ethnic background and on a local village priest. In this account from 1963 he wrote about a winter night car ride with his boss, the director of the local House of Culture:

> The road was very slippery and he told me that we were going to have an accident for sure, because he gave a lecture today on the history of religious faith, where he said many things against God. He then changed the subject, of course. He also noted this time that his brother-in-law visited him from West Germany and brought him a rosary from France, from some kind of sacred place. He didn't talk about this topic later.
>
> (ÁBTL, 3.1.2. M–28356, 231)

As was the case with this report, case officers and their superiors were often unimpressed by information like this. While these "chit-chats," as Jens Gieseke called them, had no operative value for the secret police, they do serve as great sources for researchers of everyday life (Gieseke 2010, 6; see also: Takács 2014, 124); in this case they preserved an honest moment of a believer, who struggled with his conscience for having publicly spoken against his religion.

Apart from informer's reports, files on surveilled groups or individuals also contain summary or analytical reports written by case officers or their superiors.[12] As these documents are based on information coming from multiple sources – reports by various informers, shadowing, tapping, police records from previous regimes – in theory they reflect the total knowledge the secret police had at the time about a certain group or person. Part of this knowledge – most probably due to the multiple, and often unreliable provenance of their data – often proves to be incorrect or inconsistent when we look at the details: multiple files, for example, may contain contradictory data about the prehistory of a surveilled person or get names or dates wrong.[13] Having secret police officers as their authors, these documents are written in highly politicized and ideologically laden language, categorizing and representing people according to the logic of the secret police even more strongly than informer's reports did. For example, throughout the 1950s in Hungary, clandestine Catholic youth movements were regularly labelled as "clerical fascist," while in Romania religious groups with an ethnic background often had the compound "nationalist–irredentist" as their permanent qualifier in Securitate documents. However, despite their distortions and factual inconsistencies regarding detail, on a more general level these documents can provide valuable information about the structure and operative practices of the target groups – especially if we have the possibility to read them against other sources. The Securitate file on Jehovah's Witnesses in Cluj county in Romania gives a concise summary about the local hierarchy and structure of the organization and the ways information, religious knowledge, money or material objects were circulated within this system (CNSAS, D 014428). Analytical or summary reports often include action plans for further operations, which show us how authorities tried to control and manipulate religious groups. The pressure they placed on these groups and individuals fundamentally defined the framework for their religious lives and influenced their actions and strategies.

Files also contain source types that reflect the "voice" of the targets more directly than those discussed so far. Tapped conversations, confiscated items of religious literature, personal letters, and photographs reveal the thoughts, practices and creative agency of religious groups or individuals in ways that secondary reports do not. Even confessions of the accused that were more often than not coerced and manipulated may provide several details about the ideals and practices of the religious group in question.

What can we learn, then, from secret police files about how people "met, experienced and understood religion," if we combine a critical reading of the files with the vernacular religion approach?

Vernacular religion in the archives

Scholars of vernacular religion and members of the secret services have radically different intentions when observing religious groups – the former generally intend to learn something about their subjects' religious lifeworld and worldview, while the latter desired to fit them into their own pre-existing categories as enemies. Although most communist regimes granted – even if limited – freedom of religion to their citizens, they regarded religions as rival ideologies and wanted to control their influence on the population. Thus the secret police was not so much interested in religion or religious practice itself; instead they were primarily focused on religious organizations that were unrecognized or unregistered by the authorities, on religious activity they considered as hostile, and on the influence churches or religious groups had on – especially young – people.[14] Scholars of religions, whether sociologists, historians, ethnologists or anthropologists, would have definitely come up with different field material to secret police agents; nevertheless there is much in secret police files that could inform a scholarly inquiry into everyday religious practice.

As a result of the agenda described above, files on unrecognized churches or clandestine religious groups contain abundant information on how these groups tried to escape the attention of the authorities. While for the secret police these efforts were evidence of the conspiratory nature of these communities – and, therefore, their representation in the files is probably overblown – for the student of vernacular religion they tell something about how people tried to adapt their religious lives to the power relations in their society. For clandestine Catholic groups in Hungary – but also for other persecuted religious communities – it was common practice during the entire era to disguise their meetings as excursions, group holidays, choir activities, private lessons or even dancing parties.[15] These activities provided sufficient cover for religious trainings, spiritual retreats or religious services. According to the files, groups had various methods to mask the actual nature of their gatherings. During his interrogation in 1952, György Bulányi, a central figure behind the underground Catholic youth organization, claimed that during their meetings held in private flats they always had school textbooks or cards in front of the participants to mislead accidental visitors. He also confessed that during their meetings held in the Pilis Mountains they sang folksongs or proletarian songs (ÁBTL, 3.1.9. V–14097, 142). While the latter may have been an addition to make the movement appear boldfaced or impertinent, much of what he stated is corroborated by numerous informer's reports on other groups or by later recollections.[16] In order to keep a low profile, it was also common practice to arrive and leave meeting places individually or in pairs, and to behave very quietly when there. Groups could be extremely resourceful at avoiding being caught. According to a non-literal transcript of a tapped conversation between leaders of an underground Catholic youth group, on one occasion the participants of a meeting acted as if at an engagement party when they were suddenly raided by the police: they chose a groom, put a ring on his finger, started to dance, played music and gave toasts. Although the policemen were suspicious, the youngsters had an answer to all their questions so they left without taking any measures against them (ÁBTL, 3.1.5. O–11959/4a, 97).

Persecuted religious groups were equally cautious in their internal communication, most of them followed complex strategies to transmit their messages or religious materials. A common strategy was to rely on oral communication, if possible, using a network of trusted couriers, and to use coded language or ambiguous wording if writing was unavoidable.[17] A good illustration for this comes from a case officer's note written after an informer's report on a Hungarian underground Catholic group. In his note, the case officer quotes the euphemistic content of a postcard about a meeting that was to take place "in the backroom of the little tavern in Tabán at 3pm to which I also invited uncle Pista to entertain the company" and deciphers its meaning: the backroom stands for the sacristy of a church in Tabán, Budapest and uncle Pista for István Eglis, a leading figure in the movement (ÁBTL, 3.1.5. O–11959/4, 99). It was also common practice for corresponding members to send and receive letters from and to other people's – relatives or acquaintances – addresses.[18]

Adaptation strategies also included the withdrawal of ritual activity to the domestic sphere. In the case of some groups this also meant the establishment of more or less permanent places of worship out of the public eye, mostly in the houses of their religious leaders, sometimes literally underground (see Kapaló 2018). The Hungarian secret police archive holds comparatively less information on secret places of worship than its Romanian, Moldovan or Ukrainian counterparts, probably due to the different religious landscape of the country. A notable exception is the house church of a Pentecostal splinter group in Budapest, the focus of Povedák's chapter in this volume (see Chapter 11), of which the secret police made a thorough photo documentation during a raid.

Monastic orders and apostolic movements that were banned under communist regimes represent another case of forms "domestic religion."[19] After the dissolution of their communities, most of their members had to reintegrate into secular society, find secular jobs and take up secular lifestyle.[20] Nevertheless, many of them chose to continue to live true to their vows and tried hard to reconcile their monastic duties with their secular ones. Since the secret police was eager to track down everybody who led a "forbidden monastic life," we have some information on how this was done: ex-members tried to keep close contact with each other or even lived or worked at the same place, they went to church every day before or after work and lived modest lives. An informer's account about the daily routine at the Solidarity cooperative, established in Hungary 1953 especially with the aim of providing work for former monastic members, tells us that they lived "in a certain monastic order" as they attended mass every morning, read and discussed the Bible together before work, prayed together before and after meals and recited hymns every afternoon (ÁBTL, 3.1.2. M–20223, 153).[21]

Those belonging to persecuted religious groups were not the only ones who chose to hide their religious activity from the public. While in theory people could freely participate in the rituals of recognized churches, in Hungary the state discouraged people from being actively religious in many ways. Observing one's religion could hinder one's carrier or lead to other kinds of disadvantage or retribution; therefore, many of those who wanted to fulfil their religious duties but at the same time sought to avoid conflict with the authorities had to be religious secretly. A particularly telling illustration for this is a literal transcription of a personal letter that comes from a documentary file on a clandestine Catholic movement (ÁBTL 3.1.5 O–11959/4, 73–4).[22] The letter dates from 1955 and was written by a woman, a first-time grandmother, who amongst other family matters gave an account of her grandson's baptism:

> The baptism took place on 4th December, on the wedding anniversary of our son. It was beautiful. Feri, the grandfather did everything. He was working without stopping from 9 am to 4 pm, producing the most delicious and beautiful sandwiches. There was wine and coffee. The whole family was here, 22 people altogether. The child was baptised by a Piarist priest [name]. The baptism ceremony was here at our home. Feri has erected a beautiful altar. He made it so exceptionally nice that everybody was weeping with emotion. My entire home looked like a stage. Everything was shining brightly. [The priest] gave a beautiful sermon. He included the rise of the new stars, which sometimes intrude into families, but will shine only briefly, because people will soon realise that these stars are fake. Anyways, I kept his speech and will read it when I have the time.

Concerning the study of vernacular religion, this letter is valuable for several reasons. It provides first-hand information on ritual creativity, ritual expectation and the power of materiality in rituals: it shows that this family felt the necessity to turn their everyday environment into a sacred place for a "proper" baptism, it recounts how this was done and also intimates the emotional reactions it had triggered. It is also a good illustration of the silent resistance against the regime, not only because of the baptism itself, but also because of the obvious anti-communist allusions made by the priest and the significance the writer had attributed to them. In conducting the home baptism, the family took a serious risk of which the writer was apparently very much aware, since she closed her letter by asking "please burn this letter after reading."

Although the secret police was not particularly interested in religious rituals per se, informers sometimes provided descriptions of rituals. However short and dry these accounts are, they show us something about grassroots ritual creativity. An informer reporting from a village about the local activity of KALÁSZ, a Catholic movement for rural girls, claimed that couples were granted a special "KALÁSZ wedding ceremony" if they chose to marry in the church.[23] This meant that the couple entered the church between the lines of unmarried girls, special KALÁSZ and Virgin Mary banners were placed at the altar, and after the ceremony the bride was initiated as wife in a special ritual (ÁBTL, 3.1.2. M–20223, 385). Another informer writing in 1961 (ÁBTL, 3.1.2. M–30014, 130–1) about a Baptist community from a Northern Hungarian village described the group's baptism ceremony as follows:

> During immersion the preacher entered the baptismal basin, the person to be baptised, clad in a long white shirt, steps into the basin, and the preacher immerses them backwards into the water while saying "I baptise you in the name of the Lord." Once a year they [the community] have a meeting when they put out all the lights and meditate, that is, pray in the dark. Villagers named this night a frisking night ...

The final sentence touches on a topic also present in the files: attitudes towards religion and religious people. Since the secret police was very much interested in how much influence the churches had in society, informers were often instructed to report on the intensity of religious observance, whether the particular church's influence on the population was growing or decreasing, if priests were liked or disliked by their communities. The picture we get from these reports – often provided by priest-informers – is rather mixed. According to an informer from the early 1960s, a Roman Catholic priest serving in a small town complained about the inhabitant's general disinterest in religion and praised religiously more active village communities (ÁBTL 3.1.2. M–20223, 451); at the same time a Greek Catholic village priest talked about how many townspeople observed their religion despite the difficulties this entailed, whilst "one wouldn't believe how many villagers could do without the blessings of the church" (ÁBTL 3.1.2. M–15468, 252). One village priest was reported around 1960 to have complained about losing young people because "they prefer going to football matches, to the cinema or to other events" (ÁBTL 3.1.2. M–15473, 78–80), while roughly at the same time two others talked about the popularity of their catechism classes (ÁBTL 3.1.2. M–15473, 106 and ÁBTL 3.1.2. M–36307, 109). The amount of donations to local churches also shows considerable commitment from people: in the late 1950s to early 1960s two new church buildings were erected near Máriapócs, a Greek Catholic pilgrim site and religious centre in the east of Hungary, both of them mostly financed from private donations (ÁBTL 3.1.2. M–15473, 78–80 and 94–6). According to these reports the generosity of congregation members made up for the lack of subsidies from authorities, and in some places, people also contributed to the income of priests, because they "knew that otherwise they would be left without a pastor" (ÁBTL 3.1.2. M–15473, 78–80). Financial matters on the other hand could also lead to conflicts between priests and villagers; for example, a report from 1970 stated that "people especially don't like to pay," while another claimed that a certain priest was only tolerated because he asked for donations only when it was really necessary (ÁBTL 3.1.2. M–36307, 443 and 212).

Several informers from the end of the 1950s reported that rural party members were regular churchgoers, at one place even paying considerable donations for a new church building (ÁBTL, 3.1.2. M–15473, 127–8). These examples suggest that the rift between the local communist elite and the church was not as accentuated as one would suppose; there were also cases when people who were implicated for their religious activity avoided retribution because of the support of their ties to local powerful men.[24] This does not mean, however, that the authorities did not try to counteract the church's influence: in 1957 a priest allegedly got into trouble for marrying a party functionary before the couple was married by civil law even though he was encouraged to do so by the local council president (ÁBTL, 3.1.2. M–15468). An informer's suggestion to distract pupils from involvement in religious activity by introducing afternoon screenings at the cinema was also greeted with approval from his superiors (ÁBTL, 3.1.2. M–15468, 205).

The secret police in Hungary was also highly interested in the financial situation of priests, since especially after 1956 economic crimes offered one of the few legitimate pretexts on which priests or religious institutions could be convicted (Tabajdi–Ungváry 2008, 215). It is clear from the files that many priests faced financial difficulties; their salaries were low and frequently withheld for various misdemeanours, and thus many of them had to rely on the support of their congregations.[25] According to the reports, it was not unusual for a priest to earn additional income from some kind of agricultural activity – we know about at least two, who kept bees –, and several of them were disapprovingly described as good businessmen (ÁBTL, 3.1.2. M–15468, and ÁBTL, 3.1.2. M–28356).[26] Certain "suspicious" business activities were closely connected to standard spiritual services and were part of the usual economy of the church. For example, a village priest was reported to sell gas stoves he received from abroad to local villagers. According to the report he claimed to get the stoves from former villagers relocated to Germany, for which he said masses for their dead relatives in return. Authorities nevertheless did not give credit to this explanation and firmly believed he was working for his own profit (ÁBTL, 3.1.2. M–28356, 256). These reports, together with the ones relating to spare time activities and social ties of village priests help us to draw a picture of the lower clergy as a social class.

Informers – though often indirectly – also captured moments when people negotiated religion or religious beliefs. Attitudes towards expressly religious people or members of religious minorities were often negative, which, as the reports suggests were probably due to their proselytising activities. In the 1950s, young, urban members of clandestine Catholic movements frequently complained about how hostile their environment – fellow students, colleagues, superiors – were against them and their worldview; as one informer reported: "she told me that notwithstanding her patience and attempts to avoid conflicts, her colleagues found her dislikeable, and she couldn't make Christian life attractive to them" (ÁBTL, 3.1.5. O–11959/4a, 73). As another report states, a Baptist glazier was also regularly mocked by his colleagues for belonging to a "sect," which he accepted "with Biblical citations and religious conviction." From the same file we also learn about a Jehovah's Witness who, while working in the fields, read out the Bible to fellow villagers in vain, "because people generally thought the whole family was nuts, and only laughed at them." Therefore, as the informer notes "their activity in the village is not dangerous, since no one takes them seriously" (ÁBTL, 3.1.5. O–14916, 79 and 64).

A report given by informer Bátori about a conversation he had about religious miracles when returning from the shrine at Máriapócs on a horse-cart in the summer of 1958 stands out for its degree of elaboration and vividness. When talking about the shrine's miraculous Virgin Mary statue, one of his fellow-passengers, an emigrant visiting from Canada – and Bátori's main target at the time – claimed that he was, in fact, an atheist and only visited the indulgence day of the shrine because his wife asked him to pay votive masses for her. He went on to give rational explanations for weeping Virgin Mary paintings and told a story about how priests in Czechoslovakia faked a Virgin Mary miracle by moving her painting on a string. Bátori stepped into the conversation and "enlightened" the other passengers, that one of their common acquaintances also attributed the healing of her granddaughter's leg to the Virgin Mary of Máriapócs:

> The kid had to use crutches. In the church, however, she slid from her grandmother's lap and started to wriggle on the floor. Thereupon I pointed out that this superstition was refuted by the nearby tuberculosis hospital. Her leg was treated there and that is why her condition improved. Neither is it a 'miracle' that is helping her this summer, but the fact that she is being treated in the hospital.
>
> (ÁBTL, 3.1.2. M–15468, 147)

The apparent irony in this little vignette – people disclaiming miraculous events after participating in a major religious pilgrimage – opens up alternative interpretations: it could be read as a genuine expression of disbelief, but also as a reflection of what kind of attitude people thought they should express towards matters of faith when in the company of people they probably could not fully trust.

Informer's reports also reflect that there was one aspect of life where adherence to religious rituals seemed stronger: death. According to one example dating from 1959, a funeral of a young girl "almost turned into a scandal" because she was buried without a priest, with one person exclaiming: "this child has not even been baptised, let's not bury her as a pagan, let's pray the Credo" (ÁBTL, 3.1.2. M–15468, 252). In another file, a priest informer wrote about the boisterous reception of the civil funeral service:

> The relatives of the dead person, that is her husband, is very angry at the priest, because he did not ring the bells for the funeral and did not hand

> out the church banners for the ceremony. It was impossible to explain to the relatives that bells and banners don't go with the civil funeral.
> (ÁBTL, 3.1.2. M–42002, 35)

Finally, reports may also give us a sense of how people struggled to adapt their religious life to an anti-religious environment and how religion informed their daily lives and the way they understood their position in the world. There are accounts of uncertainty and perplexity when it came to fulfilling both one's ritual obligations and the obligations of a socialist citizen. In 1954, a priest-informer reported, for example, that a woman asked him in the confession booth if her daughter was allowed to do the extra work she was assigned in her factory on a compulsory religious holiday (ÁBTL, 3.1.5. O–11959, 75), and young Catholic activists also sought advice from their spiritual father (a secret police informer) on how to fulfil their duty to advocate faith without being ridiculed by their peers (ÁBTL, 3.1.5. O–11959/4a, 62). Many, on the other hand, found solace in understanding their persecution in terms of religion, seeing communism either as a temporary punishment by God or God's tool to convert people to the faith (ÁBTL, 3.1.5 O–11959/4, 222; ÁBTL, 3.1.5. O–11959/4a, 142 and 143).

My aim here was to show the potential of secret police files as sources for the study of vernacular religion. As these examples demonstrate, for all their limitations and shortcomings these documents provide varied information about vernacular religious life. When read with a critical approach they reveal several aspects of religiosity under communism: most notably the ways in which religious groups and individuals adapted to oppression and developed strategies to deflect the attention of the authorities, but also expressions of spirituality or the position and role religion, churches and their representatives had in a socialist society. The considerable lack of ethnographic data from this period makes secret police files even more valuable; they provide us with a rare and unique window on how religious people experienced their faith during communism and by applying the vernacular religious approach to these files we are able to move away from showing religious subjects simply as the victim of the regime and point instead to their resilience and agency.

Acknowledgement

The research for this chapter was funded by the European Research Council (ERC) under the European Union's Horizon 2020 research and innovation programme No. 677355.

Notes

1 For more on the terminological debate surrounding the concepts of folk and popular religion see Badone (1990), Dinzelbacher (1997) and Kapaló (2013).

2 For more on the concept and theory of vernacular religion see also Primiano (2001, 2012), Bowman (2003, 2004a, 2004b) and Bowman–Valk (2012).
3 In communist Hungary, research on religious practices were not encouraged by the authorities, especially in the first two decades of the regime, therefore there are only a few scholarly studies from this period and there is also a parsity of contemporary ethnographic data.
4 I would like to express my gratitude to the Hidden Galleries project team, James A. Kapaló, Iuliana Cindrea-Nagy, Kinga Povedák, Anca Şincan, Dumitru Lisnic, and to our external member, Tatiana Vagramenko for their valuable insights and advices. I would also like to thank Ádám Mézes for his insightful comments to an earlier version of this paper.
5 As Tibor Takács noted, historians often inadvertently reproduce this logic by unreflexively taking up the language of the files (Takács 2014, 10).
6 On the involvement of Hungarian churches with the secret police see: Tabajdi–Ungváry 2008.
7 Phrases like "the agent reported" indicate that the report was noted down by someone other than the informer. Grammatical errors, spelling mistakes or linguistic styles that are at odds with the educational level of the informer could also be signs of a different author (see Pihurik 2011, 149). Notes and evaluations following a report may also point to the differences between the orally given account and its written version: it is not rare for case officers to note that the informer had said more about a subject during their conversations than was included in the written report.
8 Informer's reports were "secondary accounts" also in the sense that they often conveyed information based on gossip and unsupported hearsay. This is indicated by the presence of indirect speech with structures like "I heard", "it is said", "allegedly" (see Gervai 2015, 173).
9 The irony is that whatever and however informers wrote, they could not defy the logic of the secret police. As Péter Esterházy argued in his captivating work about his father's informer's files, there's no such thing as a harmless report: reports already did something by having been written. Depicting someone as neutral or even friendly to the regime, for example, may have led to their roping in, while meaningless, "empty" accounts together could always build up to something meaningful (Esterházy 2002, 92; 79; 85).
10 László Borsányi, a Hungarian cultural anthropologist and informer of the Hungarian secret police has dismissed any parallels between doing ethnographic fieldwork for academic purposes and doing surveillance for the secret police stating that whereas anthropologists had the freedom to choose their field and topic of research and knew what they were looking for, informers were only told the target of their surveillance but not the reason for it (Borsányi 2009, 67). There is ample evidence in the files to contest his claim, but there must have been cases when informers did not exactly know why the secret police was interested in a certain person.
11 See also Esterházy on how his father was instructed to always include in his written reports the identity of his sources and the circumstances under which information was obtained; especially in reports about the overall mood of the public (Esterházy 2002, 67).
12 About the path of information within the system see, for example, Gyarmati (2014) and Verdery (2014, 40–4).

13 This happened in the case of Mihály Virasztó, former religious specialist of the Turan Believers of One God: according to some documents his father was a tax officer, according to others a peasant. His files were also inconsistent about the time he spent in prison before and during WWII and the exact dates of his incarceration (ÁBTL, 3.1.5. O–14980/18; 3.1.9. V–149713; 3.1.9. V–153994).

14 A summary report in a file on one of the Hungarian clandestine Catholic religious movements from the 1950s claims that the movement used religion as their main tool for masking their 'hostile activity' stating that they recruited new members with the help of religion and hid their attacks on people's democracy behind Catholic ethical and theological arguments (ÁBTL, 3.1.5. O–11959/4, 193–194).

15 ÁBTL, 3.1.5. O–11959/4; ÁBTL, 3.1.5. O–11959/4a; ÁBTL, 3.1.5. O–10203; 3.1.9. V–14097; ÁBTL, 3.1.5. O–16252/2a; Bögre–Szabó 2010, 355; For other groups see for example: Petrás 2017 and this volume (on Hungarian Jehovah's Witnesses); Huhák (Campers – http://hu.culturalopposition.eu/registry/?uri=http://courage.btk.mta.hu/courage/individual/n31559&type=collections).

16 According to an informer's report from another file, children participating in such excursions had to wear pioneer ties so that they could use public transport as a group without attracting attention (ÁBTL, 3.1.5. O–11959/4a, 23). In some cases there was more to masking measures than providing a cover up: in her recollections, a member of an apostolic movement said that she received religious training from her spiritual leader in the form of German language lessons so that none of them had to lie if they were caught (Bögre–Szabó 2010, 360).

17 A summary report on the Jehovah's Witnesses of Cluj county in Romania gives a full overview of the group's communication strategies: they only used coded reports, employed couriers who met with the leaders in crowded public places and used prearranged signs to get in touch with one another (CNSAS, D 014428).

18 See for example: ÁBTL, V–14097/3, 100.

19 For more on domestic religion in communist societies see: Kapaló (2018).

20 Reintegration was especially difficult for nuns because there were considerably fewer church positions for them than for monks, who could go on working as parish priests or chaplains.

21 On the Solidarity Cooperative see: Bögre–Szabó 2010, 99–100 (footnote 48) and 284–8.

22 The file does not contain any information about the identity of the corresponding parties (apart from their names) or about their connections to the movement.

23 KALÁSZ (Association of Catholic Girl's Clubs) was founded in 1935–1936 with the aim of helping village girls become devoted Catholic mothers (Magyar Katolikus Lexikon – http://lexikon.katolikus.hu/K/Katolikus%20Leánykörök%20Szövetsége.html – accessed on 1 May 2019).

24 See, for example, ÁBTL, 3.1.2. M–28356/1 103. I also know of a similar case from ethnographic fieldwork in Püspökszilágy, Hungary, where the positive evaluation by the local council leader saved the founder of a neo-protestant splinter group from harassment by the police.

25 This support sometimes consisted of supplies of food such as wheat or flour. See for example: ÁBTL, 3.1.2. M–26516/1, 119.

26 This was not unusual in the pre-communist era either.

Archival sources

Állambiztonsági Szolgálatok Történeti Levéltára [Historical Archives of the Hungarian State Security] (ÁBTL), 4.1. A–3253; 3.1.2. M–23166; 3.1.2. M–28356; 3.1.2. M–28356/1; 3.1.2. M–15468; 3.1.2. M–26516/1; 3.1.2. M–22846/1; file 3.1.2. M–20223; 3.1.2. M–30014; 3.1.2. M–15473; 3.1.2. M–36307; 3.1.2. M–42002, 35; 3.1.5. O–14980/18; 3.1.5. O–11959/4; 3.1.5. O–11959/4a; 3.1.5. O–10203; 3.1.5. O–16252/2a; 3.1.5. O–14916; 3.1.9. V–149713; 3.1.9. V–153994; 3.1.9. V–14097; 3.1.9. V–14097/3;

Consiliul Naţional pentru Studierea Arhivelor Securităţii [National Council for the Study of the Securitate Archives] (ACNSAS), D 014428.

References

Badone, Ellen. 1990. “Introduction.” In: *Religious Orthodoxy and Popular Society*, edited by Ellen Badone, 3–23. Princeton: Princeton University Press.

Borsányi, László. 2009. From an Emic Perspective [Émikus perspektívából]. *AnBlokk* 3: 64–7.

Bowman, Marion. 2003. “Vernacular Religion and Nature: The “Bible of the Folk” Tradition in Newfoundland.” *Folkore* 114 (3): 285–95.

Bowman, Marion. 2004a. “Procession and Possession in Glastonbury: Continuity, Change and the Manipulation of Tradition.” *Folklore* 115 (3): 273–85.

Bowman, Marion. 2004b. “Taking Stories Seriously: Vernacular Religion, Contemporary Spirituality and the Myth of Jesus in Glastonbury.” *Temenos* 39–40: 125–42.

Bowman, Marion–Valk, Ülo. 2012. “Introduction: Vernacular Religion, Generic Expressions and the Dynamics of Belief.” In: *Vernacular Religion in Everyday Life: Expressions of Belief*, edited by Marion Bowman and Ülo Valk, 1–19. Abingdon & New York: Routledge.

Bögre, Zsuzsanna–Szabó, Csaba (eds). 2010. *Ruptures. Nuns in Communism.* [*Törésvonalak. Apácasors a kommunizmusban*]. Budapest: METEM–Szent István Társulat.

Dinzelbacher, Peter. 1997. *'Volksreligion', 'gelebte Religion', 'verordnete Religion. Zu begrifflichen Instrumentarium und historischer Perspektive. Bayerisches Jahrbuch für Volkskunde.* München: Kommission für bayerische Landesgeschichte bei der Bayerische Akademie der Wissen. 77–95.

Esterházy, Péter. 2002. *Revised Edition* [*Javított kiadás. Melléklet a Harmonia Cœlestishez*]. Budapest: Magvető.

Farkas, Gyöngyi. 2006. Informer's Reports, Interrogation Minutes, Petitions. Possible Sources for Social History Writing [Ügynökjelentések, kihallgatási jegyzőkönyvek, kérvények. A társadalomtörténet-írás lehetséges forrásai]. *Aetas*, 21 (4): 146–70.

Gervai, András. 2015. *A Secret Hungary. The Society as "Target"* [*Titkos Magyarország. "Célszemély" a társadalom*]. Budapest: Kalligram.

Gieseke, Jens. 2010. State Security and Society. An Argument for a Joint Research [Állambiztonság és társadalom – érvek az együttes vizsgálat szükségesssége mellett. A NDK Állambiztonsági Minisztérium történeti kutatásának állása]. *Betekintő* 2010/3. http://betekinto.hu/sites/default/files/betekinto-szamok/2010_3_gieseke.pdf – accessed on 4 April 2019.

Gyarmati, György. 2014. "What Can We Study in Secret Security Informer's Files and What Cannot?" ["Mire jók az állambiztonsági ügynökiratok, és mire nem?"] In: *The Faces of the Informer: Everyday Collaboration and the Informer-issue* [*Az ügynök arcai. Mindennapi kollaboráció és ügynökkérdés*], edited by Sándor Horváth Sándor, 65–87. Budapest: Libri.

Horváth, Kata. 2009. "The Name Borsányi. The Borderline between Political and Scientific Surveillance" ["A Borsányi név. A politikai és a tudományos megfigyelés határai"] AnBlokk 2009 (3): 30–8.

Kapaló, James A. 2013. "Folk Religion in Discourse and Practice." *Journal of Ethnology and Folkloristics* 7 (1): 3–18.

Kapaló, James A. 2018. "Domestic Religion in Soviet and Post-Soviet Moldova." In: *Religion im Kontext/Religion in Context: Handbuch für Wissenschaft und Studium*, edited by Annette Schnabel, Melanie Reddig and Heidemarie Winkel, 305–21. Baden-Baden: Nomos.

Kula, Marcin. 2004. "Was ich aus den legendären „Mappen" erfahren möchte." In: *Die Überlieferung der Diktaturen. Beiträge zum Umgang mit Archiven der Geheimpolizeien in Polen und Deutschland nach 1989*, edited by Bensussan, Agnès – Dakowska, Dorota – Beaupré, Nicolas. 195–203. Essen: Klartext Verlag.

Laczó, Ferenc. 2009. A Monumental Petty Game. Review: Rainer M. János. 2008. In a Web of Reports. József Antall and the State Security Men, 1957–1989. Budapest: 1956-os Intézet. [Nagyszabású kisszerű játszma. Rainer, M. János. 2008. Jelentések hálójában. Antall József és az állambiztonság emberei. 1957–1989. Budapest: 1956-os Intézet.] *BUKSZ* 21 (1): 3–7.

Luehrmann, Sonja. 2015. *Religion in Secular Archives. Soviet Atheism and Historical Knowledge.* New York: Oxford University Press.

Petrás, Éva. 2017. "The History of the Jehovah's Witnesses between 1945 and 1989" ["Jehova Tanúi története 1945 és 1989 között"]. In: *The History of the Hungarian Church of Jehovah's Witnesses from the Beginnings to the Present* [*A Magyarországi Jehova Tanúi Egyház története a kezdetektől napjainkig*], edited by Csaba Fazekas et al., 203–69. Szabolcs. Budapest: Gondolat.

Pihurik, Judit. 2011. "Undermining People's Democracy in a Szekszárd Wine Cellar" ["A népi demokrácia aláaknázása egy szekszárdi borospincében"]. *Századok* 145 (1): 143–60.

Poenaru, Florin. 2013. "Contesting Illusions: History and Intellectual Class Struggles in (Post)socialist Romania." Ph.D. Diss., Central European University.

Primiano, Leonard. 1995. "Vernacular Religion and the Search for Method in Religious Folklife." *Western Folklore* 54 (1): 37–56.

Primiano, Leonard. 2001. "What is Vernacular Catholicism? The "Dignity" Example." In: *Politics and Folk Religion*, edited by Barna Gábor, 51–8. Papers of the 3rd Symposium of SIEF Comission of Folk Religion. Szeged: Department of Ethnology, University of Szeged.

Primiano, Leonard. 2012. "Afterword: Manifestations of the Religious Vernacular: Ambiguity, Power, and Creativity." In: *Vernacular Religion in Everyday Life. Expressions of Belief*, edited by Marion Bowman and Ülo Valk, 382–94. Abingdon & New York: Routledge.

Rainer, M. János. 2008. *In a Web of Reports. József Antall and the State Security Men, 1957–1989* [*Jelentések hálójában. Antall József és az állambiztonság emberei*. 1957–1989]. Budapest: 1956-os Intézet.

Tabajdi, Gábor–Ungváry, Krisztián. 2008. *Past Hushed Up. The Party-state and Internal Affairs. The Workings of the Political Police in Hungary 1956–1990* [*Elhallgatott múlt. A pártállam és a belügy. A politikai rendőrség működése Magyarországon 1956–1990*]. Budapest: 1956-os Intézet–Corvina.

Takács, Tibor. 2013. *Informers on Informing: Informer's Memoirs from the Kádár-era* [*Besúgók a besúgásról. Ügynök-visszaemlékezések a Kádár-korszakból*]. Budapest: L'Harmattan.

Takács, Tibor. 2014. "Studying the Informer-network from a Social Historical Perspective" ["Az ügynökhálózat társadalomtörténeti kutatása"]. In: *The Faces of the Informer. Everyday Collaboration and the Informer-issue* [*Az ügynök arcai. Mindennapi kollaboráció és ügynökkérdés*], edited by Sándor Horváth, 107–28. Budapest: Libri.

Ungváry, Krisztián. 2014. "Undervalued Sources" ["Források és alulértékelésük"]. In: *The Faces of the Informer. Everyday Collaboration and the Informer-issue* [*Az ügynök arcai. Mindennapi kollaboráció és ügynökkérdés*], edited by Sándor Horváth, 89–105. Budapest: Libri.

Vățulescu, Cristina. 2010. *Police Aesthetics. Literature, Film, and the Secret Police in Soviet Times*. Stanford: Stanford University Press.

Verdery, Katherine. 2014. *Secrets and Truths. Ethnography in the Archive of Romania's Secret Police*. Budapest and New York: CEU Press.

Verdery, Katherine. 2018. *My Life as a Spy. Investigation in a Secret Police File*. Durham and London: Duke University Press.

11 Photographs of the religious underground

Tracing images between archives and communities

Kinga Povedák

Introduction

In this chapter, which is based on an in-depth analysis of a single secret police file, I approach the question of how to deal with police photography in the study of religious culture? Are photographs that were intended to capture reality from a certain ideological perspective capable of opening up new layers of the past? I examine whether it is possible to gain new insights about religious culture during the years of dictatorship with the help of the images and artefacts, referred to by Kapaló as "hidden galleries" (2019, 88), enclosed within the secret police archives. Are photographs we find there more reliable than texts? In this chapter, I seek to demonstrate that secret police photographs are not only suitable for illustrating articles as complementary elements, but they also have significantly more potential. Through a case study of a clandestine religious community, I explain the context and production of photographic images situated in a single secret police file and discuss how these images are presented in the file. More importantly, I liberate or "repatriate" photographs from the archive and, through the process of photo-elicitation with community members, allow alternative narratives to emerge.

The "József Németh" case

In order to escape the attention of the communist state and the eyes and ears of the secret police, some religious groups in Hungary attempted to hide their activities. Clandestine religious rituals, base communities or prayer group meetings were only sporadically documented by participants at the time and there are no precise descriptions or data on how these groups operated during communism. There is scarce knowledge of the practices that developed within the framework of everyday or vernacular religiosity (see Hesz, Chapter 10, this volume) in these underground religious groups. Aware of the lack of sources and the methodological constraints this poses, I was extremely excited to find a well-documented description of a religious

Figure 11.1 Crime scene photograph of the electric organ (ÁBTL 3.1.9. V-160122/24). ©Historical Archives of the Hungarian State Security.

community accompanied by 27 photographs inserted into a secret police operational file. A part of the photographs documented a church hall in every detail: separate pictures were taken of the furnishings, such as the chairs, wall clock, donation box, pictures and the electric organ (see Figure 11.1). Several pictures also show the church members sitting in the hall and the pastor preaching (see Figure 11.2). In addition, five images depict a baptism ceremony with the baptized dressed in white with an image that captures the actual ritual action (see Figure 11.3). Such visual data and resources of rituals and spaces are extremely scarce from this period in Hungary. Although it was not apparent at first glance, five of the 27 photographs depicting the baptism and eight depicting persons preaching or testifying to members of the congregation were confiscated from the community, whilst the remaining 14 were taken during a raid by the secret police. In the case file, these two sets of images are not separated, so on first glance the researcher does not necessarily feel the irreconcilable contrast between them, which only becomes evident on reading the written documents amongst which they sit. While the confiscated photographs portray religious events and ceremonies, or the encounter with the transcendent, the photographs taken during the raid were intended to operationalize the community's destruction.

Figure 11.2 Pastor Németh preaching (ÁBTL 3.1.9. V-160122/7). ©Historical Archives of the Hungarian State Security.

Figure 11.3 Baptized congregants in white robes (ÁBTL 3.1.9. V-160122/13). ©Historical Archives of the Hungarian State Security.

We learn from the file that the photographs were taken in a hidden house church, in the home of Pastor József Németh in Budapest. In 1968, Németh left the congregation of the Evangelical Christian Church – or the "Pentecostals" as they are referred to in the files – which was recognized by the State Office of Church Affairs,[1] and founded an independent congregation. At first, he wanted to keep the new congregation within the framework of the Church, but his attempts failed after long negotiations. Németh and his followers did not want to accept the restrictions imposed by the Evangelical Christian Church, which allowed them to meet only once a week under the supervision of a pastor sent from the centre. Németh's newly planted congregation, now operating without permission with 50–60 members, met three times a week in the hidden house church. The secret police considered Németh's congregation dangerous, "as it seeks to hinder the further development of a good relationship between the state and the church. He is fanaticizing its members with extreme religious views. They are trying to attract and win new people" (ÁBTL 3.1.9. V-160122, 3). Alongside the threat posed by his beliefs, Németh and his associates were also suspected of illegal profiteering. The report of June 23, 1972 highlights the relations of the forbidden congregation in the FRG (Federal Republic of Germany), from which they received aid, and specifically mentions that "they also possess a high-value electric organ from the FRG" (ÁBTL 3.1.9. V-160122, 1).

The file also includes a detailed plan of action to liquidate the congregation. As a first step, the secret service officers produced an anonymous letter[2] stating that "a citizen" had found an envelope on the street along with religious booklets and an invitation to their secret meeting. However, the alleged "citizen" did not find a church at the address provided, so he or she took the envelope to the police. To verify this, the police raided the congregation during a meeting to "catch" the members and seize evidence. The purpose of the house search was also to "assess the assets of the unlicensed congregation, to obtain data on their financial resources and related written materials" (ÁBTL 3.1.9. V-160122, 14). A staff photographer also participated in the operation. According to the descriptions, the room was 4 meters by 6.5 meters and had wood panelling on the walls, it had 55 chairs, an altar and an electric organ next to it, with 18–20 people praying, all of whom were required to show their identification papers to the officers (ÁBTL 3.1.9. V-160122, 22). In addition to booklets and a cash register containing a list of church members, religious booklets, bills, letters, and five photographs of a church ceremony were seized during the raid (ÁBTL 3.1.9. V-160122, 19).

After the raid, the pastor József Németh and treasurer Anna Sima, and later several congregants, as well as other individuals who came into contact with the congregation, were interrogated. During these interrogations, Németh spoke in detail about his conversion, his growing immersion in faith, his conflict with the leaders of the Evangelical Christian Church and then his separation from the church and the process of setting up a new congregation.

During the multiple interrogations, they were primarily asked for information about the financial functioning of the congregation, which was compared with data and numbers in the confiscated cash book. Among other things, Németh was asked about the salary he received from the congregation, the donations made in the donation box during services, and how and for what they were used. During the interrogations, it is mentioned several times that Németh had left his job in 1970 in order to dedicate all his efforts to the congregation, for which he received a monthly donation of 1,500 HUF. The interrogations of Anna Sima, the treasurer and one of the leaders of the community, focused on the circumstances of the purchase of the apartment for the purpose of setting up the secret house church, as well as the acquisition of the various furnishings.

In light of the interrogation reports the content of the 13 confiscated images becomes clear: five images show the baptism (see Figures 11.3 and 11.4), which pastor Németh performed once or twice a year in a small garden pool built specifically for this purpose. In the following photographs Németh preaches (see Figure 11.2), and other leaders of the community, such as his brother Mihály, and the congregation treasurer Anna Sima share their personal testimonies. According to the file the photographs were taken by two congregants, Zoltán Sajtos and Jánosné Hetesi.

The interrogation records state that Németh and the other congregants were cooperative throughout the process, with no significant anomalies in their confessions. They acknowledged that occasional foreign (from FRG, Czechoslovakia, Romania) guests also visited them, preached or testified, named the sources of their religious material received from abroad and acknowledged that the seized religious samizdat booklets had several anti-Soviet contents. Based on the written documents and photographs, we are dealing with a simple, straightforward storyline: Németh acknowledged that he had created a "sect" that was not recognized by either the Evangelical Christian Church nor the state; He had not worked since 1970, was supported by members of the illegal congregation, set up their house church from donations from them, and wanted to organize a "gypsy mission" without permission. In view of all this, the punishment imposed on the leaders of the congregation in 1975 seems mild: four leaders received only a warning, József Németh was sentenced to 3 months imprisonment by the Court of Budapest for the misuse of the right to freedom of association. The sentence was suspended for 3 years. Anna Sima was fined 1,500 HUF (which was about 60% of her monthly salary at the time).

The secret police had woven the images and texts into a coherent narrative. The 55 chairs, the wood panelling on the walls, the wall clock, the ornate donation box, the altar, the confiscated samizdat literature, and the expensive West German electric harmony organ were carefully documented. Although Németh was not a legally licenced pastor of the Evangelical Christian Church, the images testify that he did baptize others and preach to the community. The correspondence he received from the leadership of the Evangelical Christian Church also proved that he was aware of the illegality of his church activities. We also learn from the secret police file that Németh stole yarn from his workplace in 1957 for which he had been convicted.

Reading photographs

As Barthes noted, photography is not about what is no longer, but about what has been (Barthes 1981, 96). Following this realistic position and the arguments of those theoreticians of photography who see photographs as evidence of the real – the photographs that appear in Németh's secret police file verify the events recounted. The photographic images in secret police files, therefore, can be understood as "incontrovertible proof that a given thing happened" (Sontag 2005, 3) and inform us of moments of a reality that once existed. The secret house church did exist, baptisms were actually performed in the garden pool hidden from the outside, the baptized did indeed wear white robes and certain details of the secret police raid can be recalled with their help. Based on this approach these photographs represent proof that can contribute to our understanding of an unknown aspect of underground religious culture. Consequently, such images are valuable snapshots for the scholar of religion, portraying and documenting the unexplored religious life and the hidden forms of religious practice during communism, albeit from the perspective of the regime. This evidential nature, or indexicality, assured that "[p]hotography was considered one of the most important means by which the secret police could track their targets and gather convincing evidence of the activities and networks of those under surveillance" (Kapaló 2019, 89).

Taking this kind of evidential approach, however, as Kapaló points out, misses other important saliences that accrue to secret police photography "... photographs in the archive speak to us first and foremost about the institutional use of photography to exert power over communities" (Kapaló 2019, 104). In relation to secret police images such as those featured in Németh's file, there exists a gulf between the purpose of their creation at the time and the way they can be viewed and used today. Firstly, we should be cognizant of the fact that the repressive apparatus of communism did not intend to establish a database for future use by researchers following the overthrow of the dictatorship and neither was its purpose to record aspects of everyday life and culture of the period. The purpose of the archive was clearly political, that is, to assist the operational work of the repressive apparatus that sustained the dictatorship, and to record, textually, visually and aurally any person, community, event, circumstance that might have been dangerous to the functioning of the dictatorship. The question, then, is to what degree these images can be considered as sources, whether they can be used as authentic eyewitnesses[3] to historical events, and when do they become entirely a "studio photo" that aims to depict something contrived in order to create merely the appearance of reality.

The truth value of photography has been the focus of scepticism and debate in courtrooms as well as in other contexts, as images can be differently interpreted, and may reasonably support different and even contradictory "truths." If we apply a discursive approach and place the images next to the written sources of the files, the "objectivity" disappears from the underlying interpretation. The discursive interpretation of photography "concentrates most on the sites of production" (Rose 2016, 224). The works of theorists like John Tagg or Allen Sekula are "held together by an insistence on the power relations articulated through these practices and institutions. For both of them, visual images and visualities are articulations of institutional power" (Rose 2016, 224–5). Sekula contests the idea that photographs transmit immutable truths and emphasizes that "photographic meaning depends largely on context" (Sekula 2003, 445). As Edwards points out, photographs and their archiving have been produced and controlled through sites of authority, and the nature of photography itself is intrinsic to this powerful process. Through their mutability, photographs are able to create stories, distort identities and appropriate cultures (Edwards 2003, 83). In the case presented here, it is clear that the images have a constructed message, which can be considered a fabricated reading of reality that was intended to justify the actions of the authorities. In the case of secret police photography, the images are instrumentalized and become the powerful tools in support of the police narratives and their underlying truth claims.

As Edwards alerts us, however, "Photographs seldom have closed meanings. Rather, meanings are mutable and arbitrary, generated by their viewers and dependent on the context of their viewing" (Edwards 2003, 84). If we change perspective and approach the interrogation record texts from the dossier as "informant's" narratives and paste them next to the images, another reading emerges. The photographs become polysemic, ambiguous and opaque. Based on this other reading, pastor Németh was an active member of the Evangelical Christian Church in the 1960s, trying to spread the Word and establish a new congregation. For this reason, he applied for a loan, bought a new house so that he could set up a meeting place in his own home. However, whilst looking after the affairs of the congregation, visiting the patients and dealing with the members, he found he no longer had time for other work, he became a "full-time" pastor and the other members of the congregation voted to pay him a modest monthly salary. Although he received samizdat spiritual literature from abroad, which also included anti-communist views, he did not politicize during the church meetings nor did he have any illegal political connections. The images lined up to demonstrate and prove the illegal economic activity of the congregation lose their power and relevance in this reading as the interrogation reports revealed that the members donated voluntarily, no one instructed them to do so, and the amounts received can be traced from the cash registers. The chairs, the collection box, even the expensive electric harmony organ were legally owned by the congregation. The characters in the photographs of the rituals are indeed praying, testifying, the Bible is indeed open on the altar, and the religious organ, violin, and rattles were indeed used to perform religious songs for the visibly poor, mostly elderly members of the congregation.

In order to prompt the photographs to speak in another way, we have to immerse ourselves in the situation of the creator and the given cultural and political context. These documents were created and documented based on a fabricated narrative and as such the contemporary structures and prefigurations must be peeled off the text (Gyáni 2010, 34–5). The stillness of photographs – says Edwards – invites certain ways of weaving stories around them. Their meanings are "mutable and arbitrary, generated by their viewers and dependent on the context of their viewing, their relationship with written or spoken 'texts,' and the embodied subjectivities of their viewer" (Edwards 2003, 84). According to this understanding we have the possibility to strip both the secret police and the victim narrative from the opposing readings.[4] Even though there is no single "correct interpretation," we can find new readings of the reality behind the images, as well as details that the images – accidentally or intentionally – do not speak of, that is, details that at present we have no idea ever existed or happened. The interpretation of the images cannot be complete, however, without them. Photo elicitation as a research method can help with this.

Photo elicitation

So far we have uncovered two divergent readings of the same set of photographic images found in the secret police file. There are several ways to resolve the differences between the two. The first obvious option is to conduct oral history interviews. Through oral history, a personal reading of past events opens up a bottom-up perspective that can reveal how certain political-economic-cultural processes have transformed and been experienced in everyday life. In our case, the validity of the oral history method is strengthened by the fact that due to the relatively short time that has elapsed since the creation of the secret police file, it is still possible to supplement the archival data with oral history interviews. However, as time passes, we find fewer memories, and stories become more and more obscure. The change of political system that has taken place in the meantime, the multiple changes in attitude towards the dictatorship, including a certain degree of nostalgia for the Kádár regime (1956–89), means that oral history interviews conducted today contribute to a fragmented and constructed knowledge. Due to its subjectivity, the oral history method is not primarily aimed at searching for "historical truth," but at "democratizing" historical events and exploring their experiential dimension. However, oral history is essentially an interview, in which a personal story unfolds along the researcher's pre-structured questions. In relation to Németh's case file, it was possible to deploy another method, which is in some ways similar to oral history, that places photographic images at the centre of the research process.

Photo elicitation emerged from the classic power relations of anthropology, its methods and goals – says Edwards – were developed as a methodological tool to trigger memories and glean cultural information (2003, 87). Collier was first to introduce this method in a much-cited article from 1957 and later in several of his books. The essence of the method is that during photo elicitation, the researcher does not ask questions but allows the photograph to replace the question. In his study of the method, Douglas Harper briefly states that photo elicitation is "based on the simple idea of inserting a photograph into a research interview" (Harper 2002, 13). This evokes the personal experiences and impressions of the observer making the photograph an active participant in the dialogue. In this way, the photograph becomes a social actor, impressing, articulating and constructing fields of social actions and relations (Edwards 2003, 88). In photo elicitation, people speak by photographs (Pink 2001, 74) and photographs and people perform histories together (Edwards 2003, 89) allowing participants to articulate histories in ways that would not have emerged in that particular figuration if the photograph had not existed (Edwards 2003, 88). It is both the indexicality of photographs, the idea of "what has been" (Barthes 1981, 85), along with photography's ability to trigger memory that is utilized though the method.

Photo elicitation as a method thrusts images into the centre of a research agenda (Harper 2002, 15). Perhaps the most significant and important advantage of the method is that topics can emerge when looking at the photographs without the researcher having had any prior knowledge of them. In Rose's words "while ordinary interview talk can explore many issues, discussing a photograph with the interviewee can prompt talk about different things, things that researchers hadn't thought about" (Rose 2016, 315).

In her exploration of visual methodologies, Rose (2016, 315–16) points to four important benefits of using photography in research in the social sciences. It is worth recounting these briefly as they each have relevance for the use of images from secret police archives. Firstly, *photographs encourage different insights, not just more but different, into social phenomena* and they have potential for opening alternative histories. Consequently, a different kind of knowledge is evoked.

Photo elicitation also *encourages talk that is more emotional, more affective more ineffable.* In our case, perhaps most importantly, it is easier to talk about sensitive topics in this way. As Sztompka aptly puts it, photo elicitation is like looking at photos in a family circle, while oral history can be more like an exam or questioning (Sztompka 2009, 83). While standard interviews tend to take place face-to-face, the researcher and participant often sit shoulder-to-shoulder when focused on the image before them (Williams and Whitehouse 2015, 306). The difference in mood between the two can help reach different depths of the personal sphere – even the "intimate" inner feelings and events.

Rose also emphasizes the obvious fact that *visual materials are particularly helpful in exploring everyday, taken-for-granted things.* Due to the selective and imperfect nature of our memory, the objects, clothes, decorations, etc. that appear in the pictures in many cases are stored only latently, requiring stimulants to activate. A photo can raise such memories and bring them to life.

The final advantage of photo elicitation according to Rose is that it *demands collaboration*. As opposed to a certain hierarchical relationship between the oral historian and the interviewee in classic oral history interviews, photo elicitation promotes a kind of "reciprocal ethnography" (Lawless 2019) allowing agency and active collaboration from the research participants. With regard to sensitive material in secret police files, it is particularly important that photo elicitation shifts the researcher-participant power dynamic in this way (Williams and Whitehouse 2015, 306). The informant in photo elicitation is less likely to try to give more and more perfect answers to the researcher's questions, but – as Sztompka discusses – it can unfold as "experience-oriented" conversation of equal parties, during which personal feelings, experiences and memories come to light. As Harper concludes, if the photo elicitation interview goes well "the person being interviewed sees himself or herself as the expert, as the researcher becomes the student" (Harper 2012, 157).

For the reasons outlined here, the most important results of the photo-elicitation method are "emotional revelations, psychological explosions and powerful statements of values" (Collier 1967, 62) that might otherwise be impossible to obtain. This collaborative relationship works even if we are not talking about photos taken of the interviewees themselves. Through the re-engagement with and re-cognition of lost images, photo elicitation can help ensure research is not only about loss, but instead also about empowerment, renewal and contestation (Edwards 2003, 86).

Although photo elicitation has many research-enhancing benefits and is now a widespread method in the social sciences, it is only slowly taking root in research by scholars of religions and is still rarely used.[5] This methodological deficit is especially true in research on religions in the countries of the former Soviet bloc. During communism, research on religions meant primarily a Marxist analysis of religious history and ethnography, when it dealt with religion at all, focused mainly on the exploration of archaic elements, superstitions and pre-Christian beliefs, that is, the religious culture of the past. As very few contemporary sociological or anthropological works on religion were produced during the years of communism, we have virtually no knowledge of the transformation of religious culture during these decades. By taking an anthropological approach, the photographs we find in secret police archives can provide an insight into the vernacular religiosity (see Hesz, Chapter 10, this volume) of the time, evoking and portraying the mundane, the everyday, the quotidian and a glimpse of the materiality of the religious experiences (see Kapaló, Chapter 12, this volume).

Photo elicitation experiences

From an anthropological perspective, archival research sheds light on only one side of the story. Photos found in archives as "raw documents" (Edwards 2001a) deprive individuals and communities of their own interpretation. Visiting and finding religious communities that appear in the secret police photographs formed an integral part of the Hidden Galleries project (see Kapaló and Vagramenko 2020) and the research undertaken with pastor Németh's community. Without having taken this step, it would have been impossible to recover their voices and narratives. Although I listed several benefits of the photo elicitation method earlier, this does not mean that there are no risk factors associated with it. While on the one hand, photo elicitation may mine deeper shafts of human consciousness than a words-alone approach, on the other hand, ethical and emotional concerns can emerge that need to be addressed.

How will the daughter of the pastor, who underwent the house search herself and whose father was interrogated by the secret police on several occasions, react to a researcher appearing on her doorstep with photographs from her father's case file? To what extent is the process affected by the fact that the previously underground community is still a minority religion, not recognized by the state as an official church? Will the previously unknown secret police photographs cause repeated trauma and negative emotions? Do the advantages of the photo elicitation method apply in such a burdened and sensitive situation? Having recalled negative emotions and memories, will the collaborative experience-centred narration give way to melancholy and alienation instead?

Before embarking on this research, it was important to keep in mind that the purpose of using photo elicitation was not to refute the agent reports nor to accept another reading that opposes the police narrative as authentic. Rather, my goal was to allow an individual reading that is independent of what is described in the file to emerge; not a counter-narrative but rather one liberated from the confines of the file. Photographic images are used to invoke and elicit new narratives without reading the context, without the burden of representation. By unstitching the archive through a photo-encounter I intend to "listen to, and above all, dialogue with the documents" (Cunha 2020, 31).

With this aim, I conducted a series of interviews with members of the community in 2017–2018. Pastor Németh had died in 2013 so my primary contact became his daughter, Lilla Gere,[6] who was mentioned several times in the file even though she was still a child at the time of the incident. During the research process, I kept in mind that even though members of the religious community under surveillance were unaware of the existence of the photographs and the contents of the secret police file, they had a right to learn about their own past and tell their own story.

As discussed earlier in this chapter, the photographs can be divided into two groups. Some were taken in line with the norms of crime scene photography, and were designed to record the environment, context, and circumstances of the crime for use as data for investigations and as evidence in the courts (see Kapaló 2019). The intention of the secret police was to collect evidence of the supposed crimes of the community. A second set of images includes photographs taken by the members of the community themselves during earlier rituals, although they were later used against them in the prosecution. The source of certain images (either prepared by the secret police or confiscated from the community) crystallized during the photo elicitation process, which confirmed several of my positive expectations mentioned earlier. All kinds of difficulties, the tension caused by the formal situation, even if it existed, vanished extremely quickly. The interviewees knew they would see images of their community that had been kept in the secret police archives, but not exactly when and where they were taken. As a result, I encountered excited anticipation rather than anxiety.

I received a virtually immediate point of access to the memory of both of my interviewees. For Lilla Gere and her husband, the images instantly revived latent elements of memory. I learned, for example, that the church hall, i.e., Németh's home, was in a three-apartment building built as a home for a female Protestant religious order in the 1930s, that looked like a bourgeois villa. Each of the three families who lived there belonged to the congregation and had planned in advance to move there. Seeing the pictures, the interviewees were delighted as if they were reuniting with friends they hadn't seen in a long time. The faces were first recalled: "Wow! She is my grandmother! Uncle Tankó! Andris' grandmother! ... Aunt Ancika, Dad, Uncle Misi, my dad's brother! Here's Daddy, oh, dear, dear! ... Old Uncle Zagyva is here too! Well, this is something!" Then, after the faces, the emotions attached to them came to light: "I remember everyone! Aunt Sándor, it occurred to me! Oh, I really loved this aunt! ... Wow! It is Eszti, and he is the Sajtos boy. Sajtos ... I think Misi ... I think they reported on us too!"

At first, the memories fluttered freely as more and more burst to the surface. It was clear that the images inspired different insights, not just more but different. Virtually all of the material in the file came to be re-interpreted and recontextualized, and the storyline of the file was contested. Perhaps naturally, the day of the raid depicted in the photographs and the file soon came to the centre of the photo-elicitation process. While we can't find any reference to this in the file, and the whole action and subsequent interrogations are portrayed as a peaceful conversation, we learned another story from Lilla:

> I remember when they rang [the door bell] and came in. It was a horrible feeling that everything was turned upside down, shattered, searched through, even our bedding. That brutality ... Mom held me back from going at them [...] I was very sorry for those old ladies. I loved them very much ... I saw my father's face, I saw he was shocked but tried to remain strong [...] Worship began, we were still praying. After the gathering, everyone came in, knelt down and prayed. I always sat in the back row with

> my mother under the collection box on one of the images. We knew there was something up because the ringing was a special thing. I remember the old aunts' terrified face [...] They were searching for money everywhere and for samizdat. We even had to take our bedding off [...] Everyone's identification was checked, they had to stay there for a long time before they were released, and the officers stayed in our house until dawn.

And then after looking at all the secret police photography, Lilla's deepest feelings came to light referring to a mental image that remained with her even today:

> There is this image that stayed with me when Dad went with them and we didn't know whether we would see each other again. Even now it makes me cry when I think of that [Lilla begins to cry] [...] For a month they came and took him away every day for interrogation.

Based on the secret police file, we find that the consequences of the house search were not serious. According to the court decision taken in 1975, József Németh was given a three-month suspended sentence. The surveillance, interrogation, house search, and the confiscation of images and religious materials did not cause the community too much trouble as both József Németh and other members of the community avoided imprisonment. However, the recollections of Lilla reveal a different, more tragic story.

> I was there during the trials and I remember I wanted to run up to and kill these people who accused my father. So, this is in me so deeply even today. [...] So this is so deep in me because [...] For many years almost every day the cars were standing in front of our house and watching ... Papa [Lilla Gere referring to Pastor Németh] was an electrician but he was not allowed back into his profession. He worked as a night watchman. It was horrible, financially. I only had one pair of trousers as a teenage girl, I will never forget that. It was very hard. But he prayed and trusted in God, but we knew they were always watching [...]

The recollection of the house search and the interrogation of her father certainly activated other, similar experiences in Lilla Gere. As mentioned earlier, photo elicitation encourages talk that is more ineffable. At the same time, the photographs of the house raid evoked further experiences of repercussions from my interviewee's later years providing an example how a particular image might encourage different insights going beyond the stories related to the secret police photographs.

> [Male informant] Tell us about your decorative [adds sarcastically] companions to high school! – Yes, when I went back to school in the afternoons the agents followed me all the way to the building by

> car. – [Male informant] And the college? – I wanted to be a teacher. I enrolled in college and at the end of my admission I was asked by the examination committee of KISZ[7] members why I am not a member of KISZ. I said that because I am a believer. So, I was told not to try again because I am blacklisted, they will never accept my application [...] What struck me is that because of my faith in God, I was stigmatized and not accepted in this society. In this society, I could not live my faith the way I wanted to, because society did not accept Christians.

The raid on the secret house church was not without consequences, the community was shattered and disintegrated. For a long time, even relatives and friends could not visit them because if there were to be an "incident," pastor Németh's suspended prison sentence would be activated. Lilla Gere recounts of her father's disillusioned state of mind as follows: "The main reason for his disappointment was that several of the believers, members of the congregation, and even Pentecostal leaders, collaborated with the power. They were paid or intimidated." József Németh was only able to found a new congregation in 1982 within the organizational framework of the Hungarian Free Christian Church.

> He got it in his heart that he needed to plant a new congregation in Erzsébet (a district of Budapest). At the end of 1974, there was a very large wave of revival among the Free Christians. At that time he joined the Free Christian Church in Budapest, in Hőgyes Endre Street, which was led by Mézes Laci. We rented a tiny Reformed prayer house.

The photo elicitation process also revealed significant and intriguing details regarding the confiscated photographs. It turned out that the photo of a young girl being baptized was actually Lilla Gere, the daughter of the pastor, and the baptism had taken place in the garden of the hidden house church, in a specially constructed font (see Figure 11.4). In several cases, the photos also gained new interpretation and details were revealed that put its characters in a new light. When my interviewees looked at the pictures of the raid (see Figure 11.5), the smile on someone's face or a simple glance into the camera captured in the image, prompted unexpected feelings and interpretations:

> Well this was the guy who came to search the house ... they just came unannounced, rang and sat down. Everyone is terrified, poor Aunt Ancika is looking straight into the camera, I still see the horror on her face today.

A wealth of new, previously unknown information relating to religious life also came to light through this research process. In connection with Figure 11.6, I learned how samizdat recordings and documents were received from abroad:

Figure 11.4 Baptism of Lilla Gere (ÁBTL 3.1.9. V-160122/10). ©Historical Archives of the Hungarian State Security.

Figure 11.5 Moments of the house raid (ÁBTL 3.1.9. V-160122/17). ©Historical Archives of the Hungarian State Security.

Figure 11.6 Searching for samizdat during the raid (ÁBTL 3.1.9. V-160122/40). ©Historical Archives of the Hungarian State Security.

> We got samizdat spiritual literature that was brought in by foreigners, by Dutch people, in a double-bottomed caravan. They were brought at night, they stopped in front of the house and it had to be quickly unloaded in secret. But these were all about God, there was nothing anti-state in them. These were translated with horrible spelling by '56 Hungarians but we were terribly happy with them, they were living testimonies. Before that, there were only cassettes and we typed them and duplicated them. [...] They were in mason jars. During the raid and the house search they were looking everywhere, even behind the bottles to see if they were there, but they didn't notice they were tucked into the mason jars.

When it came to the image of the electric organ (see Figure 11.1), they were surprised at how much importance the police attached to it. And then from the images of the instruments, they remembered what and how they were singing on church occasions. The photo elicitation also confirmed that visual materials are particularly helpful in exploring everyday, taken-for-granted aspects of religious life in the community such as worship practices.

> Is this serious? Oh, how funny ... we were so very well documented! [...] Aunt Ilonka played old Pentecostal or Baptist hymns on the organ, Uncle

> Tankó played the violin, we had a rattle drum, but back then there were only classical hymns, the new ones were still being written at that time. We used Pentecostal or Baptist songbooks.

The photo elicitation process revealed that members of the community had no prior knowledge, or only false knowledge, of several details of the secret police action. They had no information on exactly what grounds Németh and his associates had been convicted, or who reported on them to provoke the action launched against them, or who the embedded informers had been. The distrust born of these uncertainties was indelibly ingrained in the members of a congregation. During the research, interviewees mentioned certain congregants on several occasions, "he wasn't clean either, I am sure he reported on us as well." As a result, following the raid they became more cautious with new members coming to the church. Their opposition to communism remained strong even during the post-regime socialist governments, and they assumed that agents were still among them even then: "we knew who the built-in people were who pretended to be Christians but came to observe [...] and after 2002 the same people reappeared."

In parallel, their curiosity and determination to learn about their own past grew. Lilla Gere decided to publish a book about her father, including her father's poems. They asked for information on where and how to request access to their secret police files and planned to initiate a crowdsourced oral history project on their congregation during communism. By consciously starting to learn about their own past, they themselves began to reveal unknown details of the past to members of their own community and express the value of research and creating their own record:

> When I see how this works [the research process and the interviews], it satisfies me, and for me it is absolutely OK. This fits into my way of thinking, I am happy to make this a public good. I believe these things are something people need to know about.

From the very beginning, the Hidden Galleries research project, out of which this chapter grew, has focused not only on archival research, but also on bringing materials back to source communities through the framework of collaborative ethnography. As part of the collaborative ethnography tracing the images of pastor Németh's file, Lilla Gere, my key informant, was open and involved in the project. She took part in the preparation of our exhibition that displayed images from her father's file by lending us his handwritten poetry book and by giving her permission to use the transcripts of our personal communications and extracts from our interviews.

The shoulder-to-shoulder collaboration has clearly demonstrated its advantages over interrogation-type data collection. Not only the interviewees and the researcher, but also the interviewees amongst themselves cooperated with each other, building their own readings side by side, correcting each other at times and even encouraging each other to tell more and more stories. Rose's several statements about the benefits of photo elicitation were clearly confirmed, first, that photo elicitation encourages talk that is more emotional, more affective, more ineffable. Lilla Gere expressed her feelings and impressions not only about the images, but also about the photo elicitation and the person of the researcher: "Your kind personality also mattered, but you know, if some ex-communist somebody would have been ordered to come here, I am sure we wouldn't have talked to them."

Conclusion

In the case of photographic collections in secret police archives, by taking a similar ethnographic approach to that taken to colonial photographic collections, I attempted to unstitch and liberate photographs from their archival holdings by linking secret police photographic legacy with source communities to allow space for new perspectives and alternative histories to emerge (Edwards 2001b, 16). Bringing the images back to the community, through the process of photo elicitation, set in motion a new process in which the photographic images, as we have seen above, are attributed with a completely different role and significance. They remain no longer merely a document, but a stimulus of remembrance, a generator of the emergence of new historical narratives. In the case of underground religious groups hidden during the dictatorship, retelling their own stories can also strengthen community and personal identity and through such collaborative visual repatriation projects communities can become more visible and audible. Through collaborative visual repatriation we can see the formation of another "visual economy" (Poole 1997, 9–13), in which "The Archive" is decentred, extended and refigured through inclusion, recognition and liberation of the "indigenous voice" (Edwards 2003, 85). The main feature of this visual economy is the active agency of the researched community through the collaborative process of photo elicitation.

Just as Edwards found in relation to photographic collections in museums having a twofold potential, I have come to a similar conclusion concerning secret police photographs: "They are an evidential source within the communities they depict, inscribing complex layers of cultural information and knowledge, and an important site of negotiation for the development of long-term collaborative relations between museums [in our case the researcher] and communities" (Edwards 2003, 83). The photo elicitation method brought new stories and new emerging narratives to the surface in this research. The collaborative nature of photo elicitation and the emerging trust allowed alternative readings and mundane stories of underground religious life to surface that I may not have been able to access in an oral history interview.

It is important to emphasize that although this chapter focused on the images through which individual emotions and fates appeared, in addition to these, I also gained important information about minority religious culture. Transitions, relationships, and occasional tensions between individual congregations (e.g. the aforementioned wave of awakening in 1974), the material dimensions of religious culture (e.g. musical culture), and the formation of underground religiosity (e.g. samizdat literature), are all aspects that await further analysis.

Acknowledgement

The research for this chapter was funded by the European Research Council (ERC) under the European Union's Horizon 2020 research and innovation programme No. 677355.

Notes

1 Állami Egyházügyi Hivatal.
2 A copy of the "found letter" is also included in the file.
3 Peter Burke argues that images have the same historical value as texts and oral testimonies. See Burke (2001).
4 Recently, the 'truth-value' of archival texts have been questioned on many levels (Văţulescu 2010, Verdery 2014, most recently Kapaló 2019, 86). The distorting effect of interrogation reports under intimidation can be somewhat offset by photographic documents, but as we can see, photographs can also be used to support several, even contradictory, stories.
5 From the time of Collier's pioneering writing in 1956 to 2010, Williams and Whitehouse only found a total of 18 English-language studies dealing with religion that used the method of photo elicitation. In addition to these studies, the images appearing in the religious studies literature, especially in the anthropology of religion, in most cases only serve to support a given phenomenon, to prove its occurrence, or to provide a visual illustration, on the basis of which further (e.g. symbolic anthropological) analysis is possible. Even in the analysis of religious experiences, or vernacular religious practices, scholars rarely apply photo elicitation (see Williams and Whitehouse 2015).
6 I thank Lilla Gere very much for participating in the research. It is usual to anonymize research participants, however, in this case Lilla Gere and other members of the community were happy to have their names included.
7 KISZ stands for *Kommunista Ifjúsági Szövetség* which translates as Communist Youth League.

Archival source

Állambiztonsági Szolgálatok Történeti Levéltára [Historical Archives of the Hungarian State Security] (ÁBTL), ÁBTL 3.1.9. V-160122

References

Barthes, Roland. 1981. *Camera Lucida. Reflections on Photography* (translated by Richard Howard). New York: Hill and Wang.

Burke, Peter. 2001. *Eyewittnessing. The Uses of Images as Historical Evidence.* Ithaca: Cornell University Press.

Collier, John R. 1967. *Visual Anthropology: Photography as a Research Method.* New York: Holt Rinehart and Winston.

Cunha, Olívia Maria Gomes da. 2020. *The Things of Others: Ethnographies, Histories, and Other Artefacts.* Leiden: Brill.

Edwards, Elizabeth. 2001a. *Raw Histories. Photographs, Anthropology and Museums.* Oxford and New York: Berg.

Edwards, Elizabeth. 2001b. "Photography and the Performance of History." *Kronos. Journal of Cape History* 27: 15–29.

Edwards, Elizabeth. 2003. Introduction. In: *Museums and Source Communities. A Routledge Reader*, edited by Laura Peers and Alison K. Brown, 83–99. London and New York: Routledge.

Gyáni, Gábor. 2010. *The Past that Might Be Lost: The Experience as Memory and History* [*Az elveszíthető múlt. A tapasztalat mint emlékezet és történelem*]. Budapest: Nyitott Könyvműhely.

Harper, Douglas. 2002. "Talking about Pictures: A Case for Photo Elicitation." *Visual Studies* 17 (1): 13–26.

Harper, Douglas. 2012. *Visual Sociology*. New York: Routledge.

Kapaló, James A. 2019. "The Appearance of Saints: Photographic Evidence and Religious Minorities in the Secret Police Archives." *Material Religion* 15 (1): 82–109.

Kapaló, James and Vagramenko, Tatiana. 2020. *Hidden Galleries: Material Religion in the Secret Police Archives in Central and Eastern Europe*. Berlin: LitVerlag.

Lawless, Elaine. 2019. *Reciprocal Ethnography and the Power or Women's Narratives.* Bloomington: Indiana University Press.

Pink, Sarah. 2001. *Doing Visual Ethnography*. London: Sage.

Poole, Deborah. 1997. *Vision, Race, and Modernity. A Visual Economy of the Andean Image World.* Princeton: Princeton University Press.

Rose, Gillian. 2001 (2016). Visual Methodologies. *An Introduction to Researching with Visual Materials.* London: Sage.

Sekula, Allen. 2003. Reading an Archive. Photography between Labour and Capital. In: *The Photography Reader*, edited by Liz Wells, 443–52. London and New York: Routledge.

Sontag, Susan. 1977 (2005). *On Photography*. New York: RosettaBooks LCC.

Sztompka, Piotr. 2009. *Visual Sociology: Photography as a Research Method* [*Vizuális szociológia. A fényképezés mint kutatási módszer*] (translated by Márta Éles). Budapest and Pécs: Gondolat Kiadó, PTE Kommunikáció- és Médiatudományi Tanszék.

Vățulescu, Cristina. 2010. *Police Aesthetics: Literature, Film and the Secret Police in Soviet Times*. Stanford: Stanford University Press.

Verdery, Katherine. 2014. *Secrets and Truths: Ethnography in the Archives of Romania's Secret Police*. Budapest and New York: Central European University Press.

Williams, Roman R. and Kyle Whitehouse. 2015. "Photo Elicitation and the Visual Sociology of Religion." *Review of Religious Research* 57(2): 303–18.

12 Feasting and fasting

The evidential character of material religion in secret police archives

James A. Kapaló

Introduction

During the decades of communism, both the regimes within the region and scholars of religion (overwhelmingly outside the region) were engaged with the same question; how socialist modernity was impacting on religion and whether the expected demise of religion would prove fatal (see Rogers 2005, 6). Whether wished for or lamented, the assumption was that religion was in terminal decline in the Soviet Union and its satellite states, just as it was understood to be in much of the West. But as Sonja Luehrmann (2015, 12) notes, since that time "… the basic assumptions that ground the debate have shifted" and in the post-communist context we can bring new questions to research on religion under communism, and to our explorations of the documents bequeathed to us by communist regimes. In recent years, interest in the role that the memory of communism plays in society and amongst religious groups has begun to eclipse the historical study of religion under communism. Nevertheless, the persistence of religion under state sponsored secularization remains an important question for scholars of religions not least because, as Chris Hann observes, if we want to find satisfactory answers to our questions regarding the contemporary post-communist context our "inquiries cannot proceed without careful reassessment of the transmission of religious beliefs and practices in the socialist era …" (Hann 2010, 8).

The anthropological study of religion, as Rogers reminds us, "was at best difficult and at worst impossible in the socialist period" (2005, 5). Partly as a consequence of the absence of ethnographic research conducted at the time, archival research in the once secret files of the communist state, has become pivotal for scholars wishing to explore religious processes and identities during communism. In this chapter, I argue that an exploration of the material aspects of religion as represented in the archives of the secret police can offer valuable insights into the transmission of religion in communist societies. When viewed through a material lens and situated within the broader religious context and lifeworld, the texts and images in the archives reveal aspects of the reality of life in the underground that remain relatively under-explored and little analysed. Although not qualitatively the same as ethnographic sources, the reports and images compiled and composed by agents and informers, can be viewed as "surrogates" of the performances that led to their creation (Zeitlyn 2012, 469, citing Taylor 2003) in a similar way that ethnographic fieldnotes might, allowing the researcher today to access material, spatial and somatic aspects of religion that were captured by those I term here "insider-informers." Exploring material religion in the secret police files in this way, however, also invites us to reflect on the interpretational problems associated with its dual evidential status, which at the time constituted evidence of criminal or anti-state activity while today, for the scholar of religion, is transposed as evidence of religious meaning and agency. The unintended "evidential multiplicity" of material religion in the secret police archives encourages the scholar of religion to apply a "strategic methodological pluralism" (Vásquez 2017, 236, 238) that can add new layers to our understanding of the complexity, diversity and paradoxes of clandestine religion and its transmission during communism.

As Hesz (Chapter 10, this volume) observes, by shifting our viewpoint and by applying alternative methodological apparatus, namely those of the scholar of religions rather than of the historian of communism or the secret police, the archives can offer up data that is both intriguing and illuminating. Over the past decade, scholarship on religions, influenced by broader trends in the social sciences and humanities, is increasingly exploring the significance of materiality. The so-called "material turn" has inspired renewed attention towards practices, spaces, bodies, landscapes, sensory and lived experiences and their intersection with non-human agencies (see Hazard 2013; Bräunlein 2016; Vásquez 2011, 2017). Secret police archives contain a wealth of sources that refer to, represent, reproduce and capture in images aspects of the material dimension of religious lives (see Kapaló 2019; Kapaló and Vagramenko 2020). These archival sources come in many forms; written accounts such as informers and interrogation reports, lists and photographs of confiscated items; publications and devotional materials; photographs of communities and their spaces, both those confiscated from communities as well as images taken by the secret police during operations (see Povedák, this volume, Chapter 11). Despite the significant epistemological and ethical challenges associated with the use of sources compiled and composed as part of anti-religious operations, they constitute one of the few sets of historical data available for researchers seeking to understand lived religion during communism.

In this chapter, I explore one aspect of the material religious practices of a community in 1950s and 60s Romania as reflected in the secret police record. As Graham Harvey argues food, and the abstention from food, is central to religion and religious acts (Harvey 2014, 32) and this is certainly true with regards to the Eastern Orthodox tradition. Practices associated with food, or foodways, are extremely important in Orthodox Christianity for individual spiritual, communal and economic life. There are multiple occasions when special foods are prepared and consumed, including amongst others, funerals and two distinct forms of the periodic commemoration of the dead, *parastas* and *pomana* (see Geană 2005); there are complex and diverse fasting rules and traditions that many devout Orthodox follow, including obligatory periodic fasts associated with religious festivals and daily fasts performed each week; and there are also important distribution networks, charitable activities and food exchange practices, including *milostenie*, or the giving of charitable gifts to monasteries. Not least amongst the ways in which food is engaged is the act of communion with the divine through the Holy Mystery of the Eucharist, or *împărtăşanie* in Romanian, which also requires the special acquisition, preparation, consecration and consumption of foodstuffs.

During communism, most Orthodox Romanians openly continued these practices and their associated foodways to some degree or another. For groups observing the Old Calendar (see below), however, certain of these ritual meals, as well as the fasts and feasts needed to be performed secretly in order to avoid the attention of the authorities. The reports discussed in this chapter, can be read as evidence of the importance of the distribution and consumption of special foodstuffs by this community in the context of their underground religious life as well as of the significance that the secret police placed on food as material and economic value.[1]

The descriptions of this community's foodways, like all other secret police materials, were ideologically shaped by the Marxist-materialist dogmas of the regime, discursively "confining" their religious practices within a frame defined by the regime. The attention that was placed on the food transacted by the community, was in part a reflection of the importance that the regime placed on discovering and eliminating the material and economic means by which dissenting communities sustained themselves. From the early 1950s, the beginning of the period of surveillance of the so-called Inochentist-Stilist network, into the 1960s, there were a host issues that impacted on food consumption and food security for the population, including drought, grain requisitioning, collectivization and war reparations. All of these factors were referred to in the informer reports resulting from the surveillance operation against the Inochentist-Stilist group targeted in the secret police operative files. These reports, however, far from simply reporting accusations of ant-communist attitudes, parasitism or illegal hoarding of food, when read with close attention to material religious practices, instead convincingly reveal the spiritual centrality of food for this religious community and the agency of food itself in shaping the complex relations inside the group.

Making material religion "evidential" (Morgan 2017, 14) for the study of religions in the secret police archives in this way, as in all other social and historical settings, requires foregrounding "images, emotions, sensations, spaces, food, dress or the material practices of putting the body to work" (Morgan 2017, 14). In other words, in order for the texts and images in the archives to speak fully of the complexity of lived realities, we need to take special care, and intentional methodological steps, not to disembody the characters, practices and past lives we encounter in the archives. The material approach to religion, however, implies more than simply taking physical things seriously (Plate 2015, 4) or taking them as evidence of something that cannot be seen, such as belief or thoughts (see Keane 2008). In my reading of secret police files, I afford the material a status *as* primary religious phenomena, upon which beliefs may be predicated, an approach that contrasts with long-held interpretational tendencies in the study of religions (see Plate 2015).

In the case I present below, the food swallowed by the archival record speaks of the broader religious, cultural and socio-economic lifeworld of a community in 1950s and 1960s Romania. As Luehrmann, one of the few scholars to have written specifically about the problem of religion in communist-era archives asserts, documents can, and do, contain "valid insights that do more than simply perpetuate an existing regime of truth" (2015, 22). The secret police archives, as this chapter seeks to illustrate, sometimes ingested objects, materials and cultural practices that could not be fully digested into the regime of truth of the secret police or the communist state. The references to the religious foodways of this community, presented as evidence by the secret police of something secretive and hidden that needed to be exposed, also illustrate common practices that in normal circumstances would be in plain view. The fact that the food was doing things with and for the community other than economically, escaped the attention of, or was of no interest to, the secret police. Interpreted by the scholar of religions, however, the food appears as the very substance and agentive force of the community.

Material religion and secret police archives

Material approaches to social phenomenon, which have in large part grown out of the disciplines of archaeology and anthropology, represent an implicit critique of approaches that "reduce the material world to the effects of discourses, expressions of signs or symbols, ideas or ideologies" and, as Bräunlein outlines, they reflect the ongoing dissatisfaction with the constructivist approaches born out of the Derridean and Foucauldian traditions (2016, 366); traditions which had earlier laid the groundwork for the archival turn in the social sciences and humanities, including post-structuralist and post-colonial approaches to the archive. The transformational influence of the archival turn, which emphasized the archive as an expression and instrument of societal control and transformation (see Zeitlyn 2012), roughly coincided with the opening of the archives of the communist regimes of Eastern Europe and has proved pivotal for contemporary analyses of knowledge production and technologies of the self during communism, an approach perhaps exemplified by the "Soviet subjectivity" school (Fitzpatrick 2005, 8). Of the many shades of constructivism (see Vásquez 2011, 123–4), researchers working on communist archives have tended to emphasize linguistic regimes of truth, discourses, and social categories as the principal means by which to make sense of historical reality and reconstruct identities during communism.

When approaching religion in communist archives, the tendency of discursive approaches to theoretically restrict access to real bodies and material lives has been compounded by the tendency amongst scholars of religions to emphasize ideas, beliefs (largely drawn from texts) and cognitive processes over religion as lived (Harvey 2014, 33). The combination of these two factors has contributed to a reluctance amongst scholars of religions to see the secret police archives as a valuable or reliable source of data for research on religion *per se*. Indeed, the ubiquitous misrepresentations of motivations, false interpretations of beliefs and distorted presentations of religious practices discussed in several chapters in this volume (see in particular chapters by Vagramenko, Pintilescu and Petrás), suggest that data on religions in the secret police archives may only have utility for studies focussing on the discursive processes deployed as a means of social control or transformation. Despite both Foucault and Derrida having explicitly recognized the possibility for the archive to disrupt or subvert the hegemonic system that created it (see Zeitlyn 2012, 463), appreciation of this potential has been overshadowed by the implied impossibility of escaping the "evidential purpose" or intention of the secret police archive and the discredited regime that lay behind it.

In relation to research on other historical settings, a number of approaches have been developed with the aim of uncovering voices and lives lost or silenced by bureaucratic and colonial archives (see Zeitlyn 2012); Comaroff and Comaroff have advocated reading the archive "against the grain" (1992) by using traces external to the archive to re-interpret archival documents and recover lost voices, whilst Stoler's much cited approach to read "Along the Archival Grain" (2009) in order to grasp the "biases and preoccupations of the creators of archived documents" (Zeitlyn 2012, 464) can also retrieve seemingly lost subjugated or subaltern voices. In a similar vein, Sonja Luehrmann describes her attempts to "pierce through" the layers of "rhetoric and standard formulae" in Soviet documents in the hope of being able to "filter out facts" about religious life (2015, 3), explicitly rejecting the idea that communist archives speak "only of the internal workings of Soviet state bureaucracies." These approaches, which recognize that "a record may be created for one purpose but used for other ends" (Zeitlyn 2012, 463), accepts that the archive can become the means by which "traces" that were never intended to form conscious historical remains (see Assmann 2008, 98) can bear witness in the future.

Speaking more broadly about cultural memory and acts of remembering and forgetting, Assmann (2008) makes some pertinent points with regards to the nature and content of political archives. Highlighting the means by which "acts of forgetting" are enacted, which although often "violently destructive when directed at an alien culture or a persecuted minority" are not always a "successful instrument for destroying material and mental cultural products" (Assmann 2008, 98), we are reminded that violent attempts to subjugate knowledges, cultures and identities during communism largely proved unsuccessful (the persistence and re-emergence of numerous targeted religious communities attests to this). In the case of communist regimes' attempts to destroy or obliterate religion, which was pursued through very diverse means as the chapters in this volume attest, the archives of the secret police have paradoxically become the place where "traces" of persecuted groups have remained. As already mentioned, the folders in the archives contain between their covers a rich collection of confiscated items such as photographs, religious art, pamphlets, diaries, poetry and hymns. These materials sit alongside texts, photographic images, graphs, maps and tables created by the secret police in the course of their investigations. Secret police archives, therefore, represent an important resource not only for understanding both how the totalitarian state constructed an image of religious others in order to incriminate and control them, but also the unintended material traces and self-representations that have the power to destabilize both the power of the archive and the dominant historical narratives that have emerged from it (see Edwards 2001, 4).

As discussed above, actual operations against Churches and religious communities, due to the ideological imperative and operational needs of the secret police, placed enormous emphasis on the material existence and financial means of targeted communities. In many cases, it was easier to charge members of religious communities with economic rather than political crimes and for this reason evidence of the material bases of religious lives often appear in the archives very prominently (see Povedák, Chapter 11, this volume). This has proved serendipitous for contemporary scholars of religions, for the secret police archives often place a rather pronounced emphasis on religion as lived – that could be captured, catalogued, confiscated or destroyed – rather than religion as believed; the lens of the secret police was oddly in tune with the way that many contemporary scholars of religion approach their object of study.

In Assmann's terms, the revolutionary break with the communist past that happened from 1989 to 1991, changed or shifted the identity of the secret police archives from being active *political archives* to *historical archives* (Assmann 2008, 103). This distinction, however, when applied to the archives of the former secret police in Eastern Europe, obscures their political uses in the present. They do not "store information which is no longer of immediate use" (2008, 103) as Assmann supposes, but are the active concern of political interests and memory projects in the present. The constructivist approaches that have been applied by contemporary historians and political scientists to communist archives, have drawn our attention towards the enduring power of the archives to shape contemporary political, cultural and religious realities and structure historical memory (see Apor et al. 2017; Blaive 2019; Stan 2013) more effectively than they have towards the new historical questions that Hann, Luehrmann and others have highlighted relating to the transmission and lived experience of religion during communism.

This discrepancy in terms of the uses of communist archives can be accredited to the failure of historians to view the archive as a participant in the active process of religious transmission. Luehrmann comes close to this perspective when she points towards the documents in the archives as "crucial nodes in nets of relations" that can alert us to realities other than the textual truths of the secret police. The materiality of the archives in her words present "traces of the social relationships from which they emerged" (Luehrmann 2015, 3) and in light of this she encourages us to pay attention to how, where and when human actors met, occupied the same spaces, interacted, socialized and exchanged words and goods, in other words to their temporal, spatial and somatic presence. Numerous *real* people contributed to the assembled texts, images and folders in the archives from case officers, undercover agents, informers, administrators and commanding officers as well as the targets themselves, both directly through their written statements, their signatures and finger prints, and materials confiscated from them, and indirectly, and unknowingly, through references to what they said, surveillance photographs taken of them and descriptions of their activities. Each of these traces of course potentially could be fabricated or distorted, but through their totality, the sheer volume, their multi-vocality and complexity (Verdery 2014, 42), and materiality, they carry the potential to reveal much more than they distort if approached as records of performed, embodied action. When religion, which in most circumstances has an inherently performative character, constitutes the object of study and/or surveillance, this complex archival assemblage of agencies is perhaps even more apparent than in other social or cultural diverse spheres.

Related to these ideas of the performative character of religion and processual nature of the archival record, is the important observation discussed by Hesz (Chapter 10, this volume), that the work of the secret police informer, from whom a large proportion (perhaps even the majority) of archival data was derived in Romania, can be compared to that of the ethnographer. As Katherine Verdery (2014, 7), who was the object of secret police surveillance operations whilst conducting ethnographic work in Romania in the 1970s and 1980s, observed in relation to her own police file, the close examinations and interpretations of everyday behaviour and use of similar methods and techniques by the secret police, warrants their comparison with the *bona fide* ethnographer. In light of this comparison, if we views cultural (and religious) memory as a process and inherently performative in nature, as Diana Taylor (2003) argues, and ethnographic fieldwork as the means to capture the active processes of cultural transmission (see Zeitlyn 2012, 469), the performances recorded by the informer in surveillance reports, like those captured by the ethnographer, can similarly be seen as "surrogates of the events that they capture" and as "archives of the performance of research" (Zeitlyn 2012, 469).

Informers were extremely diverse, ranging from the casual and reluctant to the well qualified and diligent (see Albu 2008). Some made excellent ethnographers in the sense that they were able to provide detailed reports that contained not only the words of their targets, but also subtle observations about their demeanour and the contexts and environments within which the events they captured took place. In regard to the surveillance of religious communities, others who were recruited from within the communities and shared the religious culture of those on whom they were reporting, as in the case discussed below, were able to go even further. In this sense they were not just observers, they were also insiders to the community and participants in the rituals and life of the community they later describe in reports. In anthropological terms they could be considered as participant-observers, with their proximity and participation in the performance of religion granting them a particular authority. I am not arguing here that insider-informer reports are qualitatively the same as ethnographic sources, but certain aspects of what they report and how they report, especially where material, spatial and somatic aspects of religion are described or evoked in their texts, offer us unintended archival "traces" of religious material worlds and agencies.

Inochentist-Stilists in communist Romania

My case study relates to a group described by the Securitate in its case files as "*sectă ilegală inochentişt-stilişta*," or the illegal Inochentist-Stilist sect. Inochentism originated in the western Russian provinces of Podolia, Kherson and Bessarabia in the final decade of the Tsarist empire and following Bessarabia's incorporation into Greater Romania after the First World War, became a significant issue for the Romanian authorities (see Kapaló 2019, 105–38). The movement started to make significant inroads in other parts of Romania, beyond Bessarabia, by the early 1930s due largely to the leadership of Ioan Zlotea, a monk and spiritual father who continued to preach the message of the movement's founder, Inochentie of Balta. Zlotea, like other followers of Inochentie of Balta, rejected the religious calendar reform introduced by the Romanian Orthodox Church in 1924[2] and continued to practice according the Old Calendar in secret (see Kapaló 2019, 183). The term Stilist is derived from the term "Old Style" and was used by the Romanian authorities to refer to communities, mostly located in Moldavia and Bessarabia, that rejected the Orthodox Church's change of calendar. Following Romania's adoption of the Revised Julian Calendar, the Inochentists and the so-called Stilists (Old Calendarist Orthodox Church) were subject to violent repression at the hands of the Romanian authorities for rejecting this key symbolic component of the national project (see Kapaló 2019, 126–9). Following the communist takeover of Romania in 1945–46, Stilism had an ambiguous legal status, it was not recognized as a legal sect by the Ministry of Religions but neither was it listed alongside the Jehovah's Witnesses amongst the banned sects. As a consequence, secret police operations focussed on "unmasking enemy elements who carry out their activity under the cover of the Stilist religion" (see Chivu-Duţă 2007, 126–7).

Following the loss Bessarabia and Transnistria to the Soviet Union at the end of the Second World War, Romania became a refuge for many Bessarabians that had been associated with or had worked for the Romanian regime before and during the war. A part of these refugees from Soviet-occupied Bessarabia constituted priests, monks and nuns of the Romanian Orthodox Church, some of whom were native to those regions whilst others had been posted there from the rest of Romania (Petcu 2009, 147–8). Amongst these Romanian Orthodox refugees was a group of monks and nuns who had belonged to Inochentist networks in Bessarabia and had practiced their faith, counter to Romanian law, according to the Old Calendar. This group of refugees and returnees, devotees of Ioan Zlotea, formed the core of what the Romanian secret police came to refer to as the Inochentist-Stilist sect.

At the head of this community was C.A., a monk of the Romanian Orthodox Church who had served in Bessarabia in the 1940s and had been a spiritual child of Ioan Zlotea.[3] He first came to the attention of the Securitate in 1951 when an unsuccessful attempt was made to recruit him as an informer. His refusal was taken as proof that he was a religious "fanatic" (ACNSAS I 237454, vol. 1, 11). From this point forward he was placed under surveillance, which lasted for almost 20 years. For part of this time he served as a priest and abbot of two Orthodox monasteries. In the 1950s, he was suspected of secretly encouraging the use of the Old Calendar when he was dispatched to a village to combat the lingering "Stilism" practiced there (ACNSAS I 237454, vol. 3, 194). In 1959, after being forced to leave his monastery during the period of mass closures of Orthodox monasteries, he first set up home with another ex-monk, P. G., who later informed on C.A. and his community. Shortly after, between 1960 and 1962, C.A. built a house together with I.M., another ex-monk from Bessarabia who was also revered as a saint by the community.

I.M., whom C.A. had been "supporting with money and food" since their arrival in Romania from Bessarabia (ACNSAS I 237454, vol. 3, 197), was considered a visionary and his prophesies were communicated by letter to members of the community in different parts of the country. The *turmă*, or flock, established by C.A. was widely dispersed in at least three cities and several towns and villages in eastern and southern Romania, and was described by the Securitate as being made up of individuals who were "culturally backward." They venerated their spiritual fathers (and mothers) variously as incarnations of the prophets Elijah, Enoch, Elisha, and John the Evangelist (B. E.) and referred to C.A. as "tăticu" and I.M. as "mămica," expressions which one of the community described during an interrogation as reflecting the "familial closeness of the spiritual relationship" that existed between the followers and their priests and charismatic leaders (ACNASAS D010110, 54). The community was observed to be supplying their spiritual fathers materially with all they needed and they were reported to be living a "wealthy and carefree life" without the need to work (ACNSAS I237454, vol. 1, 11–12). Numerous reports include reference to the support offered by individuals to the two monks as *milostenie*, a form of charitable donation usually made to a monastery, whilst also interpreting the gifts of food, money and cloths as material exploitation of vulnerable people.

On July 29, 1967, C.A. was given a 6-month correctional prison sentence under article 256, of Penal Code 2, for having continued to practice as a priest after his exclusion from his monastery in 1959 (I237454, vol. 1, 35). The sentence was later reduced to 3 months on appeal on grounds of his age and that the case was only able to produce firm evidence of one serious infraction, a memorial feast to commemorate C.A.s parents at which he was said to have performed many prayers and blessings (I237454, vol. 1, 38). The archival record of the surveillance of C.A. and his followers between 1951 and 1975 stretches to several thousand pages of informers' reports, interrogations, court proceedings and communications. The many observations, accusations and pieces of evidence that were presented in the secret police case files placed a great deal of focus on the material practices of the group especially on the collection of money and foodstuffs from followers.

This long running surveillance operation relied on a group of longstanding informers, some of whom were members of the flock, close family members or monks who had served in monasteries with the two leaders. Informer D.G. actively reported on the group between 1955 and 1975, and M.O. lived with C.A. for a period of several months. These were not occasional spies but were deeply embedded in the community and trusted individuals with an intimate understanding of the groups practices. The closeness of the informers to their targets and the nature of their reports in this case serve as a reminder not to exaggerate the "social distance" of officers, agents and informers from those they described (Luehrmann 2015, 22).

Fasting, feasting and the distribution of foods

Inochentists observe all of the regular fasts of the Orthodox Christian tradition according to the Julian or Old Calendar, of which there are four main fasting periods; Great Lent, the Nativity Fast, the Apostles Fast and Dormition Fast, as well as the individual fasting days of Wednesdays and Fridays (days associated with mourning Jesus' betrayal and his crucifixion, respectively) observed in most weeks of the year. In addition, Orthodox communicants are required abstain from all food or liquid from 12 midnight prior to receiving the Eucharist and on the eve of important feasts such as Christmas (Conomos 2011, 242). Inochentie of Balta, the founder of the Inochentist movement, was a monk in the Russian Orthodox Church and in addition to the standard fasts required of lay people he introduced monastic fasting rules for his whole community. These rules required an additional weekday fast on Mondays, the day of the week dedicated to the commemoration of the angels. Associated with both penance and supplication, fasting in the Orthodox tradition is a means to brings one's passions and desires under control by turning them towards salvation and heaven and not only requires abstention from certain foods, but also from marital relations. As such, the approach to fasting adhered to by Inochentists included total abstention from meat, hard liquor and garlic as well as the total rejection of sexual relations, even within marriage (see Kapaló 2019, 88–91). This rigorous approach to fasting set followers of Inochentie apart from their Orthodox neighbours and became an important boundary marker (see Kapaló 2019, 242–3, 259). Fasting for the community discussed in this chapter, although undertaken on a personal level, was also a corporate practice that united the community in a common act of worship, devotion and supplication.

According to the wealth of insider-informer reports, the dispersed community's main reason for gathering was attendance at commemorative feasts and saints' day celebrations, including the Feast of Saint Elijah and the commemoration of the death of Ioan Zlotea, when food would be served and shared amongst the community. On these occasions they would take communion and receive blessings from *tăticu* and *mămica*. Maintaining a supply of the appropriate foodstuffs for these gatherings that conformed with their rigorous dietary restrictions required special logistical arrangements that are recounted frequently in the secret police record. One indication of this comes from an interrogation of one of C.A.'s female followers, who confessed in February 1965 to keeping records of monies collected and foods purchased and distributed.

> Also, a number of times I gathered money, about 150 lei from the "girls," with which I brought food and various objects and I sent them to help the monastery … Also, from the collected money I bought foodstuffs which I sent to C.A. and to M.I. These gifts were taken by me personally to city B. when I also gave them money that had been collected. The largest amount was 200 lei.
>
> (I509215, vol. 2, 7)

Significant for the community's supply of appropriate foodstuffs, one of the members of the community placed under surveillance 10 years earlier, M.Z., was a fisherman by trade, as the informer D.G. reports:

> He also said that in their village the "flock" consists of 7 families and they are all party members. He said that he was a fisherman and that before when he used to catch fish he sold it, and no one asked him, and now since the country in headed by the antichrist, he is only entitled to 5 kg. a week, he said that some fishermen had gone to prison over just 2 kg of fish but that he had got away with over 100 kg of fish by saying prayers [calling on] God to have mercy on me, God and the Mother of God, immaculate virgin, and [for] *tăticu* to take care of me and nothing happened to me.
>
> (I 237454, vol. 3, 276–7)

The maintenance of a steady supply of fish was vital for the community as they ate no other kind of meat. Fish was served at all gatherings outside of required fasting days or periods. The informer went on to give other examples where the fisherman M.Z. was seemingly miraculously saved from the clutches of the *miliția* whilst discovered transporting the valuable fish to C.A.

> And he said there was another time when he performed a miracle, he was at the station in town T., he wanted to leave on the ferry and he had two baskets of carp weighing about 5–6 kg each and a police officer came and asked him what he had in his baskets, he replied that he had fish, and the officer took the fish out of the basket and he also had eggs and he broke them, and he was asked where he was taking the fish? He replied that he has a child at school in city C. and he is taking him food, and then he asked for his documents and the officer saw that he is a fisherman, and he also saw his party membership card, he then gave him his documents and told him to hurry because the ferry is leaving. M.Z. put the fish back in the basket and asked the officer to pay for the broken eggs as a joke, after which he picked up the baskets and boarded the ferry …
>
> (I 237454, vol. 3, 277)

The significance of these reports from the point of view of economic surveillance is obvious, but the miraculous component of these narratives included by D.G. (something he was particularly diligent in recording as further examples will illustrate), suggest that the supply chain had spiritual significance for the community and that it involved well calculated risks that were mitigated against through party membership and acts of faith in C.A. and M.I. On another occasion, M.Z., when asked directly why he travelled so far and often to visit C.A.

> M.Z. answered why do you ask? Do you not know that we brothers must keep in touch with *tăticu* if not several times then at least once a month so that we can take communion and be anointed with myrrh for the cleansing of our soul and body and so that we can bring *milostenie* that is of great use and we tell *tăticu* our troubles and joys so that he can bless us often for the tasks we have to do.
>
> (I 237454, vol. 3, 232)

These accounts point towards both the spiritual and the reciprocal nature of the transactions engaged in by C.A.s followers. That these practices also structured relations with those outside the group is clear from comments in D.G.'s earlier report (above), where we also learn that members of the community were requested or required to become party members as a way of outwitting the "antichrist." This practice was useful for avoiding the consequences of encounters with the militia, as the story recounted above shows, but access to party members also had another function within the group as this report by informer V.I. illustrates:

> And I also tell that you "Tăticul" has in his flock different types of people – doctors, officers, teachers. Brother, he has a lot of officers' and party members' wives whose husbands know nothing about "Tăticul" but you should know brother John that they are blessed by "Tăticul" and I will tell

> you how brother: "Tăticul" and "Mămica" together with the nuns they do the mass and consecrate the bread of the host and they give it to the sisters whose husbands don't know anything just how I am telling you. And those sisters, they asked "Tăticul" to put the blessed *anafură* [host] in the food that they eat and also the holy water that has also been prepared by "Tăticul", they put it in their drinks and they drink it and they eat it and they are blessed and that is how they do it brother.
>
> (D010110, 13)

This account of the secret use of consecrated bread and holy water from 1966, which was reported by the case officer in his summary analysis reports upwards to his superiors (ACNSAS I237454, vol.1, 306), was part of a broader pattern of using the distribution of blessed foods and the surplus generated by the community to affect spiritual influence over others in society. The food produced by the community was used to infiltrate groups they wished to spiritually influence in order to counter any potential actions against them by the enemy. That this was not just a one-off incident is demonstrated by another report dated six years later. N.T. was a worker in the telegraph office who was also under surveillance in 1972 by a different informer, V.V.,

> Lately, he brings various goods such as food to the telegraph service, inviting employees to take part in the meal, and at the moment when everyone begins to help themselves to something, he begins to talk about the Lord Jesus Christ, who as he said, gives him the strength to satisfy and to support his relatives. In this way he has attracted the majority of the workers at the telegraph service, making them appreciative of N. T. He brought up in conversation that he has a uncle by the name of C.A., with whom by the way he also lives, and in whom he has great faith, considering him a saint being the only honest man with a clear conscience before God, but he is old and has suffered greatly due to Satan.
>
> (I 238346, vol. 3, 55)

These reports, and many others like them, show that food for this community represented both a commitment to and contribution towards the community as well as a means of exercising spiritual influence on the world outside. Contrary to the assumptions made by officers in their summary reports that food was being hoarded or used for profit, informers offered a vivid portrayal of the way that foodstuffs were redistributed both to members of the flock and to others as another informer's report from D.G. from September 1956 suggests:

> On the morning of August 28, I went with the aforementioned to the priest A. [C.A.], when I went to E's home and was ready to leave, N.N. arrived and was preparing to come to me, he had *cozonac* [a type of sweet cake] and *must* [unfermented grape or fruit juice] blessed by *tăticu* and

> sent specially for the brothers who fasted the fast of St. Mary, according to the old [style], which was on that day of the 28th.
>
> (I 237454, vol. 3, 268) – 5th Sept 1956

From the body of insider-informer reports accumulated over a 20-year period, and when considered within the known cultural Orthodox religious frame, we gain a clear insight into the meaning and purpose of the heavy traffic in various foodstuffs that the group engaged in. The donation of foodstuffs, in fact, served to configure, spiritually sustain and defend the group, an observation that the longstanding informer D.G. was able to articulate to the officer in charge of the case as early as 1955 when he was explaining how one becomes a member of the flock:

> The person in question also said that any citizen who wants to enter the flock cannot be chosen and placed in the book of life until the priest C.A. marks him with the seal of the Holy Spirit, and in order to be marked with the seal you need to take oil, wine, flour, and other foods to the priest, and after conducting the liturgy the priest gives alms to those that are not brothers in the flock.
>
> (I238346, vol. 1, 142)

Eschatology and food security

The surveillance of the community spanned a period in Romanian history when food security, diet and food production went through significant and dramatic changes. These included the prolonged effects of the drought of 1946–47; the quota system of food collection from the countryside to feed the growing urban population and to fulfil war reparations to the Soviet Union – partly paid in grain; the imposition of general taxes on agricultural produce, and the more than a decade long process of collectivization of agriculture (Kligman and Verdery 2011, 108–13, see also Iordachi and Dobrincu 2009). In addition, in the 1960s the rural population of Romania switched from a diet largely based on *mămăligă*, or corn mash, to bread (Scrob 2015); a change that also had a negative impact on food supply in many towns and villages. The following report, one of several similar examples, alludes to at least three of these factors in the space of a very few lines:

> [...] in the village of B., especially because of bad organization, the only business is a restaurant, if you don't go home for food you go hungry and [he said] that he was in [the town of] B. I. and did not find bread and only ate 6 pretzels all day and that bread is given only [in exchange for] a coupon. He also said that 150 wheat wagons from [the station of] B. D. were on their way to the GDR and that he had seen the documents [...]. Then *tăticu* said that it is true that today's leaders make fun of the people because the peasants work all summer in the fields to grow wheat

> and when he takes it to deliver his quota it is worth nothing and he has no right to buy bread from the city but must go with *mămăligă* in his bag (I 237454, vol. 3, 253)

Based on dozens of informer reports in the case files relating to C.A.'s community, it is clear that rumours intensified during and after the 1956 Hungarian Revolution when concerns about food security combined with speculation about the impending conflict between the West and the Soviet Union gave the reports an increasingly apocalyptic character. Apocalyptic expectation had been central to the Inochentist worldview since Inochentie of Balta first began preaching around 1908 (see Kapaló 2019, 74–106). His followers, drawing on popular belief about the End of Days, associated Inochentie with the prophet Elijah, who together with the prophet Enoch and John the Baptist would walk the earth during the Antichrist's reign, prophesying to the faithful and quenching the thirst and relieving the hunger of those they meet. For this community, C.A. had taken on the role of Elijah in the drama of the End Days and was nourishing his followers in their time of spiritual and actual need.[4]

> He told me that *tăticu* had told him [...] now a part of the world is ruled by the antichrist and that only the devil performs miracles with his crafts in order to deceive mankind and even the chosen ones of Saint Elijah [are fooled], and for us to be strong in our faith in *tăticu* and not believe in the hallucinations of the antichrist, for they will not last long. [...] And he also said that the time that the prophet spoke of has come, that the prophet Elijah will come down from heaven to earth with a *corn de prescură* [special bread used to prepare the host] and whoever will partake of it will be made holy, he said that we have tasted of the *corn de prescură* when *tăticu* shared the *corn de prescură* and that we are his chosen ones. (I 237454, vol. 3, 225)

This extract from a much longer report that goes on to describe how quotas and grain requisitioning will leave the people with nothing to eat, brings to life the events of the Eschaton as it was being experienced by this small group of believers. According to this existential brand of popular eschatology (see Harrison 1979, 228–9), C.A.'s act of feeding his flock with the bread of the host expressed in this final example goes beyond simply a means to sustain and constitute the community, it represents nothing less than their route to ultimate salvation.

Conclusion

The economic and political context within which the surveillance operation against the Inochentist-Stilists took place goes some way to explaining why the secret police files contain so many informer's reports and so much detail focusing on foodways. For this community, maintaining Orthodox ritual life according to the Old Calendar, which under ordinary circumstances would have posed few problems, became a defining feature of underground life. The food produced, blessed and distributed by individuals in the community was central to the complex network of interactions between the widely dispersed members. As the examples from reports illustrate, individuals risked arrest and imprisonment travelling around the country to supply their spiritual leaders and brothers and sisters in faith with the necessary dietary and spiritual nourishment. Communal feasting and fasting represented a pivotal aspect of the way that the community was constituted and sustained, especially in their struggle against the regime, which represented for them the Antichrist. The reciprocal relations around foodstuffs, involving religious obligations and social risks, became constitutive of the groups social relations in a way distinctive to underground life; food, one of the key "spiritual and material resources at hand" (see Vásquez 2017, 236), solved the "existential predicaments" of life lived in the underground in the End Times.

In contrast, the regime attempted to create an image of the leaders as religious charlatans who exploited economically their gullible and incredulous followers. From the archival record, however, it is possible to discern, how and why the traffic in food needed to be constant and co-ordinated; this was not primarily due to their desire to hoard food in times of shortage (although this may have also played a role too) but rather due to the need for specific foods to meet their special religious dietary requirements; when C.A. was arrested in 1965 and his house searched the stock of foodstuffs found, apart from 20 kg of fish, was very modest (1 kg of rice, 1 kg of sugar, 2 litres of oil) that was nevertheless recorded as evidence against him (I 237454, vol. 1, 35). The centrality of the distribution of food was of ultimate concern to the community not because of its worldly value but because it constituted the means by which the prophet Elijah could sustain the lives and save the souls of his followers during the reign of the Antichrist.

It was the aim of this chapter, to demonstrate how secret police files are valuable not only for historians of communism and state security, but also for scholars of lived religions. Secret police archives captured material religion in many varied ways, in this chapter I have focused solely on insider-informer reports as a means of accessing one aspect of this material lifeworld and how it related to religious transmission during communism. I have not advocated nor followed a particular theoretical approach to or method of interpretation of material religion, of which there are several (see Vásquez 2001, 2017; Hazard 2013; Morgan 2009, 2017), instead, through the brief examples, I have illustrated how alternative readings emerge when data on religion is taken seriously and not discounted simply as an reflection of the ideological vision of the regime. In the case presented here, insiders to the community (admittedly those who had chosen or been pressured into betraying the confidence of their brothers and sisters in faith) explained to an audience of secret police officers how, for their community, food was "imbricated with other agents in the production of religious efficacy" (see Vásquez 2017, 238). The distinctive transactions through food outlined in this collection of narratives help us appreciate the archival record as a genuine by-product, or surrogate, of performed human activity.

Acknowledgement

The research for this chapter was funded by the European Research Council (ERC) under the European Union's Horizon 2020 research and innovation programme No. 677355.

Notes

1 The points I make in this chapter, although they relate to the 1950s and 1960s, support the idea suggested by Andrei Pleşu (2006) that food constituted an important form of cultural resistance in late communist-era Romania where a complex "food procurement underground" evolved to overcome food shortages (see, for example, "Andrei Plesu: In Romania, daca a existat un samizdat, a fost samizdatul mancarii" 2010). Thank you to Cristina Vaţulescu for this reference.

2 The Revised Julian Calendar was adopted by the Orthodox Churches of Constantinople, Alexandria, Antioch, Greece, Cyprus, Romania, Poland, and Bulgaria at a congress in Constantinople in May 1923. Russia along with Ukraine, Georgia, and Jerusalem rejected its introduction. Today, followers of the Old Calendar in Romanian reject the term Stilist as derogatory and prefer there church to be known as the Old Calendarist Orthodox Church.

3 In order to protect the privacy of the religious community discussed in this study, I have taken additional measures to disguise their identity including removing the names of locations, cities, towns and villages, and replacing them with initial letters only. All members of the community, including the insider-informers, are referred to only by their initials.

4 On apocalyptic rumour in the Soviet countryside during collectivization in the 1920s and 30s see Viola (1990), Smith (2006) and Fitzpatrick (1994). On the significance of rumour in the context of Romanian collectivization see Kligman and Verdery (2011).

Archival sources

CNSAS – *Consilul Naţional pentru Studierea Arhivelor Securităţii* [National Council for the Study of the Securitate Archive], dosar. D010110; I237454, vol. 1 and vol. 3; I509215, vol.2; I238346, vol. 3; P057044.

References

Albu, Mihai. 2008. *The Informer: A Study on Collaboration with the Securitate* [*Informatorul: Studiu asupra colaborării cu securitatea*]. Bucharest: Polirom.

"Andrei Pleşu: In Romania, if samizdat existed, it was the samizdat of food" ["Andrei Plesu: *In Romania, daca a existat un samizdat, a fost samizdatul mancarii*"]. 2010.

Hotnews.ro. Accessed 25 March 2021. https://life.hotnews.ro/stiri-prin_oras-8051138-andrei-plesu-romania-daca-existat-samizdat-fost-samizdatul-mancarii.htm.

Apor, Péter, Horváth, Sándor and Mark, James. 2017. "Introduction: Collaboration, Cooperation and Political Participation in Communist Regimes." In: *Secret Agents and the Memory of Everyday Collaboration in Communist Eastern Europe*, edited by Péter Apor, Sándor Horváth and James Mark, 1–17. London and New York, Anthem Press.

Assmann, Aleida. 2008. "Canon and Archive. 1. The Dynamics of Cultural Memory between Remembering and Forgetting." In: *Cultural Memory Studies: An International and Interdisciplinary Handbook*, edited by Astrid Erll and Ansgar Nünning, 97–107. Berlin and New York: De Gruyter.

Blaive, Muriel. 2019. "Introduction." In: *Perceptions of Society in Communist Europe: Regime Archives and Popular Opinion,* edited by Muriel Blaive, 1–12. London, New York, Oxford: Bloomsbury Academic.

Bräunlein, Peter J. 2016. "Thinking Religion through Things: Reflections on the Material Turn in the Scientific Study of Religion\s." *Method & Theory in the Study of Religion 28 (Special Issue: A Matter of Perspective? Disentangling the Emic-Etic Debate in the Scientific Study of Religion\s)* (4/5): 365–99.

Comaroff John and Comaroff Jean. 1992. *Ethnography and the Historical Imagination*. Oxford: Westview.

Conomos, Dmitri. 2011. "Fasting." In: *The Encyclopaedia of Eastern Orthodox Christianity*, edited by John A. McGuckin, 242. Malden, MA and Oxford: Wiley-Blackwell.

Edwards, Elizabeth. 2001. *Raw Histories: Photographs, Anthropology and Museums*. Oxford and New York: Berg.l

Fitzpatrick, Sheila. 1994. *Stalin's Peasants: Resistance and Survival in the Russian Village after Collectivization*. New York: Oxford University Press.

Fitzpatrick, Sheila. 2005. *Tear of the Masks! Identity and Imposture in Twentieth-Century Russia*. Princeton and Oxford: Princeton University Press.

Geană, Georghiță. 2005. "Remembering Ancestors: Commemorative Rituals and the Foundation of Historicity." *History and Anthropology* 16 (3): 349–61.

Hann, Chris. 2010. "Introduction: The Other Christianity?" In: *Eastern Christians in Anthropological Perspective*, edited by Chris Hann and Hermann Goltz, 1–29. Berkeley, Los Angeles, London: University of California Press.

Harrison, John F. C. 1979. *The Second Coming: Popular Millenarianism 1780–1850*. Abingdon and New York: Routledge.

Harvey, Graham. 2014. "Respectfully Eating or Not Eating: Putting Food At the Centre of Religious Studies." *Scripta* 26: 32–46.

Hazard, Sonia. 2013. "The Material Turn in the Study of Religion." *Religion and Society: Advances in Research* 4: 58–78.

Iordachi, Constantin and Dobrincu, Dorin. 2009. *Transforming Peasants, Property and Power: The Collectivization of Agriculture in Romania, 1949–1962*. Budapest and New York: CEU Press.

Kapaló, James A. 2019. "The Appearance of Saints: Photographic Evidence and Religious Minorities in the Secret Police Archives." *Material Religion*, 15 (1): 82–109.

Kapaló, James A. and Vagramenko, Tatiana. 2020. *Hidden Galleries: Material Religion in the Secret Police Archives*. Berlin: LitVerlag.

Keane, Webb. 2008. "The Evidence of the Senses and the Materiality of Religion." *Journal of the Royal Anthropological Institute,* 14 (1): 110–27.

Kligman, Gail and Verdery, Katherine. 2011. *Peasants under Siege: The Collectivization of Romanian Agriculture, 1949–1962*. Princeton: Princeton University Press.

Luehrmann, Sonja. 2015. *Religion in Secular Archives: Soviet Atheism and Historical Knowledge*. Oxford and New York: Oxford University Press.

Morgan, David (ed.). 2009. *Religion and Material Culture: The Matter of Belief*. London: Routledge.

Morgan, David. 2017. "Material Analysis in the Study of Religion." In: *Materiality and Study of Religion: The Stuff of the Sacred*, edited by Tim Hutchings and Joanne McKenzie, 14–32. London: Routledge.

Petcu, Adrian Nicolae. 2009. "The Attention on the Securitate on Priests from Bessarabia and Bucovina" ["Preoţii Basarabeni şi Bucovineni în atenţia Securităţii"]. *Caietele CNSAS* 2: (1): 147–78.

Plate, S. Brent. 2015. "Material Religion: An Introduction." In: *Key Terms in Material Religion*, edited by S. Brent Plate, 1–7. London and New York: Bloomsbury.

Pleşu, Andrei. 2006. *About happiness in the East and in the West* [*Despre bucurie în Est şi Vest*]. Bucharest: Humanitas.

Rogers, Douglas. 2005. "The Anthropology of Religion after Socialism." *Religion, State, and Society* 33 (1): 5–18.

Scrob, Mircea-Lucian. 2015. *From Mămăligă to Bread as the "Core" Food of Romanian Villagers: A Consumer-centred Interpretation of a Dietary Change (1900–1980)*. PhD Thesis. Central European University.

Smith, Steve. 2006. "Heavenly Letters and Tales of the Forest: 'Superstition' against Bolshevism." *Forum for Anthropology and Culture*, 2: 316–39.

Stoler, Anna Laura. 2009. *Along the Archival Grain: Epistemic Anxieties and Colonial Common Sense*. Princeton: Princeton University Press.

Taylor, Diana. 2003. *The Archive and the Repertoire: Performing Cultural Memory in the Americas*. Durham, NC/London: Duke University Press.

Vásquez, Manuel. 2017. "Afterword: Materiality, Lived Religion, and the Challenges of 'Going Back to the Things Themselves'." In: *Materiality and the Study of Religion: The Stuff of the Sacred*, edited by Tim Hutchings and Joanne McKenzie, 235–41. London and New York: Routledge.

Verdery, Katherine. 2014. *Secrets and Truths: Ethnography in the Archives of Romania's Secret Police*. Budapest and New York: Central European University Press.

Viola, Lynn. 1990. "The Peasant Nightmare: Visions of Apocalypse in the Soviet Countryside." *The Journal of Modern History*, 62 (4): 747–70.

Zeitlyn, David. 2012. "Anthropology in and of the Archives: Possible Futures and Contingent Pasts. Archives as Anthropological Surrogates." *Annual Review of Anthropology* 41: 461–80.

Part IV

Secret police archives in post-communism

Politics, ethics and communities

13 The Patriarchate, the Presidency and the secret police archives

Studying religions in post-communist Romania

Cristian Maria Vasile

This chapter discusses the politics of the opening of the secret police archives in Romania with reference to the Romanian Orthodox Church and to a lesser degree, the Catholic (Roman Catholic and Greek Catholic) Churches, which together form the largest religious communities in Romania. Over the past three decades, the Patriarchate of the Romanian Orthodox Church and the Presidency of Romania have been entangled in disputes over the uses and meaning of the archives of the Romanian Securitate (the communist secret police). Successive presidents and various Church leaders intervened in the politics of memory and the pursuit of justice for those oppressed by the communist regime. In fact, this paper draws on my personal experience both in the Romanian Intelligence Service Archives (SRI Archives)[1] and in the Archives of the National Council for the Study of the Securitate Archives (CNSAS Archives)[2] after 1999 and 2002 respectively. This account of my experiences gained in these archives also offers an opportunity by way of comparison to talk about the ecclesiastical archives and the functioning of Romania's National Archives in Bucharest highlighting issues regarding researchers' access to the most relevant archival documents and fonds relating to the recent past of Romanian religious denominations. Finally, I will look also at the legal context and at the process of coming to terms with the controversial past of the main Christian Churches in Romania, particularly the Orthodox Church.[3]

A few words are necessary in this introduction in order to understand the relationship in Romania between the Orthodox Church, other churches and the state during communism and in post-communism. During communism, the Romanian Orthodox Church probably depended on state support to a larger extent than even the Russian Orthodox Church (Chumachenko 2002, 16–43). That was mainly because the Romanian Orthodox Church benefited from the suppression of the sister (and rival) Greek Catholic Church in December 1948, when as a result it received over 2,000 church buildings, parishes and monasteries, and welcomed within its ranks over one million believers. This move amounted to a successful but paradoxical proselytism carried out by a self-avowed atheistic regime for the benefit of the majority religion. This is not the only reason for the Church's dependence on the state, but perhaps it is one of the most significant (Stan and Turcescu 2017, 242).

The (mis)use of the secret police archives

Fierce debates took place about the functioning of the Hungarian ÁBTL and Romanian CNSAS, in particular, but in general, about East Central European national archives or agencies which preserve communist-era secret police documents. In Romania for a short period between 1992 and 2000, and prior to the opening of CNSAS, political police archival fonds or documents were accessible. Some researchers and historians tried, and partially succeeded, in approaching directly the post-communist secret service which had inherited the Securitate archives (i.e. the SRI). The SRI was headed by Virgil Măgureanu, Professor of Marxist Philosophy at the former Communist Party Academy and a close acquaintance of the first Romanian post-communist president, Ion Iliescu (1990–96; 2000–04). Speaking about access to the SRI Archives, there were two different periods: 1992–96 and 1996–2000. In the first period, Virgil Măgureanu, the head of SRI, invited his former friend and colleague historian Mihai Pelin to establish a team of researchers in order to study important documents of the Securitate, to edit them, to gather and publish relevant documents on the history of communism in Romania (the history of repression, history of the artistic and literary milieus and other topics related to the recent past of the secret police) (see Pelin 1996; Pelin 1997). Mihai Pelin and Virgil Măgureanu were accused by some historians, NGOs and also by former Securitate general and defector to the USA Ion Mihai Pacepa[4] of misusing the historical facts and documents, whilst establishing a monopoly on the SRI Archives (Pacepa 2013, 4). After 1996, in the context of the new liberal anti-communist government, access to such documents was somewhat enlarged, in the sense that more historians – even a PhD student in History as I was in 1999 – could get access to the Securitate archives held by the Bucharest-based SRI archives. So, the early 1990s moment with Măgureanu and Pelin as the main protagonists was the first political abuse or at least misuse of the secret police archives (Pacepa 2013, 4).

It is true that in East Central Europe the process of opening the archives as part of a movement for transitional justice has proved highly contentious giving rise to numerous blackmails and political manipulations. This is the case in Romania too, but one should immediately qualify this as blackmail and political manipulations through such misuse of the archives were already taking place – on a large scale – prior to the establishment of CNSAS. These early scandals included releasing political/politicized and historical information to the pro-government press in order to compromise the disobedient mass media, the political opposition, minority religious groups and even opponents from within the Orthodox Church of Patriarch Teoctist Arăpaşu (1986–2007).

A short note on the situation of Christian churches during communism in Romania is needed here in order to understand the wider frame that will be represented with the case of Teoctist. The various Christian churches had different connections to the communist party and, therefore, differing degrees of political/symbolic power. Although the so-called neo-Protestant churches (such as the Adventists and Baptists) were officially recognized by the communist governments after 1945, they were subjected to discriminatory policies that favoured the Romanian Orthodox Church (ROC). While ROC's patriarch Justinian Marina (1948–77) had a privileged relationship with communist secretary general Gheorghe Gheorghiu-Dej (1945–65) (Turcescu and Stan 2015: 80–1), none of the leaders of neo-Protestant churches could claim such political connections. In some cases the communist power even blamed the ROC hierarchy for the spread of neo-Protestant denominations, suggesting that Orthodox religious leaders failed in their attempt to use various methods of containment, mainly against Pentecostal believers (Croitor 2011, 55). Some neo-protestant groups became public pariahs and the situation was the same in the case of a few Orthodox dissenters.

Among those who defied the authority of Patriarch Teoctist – successor of Justinian Marina – were the former Orthodox nuns from Vladimireşti Convent – a monastic settlement in Southern Moldavia suppressed in the mid-1950s due both to its anti-communist allegiance and its alleged heretical practices (Enache 2005, 586–7). One should mention that Teoctist had been part of the Orthodox hierarchy during communism and had been one of the vicars of Patriarch Justinian Marina in the 1950s. Justinian (patriarch between 1948 and 1977) had levelled grave accusations of heretical practices at the convent and these doctrinal and ecclesiastical charges were used by the communist authorities to suppress the convent (Pandrea 2001, 133). The Vladimireşti nuns (or their relatives and supporters) became in post-communism fierce critics and objectors to Teoctist (Patriarch, 1986–2007) whom they considered a collaborator with the communist party and even the Antichrist (Mânăstirea Recea: părintele Ioan Iovan 2015). Meanwhile, those in political power, especially Ion Iliescu's regime and his party, probably in conjunction with the post-communist chief of SRI (the successor of the Securitate), manipulated information regarding collaboration with the political police by journalists, members of NGOs and opposition political leaders (Mungiu Pippidi 2002, 38; Tismăneanu 2014) with the aim of discrediting those that supported the nuns of Vladimireşti morally, and even financially. The nuns themselves were sued (for grave injury or insult) and needed the assistance of lawyers. On the other hand, they were defended by the liberal anti-communist press (Dragomir 1993, 391–2).

This case illustrates how the post-communist political elite initially had a monopoly on the potentially toxic information found within political police archives. The establishment of an institution to govern access to the archives in pursuit of transitional justice was considered to be the best way to overcome this situation. Furthermore, the proper means to prevent cases such as the aforementioned was to enable CNSAS, ÁBTL and other East-Central European institutions of transitional justice to reduce the possibility of blackmail and manipulation through educating the public both in terms of the history and the moral complexities of the holdings of the secret police archives in order to counter attempts at slander and vicious labelling of those who had, in fact, been victims of the Securitate.

President Iliescu and Patriarch Teoctist

One cannot understand the post-communist archival policies and the religious policies of Ion Iliescu's regime in Romania without a familiarity with the biographies of at least two individuals, Iliescu himself and Patriarch Teoctist. Preventing access to state security files was one means by which the state and the Orthodox Church sought to protect themselves from future claims made against them. Teoctist as archimandrite (superior abbot) was directly involved in the suppression of the Greek Catholic Church after 1948. On October 21, 1948, the "completion" of the spiritual unity of the Romanian people was celebrated under communist guidance. After a week, all the Greek Catholic bishops were arrested and imprisoned for some months in the Orthodox Patriarchate villa in Dragoslavele (Bucur 1998) where they received at the beginning of December 1948 the visit of Patriarch Justinian and archimandrite Teoctist who tried in vain to convince them to accept the union with Orthodoxy (ASRI, D-7755, 3, 61). Several hundred Greek Catholic clergy who denounced the alleged religious union and stood against the forced assimilation into the Romanian Orthodox Church were imprisoned. Over the next 20 years, all of the six Greek Catholic bishops died in the prisons at Sighet and Gherla, or in the Orthodox monastery of Ciorogârla or whilst under house arrest (Bucur 2003, 233–58). So, for many Greek Catholics, Teoctist is identified with their post-war tragedy. Moreover, the law on the suppression of the Greek Catholic Church came into effect on December 1, 1948 and it stipulated that all local parishes and administrative organs were united under the jurisdiction of the Romanian Orthodox Church; so, over 2000 (or even more) Greek Catholic parishes, church buildings, cemeteries and monasteries, convents were turned over to the Orthodox Church by state decree and they remained so even after 1989 when the Greek Catholic Church was reestablished (Vasile 2004, 160–321). As a consequence, many Greek Catholics sued the Romanian Orthodox Church parishes after 1989 in order to regain their 1948 ecclesiastical properties (Marcu 1997, 277). Some courts – and later the authority for property restitutions – called on experts, and even historians, to help determine the legitimacy of claims.[5] Therefore, from the official point of view, restricting access to the archives was not only about preventing historians reestablishing the biography of figures such as Patriarch Teoctist. Perhaps even more importantly, the issue was also the material dimension relating to the property restitution question (Stan 2013, 136–60).

Ion Iliescu himself had even greater problems with regard to his biography; he was the former leader of the Romanian Komsomol (the Union of the Working Youth/UTM), communist *Agitprop*, minister of the communist Youth and party chief secretary in Moldavia; and he was involved in repressive activities against student movements both in 1956–59 and in 1968 (Both 2012). It is important to point out that Ion Iliescu, who served as President of Romania from 1990–96 and from 2000–04, and Patriarch Teoctist had known each other for many years before 1989. They met during the 1970s in Iaşi (Jassy) where they were both dignitaries: Iliescu as communist party chief secretary of Iaşi County (Dobre 2004, 323) and Teoctist as Orthodox Metropolitan of Moldavia.[6] In early 1990, Teoctist survived an internal challenge as patriarch, having been accused of pro-communist stances (Buzilă 2009, 84). Teoctist returned to his office in April 1990 also thanks to Iliescu's administration. Moreover, starting in 1990 the interests of the Orthodox hierarchy in various matters began to coincide with those of the post-communist political elite. One such matter was the way to examine the records of the recent past, and history writing in general. Their stance relied on a sort of politics of fear, or politics of oblivion; a fear generated by an unusable past (Gussi 2011, 60).

It would be a mistake, however, to single out – from the point of view of undermining the transitional justice process – only the Orthodox hierarchy embodied by Teoctist. The Roman Catholic Church and even the Greek Catholic Church high clergy also had difficulties in offering an adequate response when they were confronted with the process of coming to terms with the past. The Roman Catholic prelates, at least those from the Bucharest Archbishopric, blocked access to their ecclesiastical archives by independent historians and, as far as we know, did not fully cooperate with CNSAS on transitional justice matters (e.g. in finding out if there were any informers within the Catholic archbishopric or by requesting CNSAS to offer useful information in order to establish a moral reform within its own ranks) (Răchită 2015).

On the other hand, although it was one of the main victims of the Romanian communist regime being the only completely suppressed church, the Greek Catholic Church, or its higher ranking clergy to be more precise, also showed some hesitation (*Gazeta de Cluj* 2017). It seemed that it encouraged a historiographical attack that targeted mainly the hierarchy of Romanian Orthodox Church whilst neglecting the destructive role played by the Securitate. Recently some historians and CNSAS experts have established that important and significant members of the Greek Catholic clergy (previously associated with the underground and anti-communist resistance) both at home in Romania and in exile were also (at least for a while) agents of the Securitate (Fărcaş 2017, 333).

Another sensitive issue is the fact that even some underground Greek Catholics during the communist period adopted Orthodox-like, anti-neoprotestant stances. Neo-protestants were themselves severely persecuted, were under constant surveillance and were victims of vicious labelling by both the political power and Romanian Orthodox Church's hierarchy (Vasile 2003, 121). Therefore, one can observe that members of the religious underground did not necessarily assume a more tolerant attitude towards those that were outside the narrow historical perspective represented by the March 1923 Constitution, which restrictively proclaimed that only the Romanian Orthodox Church and the Greek Catholic Church are "Romanian Churches," that is, "national Churches" (Muraru, Iancu 1995, 66).

The presidential commission for the analysis of the communist dictatorship and the Vladimireşti case

In 2006, a dozen historians and social scientists had the opportunity to write about the history of Romanian Churches in the post-war period using various archives and documents, some of them never researched before; this process set an important precedent. The Higher Defence Council decision 61/2006 granted these historians access to previously inaccessible documents (Gussi 2017, 94). In April 2006, president Traian Băsescu established a historical commission, the Presidential Commission for the Analysis of the Communist Dictatorship in Romania (PCACDR), headed by Romanian American professor Vladimir Tismăneanu, in order to draw up a report documenting the crimes of the 1945–89 period that would allow for an official condemnation of the Romanian communist regime (Stan 2013, 112). The Final Report was required to focus on the institutions and the methods that allowed the communist regime to retain control over the country and perpetuate itself over more than four decades between 1948 and 1989. It also included a chapter that discussed the fate of religious denominations under communist rule as well as chapters on ethnic Hungarians, Jews, Germans, Roma, and Greek Catholics under communism. Using new archival materials, particularly those from the CNSAS archives, the National Archives of Romania and the State Secretariat of Religious Denominations Archives, the presidential commission also tried to examine the fate of Romanian monasticism, and especially the case of Vladimireşti convent, which had been closed by the communist authorities in 1956 (Tismăneanu 2007, 277). An important document identified by the commission was the Cadre File of Teoctist, kept at the National Archives.

After 1990, at numerous ecclesiastical services and other religious anniversaries a group of nuns from the recently reestablished convent of Vladimireşti disturbed the meetings by shouting against Teoctist, who they perceived as "Anti-Christ and communist" (Vasile 2017, 244). These nuns were repeatedly silenced and even sued, but they continued to voice their views until 2006. The final report of the Tismăneanu commission, as it became known, tried to understand the origins of such disputes. In the mid-1950s, Vladimireşti convent was considered a center for spreading mysticism and gathering the "enemies of the people." Such accusations were levelled especially against two persons: the Abbess Veronica Gurău Barbu and the monk Fr Ioan Silviu Iovan, the priest confessor of the convent. The Securitate accused the Vladimireşti representatives of moral and material support for the anti-communist resistance (ASRI, D-2487, 82; Tismăneanu 2007, 277) and as a consequence, in March 1955, Abbess Veronica and Fr Ioan Iovan were arrested. At the beginning of 1956, Securitate officers took the convent by storm and the Vladimireşti monastery was suppressed. Even before the repression, the Holy Synod discouraged any Orthodox Church support for the convent by alleging that the nuns from Vladimireşti convent had breached some important Orthodox Christian dogmas. On January 25, 1955, Fr Ioan Iovan reacted to these allegations and sent Patriarch Justinian Marina a memo in which he confronted the Orthodox prelates, accusing them of cowardice and obedience to the communist authorities. Fr Iovan also mentioned that vicar Teoctist Arăpaşu had in 1952, when he was rector of the Orthodox Theological Institute in Bucharest, hindered his devotion to the Holy Eucharist and public confession. In fact, in his memo Fr Iovan criticized the Orthodox hierarchy's desire to level all attempts at emancipation amongst ROC convents and monasteries saying that:

> I know from the courses on Orthodox missionary guidance that this desire to "level" and reduce to a common denominator, for the Reverend Teoctist, then the Rector [of the Bucharest Orthodox Theological Institute] (in 1952), stopped me from frequently taking Holy Communion and hampered me in my attempt of behave like a real monk amongst the parish priests, for the sake of "unity" and "orthodoxy"[7]
>
> (ASSC, Marina, 2; Tismăneanu 2007, 276; Berindei et al. 2009, 475)

Fr Iovan's memo was mentioned and commented on in the final report of the commission (Tismăneanu 2007, 275–6).

Immediately after the official condemnation of communism on December 18, 2006, and based on the final report, the Holy Synod protested against its content. It even convinced Fr Ioan Iovan, who in the meanwhile had reconciled with the Orthodox hierarchy, to write in January 2007 to the head of PCACDR, Professor Vladimir Tismăneanu, in order to correct some assertions made in the Final Report concerning the 1950s. Soon after this moment, the Orthodox Holy Synod established its own historical commission. The latter also used I. Iovan's abjuration in order to target the work of PCACDR. Facing these new criticisms, members of the Presidential Commission admitted that oral history sources, such as Fr Ioan Iovan's, should also be used but they insisted on the authenticity of the 1955 memo containing the accusations against the Orthodox prelates. In 2009, the Presidential Commission edited a follow-up volume of the Final Report in which it published the entirety of Iovan's memo (Berindei et al. 2009, 468–85).

The Romanian presidency, the Orthodox Church, and the final report

Besides these responses, the determination of the PCACDR to resist this type of pressure was seriously challenged by the fact that in April–June 2007 the political situation worsened. On April 19, 2007, the Liberal Democrat Romanian president Traian Băsescu was impeached by Parliament which was controlled by the Social Democrats and Liberals. As a consequence, probably through the agency of his presidential advisers, trained as Orthodox theologians and philosophers, he tried also to rely on the influential Orthodox lobby for support in his political struggle against the Liberals and Social-Democrats, who had suspended him in April. In late May 2007, president Traian Băsescu attended the Pentecost liturgy at the Orthodox Metropolitanate's cathedral in Sibiu, Transylvania. After the Orthodox mass, Traian Băsescu delivered a controversial political statement, suggesting that his victory at the recent referendum was God's will. Also, he showed ostentatiously how close he was to the Orthodox hierarchy in Transylvania. Some anti-presidential political commentators compared Traian Băsescu's actions with the Fascist Legionary Movement's practices of instrumentalizing the Romanian Orthodox Church in the interwar period. Segments of the Romanian press even suggested that due to his presidential advisers, the Orthodox Metropolitan of Transylvania, Laurenţiu Streza, had been convinced to launch a process of reconciliation between president Băsescu, Liberal prime minister Călin Popescu-Tăriceanu and the leader of the Social Democrat Party, Mircea Geoană, while Romania had just experienced the political turmoil of the May 19, 2007 impeachment referendum (*Curentul* 2007). The referendum allowed Băsescu to return to his presidential office. According to these commentators, the Orthodox metropolitan's actions in working for reconciliation were biased as this had favored Băsescu.

After this episode, in mid-June 2007, at a meeting with the editorial board of the Final Report, the same presidential advisers suggested that it would be appropriate if the editors revise the final version of the manuscript in order both to add a special focus on the lower Orthodox clergy's sacrifice during communism and to diminish the allegedly excessive heroization of the Vladimireşti phenomenon. These political advisers mentioned that there was a strong dissatisfaction on the part of the Romanian Orthodox Church leadership regarding the final report; moreover, the yearly periodical of the Orthodox Church' Faculty of Theology in Bucharest had just published an extremely critical review of the report (Gabor 2016, 185) and many Orthodox journalists and clergy were putting pressure on the Romanian Presidency to repudiate the report. Furthermore, the advisers asked the members of the commission to find a solution in order to alleviate the tense climate, adding that it is not good when the Romanian Orthodox Church hierarchs curse the Presidential Report. However, the Final Report's coordinators only changed a few words, adding some references (Tismăneanu 2007, 278).[8] But when the manuscript of the final report was ready for print, in the fall of 2017, the representatives of the Romanian Presidency sent a note to the Publishing House insisting that a preface be inserted into the report. A note was added that informed the readers that only the presidential message addressed to the Parliament condemning the communist regime was entirely recognized by President Traian Băsescu, while "the report" itself[9] represented the open access work of some political scientists, scientific researchers and historians. According also to the Presidential Note, this report was only the theoretical basis for future historical studies and investigations the goal of which will be to bring other information and nuances in order to fully understand the communist past (Tismăneanu 2007, 2).

Conclusion

By way of conclusion, I will summarize the entanglements of the Orthodox hierarchy and the presidency in the politics of the archives and the interference in the Tismăneanu commission and in general, in historical writing. Before 2006 – the year when the Tismăneanu commission drafted the final report – independent historians writing on Church and state relations confronted a series of obstacles in their attempts to reconstruct/reestablish the history of religions in the twentieth century free from ecclesiastical (mainly Orthodox) guidance. It is interesting to note that in Romania, post-communist governments discovered and instrumentalized European Union rules and recommendations regarding the supervision of personal data only after winter of 2001, when historians Dorin Dobrincu and Gabriel Catalan invoked and published documents apparently linking Patriarch Teoctist to the actions of the Fascist Legionary Movement in the context of the January 1941 far-right rebellion against general Ion Antonescu (Catalan 2001, 8–9; Bichir 2001, 2). Immediately, the Social Democratic government of Adrian Nastase adopted the law on the protection of personal data and as a consequence, researchers faced more restrictions when trying to access documents mainly at the National Archives and CNSAS Archives (Monitorul oficial, no. 790, December 12, 2001). Four years later, the National Authority for the Supervision of Personal Data Processing (ANSPDCP) was established, a governmental agency set up through Law no. 102/2005.[10] This agency has the goal of protecting the fundamental rights and freedoms (especially the right of intimate, family and private life) in connection with the processing of personal data and the free circulation of these data). The problem was that initially the ANSPDCP staff tended to consider personal data – therefore, forbidden to publish – any historical documents mentioning even the date of birth (of Patriarch Teoctist, for example, as I convinced myself talking with ANSPDCP representatives in the Spring of 2007 while trying to get access to CNSAS Archives). However, in 2006 this attempt at hindering historians from accessing and using essential historical sources regarding the recent history of the main Churches failed. As a consequence, the methods used by

Church leaders, their lobbyists, including politicians and political advisers multiplied.

Probably intimidated by the aggressive Orthodox Church lobby and tired of pursuing burdensome historiographical wars, some important independent historians left this academic field of interest (namely the relationaship between religion, state and society in post-war Romania) choosing instead less controversial topics. Therefore, after a few years, Romanian historiography on post-war church-state relations became dominated by young official historians trained by the Romanian Orthodox Church. However, 2006 represented a significant moment in that probably for the first time in Romanian historiography the traditional definition of the nation was challenged (a definition centered on Orthodox religious identity). Due to the content of the final report, the tragedy that befell all groups including the Orthodox, Romanian Greek Catholics, Neo-Protestants, Roma and ethnic Hungarians was included in the so-called National Treasure of Sufferance (*tezaurul național de suferință*) under communism.[11]

Notes

1 The SRI (Serviciul Român de Informații) was established as the succesor of the Securitate in late March 1990, following interethnic clashes between Romanians and Hungarians.

2 CNSAS (Consiliul Național pentru Studierea Arhivelor Securității) was officialy established in 1999 by the law no. 187 on Access to Securitate Files and Unveiling the Securitate as Political Police, but it started to function only in 2000. It administers the archives of the former communist secret services, especially the Securitate. CNSAS develops educational programs and exhibitions with the aim of preserving the memories of victims of the communist regime. Historians and other social scientists can apply for access to Securitate's files in order to conduct research (Stan 2013, 58).

3 It is worth mentioning briefly the differing ethnic composition of the main Christian Churches in Romania. According to the last national census (2011), the vast majority of ethnic Romanians belong to the Orthodox Church (86%), while the Roman Catholics, who constitute 4.6% of the population include a mixture of ethnic Hungarians, Germans, Romanians and so on. Although in the inter-war period, the Greek Catholic Church (essentially a denomination formed by ethnic Romanians) represented 7.9% of the total number of believers in the country, in 2011 it had decreased to 0.80% (Institutul Național de Statistică din România 2013, 3–4). Between 1948 and 1989 the Greek Catholic Church was a clandestine denomination having been suppressed following the Soviet model by the communist government in December 1948. After the 1989 revolution, many former Greek Catholics remained Orthodox. Thus, for electoral and political reasons after 1989 almost all governing parties favored the Romanian Orthodox Church in its patrimonial dispute with the Greek Catholic parishes which demanded the restitution of their church buildings and other ecclesiastical properties. Even after 1989, many ethnic Romanians perceive the Roman Catholic Church as a 'foreign' denomination due to its large number of Hungarian adherants.

4 Ion Mihai Pacepa was general in the Securitate until 1978, when he defected to the West in July 1978.
5 I was approached in 2006 by advisers from the National Authority for the Restitution of Properties/ANRP asking if a few Greek Catholic parishes from Timiş County deserved the restitution of some properties.
6 Teoctist Arăpaşu served as Orthodox Metropolitan of Moldavia between 1977 and 1986.
7 In Romanian: Fr Iovan: "Cunosc încă de la cursurile de îndrumare misionară această dorinţă de «estompare» şi de aducere la numitor comun, căci Prea Sfinţitul Teoctist, pe atunci rector (1952), m-a oprit să mă împărtăşesc des şi să îmi fac pravila călugărească între preoţii de mir, de dragul de a nu ieşi din «sobornicitate» şi «ortodoxie»."
8 The authors of the 2006 final report initially characterized the works of Orthodox theologian Dumitru Staniloae as *pathetic* (Staniloae claimed in 1973 that the Greek Catholic Church – which was still an underground church at that time – was merely attempting to destroy the unity of the Romanian people). In the new version (2007) of the final report, the term was changed to *controversial*.
9 The inserted note avoided referring to it as the final report.
10 See details on the Agency's website: www.dataprotection.ro/. Accessed on 9 December 2017.
11 This concept (*national treasure of sufferance*) was spread by historians such as Violeta Barbu; see "In memoriam. Violeta Barbu (1957–2018)". *Studii şi materiale de istorie contemporană*, 17, 2018, 248.

Archival sources

Arhiva Serviciului Român de Informaţii [Archive of the Romanian Information Service] (ASRI), fond Documentar, file 2487; file 7755, vol. 3.
Arhiva Secretariatului de Stat pentru Culte [Archives of the State Secretary for Religious Denominations] (ASSC), fond Justinian Marina, file no. 2.

References

Berindei, Mihnea, Goşu, Armand and Dobrincu Dorin (eds.). 2009. *History of Communism in Romania. Documents. Gheorghe Gheorghiu-Dej Regime, 1945–1965* [*Istoria comunismului din România. Documente. Perioada Gheorghe Gheorghiu-Dej (1945–1965)*]. Bucharest: Editura Humanitas.

Bichir, Florian. 2001. *Historian Dorin Dobrincu Discovered a Document Apparently Showing that Patriarch Teoctist Participated at a Devastation of a Synagogue* [*Istoricul Dorin Dobrincu a descoperit în arhiva SRI un document din care reiese că Patriarhul a participat la devastarea unei sinagogi*]. *Evenimentul Zilei*, no. 2605, 15 January 2001, 2.

Both, Ştefan. 2012. "Ion Iliescu and Victor Atanasie Stănculescu, Responsible for the Repression of the Students' Movements in 1956" ["Ion Iliescu şi Victor Atanasie Stănculescu, în spatele înăbuşirii revoltelor studenţeşti din Timişoara, în 1956"]. *Adevărul*, 9 November 2012.

Bucur, Ion Marius. 1998. "The Situation of the Romanian Church United with Rome, Greek Catholic, during 1949–1964" ["Situaţia Bisericii Române Unite cu Roma

(Greco-Catolice) în perioada 1949–1964"]. *Studia Universitatis Babes Bolyai*, series *Theologia Catholica* 1, 88.

Bucur, Ion Marius. 2003. *Pages from the History of Romanian Greek Catholic Church, 1918–1953* [*Din istoria Bisericii Greco-Catolice Române, 1918–1953*]. Cluj-Napoca: Editura Accent.

Buzilă, Boris. 2009. *A Patriarch through the Lens of His Time* [*Un patriarh în oglinda vremii sale*]. Editura Timpul: Iaşi.

Catalan, Alexandru. 2001. *The Files of the Former Securitate Hide Terrible Secrets …* [*Dosarele fostei Securităţi ascund secrete teribile …*]. *Libertatea*, no. 3236, March 22, 2001, 1, 8–9.

Chumachenko, Tatiana A. 2002. *Church and State in Soviet Russia: Russian Orthodoxy from World War II to the Khrushchev Years.* Edited and translated by Edward E. Roslof. M.E. Sharpe: Armonk, New York.

Croitor, Vasilică. 2011. The Redemption of Memory: The Pentecostal Church during the Communist Period [*Răscumpărarea memoriei. Cultul penticostal în perioada comunistă*]. Medgidia: Succeed Publishing.

Curentul 2017. *Curentul,* 21 May 2007.

Dobre F. 2004. Members of the Romanian Communist Party's Central Committee, 1945–1989 [*Membrii CCal PCR, 1945–1989. Dicţionar*]. In: Florica Dobre et al. (eds.). Bucharest, Editura Enciclopedică.

Dragomir, Iulian. 1993. The Life of the Abbess Veronica: The Description of my Life and of the Vladimireşti Convent [*Postfaţă [Afterward]. Via ţamăicuţei Veronica. Descrierea vieţii mele şi a mănăstirii Vladimireşti*]. Bucharest: Editura Arhetip-Renaşterea Spirituală.

Enache, George. 2005. *Orthodoxy and Political Power in Contemporary Romania* [*Ortodoxie şi putere politică în România contemporană*]. Bucharest: Editura Nemira.

Fărcaş, Ion. Ioan-Irineu. 2017. *Everybody's Man. Monsignor Octavian Bârlea and the Suffering of Romanian Exile, 1946–1978* [*Omul tuturor. Monseniorul Octavian Bârlea şi pătimirile exilului românesc, 1946–1978*]. Bucharest: Editura Vremea.

Gabor, Adrian. 2006. "Short Review of the Tismăneanu Report" ["Note de lectura asupra raportului Tismăneanu"]. *Anuarul Facultatii de Teologie Patriarhul Justinian*. 2005–2006: 185–206.

Gazeta de Cluj, 2017. *Gazeta de Cluj*, 22 September 2017.

Gussi, Alexandru. 2011. *Romania Confronts its Communist Past* [*La Roumanie face à son passé communiste. Mémoires et cultures politiques*. Paris: L'Harmattan.

Gussi, Alexandru. 2017. "Paradoxes of Delayed Transitional Justice." In: *Justice, Memory and Redress in Romania: New Insights*, edited by L. Stan and Turcescu, 76–99. Cambridge: Cambridge Scholars Publishing.

Institutul Naţional de Statistică din România. 2013. "What the 2011 census tells us about religion?" ["Ce ne spune recensământul din anul 2011 despre religie?"]. www.insse.ro/cms/files/publicatii/pliante%20statistice/08-Recensamintele%20despre%20religie_n.pdf. Accessed on 10 July 2018.

Marcu, Vasile. 1997. *The Drama of the Romanian Church United with Rome (Greek-Catholic): Documents and Testimonies* [*Drama Bisericii Române Unite cu Roma (Greco-Catolică). Documente şi mărturii*. Bucharest: Editura Crater.

Mânăstirea Recea: Părintele Ioan Iovan. 2015. Recea Monastery: Father Ioan Iovan [Mânăstirea Recea: Părintele Ioan Iovan]. *Lumea credinţei,* 27 October 2005.

www.lumeacredintei.com/reviste/lumea-credintei/lumea-credintei-anul-iii-nr-10-27-octombrie-2005/manastirea-recea-parintele-ioan-iovan/. Accessed on 10 December 2017.

Monitorul oficial. 2001. Law no. 677 from 21 November 2001 Concerning the Protection of Persons with Regard to the Processing of Personal Data and the Free Circulation of These Data [Lege nr. 677 din 21 noiembrie 2001 pentru protecţia persoanelor cu privire la prelucrarea datelor cu caracter personal şi libera circulaţie a acestor date]. Monitorul oficial, no. 790, 12 December 2001.

Mungiu Pippidi, A. 2002. *Politics After Communist: Structure, Culture, and Political Psychology* [*Politica după comunism. Structură, cultură şi psihologie politică*]. Bucharest: Editura Humanitas.

Muraru, Ioan and Iancu, G. (eds.). 1995. *Romanian Constitutions: Texts, Notes, and Comparative Analysis* [*Constituţiile române. Texte. Note. Prezentare comparative*]. Bucharest, Third edition, R.A. Monitorul Oficial.

Pacepa, Ion Mihai. 2013. *The Legacy of the Kremlin: The Role of Espionage in the Communist System of Government* [*Moştenirea Kremlinului. Rolul spionajului în sistemul comunist de guvernare*]. Bucharest: Editura Humanitas.

Pandrea, Petre (eds.). 2001. *The White Monk* [*Călugărul alb*]. Bucharest: Editura Vremea.

Pelin, Mihai, Aioanei, Constantin, and Chirciu, Vergil. (eds.). 1996. *The White Book of Communism: Literary and Artistic Histories, 1969–1989* [*Cartea Albă a Securităţii. Istorii literare şi artistice, 1969–1989*]. Bucharest: Serviciul Român de Informaţii.

Pelin, Mihai, Aioanei, Constantin, and Tunăreanu, Nevian. (eds.). 1997. *The White Book of Communism* [*Cartea Albă a Securităţii*]. Bucharest: Serviciul Român de Informaţii.

Răchită, Petre. 2015. "Monsignor Ioan Robu, Accused that He was an Informant and Agent of the Securitate" ["Monseniorul Ioan Robu, acuzat că a fost informator şi agent al Securităţii"]. *România liberă*, 21 June 2015. http://romanialibera.ro/special/dezvaluiri/monseniorul-ioan-robu—acuzat-ca-a-fost-informator-si-agent-al-securitatii-382799. Accessed on 9 December 2017.

Stan, Lavinia. 2013. *Transitional Justice in Romania: The Politics of Memory*. Cambridge: Cambridge University Press.

Stan, Lavinia and Turcescu, Lucian. Eds. 2017. *Justice, Memory and Redress in Romania: New Insights*. Cambridge: Cambridge Scholars Publishing.

Tismăneanu, Vladimir, Dobrincu, Dorin and Vasile, Cristian (eds.). 2007. *Final Report* [*Raport final*]. Bucharest: Comisia Prezidenţială pentru Analiza Dictaturii Comuniste din România–Editura Humanitas.

Tismăneanu, Vladimir. 2014. "The Destiny of SRS or the Viciousness as A Way of Life" ["Destinul lui SRS sau saloperia ca mod de viaţă"]. *Evenimentul zilei*, 9 October 2014.

Turcescu, Lucian, Stan, Lavinia. 2015. "Church Collaboration and Resistance under Communism Revisited: The Case of Patriarch Justinian Marina (1948–1977)". *Eurostudia*. 10, 1: 75–103.

Vasile, Cristian. 2003. *The History of the Greek Catholic Church under the Communist Regime, 1945–1989. Documents and Testimonies* [*Istoria Bisericii Greco-Catolice sub regimul comunist 1945–1989. Documente şi mărturii*]. Iaşi: Editura Polirom.

Vasile, Cristian. 2004. *Between Vatican and Kremlin. The Greek Catholic Church during the Communist Regime* [*Între Vatican şi Kremlin. Biserica Greco-Catolică în timpul regimului comunist*]. Bucharest: Editura Curtea Veche.

Vasile, Cristian. 2017. "Coming to Terms with the Controversial Past of the Orthodox Church." In: *Justice, Memory and Redress in Romania. New Insights*, edited by L. Stan and L. Turcescu, 235–56. Cambridge: Cambridge Scholars Publishing.

14 The possibility of researching religious minorities in the secret police archives of the former Yugoslavia

Aleksandra Djurić Milovanović

Introduction

In comparison to other Eastern European countries, scholarship on religious minorities, secret police and state security archives in the former Yugoslav republics is fragmented or even non-existent. The presence of materials on churches and religious minorities in the state security archives, the anti-religious practices and operations of the state security organs and police and the role and meaning of state security archives under post-socialism are issues that remain largely unexplored. Some former Yugoslav countries lack an adequate legal basis, especially with regards to access to personal files, or have no specialized archives for secret police sources. Thus, most of the national archives in these countries preserve secret police sources in a limited space with limited possibilities for access.

Unlike most of their Central and Eastern European neighbors, for whom the end of communism was, although economically and socially disruptive, a relatively peaceful experience, the ex-Yugoslav republics experienced a decade of armed conflict. These conflicts divided societies along ethnic and religious lines, largely in accordance with the titular nations and their respective majority religions. Research on religion and identity, therefore, has understandably focused on these conflict-ridden relationships. The opening of secret police archives in this region, viewed as part of the European Union integration process and the democratization of Western Balkan societies in general, has so far been extremely tentative and piecemeal. The democratization processes after the end of communism in each of the former Yugoslav countries developed differently. In the post-Yugoslav context, each of the republics has charted a different course in terms of democratization and Euro-Atlantic integration resulting in divergent approaches to the significance, role, meaning and access to state security archives.

However, exploring other related archival collections, such as the holdings of the Ministry of the Interior Affairs, the Ministry of Religious Affairs and the Ministry of Justice and Public Administration, we can gain some insights into the way in which the state relied on state security organs in order to pursue its policies regarding religious minorities. This chapter constitutes the first attempt to review the possibility of using secret police archives as a source for scholarly research on religious minorities but also it will provide a comparative study on the presence of religious minorities in the secret police archives in former Yugoslavia.

The historiography on Yugoslavia rarely covers issues related to religious minorities and the state authorities. The subject of church-state relations in multiethnic socialist-ruled Yugoslavia is particularly significant because of the traditionally close identification of national and religious allegiances among the Yugoslav peoples, for whom religion is not simply a matter of one's personal faith but also a badge of national identity (Aleksov 1999). The scholarly literature devoted to the religious landscape in Yugoslavia is mostly focused on the complex intertwining of religious and national identity (Perica 2002; Aleksov 2006), relations with traditional churches or nation-building confessions (Radić 1995, 2002, 2012; Akmadža 2006; Roter 1976) or regional/local church histories (Hopper 1997). So-called "non-nation-forming groups" such as double minorities (those with both an ethnic and religious dimension) and smaller so-called neo-Protestant groups (like the Pentecostals, Adventists and Nazarenes) have not been the focus of academic research until recently (Djurić Milovanović 2010, 2015; Aleksov 2006; Bjelajac 2012).

Secret police sources for the study of religion in the Yugoslav context have not been explored with the exception of the introduction to a study by Radić and Mitrović (2012). These authors point to the existence of sources in the secret police archives for research on totalitarian regimes and religions but note that those sources are fragmented. As Radić and Mitrović stress, it is possible to see how the OZNA (*Odeljenje zaštite naroda*, the Department for the Protection of the People) and the UDBA (*Uprava državne bezbednosti*, the State Security Department) functioned with regards to religious communities "only by combining these sources with material available from the Federal Commission for Religious Affairs in the Archive of Yugoslavia" (Radić & Mitrović 2012, 52). Given the current degree of access for researchers to state security materials and the almost complete lack of knowledge about the scale and nature of the materials held, an important element of this paper involves exploring other related archival collections, such as those of the Ministry of the Interior, the Ministry of Religious Affairs and the Ministry of Justice and Public Administration, in order to understand the way in which the state relied on state security organs in order to pursue its policies regarding religious minorities. Alongside the aforementioned sources, my ethnographic fieldwork from 2008 with several religious minority groups in the region has provided insights into the valuable archival documents preserved by community members themselves. These private archives represent one potential way to overcome limited access to some state archival sources.

The regulation of religious minorities in Yugoslavia

Together with Slovenia, Croatia, Bosnia and Herzegovina, Montenegro and Macedonia, Serbia was one of the six constitutive republics that comprised Yugoslavia. Yugoslavia belonged to the Non-Aligned Movement, which tried to balance between the Eastern and Western Blocs during the Cold War. Under the socialist regime, religion in Yugoslavia was not prominent in public life, and was instead consigned to the private sphere (Alexander 1979; Ramet 1992; Radić 2002). In order to understand the complex situation for religious minorities in post-WWII Yugoslavia, it is necessary to have a broader picture of the relationship of the communist state with religious communities. In Yugoslavia's Constitution of January 1946, which was modelled closely on Stalin's 1936 Soviet Constitution, equal rights were to be enjoyed by all religious communities. In the religious sphere, the 1946 Constitution proclaimed two basic principles: freedom of conscience and religion and the separation of church and state. At the same time, the state prohibited the misuse of the Church for political purposes and any religious teachings and practices which were considered to contradict the Constitution.

Church-state relations after the Second World War were complex and mostly focused on the relationship with the so-called traditional churches: the Serbian Orthodox Church and the Roman Catholic Church. Religious communities were tolerated as long as neither they nor their members abused religious freedom for political purposes, i.e. they should not "under the excuse of religious teaching, act against the social system of the country, the brotherhood and unity of the people, its social development and the strengthening of its defensive power" (Aleksov 1999). In practice, this condition could be used to control almost everything related to religious teachings and activities. Such activities were controlled on the federal level by the Commission for Religious Affairs, which was established in 1945. Even though the new 1946 Constitution proclaimed the separation of church and state and freedom of religion, the reality was strikingly different. Despite the fact that both the Constitution and the Law on the Legal Status of Religious Communities (1953, 1978) were more liberal than in other communist countries, such as Romania or Russia, practice differed from these principles as elsewhere in the region: while religious communities appeared to be tolerated, in reality religion in the public sphere was forbidden.

Citizens of the Federal People's Republic of Yugoslavia (FPRY) were free to belong to any religion or religious community or none. The practice of religion was declared a private matter of citizens (Article 1). Despite constitutional acknowledgement of the freedom of conscience and religion and the equality of religions and denominations, the state and the party preserved essential tools for controlling and circumscribing these principles. Religious instruction was removed from schools in Yugoslavia as early as 1945 and religious publications were practically banned through the confiscation of ecclesiastical printing presses. Administrative matters previously in the hands of churches were taken over by the state, which also exercised strict supervision over religious schools. The churches were most successfully undermined on a financial level through the confiscation of land holdings, residences, hospitals, schools and so forth. As Aleksov argues, the rate of the population's atheisation was highest among the Orthodox and lowest among the Catholics, with the Muslims in the middle (Aleksov 1999, 15).

On the basis of Yugoslav historiography, it is clear that one must distinguish between two separate phases in Yugoslav state policy towards religious communities. The first phase started after WWII and lasted until 1948, when there were many similarities between Yugoslavia and other East European countries in terms of the policy towards religious communities. The second began during the conflict with Cominform and saw the emergence of a new state policy (Radić 2002, 652). These fluctuations affected all religious communities and had an impact on state control over religious institutions. However, it also affected Yugoslavia's unique position among other communist countries, especially after it became a member of the Non-Aligned Movement. Yugoslavia seemed more liberal than other communist countries in terms of the religious freedoms proclaimed in its constitution and laws on religions. As Aleksov stresses, "minority religious communities could be seen as a test case for an analysis of the politics of the Yugoslav state, which was usually perceived as the most tolerant among the Communist countries" (Aleksov 1999). Despite the declared policy towards religious minorities, in reality things were different. This is especially visible with regards to the pacifist Nazarenes and Seventh Day Adventists. Religious minorities in Yugoslavia were strictly controlled by the state, especially because of their international and transnational networks and missionary work. Perceived as the potential allies of foreign intervention due to their connections with communities in other countries, religious minorities were seen as a threat. Members of religious minorities were considered anti-communist and disloyal citizens: their existence was seen as illegitimate. The persecution of religious minorities during communism experienced in other Central and Eastern European societies was also present, therefore, in Yugoslavia. Religious minorities were a focus of the secret police, especially because of their transnational and international networks in Europe and the United States.

State security and religious minorities

The state security and secret police organs, the OZNA and the UDBA, played a significant role in the control and regulation of religious minorities in communist Yugoslavia. OZNA, which was the security agency of Yugoslavia between 1944 and 1946 (Dimitrijević 2010), after the adoption of the First Constitution of the Federal Republic of Yugoslavia on January 31, 1946, was according to Resanović, "organized in March 1946 by transforming the first and second division of OZNA into the State Security Department, a department inside the Ministry of the Interior" (Resanović 2011, 95). The State Security Department, or UDBA, was a major part of the Yugoslav intelligence services from 1946 to 1991 and was primarily responsible for internal security. UDBA was turned into one of six new secret services, called the State Security Service, at the federal level after 1967, with the headquarters in Belgrade. Following the new Constitution of 1974, the six republics established their own secret services, all of which existed until 1991 (Resanović 2011, 96). As Kotar stresses, "Tito employed secret services to establish his control over the delicate balance of power between republics and nationalities," while "all republics had the same organizational structure and general trends that characterized secret services" (Kotar 2009, 201). As is the case with other Central and Eastern European communist regimes, Yugoslavia pursued the classic authoritarian agenda of control through repressive means, including state security or secret police activities.

Unlike in other Eastern European countries (such as Romania, Hungary and Germany), however, access to the archives of secret police of former Yugoslav republics is still very limited with public debate on opening them still ongoing. The degree of access in each of the former Yugoslav republics is different. Belgrade has the largest archival holdings, having been the center of the secret police during the socialist period. Slovenia as the first independent state after the break-up of Yugoslavia was also the first country to grant access to the secret police files. Lustration and archival laws allowed openness of the archival material earlier than in any other former Yugoslav republics, where it is still an ongoing process.[1] Without adequate laws or political effort and will, state security archives remain closed or with limited openness as they are judged to be highly sensitive material in terms of their potential use or misuse.

In Croatia, with the changes in political system in the 1990s, secret police documents (SOA) were mostly held by the secret police until they were transferred to the Croatian State Archive. Access to these files is regulated with several Laws and requires several levels of approvals for researchers (Kudra Beroš, 2018, 160). Serbia has neither adopted a law on opening the records of the secret service nor a general law on archives.

In the Archive of Serbia, the official institution holding Secret police files, domestic and foreign researchers do not enjoy equal access rights. Serbian researchers may get permission to access the archive with recommendations from research/academic institutions they are employed by accompanied by a description of the scope of the work (publication, research paper, research project etc.).

In Slovenia, General provisions apply to all archival records, including those created by the State Security Agency of the Socialist Republic of Slovenia (*Uprava državne varnosti* or *UDV*). Since the above-mentioned records contain information that falls into the category of sensitive personal data, protected by the Slovenian archival legislation (Article 65, Paragraph 2), they are not accessible without limitation. It is important to note that data about a person's religious affiliation also falls into the category of protected personal data. The accessibility of complete records (i.e. all the personal data) is determined by the date of death of a person – the data/documents are inaccessible for a period of 10 years after the individual's death. In accordance with archival law (Article 65, Paragraph 4), such documents are accessible only in a form of copies, on which all the protected sensitive personal data have previously been made unreadable (i.e. blackened). In special cases, exceptional access can be granted to researchers and journalists, who prove that the use of sensitive personal data is indispensable for the completion of their study/article. Such permission is granted through an administrative procedure; therefore, a researcher is obliged to prepare a special request (in the Slovenian language) in accordance with the stipulations of The Protection of Documents and Archives and Archival Institutions Act, Article 66, Paragraph 2 and 3.

In order to identify local and regional differences with regard to treatment and attitudes towards particular religious minorities it would be necessary to conduct comparative research in all republics. Such insights would also open many methodological, ethical and legal questions on religious groups and their activities during communist Yugoslavia. Recently the European Parliament asked from the Republic of Serbia to fully open its secret police archives as one of the EU access requests.

Archival data on religious minorities

During the communist period, some religious minority groups avoided leaving any written documents or other material traces of their community's history. This was especially noticeable in the Nazarene community, whose history is difficult to trace in archival sources. Other Neo-Protestant groups in Yugoslavia had a similar "hidden identity." The marginalization of religious minorities in Yugoslavia, such as Seventh Day Adventists, Baptists, Nazarenes, Pentecostals and Jehovah's Witnesses, took place because of their international and transnational networks and missionary work. Some individuals were persecuted for their pacifism (Nazarenes, Jehovah's Witnesses and Seventh Day Adventists) and condemned to long and repeated prison sentences (Bjelajac 2012, 79–91). The Nazarenes came to the attention of state authorities because of certain doctrinal and communal principles, such as their refusal to vote and carry arms, resistance to collectivization and the distribution of land previously owned by Germans, rejection of newly formed mass political organizations and disinclination to hand over alleged agricultural surpluses (Aleksov 1999, 26). Alongside the "nation-defining" religions in Yugoslavia, religious minorities (usually multiethnic in their structure) were perceived as socially subversive and dangerous. The state found it hard to subordinate the Nazarenes to its political authority or infiltrate them because of their close communal bonds and their concept of the priesthood of all believers. The Nazarenes were monitored by state officials, and many reports reveal their growth or decline and the locations of their churches (usually in private homes). According to the 1953 census, there were 15,650 Nazarenes in Yugoslavia. They were perceived as disloyal citizens who were unwilling to take oaths of allegiance or defend their country by joining the army. Nazarenes were considered to be unpatriotic and anti-communist and were therefore a direct threat to the system: they questioned the militarization of the Yugoslav citizenry through compulsory military service. Aleksov argues that an essential component of Yugoslav communism was so-called "nationwide and social self-protection":

> according to this doctrine, all citizens were regarded as soldiers or parts of defense while the Yugoslav army was held as a guardian of the Yugoslav communist system: brotherhood in unity insisted that it was the duty of citizens to defend their country, if need be, by taking up arms.
>
> (Aleksov, 1999)

Whether one accepted or rejected military service became the most important test of the Nazarene doctrine of nonconformity – this, together with other problems created by cooperation with the communist state, caused significant levels of emigration. This kind of treatment was intended to silence political opposition and frighten them into compliance. The length and harshness of imprisonment for conscientious objection in Yugoslavia had little parallel in any other country. The Nazarenes fled *en masse* to escape this extreme situation. Tito's decision to reduce the length of imprisonment for religious conscientious objectors and open the borders in the 1960s eased the situation of the Nazarene community (Djurić Milovanović 2017a).

The material related to the activities of religious minorities in the secret police archives is very modest. In the Archive of Serbia (the special section for BIA documents), the existing material on clerical activities contains one report on the number of the Nazarenes, Adventists, Baptists and members of the "Christian Community" in 1946. In the county of Novi Sad (Vojvodina), there were 792 Nazarenes, 327 Adventists, 218 Baptists and 93 members of the Christian Community (AS, BIA, 124, Kler, Report 8 August 1946, 1). The Nazarenes were considered the most numerous "sect" they had no interest in political activities and were very loyal to their community. They are described as pacifists who did not proselytise and were "not dangerous to their environment": however, some of them did refuse to vote or become members of a syndicate (AS, BIA, 124, Kler, Report 8 August 1946). The report provides details on the localities near the city of Novi Sad where Nazarene communities could be found, as well their occupations and the names of their leaders. In the report on the Adventists, the secret police agents emphasized their ethnically mixed community structure. Labelled as "religious fanatics," the members of the Adventist community were described

> as non-alcohol drinkers [and] non-smokers who do not eat pork. They practice adult baptism, usually in rivers or lakes in the presence of other

> sect members. The number of community members is decreasing since their youth is joining the Young Communist League of Yugoslavia (USAOJ). The Adventist community does not receive any donations of books or money from abroad.
>
> (AS, BIA, Kler, 124, 5–7)

In terms of the Baptist community, the secret police reported their connections with foreign missions in the United States: "the sect is financed from America. They were quite numerous before WWII; however, their membership is decreasing. Some of them are Hungarians, mostly peasants" (AS, BIA, Kler, 124, 7–8). For each of these communities, the same evaluation is made: "they have no influence on the people."

Members of the Neo-Protestant communities were described as having "low political awareness and [being] anational." Secret police agents were especially interested in the international collaboration of these groups and focused on their leaders. Thus, they proposed a guide for collecting and analysing material collected in the field, divided into a) counter-intelligence work and b) intelligence work. During counter-intelligence work, the agent had to be familiar with the teachings of the particular "sect," have detailed information on their organizational structures and methods of religious propaganda, follow closely the work and networks of the religious leaders and control religious activities and rituals that preached activities against the government. During intelligence work, the agent had to influence the "sect's" leadership towards working for the benefit of the country and being a model organization (AS, BIA, *Kler*, 124, Report on "Religious Sects" 1945).

In an OZNA report from 1945, it is emphasized that almost all the religious sects had their headquarters somewhere abroad.

> They often preach against the new Yugoslavia and especially against its political leaders. The focus of their enemy activity is propaganda and espionage for foreign agents. They forbid their members from participating in the political life of the country or in the people's front and from voting or [being in] the military. It is our duty to stop the activity against our country. However, we need to pursue good tactics in our activity so nobody can say we are doing something against this sect.
>
> (AS, BIA, *Kler*, 124)

Alongside the Nazarenes, Adventists and Jehovah's Witnesses, the secret police in Yugoslavia reported on the God Worshipper Movement, a renewal movement within the Serbian Orthodox Church that spread widely in the interwar period.[2] Described as "religious fanatics," this organization allegedly worked in secret and was connected with reactionary movements. Secret police agents were especially interested in the international collaboration of these groups and focused on their leaders.

Secret police in relation with small religious communities was interested in several segments:

- Enemy propaganda (translation of publications, printing material).
- Influence to youth (educational camps, sports events and excursions).
- Contacts with communities from abroad (foreign tourist visits etc).

These activities were especially noticeable among Methodist in Macedonia, Jehovah Witnesses in Slovenia and Adventists in Serbia and Croatia. Mass gatherings with children and youth were in the focus of secret police in Yugoslavia. Especially during holidays religious communities would organize gatherings with sports activities, seminars or movie projections. Contacts with foreign countries were perceived as dangerous and hard to control by state security. During 50s number of religious leaders from abroad were allowed to come to Yugoslavia (after 1956). For example, in 1959, 97 religious officials visited Yugoslavia. Their activities during visits were monitored and many reports have been preserved on their statements or other activities during their stay. Financial donations from abroad had significant role in building new prayer houses, or printing books, newspapers or other material. After 1959 small religious communities were in the focus of the state and police. They were controlled at several levels, aiming to weaken their contacts with foreign countries and the packages that were arriving (In 1957 almost 13000 Bibles in Serbian language published by British Bible Society were confiscated).

Files entitled "Imprisonment," "Emigration," "Goli Otok," "Prisoner Lists" etc. contain no data on the religious backgrounds of convicted men during the communist period or on the religious affiliation of émigrés. One possible source on the imprisonment of Nazarenes and Seventh Day Adventists on Bare Island (*Goli Otok*) or other prisons in Yugoslavia is the holdings of the Military Archives in Belgrade. Nevertheless, the verdicts of military courts in cases of conscientious objectors (Nazarenes, Jehovah's Witnesses, Seventh Day Adventists) are not available to researchers:

> The Archives of the Military Courts are considered open, but cannot be used for scientific and research purposes, publishing and other individual needs. The judicial authorities of the Republic of Serbia have a right to access documents in order to determine the rights of physical and legal entities for various reasons if such is not contrary to the Law on Personal Data Protection.
>
> ("Official Gazette of the Republic of Serbia," No. 97/08, 104/09, 58/10)[3]

The possibility of assessing these records could fill the gap in existing oral testimonies from community members and make up for the lack of available sources in the secret police archives. However, personal files in the Secret

Police Archives in Belgrade are not available for the researchers, thus only reports on religious communities are available. It is also important to emphasize that the data available in these reports on the particular religious minority community depended on the regional presence of the community (example northern Serbian province of Vojvodina). The reports of the Commission for Religious Affairs contain information on their illegal emigration activities after being realized from the prison (AS, Republic Commission for Religious Affairs, G-21, F 34). According to 1954 report, 50 Nazarenes illegally escaped from the country and almost the same number was caught during their escape. In the same year the State Secretary for Peoples Defence proposed more rigourous prison sentences for the Nazarenes since the number of illegal emigrants increased.

From the secret police archives to the religious community archives

During fieldwork with religious minorities, their often-traumatic experiences during the communist era reveal not only the richness of preserved memory, but also their personal archival material: this, to a certain extent, could be a substitute for the unavailable sources in the archives. Documents related to imprisonment or verdicts from the military courts have been well preserved among diasporic communities. Thus, ethnographic fieldwork among religious minorities can bring to light official documents kept as part of their personal archives, alongside oral narratives, pictures and books. Given the lack of access to archival sources, researchers can potentially return to these communities in order to find documents as "the missing pieces" and explore the impact of the communist regime on religious minorities in any given period.

This is especially the case with the Nazarene community and their diaspora across the Atlantic (Djurić Milovanović 2017a, 2017b). Documents on the imprisonment of the Nazarene men could be found in the holdings of the Military Archives of Serbia in Belgrade. Nevertheless, the verdicts of military courts in cases of conscientious objectors (Nazarenes, Jehovah's Witnesses, Seventh Day Adventists) are not available to researchers.[4]

In the Secret Police Department of the Archives of Serbia there are files with names and lists of prisoners (including *Goli Otok*), however without any data on reasons for imprisonment or religious background. Thus, without knowing names of Nazarenes condemned to prison sentences it is hard to find those data in the files of imprisoners.

Applying this "alternative methodology" leads researchers to other sources and legal documents kept by community members (documents related to their emigration, official letters from their sister communities abroad etc.).[5] This could be a potential way to overcome limited access to some archival sources. Another question stays open, how can we, as researchers, use these documents or is the community willing to share them for the purposes of our own research.

Conclusion

In researching the history of minority religious groups in Yugoslavia several important aspects need to be taken into account. After the break-up of Yugoslavia archival sources and documents were divided between countries and a number of files was destroyed. Since access to the secret police archives in ex-Yugoslav countries is still under question, the only way forward currently available is to combine the fragmentary archival material from these holdings with archival sources from other institutions (especially the Federal Commission for Religious Affairs) and the results of ethnographic research and oral histories from the religious communities themselves. This paper offers the first attempt to review the possibility of using secret police archives as a source for scholarly research on religious minorities in the former Yugoslavia. Providing an example of personal archives in the religious communities is one of the possibilities to overcome obstacles in access and closeness of the official archives. Religious minorities represent a valuable resource for analyzing the relations between the state and religious groups during the communist period. The public debate on openness is ongoing and has thus far been inconclusive. The discourse on the necessity of releasing secret police files has resulted in both new limitations and some openness in Serbia, Croatia and Slovenia. However, using what is available in these archives relating to religious minorities is a pioneering research that could bring a new perspective on religious minorities in Yugoslav society. Comparative research on religious minorities in the former Yugoslav Republics could also allow for new insights on the experience of religious minorities under communism. Including the former Yugoslavia in the framework of research being conducted in other countries such as Hungary, Romania and Moldova would open up perspectives on the historical and contemporary aspects of religious pluralism, tolerance, the position of religious minorities in post-communist societies and the development of democracy and social transformation after the fall of communism.

Notes

1 In 2014 there was a Referendum in Slovenia on the availability of the archival documents online. Published content does not contain sensitive personal information, or if they do, are anonymized. For more details visit: www.arhiv.gov.si/si/uporaba_arhivskega_gradiva/citalnica_arhiva/objave_arhivskega_gradiva_sluzbe_drzavne_varnosti/informativni_bilteni_sdv/ (accessed on 27 February 2019)
2 For more on the God Worshiper Movement, see Djurić Milovanović & Radić (2017).
3 www.vojniarhiv.mod.gov.rs/sadrzaj.php?id_sadrzaja=102&active=tekst (accessed on 18 February 2018).
4 www.vojniarhiv.mod.gov.rs/sadrzaj.php?id_sadrzaja=102&active=tekst (accessed on 18 February 2018).

5 The Nazarene community in US – Apostolic Christian Church gave all the community records and documents to the Virginia Historical Society in Richmond (www.virginiahistory.org/collections-and-resources/how-we-can-help-your-research/researcher-resources/finding-aids/apostolic).

Archival sources

Arhiv Srbije, Bežbednosno informativna agencija [Archive of Serbia, Security Information Agency] (AS, BIA) – Fond 124, *Kler* Report "Religious Sects" (1945).

Arhiv Srbije, Republička komisija za verska pitanja [Archive of Serbia, Republic Commission for Religious Affairs] – Fond 34, G-21.

References

Akmadža, Miroslav. 2006. "Politics of the Communist Regime in Yugoslavia towards Religious Groups 1945." In: *Dividing Croation History* [*Razdjelnica hrvatske povijesti*], edited by Nada Kisić Kolanović et al., 257–70. Zagreb: Hrvatski institut za povijest.

Aleksov, Bojan. 1999. "The Dynamics of Extinction: the Nazarene Religious Community in Yugoslavia after 1945." MA Thesis, Central European University, Budapest.

Aleksov, Bojan. 2006. *Religious Dissent between the Modern and the National – Nazarenes in Hungary and Serbia 1850–1914*. Wiesbaden: Harrassowitz Verlag.

Alexander, Stella. 1979. *Church and State in Yugoslavia since 1945*. Cambridge: Cambridge University Press.

Bjelajac, Branko. 2012. "The Persecution of the Nazarenes in Yugoslavia 1918–1941." *International Journal for Religious Freedom* 5 (2): 79–91.

Dimitrijević, Bojan. 2010. "The Formation of the OZN in Serbia and Belgrade and the Liquidation of the People's Enemies in 1944" ["Formiranje OZN-e u Srbiji i Beogradu i likvidacije narodnih neprijatelja 1944"]. *Istorija 20. veka*, 2: 9–28.

Djurić Milovanović, Aleksandra. 2010. "Conservative neo-Protestants: Romanian Nazarenes in Serbia." *Religion in Eastern Europe*, 30 (3): 34–43.

Djurić Milovanović, Aleksandra. 2015. *Double Minorities in Serbia. Distinctive Aspects of the Religion and Ethnicity of the Romanians in Vojvodina* [*Dvostruke manjine u Srbiji. O posebnostima u religiji i etnicitetu Rumuna u Vojvodini*]. Belgrade: Institute for Balkan Studies SASA.

Djurić Milovanović, Aleksandra. 2017a. "Alternative Religiosity in Communist Yugoslavia: Migration as a Survival Strategy of the Nazarene Community." *Open Theology* 3: 447–57.

Djurić Milovanović, Aleksandra. 2017b. "On the Road to Religious Freedom. A Study of the Nazarene Emigration from Southeastern Europe to the United States." *Revista de Etnografie si Folclor* 1–2: 5–27.

Hopper, David John. 1997. *A History of Baptists in Yugoslavia 1862–1962*. Fort Worth: Southwestern Baptist Theological Seminary.

Kotar, Tamara 2009. "Slovenia." In: *Transitional Justice in Eastern Europe and Former Soviet Union. Reckoning with the Communist Past*, edited by L. Stan, 200–21. London: Routledge.

Kudra Beroš, Viktorija. 2018. "UDBE Files as a Problematic Object for the (Re)construction of Croatian National Identity" ["Dosijei UDBE kao probematičan objekt (re)konstrukcije hrvatskog nacionalnog identiteta"]. *Etnološka tribina* 41: 159–73.

Perica, Vjekoslav. 2002. *Balkan Idiols: Religion and nationalism in Yugoslavia.* Oxford: Oxford University Press.

Radić, Radmila. 1995. *Faith against Faith – the State and Religious Communities in Serbia 1945–1953* [*Verom protiv vere – država i verske zajednice u Srbiji 1945–1953*]. Beograd: INIS.

Radić, Radmila 2002. *The State and Religious Communities*, 1945–1970 I/II [*Država i verske zajednice 1945–1970* I/II]. Belgrade: INIS.

Radić, Radmila and Mitrović, Momčilo. 2012. *Minutes from the Sessions of the Commission for Religious Affairs of the People's Republic of Serbia 1945–1978* [*Zapisnici sa sednica Komisije za verska pitanja NR/Sr Srbije 1945–1978*]. Beograd: INIS.

Ramet, Sabrina Petra. 1992. *Adaptation and Transformation in Communist and Post-Communist Systems.* Boulder: Westview Press.

Resanović, Aleksandar. 2011. "Secret Police Records – The Case of Former Yugoslavia with the Reference to the Case of Serbia." *Südosteuropa Mitteilungen* 5–6: 94–100.

Roter, Zdenko. 1976. *Religion and Church in Slovenia* [Religija i crkva u Sloveniji]. Zagreb: Školska knjiga.

15 If sex were a factor …

The Securitate archives and issues of morality in documents related to religious life

Anca Şincan

The issue of morality represents an important factor in the analysis of the archival documents related to religion in communism because morality formed an important element in the construction of Secret Police case files on individuals connected to religious life. This chapter presents an overview of the way in which morality and sexuality permeated the *Securitate* documents on religious life in communist Romania, how morality and sexuality was used in designing individual files and the reasons behind their use. It seeks to answer questions related to the disappearance of the moral standard in other archives that dealt specifically with religion in communism (i.e. the Secretariat for Religious Denominations, Church archives) and what they were replaced with.

When the veil of privacy is lifted, and the secret is no more, a rich picture unfolds for the researcher. Privacy was non-existent for the officers and informants and there is little that cannot be unearthed from their reports and documents. Access to mail, surveillance recordings, notes from informants in networks that surrounded the surveilled individual in gradually wider circles (family, neighbors, co-workers), visual elements (photographs and more seldom videos, maps, drawings) all present aspects of private life that grant the reader (the officer and nowadays the researcher) power over the individual. The opening of the Secret Police archives controversial as it was with files used for political agendas and show trials (Stan 2002, 2004) provided a public reenactment of the materials found in surveillance files. Blackening out of names, the minimal protection offered by the archival institutions to the actors that surface in surveillance files, does little to afford the subject the privacy he or she believed his or her actions were carried out in.[1] In the case of the clergy and church members alike, the moral stick they are measured against in relation to their case files is higher than for the rest as moral integrity was a requirement of their position. This made surveillance files of religious actors an even more powerful instrument of blackmail and control by the secret police when needed. They also made these files key instruments in the public debates on the relationship with the secret police of the clergy (Turcescu and Stan, 2005).

The Romanian Secret Police was one of the most comprehensive apparatus of repression in the Eastern bloc. It was used in two chronological stages, as

Dennis Deletant describes, “first to eliminate opponents in the drive to consolidate power and secondly to ensure compliance once revolutionary change had been effected” (Deletant, 1995, 1). The extensive surveillance was all encompassing including elements of private life and constructing narratives about the subjects of investigation. Files that were “constructed” (made-up) were frequent and the image of the person was most times distorted, an inverted Dorian Grey like image where the mirror of the document only showcased the evil and the grotesque. (See Katherine Verdery’s ethnography of her individual file for a close up look at the techniques and tropes introduced by the secret police in constructing her biographical narrative of the time she spent in Romania as a researcher, Verdery, 2018.)

This overview of the way in which morality permeated the *Securitate* documents on religious life in communist Romania is discussed through three case studies. They were selected to exemplify the way in which sexual behaviour played into the construction of the individual files regarding religious life. Morality related to sexuality played a significant role in shaping secret police responses to recalcitrant clergy as it was an easy means of control. In this sense, it was one of the first tropes the Secret Police and the inspectors for religious denominations went for alongside political affiliations or leanings. Most of the personal files of spiritual leaders, important clergymen and church hierarchs have short inserted characterizations that discuss sexual preferences or peculiarities of behaviour, such as *Îi plac mult femeile* – [he likes women very much] in the form of brief notes in the margins of the document asking for more information or to add information, respectively (ACNSAS I95070, 1). Often one finds “unknown” inserted regarding sexual life. This kind of entry in itself reflects a moral judgement on the part of inspector/ *Securitate* officer as it does not imply that the clergyman is morally correct but rather that the officer has not yet been able to discover the particular preferences or promiscuous acts that would complete the file.

Researching questions of religious life in communist archives, I have noted that with few exceptions the issue of morality remains important mainly to the Secret Police. Morality as found in the documents created by the Department for Religious Denominations personnel had a wide definition covering but not restricted itself to honesty, trustworthiness, and religious orthodoxy. Sexual behaviour on the other hand is less present. It is almost entirely absent from Church archives. Letters from parishioners could contain complaints that refer to sexual behaviour. However, issues arising from problems of sexual behaviour are addressed with silence and were frequently solved by external authorities.

Understandings of morality in communist-era archives on religion

There are several archives that host documents related to religious life in communist Romania. Some of them are state archives that have different degrees of accessibility for the researcher. The National Archives (both the central and local archives) preserve the administrative view of religious life.

Similar documents can be found at the archive of the State Secretary for Religious Affairs that has inherited the archival collection of the Communist Ministry for Religious Denominations, later the Department for Religious Denominations. However, these archival materials offer a more thorough view of religious life both at local and central level. The Ministry/Department for Religious Denominations documented the relationship between state and church at an administrative level as the state institution was responsible for imposing new set of rules and regulations on religious life. In order to impose the new legislative requirements on religious communities and supervise their administration, the Ministry for Religious Denominations retained a significant number of inspectors, both locally and centrally who worked collecting information on religious life (Şincan 2017a; Csongor 2017), imposing the state regulations, monitoring problematic situations in religious communities and ensuring a link between the local religious community, institutional religion and the state. Based on the information collected by the inspectors and information coming from the Secret Police, the ministry designed and redesigned religious policy.

Morality played a significant role in the tableau of collected information that the inspectors sent to the center. However, aspects of private life and sexuality rarely made their way into the definition of morality. There were two types of morality, conflictual in their nature, that make their way into these documents. One was based on ideology, was new and required explanation and understanding for the state employee as much as for the supervised religious communities. It was connected for instance with the break with traditional roles and values, the position of women in society, and the relaxation of promiscuity regulations in relation with family life (Field 2007).

At the same time, because of the area of interest of the ministry, the other type of morality that the documents refer to was religious. The descriptions of the characteristics of communities, biographies of clergymen and hierarchs and descriptions of potential problematic situations all include religiously defined judgments. Respect for religious rules and regulations were imposed by secular authorities as well, especially with regard to splinter groups from the legally recognized denominations that the central administration of religious denominations could not reach. In the 1960s for instance when the Department for Religious Denominations' inspectors supervised the administrative and religious local meetings of the legally recognized religious denominations, they made sure any potential religious slights were eliminated beforehand from the discussions. In a letter to the Department a local inspector from Braşov described his act of censure the presentation on the Orthodox Liturgy made by a lecturer at the Lutheran church Deans meeting on account that the subject could be regarded as inflammatory by the Orthodox Church and also insulting.

> Discussing such subjects, the note said, from the Lutheran position could be seen by the Orthodox believers and clergy as attacks on their faith and

> could lead to frictions and tensions between clergy and believers. We recommend tactfully that the subject should be replaced.
>
> (ASSC DP 88, vol. 4, 1961, 71)

Punishment was imposed on members of religious groups, sanctioned by the ministry or by local inspectors, on issues related to moral and religious deviations.

In the author's experience, privacy and sexuality rarely make their way into the archival documents created and preserved by religious institutions themselves.[2] Morality carries a religious definition in such archival documents and while the information in the document may be biographical, they shied away from details of private life and were concerned rather with public behaviour and orthodoxy of religious practice. In the rare cases when privacy was discussed in these documents it was masked behind religious language.

The relationship between private life and morality in the Secret police archives, however, is markedly different. In her analysis of the distinctions between state archives and the secret Police archives, Katherine Verdery noted that while in state archives people try to be preserved, in the documents of the Secret Police archives "(...) rather than resisting their exclusion, most people who find themselves in this archive would much rather not be there" (Verdery 2014, 36). This particularity of the Secret Police archives is exemplified by their treatment of morality for it is the Secret Police archival material that preserves and gives access to a wide range of private matters that people would really rather not be present there. In the case of the documents on religious life, morality has a new definition that is neither ideological nor religious, although it has elements of both. The use of the problem of morality was the driving force behind collecting information on an individual's private life. While the purpose of discussing morality in the documents collected by ministry employees and those from the archives of religious institutions is to correct behaviour that is deemed morally wrong (irrespective of the definition of morality, religious or ideological) the purpose of the discussion of morality, privacy, sexual life in the documents created by the *Securitate* officers was for coercion. In contrast, for the ministry and for the central administration of the church, the documents led to sanctions that could translate into salary reductions, personnel movement, or being demoted down on the hierarchical ladder. In many cases, information on moral misbehaviour could bring together the state and the church hierarchy in employing punitive measures. The contents of the Secret Police documents that discussed morally corrupt behaviour led to very different outcomes. Their value was in their secrecy, their use was not in correcting behaviour but rather in maintaining said behaviour in order to be used as blackmail. When the veil of secrecy is lifted the purpose again was rarely correctional. In most cases, a moral problem became known as part of a slander campaign. Physical abuse, especially, was not corrected and there are instances when sexual violence was encouraged, or sexual acts were staged to entrap the individual into collaborating with the secret police in order not to receive legal punishment for his/ her acts (ACNSAS D69, vol. 35, 110–28).

Another type of morality relates to the behaviour of the communist inspectors for religious denominations and the secret police officers charged with the supervision of religious life. The regulations that norm the private life of the communist man or woman become more restrictive even when it regards the state administration of religious life. There is a moral behaviour that is sanctioned by the communist ideology. Chronologically the type of morality that was imported from the Soviet blueprint was a constricting one, a traditional view of the sexual behaviour and family life and while this came on a wave of women empowerment with access to education, the expanse of divorce, help in child rearing all in an effort to expand the work force the private life values remain in the conservatism of the earlier decades. Even the involvement of women within the process of building communism entailed jobs that linked them with the private sphere. (Hoffmann 2003, 24).

For the communist private life of the 1950s an ideological code of behaviour was imposed where *tradition* and *progress* collided:

> [...] instilling Communist morality, a much-propagandized code of morality and behavior was supposed to govern all aspects of life. It required political loyalty, hard work and the proper conduct of private life. Professionals and moralists in a variety of fields determined which attitudes and behaviors constituted a correct Communist private life, putting forth specific instructions about sex, love, marriage and child rearing. Again, trade unions, the party, the Komsomol and voluntary organizations were supposed to help enforce these standards. Communist morality resembles a screen window: slightly pliable with holes that allow some permeability.
>
> (Field 2007, 5)

Deborah Field quotes The Moral Code of the Builder of Communism from 1961 where family life, moral purity, simplicity and modesty in social and personal life, concern for the upbringing of children were among the tenets that the Soviet system was imposing upon its cadres (Field 2017). This code of conduct, at least at the level of discourse, is interiorized by the communist cadres dealing with religious life. Requirements were made by superiors that the inspectors that have to deal currently with issues related with religion, religious communities, clergy, church hierarchy should adhere more to the moral conduct required by the party.

Case studies

With access to secret police surveillance and informers' files on individuals belonging to religious communities (either legally recognized or underground religious movements), it is possible to illustrate the various approaches that the secret police and the Ministry/Department for Religious Denominations had in dealing with moral issues, sexual life and privacy. My first case outlines a story fabricated by the Secret Police where the morally corrupt act may or may not have happened but was gradually constructed by the *Securitate* officers with help from informers selected from within his entourage through blackmail and corruption. This type of file, which constructs doubt through innuendos, was a last resort when all else failed to ensure control over the individual. My second case study relates to the involvement of the *Securitate* in the story, and the use of the findings to create an environment of distrust for the surveilled clergyman that had been accused of sexual relations and sexual perversions. The behaviour of the *Securitate* employees as moral censors that decided what type of punishment the clergymen received for his sexual exploits. In this case no legal actions were taken even if the file discusses instances of violence. And finally, I am discussing the moral code enforced on the state employee dealing with religious denominations, and the consequences of the break of said moral code for the secret police offices or state inspector for religious denominations.

The constructed file

The secret police archives have been described as "a staggering tableau of human depravity and woe" (Kotkin, 2002: 36). The files demonstrate how the regime was often caught up in its own internal falsifications (Kotkin, 2002: 36). Any analysis of the file needs to include a discussion on "the function of the file under the communists, with its current usages under the radically different economic and political conditions of a late-capitalist global economy" (Lewis 2003, 380). Some of these files could be looked at as a form of "hostile biography" (Lewis, 2003) where the highlight was to a darker behavioural side and when that was missing to a manipulation of facts and, indeed, fabrication. Especially with regards to morality, privacy and sexual behaviour, in these particular documents one needs to follow different guidelines in reading them. The use of the file during communism is sometimes very similar with the use of the same file by the researcher in post-communism, and therefore, a discussion on the researcher's objectives (a self-analysis) should accompany a thorough investigation on the file itself.

To showcase this precise problem, my first case study refers to a "constructed" file of an Orthodox Church hierarch accused of engaging in homosexual behaviour. The personal file illustrates the way in which morality is used by the *Securitate* officers when they put together the file to achieve control over the individual it refers to (ACNSAS I005555, vol 1–3). Even after triangulating the data in the file and placing the documents in comparison both chronologically – the individual profile that was created by the interwar Secret Police – or with similar individuals and situations, I cannot be certain that this was a fabricated accusation or that the image that surfaces from the file does not represent, at least partially, the reality. I can, however, when discussing these documents talk about a constructed story. The file does not present a neat sequence of events that the Secret Police came across in their normal surveillance process but rather one that is put together by the Secret Police by blackmailing/rewarding the associates of the individual when every other means of control available to the Secret Police had failed (ACNSAS I005555 vol. 3, 1).

The individual about which the file speaks, who was high in the leadership of the Orthodox Church escaped, through various networks he had joined and/or created along an impressive career in the public sphere, the ideological restraints put in place to regulate the leadership of the Romanian Orthodox Church in the immediate aftermath of the communist regime coming to power.

The person in question has two other files, one produced by the Serviciul de Informaţii Externe (the Foreign Intelligence Service) and one opened by the Siguranţa (the Interwar Secret Police) and taken over by the Communist Secret Police. The three volume Informative File that was taken over from the Interwar Secret Police was dedicated to the biography and activity (public and private) of the hierarch until the early 1950s. From the three volumes, the first two discuss his past and present public political and religious activities and his connections with the communist political environment. The third file was dedicated to the alleged sexual life of the individual. The usual accusations of collaboration with the Iron Guard and/or with interwar political parties do not appear at all. In the first pages, the Secret Police officers offer the reason this file is constructed: their failure to control this particular church personality (ACNSAS I005555 vol. 3, 1–2) as he had negotiated his hierarchical position directly with members of the political administration.

The file describes a sexual triangle and is composed strictly from confessions of three persons directly linked to the individual. The accounts are overly detailed (dates, descriptions of meetings, description of sexual encounters, characterizations of the persons involved). The file spans several months chronologically in 1953, it refers only to the present with no incursions into the past activities of the person and it concerns only the three persons and the individual under surveillance. However, no actual surveillance took place to corroborate or verify the accounts of the three informants. The accusation refers to homosexual acts and the descriptions are given by two persons that are presumably involved in the acts and an outsider who witnessed and corroborated parts of their story. While the file does not contain any document that would clarify whether this is a real story or a constructed one (a false account) there are several ways in which the researcher can ascertain that we are dealing with a false constructed story.

Firstly, the story is never used in any attempted blackmail over the individual. That in itself would not say that much. However, when taken together with the informant/collaboration files for each of the three informants that offer this particular story, and given the fact that they quickly advanced up the hierarchical ladder of the church in the years that followed, this suggests that the files may have doubtful contents.

Neither of the other two files on this person discuss possible sexual misconduct. The person in question was at the end of his life at the time and the descriptions suggest that he was an involved participant. The chronology of the file does not match the parallel surveillance file that was kept by the officers of the Secret Police. As far as one can tell, the information on this file had no repercussion on the activity (religious or public) that the individual conducted after the file was created and it is highly doubtful the person was ever made aware of the contents of the file.

The direct involvement of the Secret Police in the documents in the file is nonexistent. Their only role appears to be one of couch psychologists that lead a discussion gradually into progressively revealing activities going on from a scholarship offered to a poor young orphan to attend the Seminary (ACNSAS I005555 vol. 3, 12) to sexual intercourse that was never admitted by the informant but was only implied (ACNSAS I005555 vol. 3, 83) and was described by the other informant in the file.

Why would a file discussing the sexual life of this particular individual need to exist? Why use a story about his private life and not one connected with the political life of the individual that would have been sufficient for the Secret Police? The answers are problematic. However, because of the moment when this file was put together, so close to the end of the individual's life, this could be a file that speaks more about the three informants than about the individual after whom the file is named. That would also explain why homosexuality was used in place of sexual relations with women. The public repercussions would have been greater for the individual but greater would have been the risk for the Secret Police that the story would have been made public because of it being so distinct from the information the public had on the church hierarch. However, because the informants confessed to these illegal acts, it meant that the Secret police had complete control over them. The control the Secret Police and the state administration had over at least one of the informants in the file and his rapid ascension, after the death of the hierarch, in the administration of the Church could account for at least one use of the documents found in this third volume. Moral judgment does not play a role in constructing this file. The acts described are illegal under the communist legal framework and thus an ideological judgement is imposed rather than a religious one in this case.

Using "moral deviancy"

Of the efforts that the secret police put in to control the activity of oppositional religious groups, blackmail and rumor spreading make up an important part. Private life was an inexhaustible source and in the case of clergymen, the secret police paid particular attention to morality and sexual behaviour. The *Securitate* had multiple uses for this type of information. As noted in the previous case, this information could serve to coerce the individual into collaborating, it could also be an insurance for the *Securitate* agents and not be used at all, it could help the agents to discredit the individual, feed rumours and create situations where the morally deviant behaviour would be revealed.

This was the case with an individual member of the hierarchy of an underground religious group who was outed to the secret police by the new partner of his former presumed lover. The informant spoke of sexual perversion detailing sexual positions and sexual acts that his partner, the former mistress of the religious leader told him in confidence. Upon discovering this sexual relationship between the religious leader and one of the women of his close circle the secret police local office created a surveillance plan that included placing the woman under surveillance to ascertain whether her relationship with the religious leader was ongoing and what that relationship entailed, and to thoroughly check of the information received so far from the woman's new partner to verify his claims of sexual perversion (ACNSAS I3470 vol. 3, 280). A surveillance microphone was installed immediately and with it, confirmation of the relationship. A new plan was drawn up on the basis of the findings which included the use of the information and the steps the secret police officers needed to take. Encouraging the continuation of the sexual behaviour of the individual served their purposes. Thus, their findings remained unknown to the individual. Gradually information was released reaching through informants to members of the religious leader's network and through them it spread out to his close community (ACNSAS I3470, vol. 3–4). The reasoning of the secret police is outlined in the various action plans regarding the individual. The plans talk about discrediting his religious activity and encouraging a distance between him and his community.

This file reveals the position that the secret police took towards the deviant moral behaviour itself. One can see here how morality is used by the secret police officers to discredit the individual. Outing the individual is seldomly the case. The information of his sexual activity is important on several levels. It speaks of dishonesty, the moral authority of the religious leader challenged the secret police can work on replacing him with their own informants, it could lead to dismantling underground communities that rely on trust and moral authority to survive the actions of the totalitarian state. Also, it is important to note that their use of the file was not correctional. The woman that was supposedly involved in a "deviant sexual act" was not protected by the state official. Moreover, the agents tried to ensure the continuation of the said behaviour so they could continue using the elements of private life to construct their policy towards the underground community.

A moral code of conduct for the state employee dealing with religious life

The final example is a case study that offers an insight on how morality became a requirement for communist state employees whose job it was to monitor religious life. It seems from this case that the moral behaviour required for the position they filled was a mirror of the ideal morality of communities they were employed to supervise and control. I suggest that this represents an expansion of the ideological morality to encompass traits found in religious morality.

Gheorghe Nenciu was an inspector and the acting director of the Department of Religious Affairs in the late 1970s. Set to become the next director he was fired from the Department and after an inhouse trial the communist party cell in the Department for Religious Denominations excluded him from the Party. He was accused of helping an orthodox monk climb the hierarchical ladder to the position of auxiliary bishop in exchange for a large sum of money (Şincan 2017b, 317). His story as a state specialist in religious life that became entangled in corruption and blackmail is in itself important as it stands in for the decay of the Party elite itself in the final decades of the regime in Romania. However, I am using Nenciu's example here to illustrate the importance of morality and a clean family life for the communist state employee in general and the one dealing with religious life in particular.

The file on Nenciu (ASSC fond Departamentul Cultelor, file Gheorghe Nenciu)[3] contains several of his autobiographies and biographies that were used in the trial for his exclusion from the Party and they create a portrait that should have been "of a communist success story for the communist administration" (Şincan 2017b, 325–6). He started from the bottom of the hierarchical ladder, a Party intellectual when the Party had few such men, he managed to climb the hierarchical ladder over the 25 years he was in the Ministry of Religious Affairs and later the Department for Religious Denominations. However, the biographies bring forth an ideologically corrupt individual that was "too friendly with the religious communities he was supposed to supervise," and who was inclined to compromise and negotiate away the problems and infringements of regulations committed by religious actors. He was also "becoming bourgeois" having a car and a network of well-off friends and having sent his daughters to study in the West (ASSC fond Departamentul Cultelor, file Gheorghe Nenciu, 7). While the main accusation was the acceptance of a bribe, these other accusations made a compelling argument for his exclusion from the Department and from the Party.

One of the final accusations in the biographies that his colleagues wrote in the file that contributed to his demise relates to his family life and his adulterous relations with several women. Placed among the most important accusations in the process that led to his exclusion from the Party and found in most of the character references offered by his colleagues, his adulterous life was brought forth to show that a morally correct life was of the upmost importance for a leader of the party but mostly for someone in charge of controlling, regulating and administering religious life.

Two complaints about sexual encounters with women while the inspector was on delegation, coupled with several complaints of partying and drunkenness over more than 15 years surfaced to be integrated into the biographies and led to the questioning of his private life and the accusations of blurring the lines between being a state official and cohorting with members of religious communities.

In this particular case study, the reader of the file is faced not just with Nenciu's breaking of the communist moral code discussed earlier but also with the public vilification of the person breaking the moral code. One of his colleagues when discussing Nenciu's private life complains: "We had no idea whom we sat next to all these years" (ASSC fond Departamentul Cultelor, file Gheorghe Nenciu, 30). *Securitate* officers and local inspectors informed the ministry on at least two separate occasions that the behaviour of the inspector went against not only ideological requirements for morally upstanding citizens, but also for cadres dealing with religious life (ASSC fond Departamentul Cultelor, file Gheorghe Nenciu, 28). They were supposed to mirror the communities and individuals they were administering and having authority over.

The power of this accusation is evident in the file not only because of its omnipresence in the biographies and the minutes of the trial for exclusion from the Party and the Department, but also, given the opportunity to defend himself, this was the accusation he chose to start with. This speaks of the impact of morality on the construction of an upstanding and committed communist for Nenciu's trial was first and foremost about his exclusion from the Party.

In his defence, Nenciu gives value and meaning to morality and speaks of the Party using religious terminology. He admits certain lapses in judgement with regards to the accusations of corruption hoping to be able to preserve his position inside the Department:

> I told you from the very beginning that there is plenty to be said. You should know that I understand with communist piety [*evlavie comunistă*] and paid great attention to everything that has been said [during this meeting]. I understand that I have to keep stoking this fire that burned inside of me this evening. [...] On the one hand, it is fair that for everything that I have done, deeds incompatible with the position of a communist tasked with political work, I should not be with the Department for Religious Denominations anymore. On the other hand, it would be great if I could serve my punishment here, so I could be controlled by the people who showed me the truth. However, I know that the party is everywhere and my only possibility of rehabilitation [...] is to work so that the party can judge if I overcome the mistakes I made in my work and if I honored my pledge to give to the party everything I have good in me.
>
> (ASSC fond Departamentul Cultelor, file Nenciu Gheorghe, 41)[4]

The only real challenge he brought to the accusation is the one related to moral accusations. He based his defense on the personal relationships he has within the Department. "Here there are people that know me so well I cannot hide my sins from them" [...] "I have lived in your midst for over two decades, you know me and my family life, how can you think I could have done the things you accuse me of" (ASSC fond Departamentul Cultelor, file Nenciu Gheorghe, 26). One can note also, a hybridization of the definition of morality that includes religious elements and religious language. Nenciu spoke of sins and not mistakes, he spoke about the fire of truth burning inside of him, the communist conscience, his self-criticism builds upon the confession within the church with a hierarchy of sins where his defense of his moral behaviour was left for the final part of his argumentation for keeping his job, but, more importantly his place within the party. The importance of a morally correct behaviour was paramount for the inspector, and he defended the *orthodoxy* of his moral conduct to the end.

Conclusion

What are we researchers to do with this "tableau of depravity, this den of iniquity" (Kotkin, 2002) that is the secret police archive? What can anyone use from these files considering the manipulation and distortion of the facts that is often times clear and abundant. I suggest that there are indeed several important avenues worth exploring in relation to questions of morality and sexual behaviour that surface in the documents created by the *Securitate*.

As the selected case studies suggest, morality and sexual behaviour has a prime role in the construction of the secret police file with regards to religious life. The understanding of morality is primarily connected with sexual behaviour, promiscuity, perversity (as it was understood in the communist legal framework). Moral behaviour was important for the secret police mainly because it was important in society. The religious communities with their traditional outlook upon morality would react to any misconducts with regards to moral behaviour. This in turn would help the secret police for knowing of the sexual misconduct and immoral behaviour through surveillance they could force the individual in cooperating with the secret police. Also, as the first case suggests, the moral component was so important that the secret police will when all means of controlling the individual are exhausted construct a story of sexual misconduct and when needed use it to compromise that persons standing in society.

However, many of these files were used since the opening of the archives in Romania as information source for biographies that loosely can be called "popular history" where the private and even sexual life of the actors was romanticized, and innuendos helped in bypassing the regulations regarding private life in secret police documents in Romania. One such example is Tatiana Niculescu's biography of the monk Arsenie Boca that is a fictionalized close-reading of the file of worshiped saint-like figure in today popular culture that questions, following the secret police officers his relationship with a woman close to him (Niculescu, 2018).

We also learn that the secret police's surveillance is particular. The officers do not surveil the person to correct behaviour according to legal enforcements or to prevent violence against other individuals. As seen from the second example the secret police encouraged and created the environment for a possible violent act to continue when it served their purpose.

The final example brings about the understanding of "communist morality," the moral guidelines that impact the behaviour of the state employee, the secret police officer or, as this case offers, the inspector for religious denominations. One can see that the conduct of the communist administration is regulated strictly by a code that was imported and implemented from the external center, the Soviet Union. One can also note that there is a hybridization in the definition of morality that imports religious elements and terms.

Another important discussion should revolve around definitions of concepts like privacy, morality and sanctioned religious behaviour. When the *Securitate* officers took on a role of moral censor, are we faced with a personal definition on morality or is this is a definition that comes from a set of communist regulations that the officer learned beforehand? Was this a personal judgement call or was this judgement taught and required? The role of the *Securitate* officer as moral censor and judge is in itself telling and the hybridization between religious, ideological and personal morality norms offer us a window on discussions on communist orthodoxy. Moreover, as the current readers of these files, are we imposing similar personal definitions of good and bad, moral, and immoral onto behaviours and narratives in the archival documents? Are we behaving as moral censors ourselves? Self-reflection on the part of the document reader's in terms of her/his objectivity, whether a *Securitate* Officer or a present-day researcher, is paramount, especially in the case of the regulations regarding the access to files of CNSAS researchers which are offered access to the file in its entirety.

Acknowledgement

The research for this chapter was funded by the European Research Council (ERC) under the European Union's Horizon 2020 research and innovation programme No. 677355.

Notes

1 In the case of the Archives of the National Council for the Study of the Archives of the *Securitate* (here forth ACNSAS) the researcher receives the entire file without the privacy mechanisms put in place (blackened names for instance). The privacy mechanisms are activated only on the copies of the documents.
2 I have conducted research in the Archives of the Patriarchal See of the Romanian Orthodox Church, the Archives of the Romanian Orthodox Church Archbishopric of Alba Iulia and the Romanian Orthodox Church Deanery in Tîrgu-Mureş.
3 At the time of writing, this file had not yet been processed by the archives.
4 Biroul Organizaţiei de Bază PCR, Stenograma adunării generale a Organizaţiei de bază din 26 XII 1977.

Archival sources

Arhiva Consiliului Național pentru Studierea Arhivelor Securității [The Archives of the National Council for the Research of the Archives of Securitate] (ACNSAS), D69; I 95070; I005555; I3470

Arhiva Secretariatului de Stat pentru Culte [Archives of the State Secretary for Religious Denominations] (ASSC), fond Departamentul Cultelor (DP), file 88; file Gheorghe Nenciu (at time of writing this file had not yet been processed by the archive)

References

Csongor, Jánosi 2017. "Path Finding in the Communist Regime: Árpád Mózes Szabó (1927–1987)." *East Central Europe* 44: 128–47.

Deletant, Dennis. 1995. *Ceaușescu and the Securitate. Coercion and Dissent in Romania (1965–1989)*, London: Routledge.

Field, Deborah A. 2007. *Private Life and Communist Morality in Khrushchev's Russia.* New York: Peter Lang.

Field, Deborah. 2017. "The Moral Code of the Builder of Communist." In: *Seventeen Moments in Soviet History: An On-line Archive of Primary Sources*. Available at: http://soviethistory.msu.edu/1961-2/moral-code-of-the-builder-of-communism/ (Accessed on 10 November 2017).

Hoffmann, David L. 2003. *Stalinist Values, The Cultural Norms of Soviet Modernity, 1917–1941*. Ithaca, London: Cornell University Press.

Kotkin, Stephen. 2002. "The State-Is It Us? Memoirs, Archives, and Kremlinologists." *The Russian Review* 61 (1): 35–51.

Lewis, Alison. 2003. "Reading and Writing the Stasi File: On the Uses and Abuses of the File as (Auto)biography." *German Life and Letters* 56 (4): 377–97.

Niculescu, Tatiana. 2018. *Ei mă consideră făcător de minuni. Viața lui Arsenie Boca.* [They see me making miracles. The life of Arsenie Boca]. Bucharest: Humanitas.

Stan, Lavinia. 2002. "Moral Cleansing Romanian Style." Problems of Post-Communism, 49 (4): 52–62.

Stan, Lavinia. 2004. "Spies, Files and Lies: Explaining the Failure of Access to Securitate Files." *Communist and Post-Communist Studies.* 37: 341–59.

Șincan, Anca. 2017a. "Stuck in the Middle: The Inspector for Religious Denominations as Mediator between the Religious Community and the State at the Installation of the Communist Regime in Romania." *East Central Europe*. 44: 128–47.

Șincan, Anca. 2017b. "The Portrait of N. Departing the Communist Orthodoxy" ["Portretul lui N. Despărțirea de ortodoxia comunistă"]. In: *Ne trebuie oameni' Elite intelectuale și transformări istorice în România modernă și contemporană*, edited by Cristian Vasile, 317–36. Târgoviște: Editura Cetatea de Scaun.

Turcescu, Luciana and Lavinia Stan. (2005) "The Devil's Confessors: Priests, Communists, Spies, and Informers." East European Politics and Societies, 19, (4): 655–85.

Verdery, Katherine. 2014. *Secrets and Truths: Ethnography in the Archive of Romania's Secret Police*. Budapest: Central European University Press.

Verdery, Katherine. 2018. *My Life as a Spy. Investigations in a Secret Police File.* Durham & London: Duke University Press.

16 Redeeming memory

Neo-Protestant churches and the secret police archives in Romania

Iuliana Cindrea-Nagy

Following the fall of the communist regime in Romania, efforts were made by numerous historians and theologians to produce, based on research done in the archives of the former secret police, a literature that would encompass the sufferings and repression endured by the various religious communities present in the country. The present article examines the manner in which members of various religious minorities, namely the neo-Protestant churches, dealt with the past of their own communities, the importance they ascribed to the archives of the former secret police and how they utilized state security files to write histories of their communities during the communist regime. Some have used the archives as a means to highlight the sufferings and persecutions that these religious minorities endured in an effort to fill the pages of history left blank, whilst others have seen it as the sole repository of the truth about the past and took the responsibility upon themselves of exposing the names of all those community members who collaborated with the Securitate.

The Romanian Orthodox Church was the first to take the stage in creating a distinctly "sacred narrative" out of state repression that culminated in the development of the so-called *prison saints* movement[1] (Ciobanu 2017, 215). In doing so, the Orthodox Church succeeded in silencing other religious communities by dominating the public discussion on religious persecution and by generating a discourse that, as Monica Ciobanu stresses, only emphasized its own repression (Ciobanu 2017, 232). Faced with the need to come to terms with its recent past in the early post-communist years and as an attempt to legitimize its "recasting as a public religion" (Conovici 2013, 109), the Church adopted certain discursive strategies that pointed instead to its history during the interwar period and to its contribution to the creation of the Romanian nation. The process of transitional justice[2] was initiated in Romania in the early 1990s (Stan and Turcescu 2007, 65) and the Romanian Orthodox Church, as well as processing the legacy of its indisputable sufferings during communism, has also been confronted with the need to confess aspects of its controversial past. However, instead of leading the way towards the moral rebirth of the country, as many Romanian intellectuals expected it to do (Stan and Turcescu 2007, 88), the Church tried to restrict public access to its archives, while also impeding the background verification of its priests by the National Council for the Study of the Securitate Archives.[3] This made the Church even more susceptible to public criticism. This chosen silence on the part of religious actors, that would otherwise be socially vocal and visible, was interpreted as an act of fear that was due to the Church's awareness of its tainted past (Cişmaş 2017, 303). The opening of the secret police files in 1999 revealed the active collaboration with the communist regime of members of other religious denominations in the country, including neo-Protestant[4] communities, which had until then been shielded from the level of scrutiny and public scandals that had affected the Orthodox Church (Stan and Turcescu 2007, 89).

Unlike the Orthodox Church, which has been accused by scholars and historians of trying to keep under lock and key important documents that could bring to light controversial issues, contributing to what Cristian Vasile calls the "politics of fear" (Vasile 2017, 235), in the case of these religious minorities, mainly neo-Protestant communities, the process of "purification"[5] appears to have been a voluntary act, conducted by some members of the communities themselves. They considered it a step forward necessary for healing from the sins of the past, without which the true existence of the communities would have been endangered (Mitrofan 2007, 9).

Standing in the shadow of the Orthodox Church

For a long period of time, the Orthodox Church denied scholars access to documents that might have negatively affected its image, contributing to a so-called "silencing of the archives" (Şincan 2012, 144; Trouillot 1995, 26). During the early post-communist years, the Church admitted to a form of cooperation with the communist regime, cooperation that was considered more a "survival strategy" that was necessary in the face of a system that wanted to completely eliminate any form of religion from public life; all things considered, this survival was meant to be seen as a so-called act of "dissidence" to a violent, repressive regime (Conovici 2013, 117). During the 1990s, the Church declared itself a martyr of communism and began a series of actions that would support the expansion of a "memory of martyrdom" (Conovici 2013, 116). This included the publication of numerous articles, dictionaries, volumes depicting the lives and sufferings of various clergymen and monks, testimonies, documentaries and other such studies that were meant to support and legitimize its statements (Conovici 2013, 116).

While not completely denying these narratives, historians and scholars of political science have drawn attention to the fact that, at the same time, the Orthodox Church blocked the public exposure of the names of those priests who collaborated with the former secret police (Stan and Turcescu 2005, 655). Moreover, the Church was accused of turning into "saints" various political prisoners, or priestly figures who, during the interwar period, sympathized with the ideas perpetuated by the extreme right movement, the Iron Guard. Whilst trying to avoid the issue, the Orthodox Church stated that they had sympathized with the religious message of the movement, not with its political aims (Grigore 2015, 45). In an article discussing the Aiud "prison saints" phenomenon, Monica Grigore claims that the political prisoners who died there turned into venerated figures as a result of a construction,[6] and not due to a natural process, and that it all began when, instead of calling them victims of the regime, the representatives of the official religion designated them as martyrs and saints (Grigore 2015, 45).

The "prison saints movement" has resulted in large numbers of Orthodox believers participating in events, such as public mass veneration of relics, where miracles are said to have occurred, which eventually led believers into manifesting a form of veneration towards these individuals.[7] The Orthodox Church would then use these manifestations, in a circular reasoning, to justify and legitimize the need to canonize some of these political prisoners. While a controversial topic, the phenomenon marked the appearance of a narrative of self-victimization, subtly coordinated by the Orthodox Church, an act that perhaps inadvertently resulted in the marginalization of the experiences, voices and sufferings of religious minorities. Moreover, it seemed that victims who belonged to other religions, confessions and denominations were almost non-existent in the public discourse; on a platform monopolized by the Orthodox Church, their attempts at public recognition of a shared suffering have become inaudible.

The Orthodox Church's expectation to be recast as the public religion after 1989, an institutional position it had during the interwar period, is related to its historical advantage (Murgoci 2009, 26) and its close link to national identity. Its efforts to legitimize this renewed status – that of the state's official religion – posed numerous problems and by trying to consolidate a version of the communist past that portrayed it as the sole victim of religious repression (Ciobanu 2017, 234) the Church was indirectly pointing to an ideal – in its opinion – pre-communist past in which it played a significant role on both the religious and political scene. The attempt to overshadow other religions was not unintentional and the move had ramifications that go back to the beginning of the twentieth century, when the appearance of other religious minorities was perceived as a threat to the Orthodox Church's authority.

During the interwar period, there was a clear distinction made between the right belief of the Orthodox Church and the heretical teachings of the sects (see Sonja Luehrmann 2015, 11), such as the neo-Protestant groups. In a speech held in Parliament on the occasion of the 1928 legislative changes, D. Turcu, an Orthodox priest, accused the neo-Protestant minorities, such as the Adventists, Baptists, of endangering the safety of the state and its newly gained identity (Our church and Minority Religions 1928, 79). Just one year later, in the magazine *Church and School* (Biserica și Școala) there was an article entitled *The Dangers that await us* (Primejdii ce ne așteaptă) in which the above-mentioned groups were accused of trying to destroy the state by infiltrating foreign elements inside the country (Ardeoiu 1929). The Church and state's attitude towards these new religious groups, that they referred to as sects, could be justified by the fact that the latter apparently refused to be dependent on the state, they spread pacifist messages in times of conflict and war, refused to undertake military service and did not want to participate in national festivities, for which reason they were seen as aggressive (Dobrincu 2007, 595). During Antonescu's dictatorship, January 1941 to August 1944, the sects were seen as dangerous as they were perceived as undermining the purity of the Romanian nation; the 1940s marked the culmination of a process of "purification" of the country, a process which included the deportation of Jewish and Roma communities to concentration camps in Transnistria and population exchanges with Hungary and Bulgaria, and it was clear from the beginning that any belief system that was not incorporated into the idea of Romanianess propagated by nationalists was meant to disappear. During the communist era, apart from it being an atheist system that professed to reject religion altogether, the so-called sects were considered especially dangerous to the state because of their connections and relations with the outside, capitalist world. On the other hand, after a period of harsh repression, the communist regime eventually realized that the legitimacy of the Orthodox Church, as the denomination of the majority of the population, could be used to its own advantage. For this reason, the Church was tolerated by the state in exchange for its unconditional support (Cişmaş 2017, 312).

The critics of the Orthodox Church's efforts to control access to information and to create a positive memory of its history during communism did not call into question the intensity or the authenticity of the sufferings of direct victims of communist repression against the Church, but rather condemned it for failing to also admit to the dark and controversial aspects of its past, namely collaboration. *The Final Report of the Presidential Commission for the Analysis of the Communist Dictatorship of Romania* (Comisia Prezidenţială pentru Analiza Dictaturii Comuniste în România – Raport Final),[8] released in 2006, proved a major challenge for the Orthodox Church. It included a chapter on the relationship between various religious denominations and the communist authorities in which the collaboration of some Orthodox leaders with the Securitate and the communist party was not downplayed. In response to the *Final Report*, which the Church fiercely criticized, the Holy Synod formed a commission that was given the mission of defending the clergy and the Church's image (Vasile 2017, 236 and Chapter 13, this volume). Once again, the Orthodox Church refused to admit to its past mistakes and to abandon a discourse that portrayed it as almost exclusively a victim of the communist regime. The stance of the Orthodox Church was soon contested by other actors such as the Greek-Catholic Church and the neo-Protestant communities, that once again challenged the Church to examine its memory of the communist regime. While the Greek-Catholics questioned the role of the Orthodox Church in the 1948 forced dissolution of their own church, the neo-Protestant churches highlighted the fact that their ill-treatment during communism and the interwar period was sometimes backed by the Orthodox Church (Conovici 2013, 113) that felt threatened by their proselytizing actions (Final Report 2006, 455).

In a 2007 article, Radu Preda, a Romanian theologian and former Director of the Institute for the Investigation of Communist Crimes and the Memory of the Romanian Exile, expressed his objection to the negative attention that the Orthodox Church was being given, especially in the mass media, attention that encouraged people to lose sight of the fact that living under communism had meant having to make difficult decisions (Preda 2007, 779). He responded to the anticlerical voices with the following statement:

> Some have tried to compare the history of the Romanian Orthodox Church with the history of other churches and confessions, failing to see that as there is no monopoly on suffering, there is no monopoly on denunciation either. All religious groups in Romania must write a chapter of their own history during communism, about the strongest and the weakest, about confessors and opportunists. It is, after all, the most honest way of accepting the fact that the Church's holiness does not exclude the fall of its members.

The Orthodox Church, however, in its efforts to reclaim its role as the official, national church, appealed to a form of selective memory (Ciobanu 2017, 221) that generated a particular discourse. This discourse, in its turn, made it seem as if the Orthodox Church was the greatest, if not the only, victim of an atheist and extremely repressive regime, whereas the communist prisons had housed individuals of various confessions and world-views that were forced to go through the same sufferings. Limiting religious persecution to the Orthodox clergy, or even to Christian believers alone, means completely excluding the equally valid experiences and memories of people who belonged to different religions (Ciobanu 2017, 234). Moreover, by restricting or, in some cases, denying access to important documents, the Orthodox Church was, in fact, rendering difficult the reconstruction of real life stories of the many direct victims of the communist repression against the Orthodox Church and other religious communities (Conovici 2013, 121).

Healing from the past

In the last decade, various religious minorities have made efforts to come to terms with their own past. If, in the case of the Orthodox Church, the pressure to purify its memory mostly came from the outside,[9] in the case of the neo-Protestant communities this process began from within the groups themselves, and was seen as imperative. In addition to the literature depicting the sufferings and persecutions of these communities, considered an important element in the process of healing the wounds of the past, efforts were made to expose the collaborators and to give them the chance to confess their sins publicly.

The one factor that made possible this redemptive process was access to the archive of the former secret police. Immediately after the fall of the communist regime, even before access to its content was allowed, this archive had a special status among other archival sources (Poenaru 2013, 102), for obvious reasons – it was believed that it contained the truth about what happened during communism and, most importantly, why it happened. The paradoxical nature of such an expectation, namely that the products of a failed and immoral system would contain the truth about the past is discussed by Kapaló and Povedák (Introduction, this volume), with some stating that their interpretation is the task of historians, the only ones capable of distinguishing between authentic and manipulated documents (Stan 2006, 395). Both claims developed into mental constructs that Lavinia Stan characterizes as "myths" that have shaped the debate on post-communist transitional justice (Stan 2006, 388). In support of the first aspect of this, she draws attention to the fact that the secret police documents are the product of officers that looked at citizens' behaviour and attitudes through their own ideological lens, presenting a highly problematic version of reality (Stan 2006, 406). In connection to the claim that historians are the most appropriate interpreters of secret police files, however, she highlights the fact that reconstruction of the past belongs not only to historians, but also to all those who lived during communist times and had their privacy taken away by the secret police. In her own words:

> Access to secret police files democratizes truth seeking by allowing victims to control the process and ordinary citizens to contrast the truth contained in the files with their own recollection of past events.
>
> (Stan 2013, 60)

The opening of the archives of the former secret police affected many friendships and family relations as everybody could potentially become a stranger, with a different past, a different identity (Poenaru 2013, 103). For some scholars, the secret police archives are the "precursors of WikiLeaks" (Stan 2011, 326; Poenaru 2013, 103) as they have the potential to generate scandals and give public access to sensitive information. Despite all these "dangers of the archives," a thorough investigation was seen as necessary by both scholars and civil society; the archive might not contain the truth, but it certainly contains important information that, handled carefully, could lead to a more satisfactory evaluation of events.

The neo-Protestant communities started to record their history during the communist regime relatively late and their writings first took the form of memoirs, or partial attempts at writing a general history of the communities.[10] When access to the former secret police archives became possible, in the early 2000s, numerous members of neo-Protestant groups, some of whom were historians, took the opportunity to conduct more thorough research and bring to light documents that could prove the sufferings their communities had endured as religious minorities, as well as the efforts they made to oppose the vicious communist regime.

These works were often times accompanied by statements that their place in historiography was imperative, aiming to fill the blank pages of a history theretofore unwritten. From the perspective of the neo-Protestant communities, it was seen as a just and fair measure, meant to also address the wider Romanian population that hardly knew anything about these groups, much less understood them (Silveşan 2012, 19). For the most part, especially in the beginning, the need to tell the story of the sufferings that members of neo-Protestant communities had to endure was the most important task and determined the specific agenda with which historians who were members of neo-Protestant churches entered the archives. However, they were conscious that their communities were unable to escape a phenomenon that affected all structures and institutions during communism, namely that of collaboration with the secret police.

The history of the Baptists during the communist regime was approached by Marius Silveşan (2010), himself a historian and member of the Baptist Church, and developed in articles, such as *The Romanian Baptists – from Monarchic Authority to Popular Democracy* (Baptiştii din România de la regimul de autoritate monarhică al lui Carol al II-lea la regimul de democraţie populară, 2018) and various books, such as *The Romanian Baptist Church: Between Persecution, Acommodation and Opposition* (Bisericile baptiste din România: între persecuţie, acomodare şi rezistenţă, 2012). The Evangelical Christians were dealt with by Bogdan Emanuel Răduţ (2013a), a member of the community, in works such as *The History of the Evangelical Christians: Volume of Documents* and *The Evangelical Christians and the Department of Culture: Behind the Scenes of a Public Trial in Craiova* (Creştinii după evanghelie şi departamentul cultelor: din culisele unui proces public la Craiova, 2013b). The History of the Pentecostals was approached by Ciprian Bălăban, a member of the Pentecostal Church, and written in a recently published work, *The History of the Romanian Pentecostal Church. 1922–1989* (Istoria Bisericii Penticostale din România 1922–1989, 2016).

The subject of collaboration was not left unaddressed in these works, and most neo-Protestant historians and, sometimes, even members of these churches, that took the writing of a history of these communities upon themselves, dedicated at least one chapter in their works to this issue, or dealt with it in subsequent articles. However, the topic was seen as a very sensitive one and the general conclusion was that this controversial subject should be treated carefully and authors should abstain from naming people before having completed rigorous research.

The act of collaboration has been described in various ways, using expressions such as “tightrope walk” (Bălăban 2015, 71), describing the dangerous attempt on the part of the informers to keep a balanced relationship with the Securitate, while still performing their duties within their churches. Others defined it in more spiritual, yet perhaps harsher terms, such as "shaking hands with the (d)evil" (Dumitrescu 2010, 15). This assessment is often met with in neo-Protestant communities, for whom the communist regime was the work of the devil; agreeing to become an informer meant betraying your own brothers and sisters in Christ and bringing harmful consequences upon them.

The ways in which the Securitate tried to infiltrate neo-Protestant communities are described in numerous articles included in *Securitatea*, a journal that was only addressed to and available to members of the secret police. If the Orthodox Church closely collaborated with the Securitate in exchange for its protection and a privileged position among other religions, with harsh consequences for those priests who refused collaboration and openly opposed the regime, the measures taken by the secret police in the case of neo-Protestant communities were slightly different. They were designed to confuse and sow doubt in their members, which would then hopefully – from the regime's perspective – lead to their dissolution. Due to these communities' evangelizing activities, it was an easy task for the informers to pose as new converts and infiltrate their churches (Banciu 1974, 51). Recruiting collaborators among the neo-Protestant believers that were imprisoned for various crimes was another option, and the Securitate especially targeted young members (Banciu 1974, 52). If the police had any compromising information about the person that they were trying to convince to become an informer they employed blackmail and intimidation (Croitor 2010, 140), while in other cases members of a community could be recruited in order to supervize and offer information about members of other communities, in an attempt to destabilize and generate confusion amongst believers (Lungu and Medaru 1975, 32–6).

Coming to terms with the past of their own communities implied, for some members of the neo-Protestant churches, accepting both their history of opposition and the repressive measures they had to endure as religious minorities during their short history in Romania,[11] as well as the duplicitous existence of some of their brothers and sisters during the communist regime. The latter aspect, however, according to members of these communities, had to be confronted so that the past mistakes could be redeemed, the memory purified and the people who compromised themselves could be offered and receive forgiveness. Few of those who collaborated, however, came forward to confess their "weakness" and, as Paul Negruț, the former president of the Romanian Baptist Community, stated in his 2006 address in the opening of the National Conference:

> The Baptist community carries within itself a mixture of traitors and martyrs and it never had a moment of public confession, purification, forgiveness, redemption and reconciliation.
>
> (Negruț, 2006)

As the Pentecostal pastor Gheorghe Rițișan claims, having been given the chance to confess and, perhaps out of fear and shame of facing the consequences of their actions, having failed to do so, these former collaborators "had to be exposed" so that the faces of the true victims of communism could be brought to light (Croitor 2010, v). The agenda of some members of neo-Protestant communities thus changed; when entering the archives, they had a different purpose, that of "healing the badly closed wounds of the past" (Hayner 2011, 145) by exposing them and giving their brothers and sisters, who "sold their souls to the devil," the chance to repent and be forgiven (Mitrofan 2009a, 180). They took on the stance of what Florin Poenaru would call "historians as priests"[12], meaning that they assumed the function of priests, offering understanding and forgiveness and claiming that it was their responsibility to heal what was left unhealed and to mediate between the victims and perpetrators (Poenaru 2013, 103).

Redeeming the memory of a painful past

From 2006 onwards, a series of published works have shaken the neo-Protestant communities in Romania. Written by important members of these churches, some of whom were preachers, these works were the result of a more or less thorough research conducted in the archives of the former secret police. The motivation behind these attempts was frequently mentioned within the pages of these works, and it stated that "the church should be the first one to bring to light the wrongdoings of the past in order to reflect the truth" (Mitrofan 2009b, 166) because "it was the only way it could make peace with its past" (Croitor 2013, 366). Another purpose, however, was of exposing the names of people who had collaborated with the secret police while they were still performing their everyday tasks within the churches they belonged to. Taken out of context, some of these works seemed like vengeful attempts to purify the neo-Protestant communities of their weakest individuals. For some members it was difficult to comprehend that such an endeavour could come from within the communities themselves; for others, these attempts were nothing more than a "terrorist attack" against the neo-Protestant churches (Vaisamar, 2010), an act of treason meant to break down these already small communities.

Some of the most controversial works were those of Daniel Mitrofan, a member of the Baptist Church who wrote two books addressing the subject of collaboration, namely *Pygmies and Giants* (Pigmeiși uriași, 2007) and *Steps* (Pași, 2010). The Baptist community had mixed feelings regarding the publishing of these books, especially due to the fact that they seemed to have been written with the sole purpose of unmasking the former informers within the community whilst also trying to prove that more than 70% of the leaders of the Baptist Church collaborated in one way or another with the Securitate (Silveșan, 2010). Moreover, Mitrofan was accussed of using the information he acquired from the archives in a selective manner and of trying to manipulate it in order to serve his own purposes (Silveşan, 2010). Apart from these books, he would frequently publish online articles discussing controversial topics, such as the 2009 article, figuratively called *The Tip of the Iceberg* (Vârful Icebergului), in which he exposed the names of some of the most important preachers whom, he alleged, collaborated with the communist authorities, whilst also encouraging his supporters to continue his work:

> Create blogs, publish files, make all data available, make connections and do not be intimidated by those who try to discourage you from bringing to light the things that happened in the dark.
>
> (Mitrofan, 2009c)

His actions generated various responses from those he accused in his writings, some of whom imputed to him the fact that he intentionally avoided pieces of information from their files and only made available those parts that would put them in a negative light (Prologos, 2008). The fact that his book, *Pygmies and Giants,* appeared before the elections for the administration of the Baptist community was another problematic issue.

Apart from the numerous criticisms he received, some of which were connected with the manner in which he (mis)used the secret police archives, or disregarded some of its policies and regulations[13] generating the so-called *Dosariada*[14] phenomenon, an improvised form of lustration, within the Baptist community, the reality was that his works had a deeper effect. They encouraged people to go through a process of moral introspection, irrespective of how his initial intentions, as reflected in his writings, came across. The silence that followed was disappointing and devastating for some members of the community (Cruceru, 2011a); not only were the names exposed in a chaotic manner, but also those who knew their guilt still refused to come forward, thus contributing to the ongoing proliferation of a widespread climate of suspicion. Ironically, some members of the Baptist community asked for a public confession of the kind made by the Orthodox Metropolitan Nicolae Corneanu,[15] claiming that such examples have yet to happen in the Baptist Church (Cruceru, 2011a).

A similar process took place within the Pentecostal Church in early 2010. Vasilică Croitor, a Pentecostal preacher from Constanța, published a well-researched book, which he metaphorically called *Redeeming the Memory* (Răscumpărarea memoriei) implying from its title his intention of cleansing a dark memory through the same process, namely that of exposing the names of those who had not confessed their past mistakes. It was the same story as in the case of the Baptist Church: due to the fact that a voluntary admission of past collaboration was a difficult thing to do, a public exposure of the guilty ones was seen as necessary. However, his work comes across as more thoroughly researched and written in a less condemnatory tone. In the introduction to the book, Croitor lists the most important arguments that made the publishing of his work a sine qua non initiative:

> *Redeeming the Memory* should not have been published! It should have been the Church's duty to act immediately after the fall of communism. *Redeeming the Memory* should have been the consequence of a laborious trial initiated by the Church and its results should have been published in a report. This book should not have been written now! The church should have kept one step ahead of society by offering a model and showing the way to redemption ... This book should not have been written by me! Tens of researchers should have been invited to thoroughly analyse the communist period ... This book should not have been written in the form of a public exposure! This should have been the last resort to be taken. It was needed due to the former collaborator's lack of will to confess their mistakes, and to our incapacity to create a healthy, forgiving environment for them to do so.
>
> (Croitor 2010, xvii)

Irrespective of his intentions, his effort was followed by various negative reactions; one such example was the attitude of Ioan Ceuţă, a member of the Pentecostal Church, who accused Croitor of having commited an "act of terrorism" while also expressing his intentions to take him to court for shaming the entire Pentecostal community (Vaisamar, 2010). Other critics, however, pointed out his ill-intended determination to expose the names of those members who were still active within the community; as a result, after the book was published, the leaders of the Pentecostal Church resigned (Jarnea, 2014), retiring from the functions they had within the church. Newspapers around the country published articles introduced by titles such as *The Pentecostals Expose Their Brothers* (2010), which only gave way to further accusations against the author for allowing, even enabling, the portrayal of a negative image of the Pentecostal Church in Romanian society.

In order to set aside the arguments, or the so-called "myths," regarding the futility of exposing the names of those who collaborated with the Securitate, Croitor dedicates more than 10 pages to dealing with each "myth," finding reasons to maintain that such an endeavour was, in fact, more than necessary (Croitor 2010, 357–70). His actions were defended by younger members of the church, demonstrating that his intentions of redeeming the memory so that the younger generation would be given a new beginning seemed to hold true.[16]

The last neo-Protestant community that I will deal with in the present article, which went through a similar process of purification, is the Adventist Church. Due to its pyramidal structure,[17] different from the congregational structure of the Baptists or Pentecostals, the Adventist Church was more prone to the communist regime's invasive measures (Dumitrescu 2010, 24). In his article, entitled *Shaking Hands with the (D)evil*, Cristian Dumitrescu attempts to address the issue of collaboration, which he admits he was confronted with on numerous occasions (Dumitrescu 2010, 15). However, in his conclusions he states:

> The question regarding the morality of such cooperation must be judged against the prospect of the Church's survival under Satan's relentless attacks. The understanding of the Great Controversy offers the correct perspective. In my opinion the issue should not be "if" but "how far" the Church should go to shake hands with an oppressive regime.
>
> (Dumitrescu 2010, 32)

In other words, one should abstain from passing judgment on decisions made by individuals or institutions who lived under a repressive regime.

However, in 2013, Gheorghe Modoran, author of other articles dealing with the fate of the neo-Protestant communities during communism,[18] also a member of the Adventist Church and a historian, published a controversial book (Modoran 2013), *The Church through the Red Desert (1944–1965)* (Biserica prin pustiul roşu. 1944–1965),[19] a history of the Adventist Church, written after years of research in the archives of the former Romanian secret police, as well as in the archives of other institutions. What singularizes his endeavour, however, is that he avoided exposing the names of people who were still alive or, if they were, they had already retired from their functions within the church. For some people, this was considered a wiser option than that of trying to purify an entire clerical apparatus by publicly exposing their names (Jarnea, 2014). His critics, however, challenged his statements and the information he revealed in his work with complex questions regarding the extent to which one should consider the former secret police archives as repositories of truth (The Church through the Red Desert 2014). Others have accussed him of violating the policy of the Romanian Secret Police archives by publishing controversial information regarding various individuals, who were still alive, without contacting them beforehand. In a public letter, entitled *Letter for my informers*, resembling the title of the book written by the Romanian philosopher Gabriel Liiceanu,[20] Ungureanu Emanuel-Dumitru, himself a researcher and member of the Adventist community, critiqued the Church's leadership for allowing the publication of Modoran's thesis. His argument was that the latter manipulated the information contained in the archival documents and publicly exposed the private lives and conversations of numerous individuals, thus becoming himself an informer (Ungureanu, 2014).

Conclusion

All of the cases discussed above bring to light the conflicting emotions and values encountered when trying to come to terms with a painful past. Due to their self-proclaimed moral high ground, the churches, irrespective of the confession in question, fell victim to their own silences and omissions; proclaiming that these mistakes were the result of "human weakness" proved to be insufficient and perhaps even unfair towards all the direct victims of the repressive methods that the communist regime used against religious communities.

While the Orthodox Church, for a long period of time, clung to a positive memory of its own past, blocking any attempts at reassessing its role and of reshaping the discourse that turned it into an almost exclusive victim of the communist regime, the neo-Protestant communities rushed into the archives in a quest for a true history of their own past. The need to confess the sins of the past was a "burden" felt by all and was often described in biblical terms as an act of redemption; however, a process that was expected to come naturally was stunted by the former collaborators' reluctance to come forward. This was the moment when various members of the communities took upon themselves the public exposure of the names of collaborators in order to give them a chance to apologize, to be forgiven and, perhaps, in some cases, to punish them.

The value of their work was contested, and the methods they used have been fiercely criticized. Was this the only option left? According to some of them, it was, especially when exposing these issues was also an act of justice to all the other victims of the communist regime. Their works were intertwined with numerous efforts on the part of other church members who called for a public confession of those who knew their own guilt (Cruceru 2011b, 11). For others, these public exposures proved overwhelming and made them question how one could put to shame one's own brothers and sisters in Christ? In answer to this question, the authors replied with another question: how could those brothers and sisters do what they did, in their turn, to their own brothers in Christ?

The priests, pastors, ministers, rabbis, and all other religious leaders that have been identified as former Securitate informers were criticized for remaining silent in a time when recognition and apologies were needed. The Orthodox Church was blamed for avoiding an apologetic stance, seen less as the simple words of an apology[21] and more as the "transmission of a history that clearly states the wrongdoings" (Wolfe 2014, 74). Since 2006, the first moment when the Church's official history was challenged, it has not expressed repentance as an institution, nor has it addressed its past wrongdoings at an institutional level (Cişmaş 2017, 316). Only a few individual clerics have come forward in order to confess their tainted past and asked the wider society for forgiveness. The situation is no different for the neo-Protestant communities; for fear of facing the consequences of their actions, many former informers missed the opportunity to reveal their past and to express remorse immediately after the fall of the communist regime. However, silenced for two decades on a platform monopolized by the Orthodox Church and shielded from the public backlash that the latter received, the neo-Protestant churches understood that it was time for them to honestly face their past, with its best and worst aspects. The books written by the neo-Protestants, in which they publicly address the issue of collaboration, do not find equivalent in the Orthodox Church's historiography (Vasile 2010).

The quest for truth and redemption was seen as a "witch hunt" rather than as a step forward. What was expected of the Orthodox Church was expected of the neo-Protestant communities, as well. The fact that the archive of a former secret police which, in its turn, was the product of a corrupt, immoral system, was the main instrument used to bring the truth to light makes the issue even more complicated. The fascination with the purification of memory led to the proliferation of a climate of suspicion and fear. Ironically, this is exactly what the Securitate was blamed for; in the words of Florin Poenaru, "by inscribing the Securitate files as sites of truth about the past, post-communism simply prolonged its logic into the present" (Poenaru 2013, 104). To this, we can only add that the churches still have to walk a long road to redemption and acceptance of their own painful past, a road that is only made bearable by their members' belief that there is still a chance to receive and offer forgiveness.

Acknowledgement

The research for this chapter was funded by the European Research Council (ERC) under the European Union's Horizon 2020 research and innovation programme No. 677355.

Notes

1 Defined by Monica Ciobanu as a term that includes religious associations that promote the canonization of clergy or other Christian believers who were persecuted by the communist regime (Ciobanu 2017, 230).
2 Transitional justice strategies pursued in Romania are lustration (banning former communist decision-makers from post-communist public life), court trials, access to the former secret police archives, the presidential history commission, memorialization, and property restitution (Stan 2006, 383).
3 The National Council for the Study of the Securitate Archives, an institution established in 1999, is the authority that administrates the archives of the former communist secret police in Romania.
4 The term neo-Protestant refers to the Baptists, the Pentecostals, the Evangelical Christians and the Adventists. These communities usually refer to themselves as Evangelicals; however, in order to avoid confusion, in Romania the neo-Protestant term is generally accepted as a more proper term to refer to these communities.
5 The term purification, in this context, is used to refer to the cathartic effect that digging up the truth about a difficult past is sometimes expected to have.
6 The politics of saint-making is not limited to Romania and it is a phenomenon that appeared in both Orthodox (see Christensen 2018 and Bodin 2009) and non-Orthodox countries (see Anttonen 2004).
7 For example, exposure to miracles performed by the bone remains of the former political prisoners, intentionally referred to as "relics" (Grigore 2015, 38).

8 The Commission's purpose was to identify the institutions and methods that made possible the human rights crimes and abuses during communism (Vasile 2017, 236).

9 Here I should mention the initiative of the Group for Reflection on Church Renewal, a seven-member group, initiated by Andrei Andreicuț, Bartolomeu Anania and Dumitru Stăniloae, three important members of the Orthodox clergy, in January 1990. It was meant to regenerate the Church leadership by replacing its tainted leaders. However, the action was interpreted as an insulting attack against the Orthodox Church and the group ceased to exist soon after it was created (Stan and Turcescu 2007, 82).

10 See, for example, *The History of the Romanian Baptists. 1856–1989 (IstoriaBaptiștilor din România. 1856–1989)* by Alexa Popovici (2007), published in three volumes.

11 Most of the neo-Protestant communities that are present in Romania appeared in the country during the 19th century.

12 Based on the manners in which historians approach archival documents, Florin Poenaru offers three types of stances, namely "the historian as priest", "the historian as judge", and "the historian as inquisitor".

13 Mostly connected with the issue of revealing the names he found in the files in the absence of a thorough investigation and without contacting the people who were still alive.

14 A phenomenon that refers to the studying of the files of people who stand for higher positions within society in order to see if they collaborated with the Securitate, in which case they were denied the right to obtain such positions.

15 Nicolae Corneanu was one of the first Orthodox hierarchs who confessed his collaboration with the secret police, a gesture that transformed him into a beacon of moral honesty and integrity. Due to his willingness to admit to his past mistakes, Corneanu was not criticized when he later called on to others to admit to their own collaborations (Stan 2013, 79).

16 One of the supporters of Croitor's book is Emanuel Conțac, a young lecturer at the Pentecostal Theological Institute in Bucharest who is also the administrator of a website called *Vaisamar*, referenced in the present article, where numerous young people, members of various neo-Protestant churches, expressed their positive opinion about the publishing of the book.

17 The Seventh-day Adventist Church is organized on more levels, starting from the local church, an organized body of individual believers, and going up to the General Conference, the world headquarters of the Seventh-day Adventist Church, which includes all members and organizations. This particular structure proved to be problematic during the communist regime as connections with the world leadership were cut. Isolating a national or local church from the General Conference was a way used by the regime to gain control over the structure of the church (Dumitrescu 2010, 32).

18 Such as *The Neo-Protestant Confessions during the Communist Regime: 1945–1965* (*Confesiunile neoprotestante din România în perioada regimului comunist: 1945–1965*) published in *Romanian Political Science Review*, vol. VII, no. 3, 2007, 655–73.

19 Biserica prin pustiul roșu [translation by the author].

20 Gabriel Liiceanu wrote a book entitled *My Dear Informer* dedicated to the person who gave information about him to the Securitate during the communist regime.

21 In late 1989 Patriarch Teoctist delivered an apology for the mistakes of the Orthodox Church during communist years, an apology that was described as "halfhearted" by Lavinia Stan (Stan and Turcescu 2007, 71).

References

Anttonen, Pertti. 2004. "A Catholic Martyr and Protestant Heritage: A Contested Slite of Religiosity and its Representation in Contemporary Finland." In: *Creating Diversities: Folklore, Religion and the Politics of Heritage*, edited by Anna-Leena Siikala, Barbro Klein & Stein R. Mathisen, 190–221. *Studia Fennica Folkloristica* 14. Helsinki: Finnish Literature Society.

Ardeoiu, Ioan. 1929. "Danger Awaits Us" ["Primejdii ce ne aşteaptă"]. *Biserica şi Şcoala. Revistă bisericească şi culturală* 42: 13.

Banciu, Ion. 1974. "Firm, Co-ordinated Measures are Needed Against the Activity of Jehovah's Witnesses" ["Sunt necesare măsuri ferme, conjugate, împotriva activităţii iehoviste!"]. *Securitatea* 3: 50–3.

Bălăban, Ciprian. 2015. "Sandru Trandafir – The Art of Walking the Tightrope in Relation to the Securitate" ["Trandafir Sandru- arta mersului pe sârmă în relaţie cu Securitatea"]. *Caietele CNSAS*, 8 (2) (16): 71–89.

Bălăban, Ciprian. 2016. *The History of the Pentecostal Church in Romania (1922–1989): Institutions and Charisma* [*Istoria bisericii penticostale din România (1922–1989). Instituţii şi harisme*]. Oradea: Editura Scriptum and Cluj-Napoca: Editura Rosoprint.

Bodin, Per-Arne. 2009. *Language, Canonization and Holy Foolishness: Studies in Postsoviet Russian Culture and the Orthodox Tradition*. Stockholm: Stockholm University Press.

Christensen, Karin Hyldal. 2018. *The Making of the New Martyrs of Russia: Soviet Repression in Orthodox Memory*. London & New York: Routledge.

The Church Through the Red Desert – Gheorghe Modoran, Virgil Peicu, Lucian Cristescu [Biserica in pustiul roşu – Gheorghe Modoran, Virgil Peicu, Lucian Cristescu – 11.02.2014]. 2014. Speranţa TV. Available at: www.sperantatv.ro/web/biserica-in-pustiul-rosu-gheorghe-modoran-virgil-peicu-lucian-cristescu-11-02-2014/ [Accessed 23 November 2017].

Ciobanu, Monica. 2017. "Remembering the Gulag: Religious Representations and Practices." In: *Justice, Memory and Redress in Romania: New Insights*, edited by Lavinia Stan and Lucian Turcescu, 214–35. Newcastle: Cambridge Scholars Publishing.

Cişmaş, Ioana. 2017. "Reflections on the Presence and Absence of Religious Actors in Transitional Justice Processes: On Legitimacy and Accountability." In: *Justice, Mosaics: How Context Shapes Transitional Justice in Fractured Societies*, edited by R. Duthie, and P. Seils, 302–43. New York: ICTJ.

Conovici, Iuliana. 2013. "Re-Weaving Memory: Representations of the Interwar and Communist Periods in the Romanian Orthodox Church After 1989." *Journal for the Study of Religions and Ideologies* 35: 109–31.

Croitor, Vasilică. 2010. *The Redemption of Memory: The Pentecostal Religion in the Communist Period* [*Răscumpărarea memoriei. Cultul penticostal în perioada comunistă*]. Medgidia: Suceed Publishing.

Cruceru, Marius. 2011a. "Baptists between Collaboration and Resistance" ["Baptiştii între colaboraţionism şi rezistenţă ambiguă"]. Available at: http://oglindanet.ro/baptistii-intre-colaborationism-si-rezistenta-ambigua/ [Accessed 14 December 2017].

Cruceru, Marius. 2011b. "Speak Kindly of God. Practice Living in Truth" ["Despre Dumnezeu numai de bine. Exerciţiu de trăire în adevăr"] [pdf]. Available at: https://patratosu.files.wordpress.com/2007/01/despre-dumnezeu-numai-de-bine-articol-in-crestinul-azi.pdf [Accessed 15 December 2017].

Dobrincu, Dorin. 2007. "Religion and Power in Romania: State Policy towards the (Neo)protestant Confessions, 1919–1944" ["Religie şi putere în România. Politica statului faţă de confesiunile (neo)protestante, 1919–1944"]. *Studia Politica. Romanian Political Science Review* 7 (3): 583–602.

Dumitrescu, Cristian. 2010. "Shaking Hands with the (D)evil: Adventism and Communism." *Journal of Adventist Mission Studies* 6 (1): 15–32.

Grigore, Monica. 2015. "The Aiud "Prison Saints." History, Memory, and Lived Religion." *Eurostudia* 101: 33–49.

Hayner, Priscilla. B. 2011. *Unspeakable Truths. Transitional Justice and the Challenge of Truth Comissions* 2nd Edition. New York and London: Routledge.

Jarnea, Gabriel. 2014. "The Romanian Adventism or the Pathology of a Religious Confession" ["Adventismul românesc sau patologia unei confesiuni"]. [online] Available at: http://dilemaveche.ro/sectiune/din-polul-plus/articol/adventismul-romanesc-sau-patologia-unei-confesiuni [Accessed 23 November 2017].

Luehrmann, Sonja. 2015. *Religion in Secular Archives. Soviet Atheism and Historical Knowledge*. New York: Oxford University Press.

Lungu, Gheorghe and Medaru, Vasile. 1975. "The Millennialists" ["Mileniştii"]. *Securitatea* 2: 32–6.

Mitrofan, Daniel. 2007. *Pygmies and Giants: Pages of Baptists' Persecution* [*Pigmei şi uriaşi. File din istoria persecutării baptiştilor*]. Editura Cristianus.

Mitrofan, Daniel. 2009a. "Steps" ["Paşi"]. [pdf]. Available at: https://centruldeistoriesiapologetica.files.wordpress.com/2009/09/cultul-crestin-baptist-in-comunism-h-176-200.pdf [Accessed 21 November 2017].

Mitrofan, Daniel. 2009b. "Steps" ["Paşi"]. [pdf]. Available at: https://centruldeistoriesiapologetica.files.wordpress.com/2009/09/cultul-crestin-baptist-in-comunism-g-151-175.pdf [Accessed 21 November 2017].

Mitrofan, Daniel. 2009c. "The Tip of the Iceberg of Baptist Informers" ["Vârful icebergului informatorilor baptişti"]. [online]. Available at: https://centruldeistoriesiapologetica.wordpress.com/2009/03/03/varful-icebergului/ [Accessed 21 November 2017].

Modoran, Gheorghe. 2007. "The Neoprotestant Confessions in Romania during the Communist Regime" ["Confesiunile neoprotestante din România în perioada regimului comunist: 1945–1965"]. *Romanian Political Science Review* 7 (3): 655–73.

Modoran, Gheorghe. 2013. *The Church through the Red Desert: Resistance and Compromise in Adventism in Romania during the Communist Period (1944–1965), Vol. 1.* [*Biserica prin pustiul roşu. Rezistenţă şi compromis în adventismul din România în perioada comunistă (1944–1965), Vol. 1*]. Editura Viaţă şi Sănătate.

Murgoci, Oana. I. 2009. *In Church We Trust!*. Budapest: Central European University.

Negruţ, Paul. 2006. "Revelations, Disinformation and Digressions" ["Dezvăluiri, dezinformări şi divagaţii"]. [online]. Available at: https://dezvaluiri.wordpress.com/paul-negrut/ [Accessed 14 December 2017].

Our church and Minority Religions: The Great Parliamentary Discussion about the Law on Religious Denominations [*Biserica noastră şi cultele minoritare. Marea discuţie parlamentară în jurul legii cultelor*]. 1928. Bucureşti.

"The Pentecostals Expose their Collaborating Brothers" ["Penticostalii îşi arată fraţii colaboratori"].Evenimentul Zilei. 2010. [online]. Available at: https://vaisamar.wordpress.com/2010/10/06/atacat-de-%E2%80%9Eteroristi%E2%80%9D-pastorul-ceuta-il-da-in-judecata-pe-pastorul-vasilica-croitor/ [Accessed 15 December 2017].

Poenaru, Florin. 2013. *Contesting Illusions. History and Intellectual Class Struggle in Post-Communist Romania*, Budapest, Submitted to Central European University. [pdf]. Available at: www.etd.ceu.hu/2013/poenaru_florin.pdf [Accessed 28 October 2016].

Popovici, Alexa. 2007. *The History of the Romanian Baptists (1856–1989)* [*Istoria baptiştilor din România (1856–1989)*]. Oradea: Editura Făclia.

Preda, Radu. 2007. "The Securitate and the Insecurities of its Declassification: The Communist Regime in the Memory of the Political Class, of Civil Society and the Church" ["Securitatea şi insecurităţile deconspirării ei. Comunismul în memoria clasei politice, a societăţii civile şi a Bisericii"]. *Romanian Political Science Review* 7 (3): 773–85.

The Presidential Commission for the Analysis of the Communist Regime in Romania, Final Report [Comisia Prezidenţială pentru analiza dictaturii comuniste din România, Raport Final]. 2006., Bucureşti. [pdf]. Available at: https://ia800609.us.archive.org/8/items/ComisiaPrezidentialaPentruAnalizaDictaturiiComunisteDinRomania-Raport/ComisiaPrezidentialaPentruAnalizaDictaturiiComunisteDinRomania-RaportFinal-coord.VladimirTismaneanu.pdf [Accessed 10 August 2017].

Prologos 2008. "Petru Dugulescu about *Pygmies and Giants*" ["Petru Dugulescu despre *Pigmei şi uriaşi*]. [online]. Available at: https://prologos.ro/uncategorized/petru-dugulescu-despre-pigmei-si-uriasi/ [Accessed 23 November 2017].

Răduţ, Bogdan. E. 2013a. *The History of Evangelical Christians. Volume of Documents* [*Din istoria creştinilor după evanghelie. Volum de documente*]. Târgovişte: Cetatea de Scaun.

Răduţ, Bogdan. E. 2013b. "The Evangelical Christians and the Department of Religious Cults: Behind the Scenes of a Public Trial in Craiova" ["Creştinii după evanghelie şi departamentul cultelor: din culisele unui proces public la Craiova"]. *Revista Oltenia*, 1: 124–35.

Silveşan, Marius. 2010. "Light and Shadow in the History of the Pentecostals under Communism" ["Lumini şi umbre în istoria cultului penticostal sub comunism"]. [online]. Available at: https://istorieevanghelica.ro/2010/06/ [Accessed 27 November 2017].

Silveşan, Marius. 2012. *The Baptist Churches in Romania. Between Persecution, Resistance and Adaptation (1948–1965) [Bisericile creştine baptiste din România. Între persecuţie, acomodare şi rezistenţă (1948–1965)]*. Târgovişte: Cetatea de Scaun.

Silveşan, Marius. 2018. "The Romanian Baptists from Charles II's Authoritarian Regime to the Popular Democracy Regime" ["Baptiştii din România de la regimul de autoritate monarhică al lui Carol al II-lea la regimul de democraţie populară"]. In: Studies in Ecclesiastical History [*Studii de istorie eclesiastică*], edited by Marius Oanţă, 137–70. Craiova: Editura Sitech.

Stan, Lavinia. 2006. "The Vanishing Truth? Politics and Memory in Eastern Europe." *East European Quarterly* 40 (4): 383–407.

Stan, Lavinia. 2011. "Vigilante Justice in Post-communist Europe." *Communist and Post-Communist Studies* 44: 319–27.

Stan, Lavinia. 2013. *Transitional Justice in Post-communist Romania: The Politics of Memory.* Cambridge and New York: Cambridge University Press.

Stan, Lavinia and Turcescu, Lucian. 2005. "The Devil's Confessors: Priests, Communists, Spies, and Informers." *East European Politics and Societies* 19 (4): 655–85.

Stan, Lavinia and Turcescu, Lucian. 2007. *Religion and Politics in Post-Communist Romania.* Oxford: Oxford University Press.

Şincan, Anca. 2012. "Silencing the Archive – A Methodological Insight into the Research for the Study 'A Day in the Life of an Inspector for Religious Denomination." *Anuarul Institutului de Cercetări Socio-Umane "Gheorghe Şincai"* XV: 144–55.

Trouillot, Michel-Rolf. 1995. *Silencing the Past. Power and the Production of History.* Boston: Beacon Press.

Ungureanu, Emanuel-Dumitru. 2014. "Open Letter" ["Scrisoare deschisă"]. [online]. Available at: https://remembering7.files.wordpress.com/2014/03/scrisoare-deschisa uniunedragii-mei-turnatori.docx. [Accessed 23 November 2017].

Vaisamar. 2010. "Attacked by Terrorists, Ioan Ceuţă sues Pastor Vasilică Croitor" ["Atacat de "terorişti", Ioan Ceuţă îl dă în judecată pe pastorul Vasilică Croitor"]. [online]. Available at: https://vaisamar.wordpress.com/2010/10/06/atacat-de-%E2%80%9Eteroristi%E2%80%9D-pastorul-ceuta-il-da-in-judecata-pe-pastorul-vasilica-croitor/ [Accessed 15 December 2017].

Vasile, Cristian. 2010. "The History of the Church as a Plea for Moral Reform" ["Istoria bisericii ca pledoarie pentru reformă morală"]. *Apostrof* 9 (244). [online]. Available at: www.revista-apostrof.ro/articole.php?id=1251 [Accessed 27 March 2018].

Vasile, Cristian. 2017. "Coming to Terms with the Controversial Past of the Orthodox Church." In: *Justice, Memory and Redress in Romania: New Insights*, edited by L. Stan and L. Turcescu, 235–56. Newcastle: Cambridge Scholars Publishing.

Wolfe, Stephanie. 2014. *The Politics of Reparations and Apologies.* New York: Springer.

Index

Note: Page numbers in **bold** indicate tables; those in *italics* indicate figures.

Milton Keynes UK
Ingram Content Group UK Ltd.
UKHW020106020524
442028UK00005B/4